D1035849

Bloom's Shakespeare Through the Ages

Antony and Cleopatra

As You Like It

Hamlet

Henry IV (Part I)

Julius Caesar

King Lear

Macbeth

The Merchant of Venice

A Midsummer Night's Dream

Othello

Romeo and Juliet

The Sonnets

The Taming of the Shrew

The Tempest

Twelfth Night

Bloom's Shakespeare Through the Ages

ANTONY
AND CLEOPATRA

Edited and with an introduction by
Harold Bloom
Sterling Professor of the Humanities
Yale University

Volume Editor
Neil Heims

BLOOM'S
LITERARY CRITICISM
An imprint of Infobase Publishing

Bloom's Shakespeare Through the Ages: Antony and Cleopatra

Copyright © 2008 by Infobase Publishing

Introduction © 2008 by Harold Bloom

Bloom's Literary Criticism
An imprint of Infobase Publishing
132 West 31st Street
New York NY 10001

Library of Congress Cataloging-in-Publication Data
Antony and Cleopatra / edited and with an introduction by Harold Bloom ; volume editor, Neil Heims.
    p. cm. — (Bloom's Shakespeare through the ages)
  Includes bibliographical references and index.
  ISBN-13: 978-0-7910-9630-7 (acid-free paper)
  ISBN-10: 0-7910-9630-0 (acid-free paper) 1. Shakespeare, William, 1564–1616.
Antony and Cleopatra. 2. Cleopatra, Queen of Egypt, d. 30 B.C.—In literature.
3. Antonius, Marcus, 83?-30 B.C.—In literature. I. Bloom, Harold. II. Heims, Neil.
  PR2802.A77 2008
  822.3'3—dc22   2008005229

Series design by Erika K. Arroyo
Cover design by Ben Peterson
Cover photo © The Granger Collection, New York

Printed in the United States of America

Bang EJB 10 9 8 7 6 5 4 3 2 1

This book is printed on acid-free paper.

CONTENTS
❧

Series Introduction ix

Introduction by Harold Bloom xi

Biography of William Shakespeare 1

Summary of *Antony and Cleopatra* 5

Key Passages in *Antony and Cleopatra* 19

List of Characters in *Antony and Cleopatra* 41

CRITICISM THROUGH THE AGES 45

❖ *Antony and Cleopatra* in the Seventeenth Century 47

 1678—John Dryden. From the Preface to *All for Love* 49

 1680—Nahum Tate. From "Address to Edward Tayler,"
 in *The Loyal General, a Tragedy* 50

❖ *Antony and Cleopatra* in the Eighteenth Century 53

 1759—John Hill. From "Some Remarks upon
 the New-revived Play of *Antony and Cleopatra*" 54

 1765—Samuel Johnson. From "Notes on the Plays,"
 in *The Plays of William Shakespeare* 55

 1774—Francis Gentleman. From *Bell's Edition
 of Shakespeare's Plays* 56

 1784—Thomas Davies. From *Dramatic Miscellanies* 57

❖ *Antony and Cleopatra* in the Nineteenth Century 59

 1809—August Wilhelm von Schlegel. From
 Lectures on Dramatic Art and Literature 61

1817—William Hazlitt. From *Characters
of Shakespear's Plays* 62

1818—Samuel Taylor Coleridge. From *Shakspeare,
with Introductory Remarks on Poetry, the Drama,
and the Stage* 66

1832—Anna Murphy Brownell Jameson.
From *Shakespeare's Heroines: Characteristics of Women,
Moral, Poetical, & Historical* 67

1857—Charles Bathurst. From *Remarks on the Differences in
Shakespeare's Versification in Different Periods of His Life* 69

1875—Edward Dowden. From *Shakspere: A Critical Study
of His Mind and Art* 71

1896—Georg Brandes. "The Dark Lady as a Model—
The Fall of the Republic a World-Catastrophe,"
from *William Shakespeare: A Critical Study* 75

❖ *Antony and Cleopatra* in the Twentieth Century 83

1901—George Bernard Shaw. From "Preface:
Better than Shakespear?" from *Three Plays for Puritans* 85

1909—A. C. Bradley. From "Shakespeare's *Antony
and Cleopatra*," in *Oxford Lectures on Poetry* 92

1931—G. Wilson Knight. "The Diadem of Love:
An Essay on *Antony and Cleopatra*," from *The Imperial
Theme: Further Interpretations of Shakespeare's Tragedies
Including the Roman Plays* 110

1951—Harold C. Goddard. "Antony and Cleopatra,"
from *The Meaning of Shakespeare* 163

1972—Anne Barton. " 'Nature's Piece 'Gainst Fancy':
The Divided Catastrophe in *Antony and Cleopatra*," from
An Inaugural Lecture (to the Hildred Carlile Chair
of English Literature in the University of London tenable
at Bedford College) 188

1974—Rosalie L. Colie. "The Significance of Style," from
Shakespeare's Living Art 205

1986—Northrop Frye. "Antony and Cleopatra,"
from *Northrop Frye on Shakespeare* 229

1988—Laura Quinney. "Enter a Messenger," from *William Shakespeare's Antony and Cleopatra* 244

1988—Harold Bloom. "Introduction," from *William Shakespeare's Antony and Cleopatra* 258

❖ *Antony and Cleopatra* in the Twenty-first Century 263

2000—Jacqueline Vanhoutte. "Antony's 'Secret House of Death': Suicide and Sovereignty in *Antony and Cleopatra*," from *Philological Quarterly* 263

Bibliography 279

Acknowledgments 281

Index 283

Series Introduction

Shakespeare Through the Ages presents not the most current of Shakespeare criticism, but the best of Shakespeare criticism, from the seventeenth century to today. In the process, each volume also charts the flow over time of critical discussion of a particular play. Other useful and fascinating collections of historical Shakespearean criticism exist, but no collection that we know of contains such a range of commentary on each of Shakespeare's greatest plays and at the same time emphasizes the greatest critics in our literary tradition: from John Dryden in the seventeenth century, to Samuel Johnson in the eighteenth century, to William Hazlitt and Samuel Coleridge in the nineteenth century, to A.C. Bradley and William Empson in the twentieth century, to the most perceptive critics of our own day. This canon of Shakespearean criticism emphasizes aesthetic rather than political or social analysis.

Some of the pieces included here are full-length essays; others are excerpts designed to present a key point. Much (but not all) of the earliest criticism consists only of brief mentions of specific plays. In addition to the classics of criticism, some pieces of mainly historical importance have been included, often to provide background for important reactions from future critics.

These volumes are intended for students, particularly those just beginning their explorations of Shakespeare. We have therefore also included basic materials designed to provide a solid grounding in each play: a biography of Shakespeare, a synopsis of the play, a list of characters, and an explication of key passages. In addition, each selection of the criticism of a particular century begins with an introductory essay discussing the general nature of that century's commentary and the particular issues and controversies addressed by critics presented in the volume.

Shakespeare was "not of an age, but for all time," but much Shakespeare criticism is decidedly for its own age, of lasting importance only to the scholar who wrote it. Students today read the criticism most readily available to them, which means essays printed in recent books and journals, especially those journals made available on the Internet. Older criticism is too often buried in out-of-print books on forgotten shelves of libraries or in defunct periodicals. Therefore, many students, particularly younger students, have no way of knowing that some of the most profound criticism of Shakespeare's plays was written decades or centuries ago. We hope this series remedies that problem, and more importantly, we hope it infuses students with the enthusiasm of the critics in these volumes for the beauty and power of Shakespeare's plays.

INTRODUCTION BY
HAROLD BLOOM

❧

Cleopatra is endless in her variety, as Enobarbus rightly says. Her personality is as richly expressive as Falstaff's, and hers is the most challenging role for an actress in all of Western drama. So dazzling is she that she eclipses Antony, who in most Shakespearean plays would be the dominant characterization. It is the perpetually changing glory of *Antony and Cleopatra* that the public world, from Rome to the Parthian border, constitutes a third prevailing presence in this overwhelming play. That may be why Shakespeare gives us so major an ellipsis: We never see Cleopatra and Antony alone on stage together, free of their entourages. There is one moment only in the wings, when Antony is rightly furious at her pragmatic treachery, but it tells us nothing about their intimacy.

Treachery is quite mutual between Cleopatra and Antony, since their relationship is as much political as it is erotic. Each is aging, though Antony's tendency to decline is sharper in its way down and out than Cleopatra's, since she shares with Falstaff a gallant denial of time. Bewildered by his own falling fortunes, Antony at last doubts his own identity. Cleopatra's inner self, for all her outward metamorphoses, keeps her vision of herself constant.

Shakespeare, from *Romeo and Juliet* onward, covertly invents a new meaning of eros, which is that it comes into being when desire is death. At the drama's close we have to understand that their authentic mutual love has destroyed both the protagonists. Cleopatra's self-staged death has a sublimity denied to Antony's since his bungled suicide repeats his developing ineptitude throughout. The impression that Cleopatra has been sustaining Antony hardly can be avoided. His end crosses tragedy with pathos; hers is wonderfully stylized, and goes beyond tragedy.

Shakespeare's mastery of the heterocosm he creates in this play is astonishing, even for him. Something vital in the dramatist is lavished here, and he will not again write tragedy with this intensity of invention. The contrast between *Antony and Cleopatra* and *Coriolanus* is startling. Exuberance of being, the wonder of Cleopatra and of Antony, is wholly absent from the great killing-machine and mother's boy Coriolanus. Personality makes a last stand in *Antony and Cleopatra* and expands until it bursts. Even Prospero, the magus of *The Tempest*, lacks the energetic overflow that goes from Falstaff through Cleopatra.

Huge as *Antony and Cleopatra* is, nothing in it can be spared. Rammed with life, for me it competes with *Henry IV, Part 1* as Shakespeare's most comprehensive work. I cannot judge which drama is wealthier, since both cover a cosmos, mixing politics, warfare, and the personal into an amalgam that baffles our analytical powers. Only Hamlet is worthy to stand with Falstaff and Cleopatra as *a* total consciousness. Iago is veiled, even from himself, and Lear transcends our apprehension, as do his Fool and the enemy brothers, Edmund and Edgar.

Shakespeare's supremacy over all other writers, even Dante, Cervantes, and Tolstoi, is evidenced in virtually every scene of this vast play. Every production I have attended has travestied it. Is there no director who will allow Shakespeare to be Shakespeare? High-concept directors have no hope of attaining Shakespeare's conceptual abundance, and the consequences are dismal. Since Cleopatra is a self-dramatizer, hers is as difficult a part to play well as any in Shakespeare. Antony's role is scarcely simpler. His personality is not as infinite, but the aesthetic beauty of his descent from grandeur into pathos demands an artistry very rare even in major actors. And the third protagonist, the struggle between East and West, has a prophetic quality that is disturbing for us at this time when Islam and the West move toward a disaster of confrontation.

As with *Henry IV, Part 1*, this play is supremely comic, depending upon the reader's own perspective. If you want to regard Falstaff as only a rancid old roisterer, the loss is entirely yours. Should you behold Cleopatra as a royal whore and Antony as her decadent gull, the splendor squandered is again your own. Shakespeare offers his audience everything, on many levels, as do his peers Dante and Cervantes, or in another mode, Montaigne. No creator ever has been less tendentious; he has no design upon you. He holds the mirror up not only to what is natural in you, but to your occult or secret self, you own genius or daemon. *Antony and Cleopatra* may be the largest of those mirrors, and the most salutary in this bad time.

Biography of
William Shakespeare
🙦🙤

WILLIAM SHAKESPEARE was born in Stratford-on-Avon in April 1564 into a family of some prominence. His father, John Shakespeare, was a glover and merchant of leather goods who earned enough to marry Mary Arden, the daughter of his father's landlord, in 1557. John Shakespeare was a prominent citizen in Stratford, and at one point, he served as an alderman and bailiff.

Shakespeare presumably attended the Stratford grammar school, where he would have received an education in Latin, but he did not go on to either Oxford or Cambridge universities. Little is recorded about Shakespeare's early life; indeed, the first record of his life after his christening is of his marriage to Anne Hathaway in 1582 in the church at Temple Grafton, near Stratford. He would have been required to obtain a special license from the bishop as security that there was no impediment to the marriage. Peter Alexander states in his book *Shakespeare's Life and Art* that marriage at this time in England required neither a church nor a priest or, for that matter, even a document—only a declaration of the contracting parties in the presence of witnesses. Thus, it was customary, though not mandatory, to follow the marriage with a church ceremony.

Little is known about William and Anne Shakespeare's marriage. Their first child, Susanna, was born in May 1583 and twins, Hamnet and Judith, in 1585. Later on, Susanna married Dr. John Hall, but the younger daughter, Judith, remained unmarried. When Hamnet died in Stratford in 1596, the boy was only 11 years old.

We have no record of Shakespeare's activities for the seven years after the birth of his twins, but by 1592 he was in London working as an actor. He was also apparently well known as a playwright, for reference is made of him by his contemporary Robert Greene in *A Groatsworth of Wit*, as "an upstart crow."

Several companies of actors were in London at this time. Shakespeare may have had connection with one or more of them before 1592, but we have no record that tells us definitely. However, we do know of his long association with the most famous and successful troupe, the Lord Chamberlain's Men. (When James I came to the throne in 1603, after Elizabeth's death, the troupe's name changed to the King's Men.) In 1599 the Lord Chamberlain's Men provided the financial backing for the construction of their own theater, the Globe.

The Globe was begun by a carpenter named James Burbage and finished by his two sons, Cuthbert and Robert. To escape the jurisdiction of the Corporation of London, which was composed of conservative Puritans who opposed the theater's "licentiousness," James Burbage built the Globe just outside London, in the Liberty of Holywell, beside Finsbury Fields. This also meant that the Globe was safer from the threats that lurked in London's crowded streets, like plague and other diseases, as well as rioting mobs. When James Burbage died in 1597, his sons completed the Globe's construction. Shakespeare played a vital role, financially and otherwise, in the construction of the theater, which was finally occupied sometime before May 16, 1599.

Shakespeare not only acted with the Globe's company of actors; he was also a shareholder and eventually became the troupe's most important playwright. The company included London's most famous actors, who inspired the creation of some of Shakespeare's best-known characters, such as Hamlet and Lear, as well as his clowns and fools.

In his early years, however, Shakespeare did not confine himself to the theater. He also composed some mythological-erotic poetry, such as *Venus and Adonis* and *The Rape of Lucrece*, both of which were dedicated to the earl of Southampton. Shakespeare was successful enough that in 1597 he was able to purchase his own home in Stratford, which he called New Place. He could even call himself a gentleman, for his father had been granted a coat of arms.

By 1598 Shakespeare had written some of his most famous works, *Romeo and Juliet*, *The Comedy of Errors*, *A Midsummer Night's Dream*, *The Merchant of Venice*, *Two Gentlemen of Verona*, and *Love's Labour's Lost*, as well as his historical plays *Richard II*, *Richard III*, *Henry IV*, and *King John*. Somewhere around the turn of the century, Shakespeare wrote his romantic comedies *As You Like It*, *Twelfth Night*, and *Much Ado About Nothing*, as well as *Henry V*, the last of his history plays in the Prince Hal series. During the next 10 years he wrote his great tragedies, *Hamlet*, *Macbeth*, *Othello*, *King Lear*, and *Antony and Cleopatra*.

At this time, the theater was burgeoning in London; the public took an avid interest in drama, the audiences were large, the plays demonstrated an enormous range of subjects, and playwrights competed for approval. By 1613, however, the rising tide of Puritanism had changed the theater. With the desertion of the theaters by the middle classes, the acting companies were compelled to depend more on the aristocracy, which also meant that they now had to cater to a more sophisticated audience.

Perhaps this change in London's artistic atmosphere contributed to Shakespeare's reasons for leaving London after 1612. His retirement from the theater is sometimes thought to be evidence that his artistic skills were waning. During this time, however, he wrote *The Tempest* and *Henry VIII*. He also wrote the "tragicomedies," *Pericles, Cymbeline,* and *The Winter's Tale.* These were thought to be inspired by Shakespeare's personal problems and have sometimes been considered proof of his greatly diminished abilities.

However, so far as biographical facts indicate, the circumstances of his life at this time do not imply any personal problems. He was in good health and financially secure, and he enjoyed an excellent reputation. Indeed, although he was settled in Stratford at this time, he made frequent visits to London, enjoying and participating in events at the royal court, directing rehearsals, and attending to other business matters.

In addition to his brilliant and enormous contributions to the theater, Shakespeare remained a poetic genius throughout the years, publishing a renowned and critically acclaimed sonnet cycle in 1609 (most of the sonnets were written many years earlier). Shakespeare's contribution to this popular poetic genre are all the more amazing in his break with contemporary notions of subject matter. Shakespeare idealized the beauty of man as an object of praise and devotion (rather than the Petrarchan tradition of the idealized, unattainable woman). In the same spirit of breaking with tradition, Shakespeare also treated themes previously considered off limits—the dark, sexual side of a woman as opposed to the Petrarchan ideal of a chaste and remote love object. He also expanded the sonnet's emotional range, including such emotions as delight, pride, shame, disgust, sadness, and fear.

When Shakespeare died in 1616, no collected edition of his works had ever been published, although some of his plays had been printed in separate unauthorized editions. (Some of these were taken from his manuscripts, some from the actors' prompt books, and others were reconstructed from memory by actors or spectators.) In 1623 two members of the King's Men, John Hemings and Henry Condell, published a collection of all the plays they considered to be authentic, the First Folio.

Included in the First Folio is a poem by Shakespeare's contemporary Ben Jonson, an outstanding playwright and critic in his own right. Jonson paid tribute to Shakespeare's genius, proclaiming his superiority to what previously had been held as the models for literary excellence—the Greek and Latin writers. "Triumph, my Britain, thou hast one to show / To whom all scenes of Europe homage owe. / He was not of an age, but for all time!"

Jonson was the first to state what has been said so many times since. Having captured what is permanent and universal to all human beings at all times, Shakespeare's genius continues to inspire us—and the critical debate about his works never ceases.

Summary of
Antony and Cleopatra
୫ଛ

Historical Background

The action of *Antony and Cleopatra* is complicated by the historical, political, and military contexts in which the play occurs. In 42 B.C.E. Marc Antony, Octavius Caesar, and Aemilius Lepidus defeated the armies of two of the assassins of Julius Caesar, Brutus and Cassius, at the battle of Philippi. Their victory made them the rulers of Rome and, consequently, of all of Rome's possessions, essentially the world known to them at that time. Although the three men formed a triumvirate, they were not united. Octavius in particular sought to gain sole control and total power; in fact, he succeeded. He transformed the Roman Republic into the Roman Empire and became the first Roman emperor, Augustus Caesar, after defeating Antony and Lepidus. In order to achieve his purpose, Octavius had to defeat not only his enemies but also his partners. Accordingly he fought not only Sextus Pompeius—the son of Pompey the Great, who had been an ally of Julius Caesar before they became enemies—but also his fellow triumvirs Lepidus and Antony.

Antony, a follower of Julius Caesar and older than Octavius, was known for his greatness as a soldier. After the defeat of Julius Caesar's assassins, he went to Egypt, where he met Cleopatra. She had been the lover of both Julius Caesar and the first Pompey, and, like Antony, she was no longer young. But, in the play, Cleopatra's beauty and sexual allure are, if anything, enhanced by her maturity. Antony falls in love with her and is transformed and torn by that passion. So is she.

Antony and Cleopatra is a vast drama. Its action spans the world from Rome to Egypt and ranges from intimate to epic. Action takes place on land and at sea. Characters exist in past, present, and future, as they are and as they are imagined to be. Antony, Cleopatra, Pompey, and Octavius Caesar are monumental historical personages who are presented both as earthbound human beings and as timeless, mythic figures.

Act I

Antony and Cleopatra begins (scene 1) in Egypt, in Cleopatra's court. There is a disjunction between what the audience sees and hears as the play begins. In pomp and splendor, Queen Cleopatra and General Antony enter, accompanied

5

by "her Ladies, the train," and "with Eunuchs fanning her." They are speaking to each other, but the audience hears only Philo, one of Antony's officers, in conversation with another of Antony's men. Philo deplores what he sees, suggesting that Antony himself has become one of Cleopatra's eunuchs. He recalls that Antony had been a general whose eyes, surveying his troops, "glowed like . . . Mars" armed for battle. But now those eyes, which commanded and subdued other men, are cast with devotion upon Cleopatra, Philo says, and Antony's heart, which once seemed to burst out of him with military bravery, now "is become the bellows and the fan / To cool a gypsy's lust."

Philo defines the opposition between love and war in war's favor. He speaks of war as a noble activity; sexual love he calls "dotage." The conflict, as Philo presents it, is not only between love and war but between commanding and complying, between being impervious to feelings and being enslaved by passion, between discipline and indulgence. Antony now is a man twisted with desire, teased and put off by Cleopatra. "If it be love," she says, as a challenge, "tell me how much." When he says, "There's beggary in the love that can be reckoned," and that she must "find out new heaven, new earth" if she wishes to find his love's limits, he is begging as much as he is boasting. But he is also laying out the trajectory of the play's action, because in the accomplishment of their love, the lovers do renounce and redefine the world. Far from subdued, Cleopatra goads Antony with his subordination to his wife and to Caesar, calling his declaration an "Excellent falsehood!" Her taunt is that he does not belong to himself, but to his wife, Fulvia, and Octavius, and that consequently he cannot commit himself to her, no matter how grand his rhetoric.

Cleopatra's coyness is the platform for Antony's love. Every taunt of hers fuels another boast of his and magnifies his desire. He is a soldier, after all, and responds to challenge. And Cleopatra is right: Antony is torn. He must go back to Rome because of his obligations there and because of his own memory of himself as a Roman, who "must break" "these strong Egyptian fetters." If she is to hold him, she must tighten his fetters not by surrendering to him but by whetting his desire with resistance.

A messenger from Octavius Caesar in Rome intrudes upon their romantic exchange; his presence irritates Antony. Cleopatra speculates on what his news is, taunting Antony: "Fulvia perchance is angry; or, who knows / If the scarce-bearded Caesar have not sent / His powerful mandate to you, 'Do this, or this; / Take in that kingdom, and enfranchise that; / Perform't, or else we damn thee.'" She not only portrays him as subordinate to Caesar but mocks their mutual enterprise. His response is pure bombast, as assertive as a soldier's charge: "Let Rome in Tiber melt. . . . Here is my space. . . . The nobleness of life / Is to do thus. . . . We stand peerless." Antony assumes the stance of passion, calls kissing greater than conquering, and asserts his independence and power. Cleopatra's disdain has achieved her purpose: They leave the stage without his having granted Caesar's messenger an audience.

In scene 2, Cleopatra's attendants are amusing themselves by having a soothsayer tell their fortunes. Cleopatra enters but leaves again before Antony can speak to her. Amid the general merriment Antony receives several chastening pieces of news: His wife and his brother warred first against each other, then jointly against Octavius Caesar, who defeated them; his own forces were defeated in the Middle East by Labienus; Pompey is at the head of a force moving against Octavius, who is still allied with Antony and counts on his aid; and his wife has died. Antony's Roman obligations seem to triumph over the sensuous delights of Egypt and Cleopatra's magnetism. He tells Enobarbus, one of his soldiers, to inform his captains that they are returning to Rome.

In scene 3, Antony informs Cleopatra that he is leaving Egypt, that Pompey is readying an attack on the triumvirate, and that Fulvia is dead. The news of Pompey's maneuver is intended to give Cleopatra the reason for his departure; the news of Fulvia's death is meant to allay her anxiety regarding his return. As Enobarbus has warned him, Cleopatra does not take his announcement well. She is petulant and self-pitying; she taunts him with his lack of feeling for his dead wife and for herself too.

Antony and Cleopatra have appeared together in each of the first three scenes. In each, they have been far more quarrelsome than affectionate: She mercilessly belittles him and is argumentative, cynical, and distant; he continually attempts to conciliate her, declaring his devotion, but to no avail. Now Cleopatra tells Charmian that her contrary behavior is an act. Whether it shows her actual love for Antony or her desire to put him completely in her power is not clear, nor is the distinction between those two conditions.

In scene 4 the setting shifts to Rome, where Octavius Caesar is criticizing Antony to Lepidus in much the same terms as Philo did in scene 1. Although his comments are about Antony, Octavius frames them to focus on himself. Antony, Octavius asserts, is responsible for Octavius's condemnation. By indulging the Egyptian side of his nature, Antony deprives Octavius of what he needs to battle against Pompey. Octavius presents a picture of the Antony who once had been a soldier able to endure and overcome the harshest conditions as a reproach to what he calls Antony's "lascivious wassails," but his condemnation is not of the moral sort; it is only framed in moral terms. Antony's offense is practical. He is needed "i' th' field. . . . Pompey / Thrives in our idleness." Antony does not physically appear in the scene, but his image haunts it as Octavius describes both the present-day debauchee in Egypt and yesterday's super-soldier. Octavius Caesar is putting together a case against Antony.

Just as Antony exists for Octavius more as an image than as a man, so too in scene 5 is he present in image to Cleopatra, though physically absent. In her idle reverie Cleopatra constructs an image of heroic proportions, now as a voluptuous and powerful lover. For both Cleopatra and Octavius, Antony exists at least as much as an idea as an actuality. The Antony whom Cleopatra evokes in solitude is not the man who has been with her during the first three scenes of the play—who was torn, indecisive, off-balance, frustrated, impotent, and blustering. Nor are the attitudes she expresses now—submissiveness, desire, adoration—the ones she showed then. Thus, by the end of Act I, Shakespeare has established a double perspective on Antony: There is the man who appears on the stage, and there is his essence: the image that rises from him, detaches itself, and replaces his actuality.

Act II

The second act begins (scene 1) in Messina, where Pompey, with his lieutenants, is setting forth his strategy of a naval attack against Octavius Caesar's forces. He is particularly optimistic because he believes that Antony is still in Egypt and thus not a power he must contend with. Pompey's manner of speaking about Antony suggests that Antony exists for him as he does for Octavius and Cleopatra, as a figure of erotic intensity as well as a real man. When Pompey learns that Antony has left Egypt and is expected in Rome, he regards it not as a matter to dread but a compliment to the seriousness of his own power: ". . . let us rear / The higher our opinion, that our stirring / Can from the lap of Egypt's widow pluck / The ne'er-lust-wearied Antony."

Scene 2 finds Enobarbus is in Rome in the house of Lepidus, the third triumvir. The two men are discussing the meeting that Antony has come to Rome to have with Octavius Caesar. Lepidus hopes to serve as a mediator reconciling the two other triumvirs and counseling them to mount a defense against Pompey's attack. Lepidus asks Enobarbus "to entreat your captain / To soft and gentle speech." But Enobarbus declines, conceiving of Antony in his glory and grandeur. When Antony and Octavius enter from opposite sides of the stage, however, it is the very tractable and fallible Antony who appears. Antony projects an attitude designed to mollify Caesar, not very different from the one he showed in his encounters with Cleopatra. And just as he put himself at Cleopatra's mercy by a kind of erotic braggadocio, so he impulsively binds himself to Caesar. Antony's reckless disregard for consequences suggests, without illuminating it, a terrible confusion in his soul.

Point by point, Octavius enumerates the wrongs he feels Antony has committed against him: the war that Antony's wife and brother waged against him, Antony's contempt for the messengers sent to Alexandria, and his failure to supply Octavius with arms. Antony accepts each indictment, explaining his failings and excusing himself. Before Octavius can respond, one of his generals, Maecenas, suggests that the two "enforce no further / The griefs between" them but "forget them quite" and "remember that the present need / Speaks to atone you." The "present need" is that they form an alliance against Pompey. Enobarbus states the matter in his own, blunt way: "If you borrow one another's love for the instant, you may, when you hear no more words of Pompey, return it again: you shall have time to wrangle in when you have nothing else to do." Antony chides him for such talk, but Octavius welcomes it.

Agrippa then proposes that, in order to forge a strong bond between the two men, Antony should marry Octavius Caesar's sister, Octavia. It is not clear if this proposal has been planned by Caesar or is a spontaneous move by Agrippa, one of his closest advisers; it seems likely that it is planned. It is clear, however, that Antony's response is as spontaneous as it is ill-advised: He consents to the marriage. Thus resolved, Octavius and Antony, followed by Lepidus, quit the stage on their way to Octavia's residence. Their subordinates, Enobarbus, Agrippa, and Maecenas, remain behind, and immediately the conversation turns to the sensuality of Egypt and the glorious allure of Cleopatra. Enobarbus arouses their envy with accounts of the feasts and revels there, and particularly with his description of Cleopatra the day Antony first saw her: resplendent on her barge coming down the Nile. Bowing to reality, Maecenas says, "Now Antony must leave her utterly." Enobarbus denies this: "Never; he will not." Enobarbus's denial refers not to Antony's character, however, but to the image of Cleopatra he has created, which can stand alongside Antony's grand image:

> Age cannot wither her, nor custom stale
> Her infinite variety: other women cloy
> The appetites they feed: but she makes hungry
> Where most she satisfies; for vilest things
> Become themselves in her: that the holy priests
> Bless her when she is riggish.

Maecenas optimistically responds, "If beauty, wisdom, modesty, can settle / The heart of Antony, Octavia is / A blessed lottery to him." It seems unlikely, however, that good sense can triumph over the energy of Cleopatra's spirit.

Antony and Octavia appear with Octavius as scene 3 begins. Their meeting is brief and formal, and Antony's first words to Octavia foreshadow division, not union: "The world and my great office will sometimes / Divide me from your bosom." Accepting this pledge to Octavia (and, implicitly, to her brother), Octavius and Octavia depart.

Antony then happens upon the soothsayer, who had first appeared among Cleopatra's attendants in the jesting context of Act I, scene 2. He asks, "Whose fortunes shall rise higher, Caesar's, or mine?" The Soothsayer replies:

> Caesar's.
> Therefore, O Antony, stay not by his side:

Thy demon, that's thy spirit which keeps thee, is
Noble, courageous, high, unmatchable,
Where Caesar's is not; but, near him, thy angel
Becomes a fear, as being o'erpower'd: therefore
Make space enough between you.

It is a kind of fairy-tale answer. What the soothsayer is telling Antony is that he is not made for the terrestrial world, the world controlled by ambition and conquest; that is Caesar's sphere. Antony's true existence lies in a transcendent sphere. His spirit is "Noble, courageous, high, unmatchable," and Caesar's is not. Those qualities imbue it with intangibility, even with a delicacy that Caesar's earthbound power lacks, but which in its brute reality threatens Antony's spirit.

The soothsayer serves a double function. Within the plot of *Antony and Cleopatra*, he warns Antony of the risk that Caesar represents. As an interpreter of the plot, he provides the audience with insight into the existential force behind Antony's self-destructive behavior. Antony seems to be moved by capricious spirits. His peculiar, apparently self-defeating actions do not have a motive; they are the result of a force that he is consciously unaware of but bound by his nature to obey. When one understands that, one can begin to see Antony as a tragic hero: Antony unconsciously directs himself to a transcendent heroic destiny, which can only be realized through his destruction.

When Antony is again alone, he explains his true intention: "I will to Egypt: / And though I make this marriage for my peace, / I' th' East my pleasure lies." This is not the way to begin a marriage with Octavia or to cement an alliance with Octavius Caesar. Nor is it the path toward peace, because betrayal is present in Antony's mind from the very start. The betrayal is manifold. First, it is clear that Antony will betray Caesar and Octavia. But the marriage also betrays Cleopatra. Moreover, besides betraying others, Antony has engineered a series of self-betrayals. He betrays himself, both Philo and Octavius believe, by his devotion to Cleopatra; but more significantly, by renouncing her he betrays what is clearly becoming his deeper self.

In the next brief scene (scene 4), the triumvirs and their men prepare to do battle with Pompey.

Cleopatra waits idly in Egypt in scene 5, restlessly shifting her attention from one unsatisfactory distraction to another while Antony is away. She recalls voluptuous scenes of erotic adventures with him, culminating in a recollection of their embraces when they exchanged roles and he wore her garments and crown and she, his sword. A messenger from Rome interrupts, bringing news that Antony has married Octavia. At this, Cleopatra's pent-up energy explodes in violent anger at the messenger. She strikes him and threatens him with a knife. He meekly explains that he must report the news that is, rather than the news she wishes to hear. Her fury abates and Cleopatra dismisses the messenger.

As Charmian leads her offstage, Cleopatra is full of the dignity of her suffering: "Pity me, Charmian, / But do not speak to me. Lead me to my chamber." Though wounded, she is not defeated: "Bring me word how tall [Octavia] is," she commands her eunuch, Mardian.

From Egypt and Cleopatra, scene 6 shifts to Misenum, a port city on the Bay of Naples. Here Pompey and the triumvirs meet and come to an agreement, thus avoiding a naval battle. Octavius, Antony, and Lepidus concede Sicily and Sardinia to Pompey. In return, Pompey must police the seas against pirates and pay tribute to Rome in the form of wheat. The battle avoided, Pompey invites the triumvirs to feast aboard his galley. While Pompey seems satisfied with the agreement he has made, his chief lieutenant, Menas, is skeptical.

In scene 7, when the feast is at its height and everyone drunk, Menas takes Pompey aside and suggests that he could "cut the cable; / And when we are put off" kill the triumvirs, giving Pompey supreme power. Angry and righteous, Pompey rejects the scheme: "[T]his thou shouldst have done / And not have spoke on't! In me 'tis villany; / In thee't had been good service." Privately disgusted with his master, Menas finally joins the revels. Time shows his wisdom, however. Later in the play, the audience hears that Octavius has unilaterally "waged / New wars 'gainst Pompey" (Act III, scene 4), and later still comes the news that Pompey is dead, murdered by one of Antony's men (Act III, scene 5). Temperamental shifts, which appear so skittish in Cleopatra, are no less present in the Roman world—but there, they are dignified as policy and strategy.

Act III

Scene 1, opens in Syria where Ventidius, commander of Antony's forces in Syria, is deciding his next move. Having defeated the Parthians, Ventidius refuses Silius's advice to pursue the routed troops in their retreat and make his triumph all the greater. Saying, "I have done enough," he explains,

> . . . a lower place . . .
> May make too great an act. . . .
> Better to leave undone, than by our deed
> Acquire too high a fame when him we serve's away.
> Caesar and Antony have ever won
> More in their officer than person.

If Shakespeare had never written this scene, no one would ever know to miss it. It stands alone, isolated from the rest of the play. Yet this scene puts the rest of the play in perspective. Caesar and Antony, heroes of mythic, even godlike stature, are creatures of mystique. Their actual accomplishments are the work of their officers, not themselves. But should an officer accomplish too much and his reputation threaten to overwhelm his superior's, his service becomes an offense. Thus Ventidius ends by saying that he will notify Antony "humbly . . . what in his name . . . we have effected." Ventidius's lesson in hierarchical etiquette provides the audience or reader a lesson in perspective. More than it is about the military, political, and interpersonal events that it chronicles, *Antony and Cleopatra* is about the creation of transcendental myths and about the clash of mythic figures with one another. Furthermore, it is about the clash of identity that each of those figures endures when his or her personal myth confronts the human reality.

In scene 2 the soldiers Enobarbus (attached to Antony) and Agrippa (attached to Octavius Caesar) take leave of each other to follow their leaders. As if they had been watching the previous scene, the two mock the grandeur of their masters and review, without illusion, the fawning tributes Lepidus has paid to each. Octavius Caesar, Antony, Lepidus, and Octavia enter. Returning to the subject of Antony's marriage to Octavia, Caesar warns Antony not to betray his sister; the consequences would be dire. Antony assures Caesar he has no reason for fear (despite his own clear indication, at Act II, scene 3, that he will return to Cleopatra).

In scene 3 Cleopatra questions the messenger in her court. Afterward she is certain that Antony will return to Egypt: Octavia is no rival.

The locale jumps to Antony's house in Athens in scene 4. The newlyweds are in the midst of a conversation—or perhaps an argument. "Nay, nay, Octavia, not only that," Antony complains. He catalogs the inexcusable wrongs Octavius Caesar has done him since their marriage, not least of which is Caesar's failure to speak of Antony with the full honor Antony feels is his due. Octavia begs forbearance for her brother and understanding for herself: If the two warred against each other, she would be in a grievous position, torn by her loyalty to each. Antony's concern, however, is with his honor.

The fact that Antony really is not Octavia's resonates in his speech. Their marriage was designed to make him Caesar's, but he is not Caesar's either. He is Cleopatra's. Antony is his own only when he is differentiated entirely from Caesar and existing in a separate realm from Caesar's, one Caesar cannot enter. Nonetheless, Antony now endorses Octavia's desire to reconcile him and Caesar, and he accepts her offer to act as a go-between. Even so, he warns her that she will have to take sides: "Our faults / Can never be so equal that your love / Can equally move with them."

The brief scene 5 takes place at Octavius Caesar's house in Rome. Eros tells Enobarbus the "strange news" that Caesar, having defeated Pompey with the assistance of Lepidus, has now thrown Lepidus in prison, where he awaits execution.

Scene 6, also at Caesar's house, presents Caesar and his generals Maecenas and Agrippa in council of war against Antony, who has returned to Egypt. There Antony has made Cleopatra and her children rulers of several of the provinces that he had captured, in Caesar's estimation establishing an empire to rival his own. Octavia appears on her goodwill mission. Caesar greets his sister with righteous tenderness for an aggrieved wife. He breaks the news to her that Antony is not still in Athens, as she believes, but with Cleopatra and planning war against him.

When Antony next appears, in scene 7, it is indeed in Egypt. Cleopatra is berating Enobarbus for trying to prevent her from participating in the battle against Octavius Caesar. At Antony's entrance, the argument shifts from the question of Cleopatra's involvement to the question of venue: Will they accept Caesar's challenge to fight at sea, where he has the advantage, or will they engineer a battle on land, where Antony has the advantage? Cleopatra insists on a sea battle, and Antony refuses to recognize his disadvantage at sea despite the arguments of Enobarbus and other seasoned soldiers.

The brief scenes 8 and 9 show the rival forces preparing for the conflict at sea.

The sea battle takes place offstage, and Antony's men Enobarbus and Scarus heatedly discuss its progress in scene 10. Cleopatra joined in as a participant, commanding one of the vessels. Ironically, Antony's fleet was not at the great disadvantage that had been expected, but in the midst of the battle Cleopatra inexplicably ordered her vessel to retreat. Antony followed her, turning his ship from the encounter as well. This and not his navy's inferiority led to the breakup of his force and his defeat. Antony's ignominious defeat is a reflection of the breakdown of his soldier's character and discipline, and many of his captains with their troops now desert him for Octavius Caesar. Even the loyal Enobarbus begins to think of quitting Antony, but his loyalty prevails and he remains.

Until scene 11, Antony has been shown as a once-heroic figure in decline. Like a person addicted to and steadily destroyed by alcohol or narcotics, he struggles against an emerging sensuality that is undercutting his resolve and robbing him of his reputation. But now, after the naval battle, Antony emerges as both a seriously diminished figure and a man redefined by a fundamental transformation. "I have lost my way forever," he tells his captains. "I have a ship / Laden with gold: take that, divide it; fly, / And make your peace with Caesar." In accepting his new fate as a defeated man he takes on a new grandeur and a nobility that overcomes defeat.

Cleopatra enters shamefaced with her attendants, and Antony laments, "Wither hast thou led me, Egypt?" Cleopatra begs his forgiveness for her ship's retreat, saying, "I little thought / You would have followed." He responds:

Egypt, thou knew'st too well
My heart was to thy rudder tied by the strings,
And thou shouldst tow me after: o'er my spirit
Thy full supremacy thou knew'st, and that
Thy beck might from the bidding of the gods
Command me.

This is less a reproach to her than a confession of his passion and a recognition of how securely he is bound to her. Although he now must humble himself to Caesar, whose equal in power he had once been, Antony says he does not repent the transformation: "Fall not a tear, I say; one of them rates / All that is won and lost: give me a kiss; / Even this repays me."

In scene 12 Antony, through his ambassador, subordinates himself to Octavius Caesar and asks permission to remain in Egypt, or at least to live in Athens. Cleopatra asks to be permitted to remain queen of Egypt. "For Antony," Caesar says, "I have no ears to his request." He is, however, willing to grant Cleopatra everything on condition that she send Antony as a prisoner to him or execute him in Egypt. In addition, Caesar sends one of his own men, Thidias, to Cleopatra, instructing him to win her away from Antony. Caesar tells Thidias to promise her whatever she wishes, assuring him that women, in the best of times, are weak; when fortune is against them, even the most virtuous can be manipulated.

In scene 13, Antony tells Cleopatra Caesar's condition for her request: that she send Caesar Antony's head. She says only, "That head, my lord?" and yet her words ring with her expression of the absurdity and unreality of Caesar's proposition. Just as Octavius Caesar's victory allowed Antony to recognize his deepest allegiance—devotion to Cleopatra rather than lust for world domination—so Caesar's assault against Cleopatra compels her to reveal herself without her usual wiles. She demonstrates that she is as committed to Antony as he is to her. Thus begins the sequence of events in which Antony and Cleopatra realize their love, their grandeur, and their triumph.

Antony, less aware of her at this moment than of Caesar's gall, leaves to reply to Caesar's ambassador with a challenge to single combat. Enobarbus, always the realist, comments in an aside that Antony has lost touch with reality to offer such a challenge. Antony is the greater swordsman; Caesar is a tactician, not a soldier, and would never jeopardize himself so.

Thidias arrives. When he presents himself to Cleopatra with Octavius Caesar's conditions, Cleopatra shows herself a more cunning politician than the overconfident ambassador. Thidias tries to frame her responses and suggest her course. Caesar, he says, "knows that you embraced not Antony / As you did love, but as you feared him." "O!" Cleopatra responds with buried irony. When she does speak, it is with equivocation. "My honor was not yielded, / But conquered merely," where "conquered" suggests the depth of her love and the extent of Antony's power rather than her enforced submission, and "merely" means entirely. Enobarbus, honest and blunt as he is, has an ear unattuned to irony or second meanings. Taking her statement at face value and assuming, as Thidias must, that she is yielding to Caesar, he leaves the room, no doubt to tell Antony of his further misfortune.

The two men enter just as Cleopatra acquiesces to Thidias's request to kiss her hand. Seeing that, Antony orders Thidias to be taken out and whipped. He vents his rage against Cleopatra, not for his defeat but for what he sees as her betrayal. In his fury he cuts off each of her attempts to speak until she responds, "Not know me yet?" In this climactic phrase she reveals the meaning of all her past behavior toward him: It was teasing born of love and desire rather than dismissal. When Antony accuses her of being "cold-hearted" to him, she answers with what may be her first direct declaration of her feeling:

Ah, dear, if I be so,
From my cold heart let heaven engender hail,
And poison it in the source; and the first stone
Drop in my neck: as it determines, so
Dissolve my life! The next Caesarion smite!
Till by degrees the memory of my womb,
Together with my brave Egyptians all,
By the discandying of this pelleted storm,
Lie graveless, till the flies and gnats of Nile
Have buried them for prey!

"I am satisfied," Antony says, and his old energy floods through him. He vows to challenge Caesar yet in another battle and to celebrate one more "gaudy night" of revelry with Cleopatra. This absurd renewal of spirit despite Caesar's might pushes Enobarbus to his limit. He decides that he, too, will abandon Antony.

Act IV

As he formulates battle plans in scene 1, Octavius Caesar expresses scorn for Antony's challenge to single combat.

In scene 2, Antony addresses his men on the eve of the battle. He offers a valiant farewell, cementing their loyalty with his sentiment. Despite his emotion, he denies that he is pessimistic about their chance for victory.

Later that night, in scene 3, the soldiers on the watch hear strange music under the earth and above them. One of them says that it is the sound of Antony's guardian angel deserting him.

In scene 4, Cleopatra sentimentally fusses over Antony as he dresses for battle.

In scene 5 Antony hears the distressing news that Enobarbus, until now his most loyal supporter, has deserted him for Caesar's camp. He responds by instructing his men to send Enobarbus his belongings: "Go, Eros, send his treasure after; do it; / Detain no jot, I charge thee. Write him / (I will subscribe) gentle adieus and greetings; / Say that I wish he never find more cause / To change a master." Antony's response to Enobarbus's defection stands in sharp contrast to Octavius Caesar's behavior to his own subordinates.

Octavius Caesar, accompanied by Agrippa and Antony's former subordinates Enobarbus and Dolabella, gives orders for his battle against Antony in scene 6. He instructs Agrippa to place the soldiers who have defected from Antony in the front line "That Antony may seem to spend his fury / Upon himself." Antony himself is to be taken alive. Enobarbus already regrets his decision to abandon Antony: "I have done ill; / Of which I do accuse myself so sorely, / That I will joy no more." Immediately afterward a soldier informs Enobarbus that Antony has sent him all his treasure "with / His bounty overplus." Disgusted with himself, Enobarbus gives it all to the soldier, who remarks that even in defeat Antony "Continues still a Jove." In a second soliloquy, Enobarbus vows not to fight against Antony but to throw himself into a ditch and die of guilt and grief.

The fighting, in scene 7, favors Antony, and Agrippa orders a retreat. Despite the desertions Antony has suffered, his forces win the battle.

As a celebratory gesture in scene 8, Antony brings one of his valiant soldiers to Cleopatra to be rewarded with the opportunity to kiss her hand.

In scene 9, Enobarbus fulfills his pledge to die rather than fight against Antony.

Antony observes that Caesar's forces are preparing for battle at sea in scene 10. Caesar confirms this in scene 11.

Antony's victory is short-lived. In the next battle, in scene 12, his navy is defeated and surrenders. Antony rages, convinced that Cleopatra has joined in league with Caesar and betrayed him. (Why he now believes Cleopatra has betrayed him, with apparently less cause than in Act III, is puzzling.) When she approaches, asking, "Why is my lord enraged against his love?" he calls her a witch and cries in fury that he will kill her.

Cleopatra flees from Antony (scene 13) and with her attendants locks herself in her monument. She then sends Mardian, her eunuch, to tell Antony that she has killed herself, uttering his name as she died.

Hearing from Mardian (scene 14) that Cleopatra loved him and died for him by her own hand, Antony is overcome with despair. His rage turns to bitter grief and shame, and he longs to join her in death. He bids his servant Eros to run his sword through him. Rather than kill his master, however, Eros slays himself. More deeply shamed by his servant's valor, Antony falls on his own sword but bungles the attempt and is mortally wounded rather than killed. Beset with "a prophesying fear," Cleopatra has sent her attendant Diomedes to tell Antony she is alive. When the wounded and dying Antony learns this, his heroic spirit returns. "Do not please sharp fate / To grace it with your sorrows," he commands his guards and orders them to carry him to Cleopatra's monument.

In scene 15, Antony rests at the foot of the monument, but Cleopatra explains that she cannot come down to him lest she be taken. Instead, she and her women hoist him up to her. She tells him she is determined to join him in death rather than yield to Caesar. In a great, operatic exchange, they declare the transcendental character of their love. By snatching life and earthly power from the forces that seemed to defeat them, they will defeat those forces with their love. At last Antony dies, and Cleopatra vows to follow him in death.

Act V

The last act of *Antony and Cleopatra* begins (scene 1) with irony. Octavius Caesar sends Dolabella to Antony to "bid him yield." As soon as Dolabella has departed, Decretas arrives from Antony's camp with the news that Antony has evaded Caesar's victory by killing himself. A servant of Cleopatra arrives and asks Caesar's instructions for her.

In scene 2 Cleopatra puts into words the nature and scope of Antony's triumph and the triumph she intends:

'Tis paltry to be Caesar;
Not being Fortune, he's but Fortune's knave,
A minister of her will: and it is great
To do that thing that ends all other deeds;
Which shackles accidents and bolts up change.

Emissaries of Octavius Caesar, first Proculeius and then Dolabella, arrive in order to negotiate with Cleopatra the terms of her surrender. Proculeius assures her that Caesar wishes to be magnanimous and will meet whatever terms she wishes to request. But as he finishes his speech, Caesar's soldiers storm in and seize her; Cleopatra is now Caesar's prisoner. When Dolabella returns, he confirms Cleopatra's suspicion that Caesar will lead her captive through Rome, making a spectacle of her for his glory. Cleopatra repeatedly threatens to commit suicide rather than allow herself to be displayed as Caesar's trophy captive, but Caesar himself warns that he will slaughter her children if she does. Seeming to submit to him, Cleopatra gives him an inventory of all her wealth and asks her treasurer, Seleucus, to confirm its accuracy to Caesar. When he reports that she has withheld as much as she has declared, she flies into fury at him. Caesar, however, says he is not interested in her wealth. Assuring her of his goodwill, he leaves, apparently confident of her venality and her desire to remain alive.

But Caesar is mistaken. Cleopatra has arranged for a peasant to bring her a basket of figs, concealed in which are asps, small venomous snakes. "Give me my robe, put on my crown," she commands her serving woman Iras. "I have /

Immortal longings in me." Cleopatra approaches her death as if she were preparing for her wedding with Antony. "Husband, I come," she cries. "Now to that name my courage prove my title! / I am fire, and air; my other elements / I give to baser life." She and her women apply the smakes to their breasts and die, thus thwarting Caesar. Surveying this scene of death, Caesar proclaims the glory of Antony and Cleopatra and basks in its reflected glow.

KEY PASSAGES IN
ANTONY AND CLEOPATRA
🙰

Act I, i, 1–2

Philo: Nay, but this dotage of our general's
O'erflows the measure.

Antony and Cleopatra begins with a negation—"Nay"—and a contradiction. Philo is arguing against something Demetrius has just said and asserting that Antony's behavior is unworthy of him, that it is "dotage," akin to senile decay. The expression he uses to diminish Antony, "O'erflows the measure," suggests abundance and the action of the Nile in its annual flooding, when the river "o'erflows the measure" of its banks. Rather than suggesting impoverishment, then, the image evokes the idea of enrichment. In this way, the opening sentence immediately introduces the play's double perspective, its conflict between values, and the question of what constitutes loss and what constitutes gain.

Act I, i, 14–17

Cleopatra: If it be love indeed, tell me how much.
Antony: There's beggary in the love that can be reckon'd.
Cleopatra: I'll set a bourn how far to be beloved.
Antony: Then must thou needs find out new heaven, new earth.

Cleopatra's first words have been framed by Philo's contemptuous introduction. He has just called her a "strumpet" (a prostitute) and Antony "a strumpet's fool." Thus the way the audience hears her words is influenced by this characterization. As if to confirm Philo's insult, Cleopatra is asking Antony to quantify his love. "Tell me how much" implies that love is an item, a commodity that can be measured. Cleopatra's demand makes her sound like a common flirt. But it ought to be noted that hers is essentially the same question that Lear asks his daughters at the beginning of *King Lear*. ("Which of you shall we say doth love us most?")

19

Antony, however, does not fall for the quantitative trick of her question. Despite the hint of bombast in his reply, "There's beggary in the love that can be reckoned," he is saying that love is not quantifiable; it is a quality. He is thus entering a different realm from the one that Caesar knows, in which value can be measured by the amount of possessions accumulated.

Act I, i, 19–24

Cleopatra: Nay, hear them, Antony:
Fulvia perchance is angry; or, who knows
If the scarce-bearded Caesar have not sent
His powerful mandate to you, "Do this, or this;
Take in that kingdom, and enfranchise that;
Perform 't, or else we damn thee."

The audience first encounters Octavius Caesar indirectly through Cleopatra, who is both his rival for Antony and the negation of his value system. She grants Caesar the power he has and simultaneously mocks it. In this way she teases Antony about the nature of his allegiance. Like Philo, she begins with a contradiction. "Nay," she says when Antony avoids Caesar's messenger, "hear them, Antony." She is reminding him that, as a "triple pillar of the world" (one of its three supreme powers), he is in bondage to his own power and—it comes to the same thing—to Caesar.

Act I, ii, 147–157

Antony: She is cunning past man's thought.
Enobarbus: Alack, sir, no; her passions are made of nothing but the finest part of pure love: we cannot call her winds and waters sighs and tears; they are greater storms and tempests than almanacs can report: this cannot be cunning in her; if it be, she makes a shower of rain as well as Jove.
Antony: Would I had never seen her.
Enobarbus: O, sir, you had then left unseen a wonderful piece of work; which not to have been blest withal would have discredited your travel.

This exchange regarding Cleopatra follows Antony's announcement that he must leave Egypt. Although the word *cunning* now almost exclusively means "sly" and it is reasonable to assume that Antony is invoking this meaning, there is also a sense of intellectual ability in it. Hence Antony's sense also suggests "knowing," an older meaning of the word. Antony is accusing Cleopatra of being deliberate in her capriciousness, of having a purpose and scheming in order to achieve it—in other words, of having the same order of intellect that Caesar has and using it tactically, as he does, to advance her ends.

Enobarbus contradicts him, describing Cleopatra as transparent. Her behavior, he says, is the direct expression of her nature, not a product mediated by a scheming intellect. She is herself a strong force of nature, says Enobarbus; her displays of emotion are no more cunning than rain. Their conversation reveals that at this point in the play, Antony understands the strength and depth of his passion for Cleopatra but does not understand the nature of the force—Cleopatra—that inspires that passion.

Act I, iii, 6–10

Charmian: Madam, methinks, if you did love him dearly,
You do not hold the method to enforce
The like from him.
Cleopatra: What should I do, I do not?
Charmian: In each thing give him way, cross him nothing.
Cleopatra: Thou teachest like a fool; the way to lose him.

As if to contradict Enobarbus and substantiate Antony's claim, Charmian advises openness and Cleopatra reveals her use of cunning in her attempt to fasten Antony to her. Of course, Charmian's openness is just as much a ruse. But Cleopatra's "cunning" as it is expressed here does not suggest that her love is false or has any other end than union with Antony. The problem that a reader may encounter here involves the very nature of love: When love is defined as a desire to possess—which, no matter what its definition or context, it always seems to be—it is inextricably connected to power. Thus the complexities and ambiguities of *Antony and Cleopatra* result from the play's exploration of love and power.

Act I, iv, 25–33

Octavius Caesar: If he filled
His vacancy with his voluptuousness,
Full surfeits, and the dryness of his bones,
Call on him for't: but to confound such time,
That drums him from his sport, and speaks as loud
As his own state and ours,—'tis to be chid
As we rate boys, who, being mature in knowledge,

Pawn their experience to their present pleasure,
And so rebel to judgment.

In this conversation with Lepidus, Octavius is denouncing Antony's voluptuous dissipation. He argues that what Antony does is his own business; if Antony wants to ruin himself in revelry, it is his prerogative. But when Antony's irresponsibility affects Octavius himself, it becomes his business as well, Octavius says. The contrast Octavius makes between control (judgment) and rebellion (pleasure) sounds a key theme of the play. These opposing poles are represented by himself and Cleopatra.

Act I, v, 42–50

Alexas: "Good friend," quoth he,
"Say, the firm Roman to great Egypt sends
This treasure of an oyster; at whose foot,
To mend the petty present, I will piece
Her opulent throne with kingdoms; all the east,
Say thou, shall call her mistress." So he nodded,
And soberly did mount an arm-gaunt steed,
Who neighed so high, that what I would have spoke
Was beastly dumbed by him.

Alexas's report of the greeting Antony has sent from Rome to Cleopatra in Egypt depicts a heroic Antony unlike the man the audience has actually been seeing. But the image of Antony mounted in armor on his steed presents itself as vividly to the imagination as his actual depiction onstage has done, setting up a double image of Antony in the play.

Within this scene, Alexas's account of Antony on his horse completes his report of Antony's gift to Cleopatra: an opulent pearl, which he bestows as a symbol of the kingdoms he promises to give her. Antony's gift of kingdoms threatens Octavius Caesar's power in the world because it diminishes the magnitude of his holdings. An ironic coda to Alexas's report is that the neighing of Antony's horse prevented further human speech. It symbolically suggests that the force of Antony's animal passion overwhelms his faculty for rational discourse, which is Caesar's view of Antony.

Act II, ii, 241–246

Enobarbus: Age cannot wither her, nor custom stale
Her infinite variety: other women cloy

The appetites they feed: but she makes hungry
Where most she satisfies; for vilest things
Become themselves in her: that the holy priests
Bless her when she is riggish.

Enobarbus's summation of Cleopatra follows immediately upon his sensuous monologue describing Cleopatra on her barge on the Nile the day she met Antony. It concludes the scene in which Octavius Caesar and Antony have forged an alliance: Antony will marry Caesar's sister Octavia.

This speech, rather than describing her person, conveys the force of Cleopatra's character and its captivating effect upon men. She is presented as unencompassable and infinitely desirable because of her very instability. Cleopatra thus represents a counterforce to Caesar's aim of securing the world as a uniformly governed, predictable entity under his sole command. She is also, clearly, the antithesis of Octavia, whose "beauty, wisdom, modesty" are supposed to "settle / The heart of Antony" (247–248), not stir and inflame it.

Act II, iii, 19–24

Soothsayer: Therefore, O Antony, stay not by his side:
Thy demon, that's thy spirit which keeps thee, is
Noble, courageous high, unmatchable,
Where Caesar's is not; but, near him, thy angel
Becomes a fear, as being o'erpower'd: therefore
Make space enough between you.

Just after he has parted with Octavius Caesar and Octavia, telling her that his business may sometimes separate him from her, Antony encounters the soothsayer. He warns Antony to keep his distance from Caesar. Although Antony's spirit is "Noble, courageous high, unmatchable, / Where Caesar's is not," he says Caesar has an inherent power that overwhelms Antony. The soothsayer's account of Antony credits his character with a romantic dimension. This capacity can give depth to his passion for Cleopatra, and it can make his erratic course seem more profound than Caesar's order.

Act II, v, 20–23

Cleopatra: . . . and next morn,
Ere the ninth hour, I drunk him to his bed;
Then put my tires and mantles on him, whilst
I wore his sword Philippan.

Languishing in Egypt and bored without Antony, Cleopatra gropes for distractions. Neither music nor billiards affords any relief. Finally she finds some respite in reverie: She remembers how she dressed Antony in her garments and wore his sword as they made love. Her words not only convey the contours of her own sexual appetite but also suggest a kind of epiphany for Antony: When Cleopatra guided him through a transgression of gender boundaries, she allowed Antony to experience aspects of surrender and receptivity. These qualities lie beyond his masculine-oriented Roman identity, which defines masculinity (as represented in Caesar) by conquest. By experiencing them, Antony is enlarged.

Act II, vii, 75–82

Pompey: Ah, this thou shouldst have done,
And not have spoke on't! In me 'tis villany;
In thee't had been good service. Thou must know,
'Tis not my profit that does lead mine honour;
Mine honour, it. Repent that e'er thy tongue
Hath so betray'd thine act: being done unknown,
I should have found it afterwards well done;
But must condemn it now. Desist, and drink.

Caesar, Antony, and Lepidus are aboard Pompey's galley and drunk, celebrating a peace accord they have just reached. In this speech, Pompey is responding to a suggestion Menas has made: that they cut the cable of the ship and kill these guests.

Pompey's response is apparently high-minded ("'Tis not my profit that does lead mine honor; / Mine honor, it") and seems to represent a high and noble Roman value. But Pompey sharply undercuts this interpretation when he adds, "I should have found it afterwards well done; / But must condemn it now." It is the appearance of honor Pompey cultivates, not honor itself. Octavius Caesar is similarly concerned, throughout the play, with how he appears, as is Cleopatra. Only Antony is concerned with how he *is* rather than how he appears.

Act III, i, 12–17

Ventidius: I have done enough; a lower place, note well,
May make too great an act: for learn this, Silius;
Better to leave undone, than by our deed
Acquire too high a fame when him we serve's away.

Caesar and Antony have ever won
More in their officer than person.

On a plain in Syria—well apart from the main action of the play—one of Antony's generals, Ventidius, has won a victory and is outlining to a subordinate their army's next move. Ventidius explains to Silius that underlings must not accomplish too much. Their heroic deeds tend to diminish the luster of their masters even as they serve them. Ventidius points out that the feats for which Antony and Caesar are acclaimed were actually accomplished by their officers. Power, *Antony and Cleopatra* is once more suggesting, is a matter of image rather than fact.

Act III, v, 22–23

Antony: If I lose mine honor,
I lose myself.

Antony has just explained to his new wife, Octavia, why his differences with her brother, Octavius Caesar, are cracking their alliance. Octavia in turn has begged Antony to put aside his grievances for her sake: A rift between Antony and Caesar will cause an impossible division in her loyalty.

With these words Antony explains why he is unable to accede to her request. It is important to compare the way Antony invokes the concept of honor here and the way Pompey does so in Act II, scene 7 (lines 75–82). Pompey is concerned with appearing honorable to others. Antony is concerned not with his appearance but with his own inner sense of himself.

Act III, vi, 3–19

Octavius Caesar: I' th' marketplace, on a tribunal silvered,
Cleopatra and himself in chairs of gold
Were publicly enthroned: at the feet sat
Caesarion, whom they call my father's son,
And all the unlawful issue that their lust
Since then hath made between them. Unto her
He gave the stablishment of Egypt; made her
Of lower Syria, Cyprus, Lydia,
Absolute queen.
Maecenas: This in the public eye?
Octavius Caesar: I' the common show-place, where they exercise.

His sons he there proclaim'd the kings of kings:
Great Media, Parthia, and Armenia.
He gave to Alexander; to Ptolemy he assign'd
Syria, Cilicia, and Phoenicia: she
In the habiliments of the goddess Isis
That day appear'd. . . .

Talking to his lieutenants, Maecenas and Agrippa, Octavius Caesar is out-lining Antony's offenses against him. The manner and the matter of those offenses, although distinct, are presented as if they were inextricably con-nected, and each aspect heightens the offense. Caesar is offended by the deca-dence of the ceremony. But the military and geopolitical aspects are perhaps of even more concern to him. Antony is constructing in Egypt an eastern empire from which Caesar is excluded and a military alliance that challenges Caesar's Roman Empire. And Cleopatra, by dressing as Isis, is doing more than expressing her vanity: Her display represents an attempt to bestow divin-ity on their rule.

Act III, vi, 65–79, 82–91, and 98–99

Caesar: No, my most wronged sister; Cleopatra
Hath nodded him to her. He hath given his empire
Up to a whore; who now are levying
The kings o' the earth for war; he hath assembled
Bocchus, the king of Libya; Archelaus,
Of Cappadocia; Philadelphos, king
Of Paphlagonia; the Thracian king, Adallas;
King Malchus of Arabia; King of Pont;
Herod of Jewry; Mithridates, king
Of Comagene; Polemon and Amyntas,
The kings of Mede and Lycaonia,
With a more larger list of sceptres.
Octavia: Ay me, most wretched,
That have my heart parted betwixt two friends
That do afflict each other!
Caesar: . . .
Cheer your heart;
Be you not troubled with the time, which drives
O'er your content these strong necessities;
But let determined things to destiny
Hold unbewail'd their way. Welcome to Rome;

Nothing more dear to me. You are abused
Beyond the mark of thought: and the high gods,
To do you justice, make them ministers
Of us and those that love you. Best of comfort;
And ever welcome to us. . . .

                              Pray you
Be ever known to patience. My dear'st sister.

In his speech to his sister, Octavius Caesar joins politics and sentiment. Readers tend to scan Caesar's catalogue impatiently, but it records the strength of Antony's opposition: This very catalogue helps to justify Caesar's part in the upheaval in his sister's life. The greater part of his justification, though, is Antony's betrayal of Octavia. While Caesar's tenderness for his sister is genuine, the emotion he evokes is as much self-centered as not. After all, Antony's defection makes his offense against Octavia an offense against Caesar, and, more than symbolic, it occurs in practical, power-political terms.

Act III, vii, 1–6 and 17–20

Cleopatra: I will be even with thee, doubt it not.
Enobarbus: But why, why, why?
Cleopatra: Thou hast forspoke my being in these wars,
And say'st it is not fit.
Enobarbus: Well, is it, is it?
Cleopatra: If not denounced against us, why should not we
Be there in person?
  . . .
A charge we bear i' the war,
And, as the president of my kingdom, will
Appear there for a man. Speak not against it:
I will not stay behind.

Cleopatra's insistence on participating in the war stands in strong contrast to the obedience Octavia has just shown to her brother's command in the preceding scene. Cleopatra demonstrates the same impulse to exercise power equal to a man's in the political realm as she did in the erotic realm when she wore Antony's sword. In the political realm, however, she overreaches; her strength here does not equal the strength she can wield in the erotic realm. Antony's resulting disgrace shows that Antony values her erotic power over his military prowess.

Act III, xi, 7–24

Antony: I have fled myself; and have instructed cowards
To run and show their shoulders. Friends, be gone;
I have myself resolved upon a course
Which has no need of you; be gone:
My treasure's in the harbour, take it. O,
I follow'd that I blush to look upon:
My very hairs do mutiny; for the white
Reprove the brown for rashness, and they them
For fear and doting. Friends, be gone: you shall
Have letters from me to some friends that will
Sweep your way for you. Pray you, look not sad,
Nor make replies of loathness: take the hint
Which my despair proclaims; let that be left
Which leaves itself: to the sea-side straightway:
I will possess you of that ship and treasure.
Leave me, I pray, a little: pray you now:
Nay, do so; for, indeed, I have lost command,
Therefore I pray you: I'll see you by and by.

In this speech Antony addresses his troops after the naval defeat at Actium, which occurred only because he followed Cleopatra when she turned her ship in retreat. Unlike the public utterances of Caesar or Cleopatra, Antony's speech is not designed to manipulate them. It is an honest account of his response to his own action. Rather than asking anything, moreover, he is releasing his men from their obligation to him and giving them his treasure in compensation for their collective disgrace.

―⁓― ―⁓― ―⁓―

Act III, xi, 7–24

Antony: O, whither hast thou led me, Egypt? See,
How I convey my shame out of thine eyes
By looking back what I have left behind
'Stroy'd in dishonour.
Cleopatra: O my lord, my lord,
Forgive my fearful sails! I little thought
You would have follow'd.
Antony: Egypt, thou knew'st too well
My heart was to thy rudder tied by the strings,
And thou shouldst tow me after: o'er my spirit

Thy full supremacy thou knew'st, and that
Thy beck might from the bidding of the gods
Command me.
Cleopatra: O, my pardon!
Antony: Now I must
To the young man send humble treaties, dodge
And palter in the shifts of lowness; who
With half the bulk o' the world play'd as I pleased,
Making and marring fortunes. You did know
How much you were my conqueror; and that
My sword, made weak by my affection, would
Obey it on all cause.
Cleopatra: Pardon, pardon!
Antony: Fall not a tear, I say; one of them rates
All that is won and lost: give me a kiss;
Even this repays me. We sent our schoolmaster;
Is he come back? Love, I am full of lead.
Some wine, within there, and our viands! Fortune knows
We scorn her most when most she offers blows.

When Antony sees Cleopatra, he charges her with some responsibility for his fall. Nevertheless, he does not blame her. He rates his choice of her higher than a victory over Octavius Caesar. His declaration "Fall not a tear . . ." actually shows the sincerity of his proclamation at Act I, scene 1, when he said (lines 33–40):

Let Rome in Tiber melt, and the wide arch
Of the ranged empire fall! Here is my space.
Kingdoms are clay: our dungy earth alike
Feeds beast as man: the nobleness of life
Is to do thus; when such a mutual pair
And such a twain can do't, in which I bind,
On pain of punishment, the world to weet
We stand up peerless.

Act III, xii, 27–33

Octavius Caesar: From Antony win Cleopatra: promise,
And in our name, what she requires; add more,
From thine invention, offers: women are not
In their best fortunes strong; but want will perjure
The ne'er touch'd vestal: try thy cunning, Thidias;

Make thine own edict for thy pains, which we
Will answer as a law.

Caesar's generalization about women to the young ambassador Thidias establishes the masculinist perspective that challenges Cleopatra—and which she
defies. Caesar's recommendation of cunning suggests his Machiavellian way of
thinking. The first three lines of this passage are of particular dramatic interest
because they address a central ambiguity of the play: the question of Cleopatra's
sincerity regarding her love for Antony. Caesar's strategy inadvertently puts the
lovers to the test. It presumes that Cleopatra's desire for Antony is a caprice
rather than a passion as consuming as Antony's.

Act III, xiii, 43–46

Enobarbus: Mine honesty and I begin to square.
The loyalty well held to fools does make
Our faith mere folly. Yet he that can endure
To follow with allegiance a fall'n lord
Does conquer him that did his master conquer
And earns a place i' the story.

Enobarbus believes that Antony's judgment and his military and political power
have been "subdued" by Octavius Caesar and that his will has become "Lord of
his reason." But in this speech he nonetheless argues for staying with Antony.
By placing resolute loyalty over shifting fortune, Enobarbus suggests the virtues
of republican Rome.

His words resonate beyond himself, as well. They can be used to illuminate
Antony's course, when he followed Cleopatra as she turned her ship away from
the battle at Actium; they can illuminate Cleopatra's behavior, too, when she
follows Antony in death. Through these actions both are following "fall'n lords."
By showing their allegiance to an idea, Antony and Cleopatra deprive Caesar of
their allegiance; by defying their conqueror, they earn their places in an alternative
story that they create.

Act III, xiii, 74–78

Cleopatra: Say to great Caesar this: in deputation
I kiss his conquering hand: tell him, I am prompt
To lay my crown at's feet, and there to kneel:
Tell him from his all-obeying breath I hear
The doom of Egypt.

This is Cleopatra's response to the messenger Octavius Caesar has sent to "win" her from Antony. The difficulty, which creates a puzzle for the audience and a problem for the interpreter of the role on the stage, is to determine exactly what Cleopatra means. Is she sincere? Is she surrendering to Caesar and abandoning Antony? Is she being strategic, stalling for time, attempting to manipulate Caesar?

Certainty about Cleopatra seems impossible, but that is one of her chief characteristics. For example, when Thidias asserts that Caesar "knows that you embraced not Antony / As you did love, but as you feared him," it is unclear what Cleopatra's single "O" in response means. Even if it is an ironic rebuttal to an ignorant presumption, it points to the past, not to the present or the future. Similarly, her irony-drenched response (saying Caesar "is a god, and knows / What is most right. Mine honor was not yielded, / But conquered merely") refers to the strength of her love but not to her present course of action. Clearly Enobarbus is unable to hear the irony in it, because he exits to tell Antony how bad matters are for him. And Antony certainly sees Cleopatra as disloyal when he enters at the conclusion of her speech to Thidias and sees Cleopatra yielding to his request to kiss her hand.

―◦◦◦―　―◦◦◦―　―◦◦◦―

Act III, xiii, 154–167

Antony:　　To flatter Caesar, would you mingle eyes
With one that ties his points?
Cleopatra:　Not know me yet?
Antony:　　Cold-hearted toward me?
Cleopatra:　Ah, dear, if I be so,
From my cold heart let heaven engender hail,
And poison it in the source; and the first stone
Drop in my neck: as it determines, so
Dissolve my life! The next Caesarion smite!
Till by degrees the memory of my womb,
Together with my brave Egyptians all,
By the discandying of this pelleted storm,
Lie graveless, till the flies and gnats of Nile
Have buried them for prey!

Cleopatra's response to Antony's angry question suggests that she is—as she has always been—a supreme actress, dissembling with a purpose. When she assures Antony of her faithfulness, Antony believes her. Still, whether she is an agent of endless trickery or a woman with a firm purpose and as much political cunning as Caesar is indeterminate.

―◦◦◦―　―◦◦◦―　―◦◦◦―

Act IV, i, 1–6

Octavius Caesar: He calls me boy; and chides, as he had power
To beat me out of Egypt; my messenger
He hath whipp'd with rods; dares me to personal combat,
Caesar to Antony: let the old ruffian know
I have many other ways to die; meantime
Laugh at his challenge.

Having received Antony's challenge of single combat, Octavius Caesar responds with realism, wit, and self-possession. He recapitulates the events of the previous scene (Act III, scene 13) precisely and only enhances his own dignity by his honest reaction to the challenge. Caesar admits Antony's prowess while branding him an "old ruffian" (tit for tat against Antony's epithet, "boy") and laughs from a place of superiority.

His realism is once again evident in his order at line 15 to "feast the army." They have earned a bonus such as this, he acknowledges, but more importantly, "we have store to do't." Despite his later assertion (Act V, scene 2) that he is "no merchant," Caesar is an excellent keeper of his own accounts.

——

Act IV, ii, 23–45

Antony: Tend me to-night;
May be it is the period of your duty:
Haply you shall not see me more; or if,
A mangled shadow: perchance to-morrow
You'll serve another master. I look on you
As one that takes his leave. Mine honest friends,
I turn you not away; but, like a master
Married to your good service, stay till death:
Tend me to-night two hours, I ask no more,
And the gods yield you for't!
Enobarbus: What mean you, sir,
To give them this discomfort? Look, they weep;
And I, an ass, am onion-eyed: for shame,
Transform us not to women.
Antony: Ho, ho, ho!
Now the witch take me, if I meant it thus!
Grace grow where those drops fall!
My hearty friends,
You take me in too dolorous a sense;

For I spake to you for your comfort; did desire you
To burn this night with torches: know, my hearts,
I hope well of to-morrow; and will lead you
Where rather I'll expect victorious life
Than death and honour. Let's to supper, come,
And drown consideration.

With this exchange, Antony concludes the scene in which he bids what may be farewell to his troops. Unlike Octavius Caesar, he is not an example of calculation and reserve. He speaks to them thus, Antony says, to keep his men from being disheartened by his possible loss in the next day's battle. Antony's last words regarding supper contrast with Caesar's. Caesar observed that supplies would allow a feast; Antony pays this practical concern no regard. He wishes to "drown consideration," to live according to the impulses of feeling, not thought.

Act IV, v, 2–17

Antony: Would thou and those thy scars had once prevail'd
To make me fight at land!
Soldier: Hadst thou done so,
The kings that have revolted, and the soldier
That has this morning left thee, would have still
Follow'd thy heels.
Antony: Who's gone this morning?
Soldier: Who!
One ever near thee: call for Enobarbus,
He shall not hear thee; or from Caesar's camp
Say "I am none of thine."
Antony: What say'st thou?
Soldier: Sir,
He is with Caesar.
Eros: Sir, his chests and treasure
He has not with him.
Antony: Is he gone?
Soldier: Most certain.
Antony: Go, Eros, send his treasure after; do it;
Detain no jot, I charge thee: write to him—
I will subscribe—gentle adieus and greetings;
Say that I wish he never find more cause
To change a master. O, my fortunes have
Corrupted honest men! Dispatch.—Enobarbus!

The scene in which Antony learns that Enobarbus has defected is of particular dramatic significance because of the way it defines an audience's response to Antony from this point on. Antony has just admitted to the soldier that he had erred in rejecting his advice to fight on land rather than at sea. When he learns that Enobarbus has gone over to Octavius Caesar, Antony sends him his fortune with addition.

There is nothing tangible Antony can gain from doing this; he does it to show his esteem for Enobarbus and as a sort of apology, similar to the one he has offered the soldier a few lines before. In light of these actions, audiences must see Antony as a worthier man than Caesar, even if a weaker man in terms of earthly power.

Act IV, xii, 31–39

Antony: Ah, thou spell! Avaunt!
Cleopatra: Why is my lord enraged against his love?
Antony: Vanish, or I shall give thee thy deserving,
And blemish Caesar's triumph. Let him take thee,
And hoist thee up to the shouting plebeians:
Follow his chariot, like the greatest spot
Of all thy sex; most monster-like, be shown
For poor'st diminutives, for doits; and let
Patient Octavia plough thy visage up
With her prepared nails.

Before this scene, Cleopatra last appeared in Act IV, scene 8, celebrating Antony's victory over Octavius Caesar and offering a suit of "armor all of gold" to one of his prized soldiers. Since then, not only has she not appeared onstage, but no character has reported anything of her.

When Cleopatra reappears in scene 12, it is after Antony has lost a sea battle. This battle was not, according to the text, fought at Cleopatra's instigation nor lost because of her retreat. Yet Antony entered this scene (at line 9) crying, "All is lost! / This foul Egyptian hath betrayed me: / My fleet hath yielded to the foe." With apparently less cause than in Act III, Antony now believes Cleopatra has betrayed him.

Thus when Cleopatra enters and Antony denounces her, her question makes perfect sense; indeed, it is one the reader might echo. Antony does not answer but only threatens her with the consequences if she does not get out of his sight. She obeys him and flees. It is difficult to account for Antony's motivation in this scene.

Act IV, xiii, 3–4

Charmian: To th' monument:
There lock yourself, and send him word you are dead.

It is Charmian who advises Cleopatra to lock herself in her monument. More significantly, it is Charmian, not Cleopatra, who thinks of telling Antony that Cleopatra has killed herself, though Cleopatra then takes up the idea and embellishes it. But her last instruction, "Hence, Mardian, / And bring me how he takes my death," may be motivated less by coquetry than by a concern to see if it is safe to leave her monument. Cleopatra will have second thoughts and send Diomedes—too late—to tell Antony the truth.

Act IV, xiv, 2–22

Antony: Sometimes we see a cloud that's dragonish;
A vapour sometime like a bear or lion,
A tower'd citadel, a pendent rock,
A forked mountain, or blue promontory
With trees upon't, that nod unto the world,
And mock our eyes with air: thou hast seen these signs;
They are black vesper's pageants.
Eros: Ay, my lord,
Antony: That which is now a horse, even with a thought
The rack dislimns, and makes it indistinct,
As water is in water.
Eros: It does, my lord.
Antony: My good knave Eros, now thy captain is
Even such a body: here I am Antony:
Yet cannot hold this visible shape, my knave.
I made these wars for Egypt: and the queen,—
Whose heart I thought I had, for she had mine;
Which whilst it was mine had annex'd unto't
A million more, now lost,—she, Eros, has
Pack'd cards with Caesar, and false-play'd my glory
Unto an enemy's triumph.
Nay, weep not, gentle Eros; there is left us
Ourselves to end ourselves.

In Antony's valediction for himself, he compares his own corporal body to the ethereal clouds and thus argues against any possibility of permanence.

He represents the idea of mutability through images of evaporation. Antony also makes it clear that his ambition in the wars he fought was not for empire but to win the love of Cleopatra. His despair is not at his defeat by Octavius Caesar but at what he believes has been his betrayal by Cleopatra. Thus when he hears from Mardian that she is dead, the news reconstitutes his person and his love: Cleopatra's reported death shows that she has not betrayed him or been disloyal to their love. His suicide is spurred not by despair, but by desire.

<hr/>

Act V, i, 14–20

Octavius Caesar: The breaking of so great a thing should make
A greater crack: the round world
Should have shook lions into civil streets,
And citizens to their dens: the death of Antony
Is not a single doom; in the name lay
A moiety of the world.

From the very beginning of Act V, Octavius Caesar is acting. When he hears the news of Antony's death, he begins a funereal oration. He is playing Caesar. By paying homage to Antony, he pays greater homage to himself: It is nothing to have conquered a puny man but greatness to have prevailed over a man of Olympian proportions. But even as he speaks of Antony's greatness, Caesar diminishes it. "The breaking of so great a thing should make / A greater crack," he says, belittling Antony in his first words.

<hr/>

Act V, ii, 21–34

Proculeius: Be of good cheer;
You're fall'n into a princely hand, fear nothing:
Make your full reference freely to my lord,
Who is so full of grace, that it flows over
On all that need: let me report to him
Your sweet dependency; and you shall find
A conqueror that will pray in aid for kindness,
Where he for grace is kneel'd to.
Cleopatra: Pray you, tell him
I am his fortune's vassal, and I send him
The greatness he has got. I hourly learn
A doctrine of obedience; and would gladly

Look him i' the face.
Proculeius:　　　　　This I'll report, dear lady.
Have comfort, for I know your plight is pitied
Of him that caused it.

The conceit of acting continues in scene 2. Proculeius here responds to Cleopatra's pledge of obedience as if it were an act. In fact, he is himself dissembling. Antony, at his death, had told Cleopatra that Proculeius was trustworthy, but he was mistaken. Now Proculeius comes as Octavius Caesar's messenger. Even as he reassures Cleopatra of Caesar's benevolence, Roman soldiers burst in and seize her.

Act V, ii, 42–46

Proculeius:　　　　　Cleopatra,
Do not abuse my master's bounty by
The undoing of yourself: let the world see
His nobleness well acted, which your death
Will never let come forth.

This slight passage, spoken by Proculeius, may serve as a fulcrum for the entire fifth act of *Antony and Cleopatra*. Focus especially on "let the world see / His nobleness well acted." A reader, having arrived at this point in the play, may have become aware that nearly every significant action in *Antony and Cleopatra* has been, whatever else it is, a variety of acting. Now acting itself has become an overt part of the plot. Cleopatra has acted, whether to appear merry, petulant, angry, martyred, or sad. Antony has often presented himself with bombast. Caesar is always projecting the image of Caesar.

To say that the characters are acting does not mean that they are insincere or that they are lying. It means that they are communicating the truth of themselves by means of, as it were, a mask of themselves. They are artists of themselves, representing the actual through the mediation of their art.

When Proculeius says, "let the world see / [Caesar's] nobleness well acted," two meanings of the words "well acted" are at play. Proculeius means let the world see how noble Caesar is. But clinging to his words is the suggestion that Caesar is performing a theatrical representation of himself. The second meaning is so closely allied with the first that it can hardly be separated from it, even in paraphrase. Caesar, like an actor in a play, is nothing but the character he acts. Cleopatra must not, Proculeius insists, by killing herself deprive Caesar of this opportunity to perform his chosen role.

Act V, ii, 107–111

Cleopatra: Know you what Caesar means to do with me?
Dolabella: I am loath to tell you what I would you knew.
Cleopatra: Nay, pray you, sir,—
Dolabella: Though he be honourable,—
Cleopatra: He'll lead me, then, in triumph?
Dolabella: Madam, he will; I know't.

Proculeius's earlier remark about Caesar's "nobleness well acted" resonates ironically here, as Cleopatra realizes Caesar's plans for her. She has a very precise sense of how it will be done. It is not Caesar's "nobleness" that will be "well acted" but his victory.

Act V, ii, 139–178

Cleopatra: This is the brief of money, plate, and jewels,
I am possessed of: 'tis exactly valued;
Not petty things admitted. Where's Seleucus?
Seleucus: Here, madam.
Cleopatra: This is my treasurer: let him speak, my lord,
Upon his peril, that I have reserved
To myself nothing. Speak the truth, Seleucus.
Seleucus: Madam,
I had rather seal my lips, than, to my peril,
Speak that which is not.
Cleopatra: What have I kept back?
Seleucus: Enough to purchase what you have made known.
Caesar: Nay, blush not, Cleopatra; I approve
Your wisdom in the deed.
Cleopatra: See, Caesar! O, behold,
How pomp is followed! mine will now be yours;
And, should we shift estates, yours would be mine.
The ingratitude of this Seleucus does
Even make me wild: O slave, of no more trust
Than love that's hired! What, goest thou back? thou shalt
Go back, I warrant thee; but I'll catch thine eyes,
Though they had wings: slave, soulless villain, dog!
O rarely base!
Caesar: Good queen, let us entreat you.
Cleopatra: O Caesar, what a wounding shame is this,

That thou, vouchsafing here to visit me,
Doing the honor of thy lordliness
To one so meek, that mine own servant should
Parcel the sum of my disgraces by
Addition of his envy! Say, good Caesar,
That I some lady trifles have reserved,
Immoment toys, things of such dignity
As we greet modern friends withal; and say,
Some nobler token I have kept apart
For Livia and Octavia, to induce
Their mediation; must I be unfolded
With one that I have bred? The gods! it smites me
Beneath the fall I have.
(*To Seleucus:*) Prithee, go hence;
Or I shall show the cinders of my spirits
Through the ashes of my chance: wert thou a man,
Thou wouldst have mercy on me.
Caesar.   Forbear, Seleucus.

Cleopatra performs two pieces of theater in the final moments of the play. Seen in relation to each other, these performances represent the contrary possibilities of acting: acting as deception and acting as a sacred ritual that transports the actor to a higher truth.

This first performance is staged for Caesar. Although it is never stated in the text, it seems to be a drama that Cleopatra has arranged with her treasurer in order to deceive Caesar. She wants Caesar to think that he has conquered her, that she will submit and yield to his wishes. And she wants him to believe she is reserving her wealth for herself out of the vanity that (she is intuitive enough to sense) he attributes to women. By seeming to care about retaining possession of her wealth, Cleopatra hopes to convince him that she will not kill herself; with this deception she hopes to buy herself time enough to kill herself, despite her imprisonment. Although Caesar finally realizes he has been had, it is too late. Her plot succeeds.

Act V, ii, 210–224

Cleopatra: Now, Iras, what think'st thou?
Thou, an Egyptian puppet, shalt be shown
In Rome, as well as I: mechanic slaves
With greasy aprons, rules, and hammers, shall
Uplift us to the view; in their thick breaths,

Rank of gross diet, shall we be enclouded,
And forced to drink their vapor.
Iras: The gods forbid!
Cleopatra: Nay, 'tis most certain, Iras. Saucy lictors
Will catch at us, like strumpets; and scald rhymers
Ballad us out o' tune: the quick comedians
Extemporally will stage us, and present
Our Alexandrian revels: Antony
Shall be brought drunken forth, and I shall see
Some squeaking Cleopatra boy my greatness
I' the posture of a whore.

Critics commenting on these words often point out that in the first productions, Cleopatra was played, indeed, by a boy and that the very thing she is complaining about, ironically, is being staged at the moment she condemns it. But that is not quite so, because Shakespeare's play is not to be confused with Caesar's pageant. The poetry of Shakespeare's *Antony and Cleopatra* is transformative. It uses artifice to represent the spirit of reality, not to humiliate its persons.

Act V, ii, 280–291

Cleopatra: Give me my robe, put on my crown; I have
Immortal longings in me: now no more
The juice of Egypt's grape shall moist this lip:
Yare, yare, good Iras; quick. Methinks I hear
Antony call; I see him rouse himself
To praise my noble act; I hear him mock
The luck of Caesar, which the gods give men
To excuse their after wrath: husband, I come:
Now to that name my courage prove my title!
I am fire and air; my other elements
I give to baser life.

Cleopatra's last piece of theater, rather than a deception, is a ritual of transformation. Somehow she has arranged to have asps smuggled in in a basket of figs, carried by a peasant, and she dies by causing the venomous snakes to strike her breast and arm. She does not, however, simply kill herself. Like Antony, who said, "I will o'ertake thee, Cleopatra. . . . I will be / A bridegroom in my death, and run into't / As to a lover's bed" (Act IV, scene 14), Cleopatra now enacts an anticipatory ritual. Arrayed in her finest robes and adorned with her symbols of state, she performs her death as a ceremony of transfiguration.

LIST OF CHARACTERS IN
ANTONY AND CLEOPATRA
❧

Mark Antony is a Roman general. Along with Octavius Caesar and Lepidus, he is a member of the second triumvirate, three men who together rule over the Roman Empire—essentially, the entire world known to them. Antony is aging, and he is in decline as a soldier at the time of the play. He has also fallen in love with Cleopatra. In his passion he neglects his imperial duties and sets himself at odds with Octavius Caesar.

Cleopatra is the queen of Egypt. She is mercurial and passionate, and she commands Antony's love and desire. Though she long conceals her own love for Antony, it is deeper and more unsettling than anything she has known before. After Antony's death she commits suicide rather than allowing herself to be taken captive by Octavius Caesar.

Octavius Caesar, the grandnephew and adopted son of Julius Caesar, is young, disciplined, and on the ascent. He is determined to become all-powerful; he will, in fact, become Augustus Caesar, the first Roman emperor. He is disgusted by Antony's revels in Egypt. He is also threatened by the power base his rival is developing there, particularly when Antony bestows upon Cleopatra's heirs the kingdoms and provinces he has conquered.

Lepidus is the third member of the triumvirate, a weak and ineffectual man who is ultimately killed by Caesar on trumped-up charges of disloyalty.

Octavia is Octavius Caesar's sister. After the death of Antony's wife Fulvia, Antony marries Octavia in order to cement his alliance with Octavius. Instead, his continued relationship with Cleopatra becomes one more factor fueling their enmity.

Pompey is a Roman who opposes the triumvirate by force of arms. After negotiating a settlement with them, he is defeated in battle by Octavius Caesar and killed on Antony's orders.

Menas is one of Pompey's men. He offers to cut the cable of the barge where Antony, Lepidus, and Octavius are feasting at sea, then kill them, but is rebuffed by the self-important Pompey.

Varrius is one of Pompey's men.

Menecrates is another of Pompey's men.

Enobarbus is a soldier in Antony's army and one of his most loyal followers. He is droll and cynical. When Antony's cause seems lost and Antony himself dispirited, Enobarbus joins Octavius Caesar. Filled with remorse for abandoning the noble Antony for the calculating Caesar, he dies in a ditch.

Philo is one of Antony's men who scorns his master's transformation from soldier to lover.

Scarus is one of Antony's men.

Eros is one of Antony's men.

Canidius is a lieutenant general in Antony's army.

Decretas is a follower of Antony.

Demetrius is a follower of Antony.

Ventidius is the commander of one of Antony's armies, in Syria.

Silius is an officer in one of Antony's armies commanded by Ventidius.

The **schoolmaster** serves as a messenger from Antony to Octavius, showing how far Antony's fortunes have fallen.

Maecenas is one of Octavius Caesar's men.

Agrippa is a follower of Octavius Caesar.

Thidias is a messenger whom Octavius Caesar sends to Cleopatra to win her away from Antony. When he kisses her hand, he inflames Antony's jealous anger and suffers a whipping.

Dolabella is an emissary of Octavius Caesar, sent to Cleopatra after Antony's death to negotiate the terms of her surrender.

Proculeius is one of Octavius Caesar's men. He, too, is sent to negotiate the terms of Cleopatra's surrender after the death of Antony.

Taurus is one of Octavius Caesar's lieutenant generals.

Gallus is one of Octavius Caesar's men.

Bantering with Cleopatra's attendants, the **soothsayer** foresees a bleak future for them. Later he warns Antony of his powerlessness when he is near Caesar.

Charmian is one of Cleopatra's serving women. She commits suicide with her mistress.

Iras is another of Cleopatra's serving women.

Mardian, a eunuch, is one of Cleopatra's male attendants.

Diomedes is one of Cleopatra's male attendants.

Alexas is another of Cleopatra's male attendants.

Seleucus is Cleopatra's treasurer.

The **clown** is an Egyptian peasant who brings Cleopatra a basket of figs in which asps (small, venomous snakes) are concealed.

CRITICISM
THROUGH THE AGES

- the suicide of Antony's servant Eros (Act IV, scene 14);
- Cleopatra's difficulty in lifting Antony up to her monument (Act IV, scene 15);
- Antony's warning that Cleopatra should trust none but Proculeius (Act IV, scene 15);
- Cleopatra's apparent effort to conceal the true amount of her wealth, which is really a ruse to convince Caesar that she desires to live (Act V, scene 2);
- Cleopatra's death "attired and araied in her royall robes" (Act V, scene 2);
- Cleopatra's study of swift means of death (Act V, scene 2).

In addition to gathering incidents from North's translation, Shakespeare sometimes even incorporated North's phrasing into his verse. In one of the most interesting examples of transformation, Shakespeare used the following passage from North, describing Antony and Cleopatra's first meeting:

> She disdained to set forward otherwise, but to take her barge in the river of Cydnus, the poope whereof was of gold, the sailes of purple, and the owers of silver, which kept stroke in rowing after the sounde of the musicke of flutes, howboyes, citherns, violls, and such other instruments as they played upon in the barge. And now for the person of her selfe: she was layed under a pavillion of cloth of gold of tissue, apparelled and attired like the goddesse Venus, commonly drawen in picture: and hard by her, on either hand of her, pretie faire boyes apparelled as painters doe set forth god Cupide, with litle fannes in their hands, with the which they fanned wind upon her. Her Ladies and gentlewomen also, the fairest of them were apparelled like the nymphes Nereides (which are the mermaides of the waters) and like the Graces, some stearing the helme, others tending the tackle and ropes of the barge, out of the which there came a wonderfull passing sweete savor of perfumes, that perfumed the wharfes side.

Shakespeare fashioned North's text into a speech at Act II, scene 2 (lines 197–211), in which Enobarbus describes the same meeting:

> The barge she sat in, like a burnished throne,
> Burned on the water: the poop was beaten gold;
> Purple the sails, and so perfumed that
> The winds were love-sick with them; the oars were silver,
> Which to the tune of flutes kept stroke, and made
> The water which they beat to follow faster,

As amorous of their strokes. For her own person,
It beggared all description: she did lie
In her pavilion, cloth-of-gold of tissue,
O'erpicturing that Venus where we see
The fancy outwork nature: on each side her
Stood pretty dimpled boys, like smiling Cupids,
With divers-colored fans, whose wind did seem
To glow the delicate cheeks which they did cool,
And what they undid did.

The character of Enobarbus himself is entirely Shakespeare's invention, although Plutarch mentions that a soldier named Enobarbus deserted Antony.

Plutarch was not Shakespeare's only source. There is reason to believe that Shakespeare was influenced by Chaucer's portrait of Cleopatra in *The Legend of Good Women*, where the Egyptian queen is portrayed as sacrificing herself for love; by *The Tragedie of Antonie*, translated in 1590 by Mary Herbert, countess of Pembroke; from the French *Marc Antoine*, by Robert Garnier; and by Samuel Daniel's *The Tragedie of Cleopatra*, 1593. Daniel's 1607 revision of his play, in turn, shows signs of having been influenced by Shakespeare's.

According to an entry in the Lord Chamberlain's records of 1669, *Antony and Cleopatra* was "formerly acted at the Blackfriars," the indoor theater that the King's Men owned, in 1609 and 1642. From 1642 to 1661, however, the London theaters were closed by order of the Puritan Long Parliament. After the reopening of the theaters following the restoration of the monarchy, there is no indication that Shakespeare's original version of *Antony and Cleopatra* was performed at all. In 1677, however, John Dryden's reworking of the play, called *All for Love, Or The World Well Lost*, was first performed. Dryden's version, though it covered the same events as Shakespeare's *Antony and Cleopatra* and used many elements borrowed from Shakespeare, was truly an independent work rather than an adaptation. Some critics regard it as Dryden's best dramatic work. It held the stage until 1849, when a near-faithful version of Shakespeare's *Antony and Cleopatra* was again performed for the first time in many years.

1678—John Dryden. From the Preface to *All for Love*

John Dryden (1631–1700) was an English poet, dramatist, and literary critic who so dominated the literary scene of his day that it came to be known as the Age of Dryden. He produced the first substantive criticism of his predecessor Shakespeare. The following comes from his preface to his popular reworking of Shakespeare's *Antony and Cleopatra*.

The death of Antony and Cleopatra is a subject which has been treated by the greatest wits of our nation, after Shakespeare; and by all so variously, that their example has given me the confidence to try myself in this bow of Ulysses amongst the crowd of suitors, and, withal, to take my own measures, in aiming at the mark. . . .

. . . It remains that I acquaint the reader, that I have endeavoured in this play to follow the practice of the ancients, who, as Mr. Rymer has judiciously observed, are and ought to be our masters. . . . Yet, though their models are regular, they are too little for English tragedy; which requires to be built in a larger compass. I could give an instance in the *Oedipus Tyrannus,* which was the masterpiece of Sophocles; but I reserve it for a more fit occasion, which I hope to have hereafter. In my style, I have professed to imitate the divine Shakespeare; which that I might perform more freely, I have disencumbered myself from rhyme. Not that I condemn my former way, but that this is more proper to my present purpose. I hope I need not to explain myself, that I have not copied my author servilely: Words and phrases must of necessity receive a change in succeeding ages; but it is almost a miracle that much of his language remains so pure; and that he who began dramatic poetry amongst us, untaught by any, and as Ben Jonson tells us, without learning, should by the force of his own genius perform so much, that in a manner he has left no praise for any who come after him. The occasion is fair, and the subject would be pleasant to handle the difference of styles betwixt him and Fletcher, and wherein, and how far they are both to be imitated. But since I must not be over-confident of my own performance after him, it will be prudence in me to be silent. Yet, I hope, I may affirm, and without vanity, that, by imitating him, I have excelled myself throughout the play; and particularly, that I prefer the scene betwixt Antony and Ventidius in the first act, to anything which I have written in this kind.

⧿⧾ ⧿⧾ ⧿⧾

1680—Nahum Tate. From "Address to Edward Tayler," in *The Loyal General, a Tragedy*

Nahum Tate (1652–1715) became England's poet laureate in 1692. He collaborated with the great English composer Henry Purcell, providing the text for Purcell's opera *Dido and Aeneas,* and also produced a famous adaptation of *King Lear.*

What I have already asserted concerning the necessity of learning to make a complete poet, may seem inconsistent with my reverence for our Shakespeare. *Cuius amor semper mihi creseit in Horas* [My love for him only increases with time]. I confess I cou'd never yet get a true account of his learning, and am apt to think it more than common report allows him. I am sure he never touches on a Roman Story, but the persons, the passages, the manners, the circumstances, the ceremonies, all are Roman. And what relishes yet of a more exact knowledge, you do not only see a Roman in his hero, but the particular genius of the man, without the least mistake of his character, given him by their best historians. You find his Antony in all the defects and excellencies of his mind, a soldier, a reveller, amorous, sometimes rash, sometimes considerate, with all the various emotions of his mind. . . . But however it far'd with our author for book-learning, 'tis evident that no man was better studied in men and things, the most useful knowledge for a dramatic writer. He was a most diligent spy upon Nature, trac'd her through her darkest recesses, pictur'd her in her just proportion and colors; in which variety 'tis impossible that all shou'd be equally pleasant, 'tis sufficient that all be proper.

ANTONY AND CLEOPATRA
IN THE EIGHTEENTH CENTURY
ఏౖ

The version of the Antony and Cleopatra story that held the stage during the eighteenth century was John Dryden's *All for Love, Or The World Well Lost* (1677), which was truly an independent work rather than an adaptation. There is no record that *Antony and Cleopatra*, as Shakespeare wrote it, was ever performed in the eighteenth century, apart from six modified and shortened performances presented in 1759. These were given at the Drury Lane Theatre under the auspices of the renowned actor David Garrick. John Hill's short review of Garrick's production damned the play as inferior not just to Shakespeare's other works, but also to Dryden's version.

In 1774 the actor and dramatist Francis Gentleman wrote commentary for an edition of Shakespeare's works. In one of his notes to *Antony and Cleopatra*, he recalled Garrick's production respectfully and stated what he called "the double moral" of the play: "That indolence and dissipation may undo the greatest of men; and that beauty, under the direction of vanity, will not only ruin the possessor, but admirer also."

The great critic Samuel Johnson, in his edition of Shakespeare (1765), also provided notes and commentary on the texts of all the plays. His short "General Observation" on *Antony and Cleopatra* is not overly enthusiastic. He called the play interesting but complained that "except the feminine arts, some of which are too low, which distinguish *Cleopatra*, no character is very strongly discriminated" and that the events of the plot "are produced without any art of connexion."

In 1784, an actor and bookseller named Thomas Davies set down several of his own "observations" on the play. He noted Antony's "bright beams of a great and generous soul" and took issue with Dr. Johnson's complaints: The characters are indeed memorable and distinguished from one another, Davies asserted, and on the whole "this tragedy remains unequalled by any that have been written on the same subject."

1759—John Hill. From "Some Remarks upon the New-revived Play of *Antony and Cleopatra*"

John Hill (c. 1714–1775) was a prolific journalist, theater critic, novelist, and the subject of many satirical attacks by rival writers. The essay below attacks actor David Garrick's production of *Antony and Cleopatra*, which mainly adhered to Shakespeare's original text.

Since the penning of the preceding letter the revived tragedy of *Antony and Cleopatra* has been performed and published. With respect to the piece itself we are told in the title page that it is "fitted for the stage, by abridging only." As the length of this play was certainly an obstacle to its exhibition we are of opinion its alterations are so much for the better as they have rendered it less tedious, as well for the audience as the actors. I cannot, however, but be of opinion that this piece is inferior to most of Shakespeare's productions, and that it even gives way to Dryden's *All for Love, or the World Well Lost*, which is founded upon the same historical event. I do not mean by this to give the preference to Dryden as a greater dramatic poet in general than Shakespeare, but must own that his soft flowing numbers are more sympathetic to the tender passion which this story is so particularly animated with than the general language of Shakespeare's *Antony*.

I doubt not but this assertion will be looked upon as blasphemy by the *Garicians* and *Shakespearian-bigots*, who imagine no piece of this great poet can be less than perfection's-self, especially when it has received the polish of Roscius's pen. But I could cite several instances in this piece, as well as others that have been altered for the stage, which evince the contrary. Not to enter into a laboured criticism upon this tragedy, for which we have neither time or room, I shall only observe what must be obviously ridiculous to every auditor, Cleopatra *still* talks of playing at *Billiards*, a game utterly unknown at that period, as well as many ages after. . . .

The only addition I can perceive made to *Antony and Cleopatra* is a kind of poetical dedication (or whatever else the author chuses to call it) to a countess worthy of all titles, though anonymous. As I acknowledge myself utterly ignorant of the meaning or import of these verses I can say nothing more upon them but what will impeach my understanding and ill compliment my comprehension, for I believe they must be very fine, as they supply the place of a prologue (Mr G—k's *forte* in writing) or complimentary verses to the editor by a friend. . . .

In this form has the new-revived tragedy (so much talked of and so long expected) of *Antony and Cleopatra* appeared. To give the editor his due, the punctuation is very regular; in this, I think, his principal merit consists. That of the printer is much greater: the neatness of the type, the disposition of the parts, and the accuracy of the composing, are very striking, and these considerations apart we can see no reason for imposing an additional tax of sixpence upon the purchasers of this play, containing less in quantity than the original, which may be had for half its price.

However, this piece has already been twice performed and to crowded houses. We shall not attempt to depreciate Mr G—k in quality of an actor, or pretend to assert Mr F—surpasses, or equals him. The town is already very well acquainted with both their merit, and it were almost needless to say they both appear to advantage in their parts. Mrs Y—s's person is well suited to the character, and though she is an inferior Cleopatra to Mrs Woffington she is not without sufficient powers to procure her applause. Upon the whole we think this play is now better suited for the stage than the closet, as scenery, dresses, and parade strike the eye and divert one's attention from the poet.

―――

1765—Samuel Johnson. From "Notes on the Plays," in *The Plays of William Shakespeare*

Samuel Johnson (1709-1784) is thought by many to be the greatest literary critic in the English language. He was a poet, critic, prose writer, lexicographer, editor, and celebrated raconteur. His edition of the works of Shakespeare contained some of his famous thoughts on the plays. The following comments are taken from annotations he supplied to his text of *Antony and Cleopatra*.

[On the stage direction at Act II, scene 1: "Enter Pompey, Menecrates, and Menas"]
The persons are so named in the first edition; but I know not why Menecrates appears; Menas can do all without him.

[Note on the end of Act II, scene 1: "Our lives upon . . . "]
This play is not divided into acts by the authour or first editors, and therefore the present division may be altered at pleasure. I think the first act may be commodiously continued to this place, and the second act opened with the interview of the chief persons, and a change of the state of action. Yet it must be confessed, that it is of small importance, where these unconnected and desultory scenes are interrupted.

[Note on Cleopatra's speech at Act V, scene 2: "Be't known, that we, the greatest, are misthought / for things that others do; and, when we fall, / We answer others merits in our names; / Are therefore to be pitied."]

I do not think that either of the criticks have reached the sense of the author, which may be very commodiously explained thus:

We suffer at our highest state of elevation in the *thoughts of mankind for that which others do, and when we fall*, those that contented themselves only to think ill before, call us to *answer in our own names for the merits of others. We are therefore to be pitied. Merits* is in this place taken in an ill sense, for actions *meriting* censure.

If any alteration be necessary, I should only propose, *Be 't known, that we* at greatest, &c

[General Observation]

This play keeps curiosity always busy, and the passions always interested. The continual hurry of the action, the variety of incidents, and the quick succession of one personage to another, call the mind forward, without intermission, from the first act to the last. But the power of delighting is derived principally from the frequent changes of the scene; for, except the feminine arts, some of which are too low, which distinguish *Cleopatra*, no character is very strongly discriminated. [The critic] Upton, who did not easily miss what he desired to find, has discovered that the language of Antony is, with great skill and learning, made pompous and superb, according to his real practice. But I think his diction not distinguishable from that of others: the most tumid speech in the play is that which Caesar makes to Octavia.

The events, of which the principal are described according to history, are produced without any art of connexion or care of disposition.

—◦◊◦— —◦◊◦— —◦◊◦—

1774—Francis Gentleman.
From *Bell's Edition of Shakespeare's Plays*

Francis Gentleman (1728–1784) was an eighteenth-century actor and drama critic. He was the author of several plays and *The Dramatic Censor; or, Critical Companion* (1770), and he supplied the introduction and notes to *Bell's Edition of Shakespeare's Plays*.

Whether this play, tho' excellently wrote, has any chance for long existence on the stage, is very doubtful. Twenty years since that very able and successful Dramatic Modeller, Mr. *Garrick*, produced it under the most probable state of reformation;

yet, tho' elegantly decorated and finely performed, it too soon languished. *Antony and Cleopatra* are the chief marked characters in it: he is a flighty infatuated slave to an excess of love and luxury; she a tinsel pattern of vanity and female cunning, which work the downfal of both. A double moral may be inferred, namely, That indolence and dissipation may undo the greatest of men; and that beauty, under the direction of vanity, will not only ruin the possessor, but admirer also. . . .

When we meet two such celebrated names, and consider our author's great abilities, we are naturally led to expect a very capital piece. Those characters are accordingly very greatly supported; but the whole piece, as it stands here, seems rather too incorrect and confused for action. . . .

Notwithstanding the fifth Act wants the assistance of *Antony*, who, as a main pillar, should not have been cast down so soon, yet it is rather the most regular and affecting of the whole: *Cleopatra* in it is very consistent; and supported by an actress possessing grace, power, and feeling, must work very tragic effects.

⚜ ⚜ ⚜

1784—Thomas Davies.
From *Dramatic Miscellanies*

Thomas Davies (1712–1785) was an actor and bookseller. His book *Dramatic Miscellanies* had the descriptive subtitle "consisting of Critical Observations on several Plays of Shakespeare: with a Review of his principal Characters, and those of various eminent Writers, as represented by Mr. Garrick, and other celebrated Comedians. With Anecdotes of Dramatic Poets, Actors, &c." Davies introduced James Boswell to Samuel Johnson in his bookshop in 1763. After Davies went bankrupt in 1788, Johnson persuaded him to write his *Memoirs of the Life of David Garrick*, which was quite successful. Below are two of Davies's brief notes on *Antony and Cleopatra*.

. . . Admidst all the folly, profligacy, and mad flights of Mark Antony, some bright beams of a great and generous soul break forth with inimitable lustre. Instead of reproaching his officer for desertion and treachery, he lays the blame on his own adverse fortune, which had unhappily overthrown the principles of the best and worthiest men. This is one of our author's characteristical strokes, and perfectly suited to Mark Antony.

. . . I cannot help thinking that Dr. Johnson has been rather precipitate in deciding upon the merit of *Antony and Cleopatra*.—How can I submit to that sentence which pronounces that there is no discrimination of character in this play, except in Cleopatra, whom he considers only as conspicuous for feminine arts? Those she has in abundance, it is true; but her generous resolution to die rather than submit to embrace life upon ignoble terms is surely also worth remembering. But is not Antony highly discriminated by variety of passion, by boundless generosity as well as unexampled dotage? What does this truly great writer think of Enobarbus, the rough old warrior, shrewd in his remarks and humorous in his plain-dealing? I shall say nothing of Octavius or Lepidus, though they are certainly separated from other parts. The simplicity of the fable is necessarily destroyed by exhibiting such a croud of events happening in distant periods of time, a fault common to historical plays. But, in spite of all irregularities this tragedy remains unequalled by any that have been written on the same subject.

ANTONY AND CLEOPATRA
IN THE NINETEENTH CENTURY
❧

Having been absent from the stage for some 200 years—except for a few performances of Garrick's shortened version in 1759—*Antony and Cleopatra* was finally
produced in October 1849 at the Sadler's Wells Theatre by Samuel Phelps,
who also played Antony. Cleopatra was Eleanor Glyn. The reviews were oddly
contradictory. In two reviews, a month apart, the critic for *Literary Review and
Stage-Manager*, while praising the "*mise en scene*," deplored the production, calling the play itself "long winded and certainly tedious." Of the lead actors, the
critic wrote "the less said in the way of honesty about Miss Glyn's Cleopatra the
better" and "Mr. Phelps will not suffer in reputation . . . by having any portion
of his Antony passed over in charitable silence." In addition, he described the
actor who played Octavius as "puny, elocutionary, and effeminate" and said that
the whole company "smacks shockingly of the amateurish." The critic of the
Illustrated London News, however, wrote of *Antony and Cleopatra*, after seeing
the same performance, "this magnificent play is a masterpiece of dramatic construction" and a "wonderful drama" of ideas. He had nothing but praise for the
production and for the cast and said of Glyn's Cleopatra that it was "the most
superb thing ever witnessed on the modern stage."

On the whole, nineteenth-century literary critics examined the intricacies
of character in the play, praising in particular both the depth of Shakespeare's
portrayal of the major figures and their realism. But critics of this period seldom
lost sight of the "immorality" of the story, particularly relating to the impropriety
of Antony and Cleopatra's behavior.

The poet Samuel Coleridge, who thought the play one of Shakespeare's
greatest, provided an astute analysis of Cleopatra's character that was nevertheless
tinged with moralism: "The sense of criminality in her passion is lessened by our
insight into its depth and energy, at the very moment that we cannot but perceive
that the passion itself springs out of the habitual craving of a licentious nature,
and that it is supported and reinforced by voluntary stimulus and sought-for
associations, instead of blossoming out of spontaneous emotion."

The German critic August Wilhelm von Schlegel examined *Antony and
Cleopatra* not so much in terms of its characters but as a historical drama, necessarily

involving numerous people and locations. When Schlegel, in his criticism, speaks of characters, he often sees them as mythical. Antony and Cleopatra make him think of Hercules in bondage to Omphale.

The great essayist William Hazlitt had a somewhat lower opinion of *Antony and Cleopatra* than Coleridge had. Hazlitt wrote that the play stands not "in the first class of Shakespeare's productions," but "next to them." Like Schlegel, he saw the play's greatness in the way Shakespeare treats historical circumstances. He noted especially Shakespeare's "fine picture of Roman pride and Eastern magnificence" and the way "in the struggle between the two, the empire of the world seems suspended, 'like the swan's down-feather.'" On the other hand, Hazlitt also praised the way "the characters breathe, move, and live." He called Cleopatra's portrayal "a masterpiece," describing her as "voluptuous, ostentatious, conscious, boastful of her charms, haughty, tyrannical, fickle."

Anna Jameson, who wrote a study of Shakespeare's heroines, called Shakespeare a "worker of miracles" in *Antony and Cleopatra*. Like Coleridge, she talks of "crimes" and "passions" but also of Shakespeare's ability to make "a sense of the sublime spring from the very elements of littleness." Cleopatra, as a result, "is a brilliant antithesis, a compound of contradictions, of all that we most hate with what we most admire." In addition, she is not just brilliantly imagined but "the real historical Cleopatra."

Charles Bathurst, on the other hand, in his study of how Shakespeare's verse changed over time, called *Antony and Cleopatra* "carelessly written, with no attempt at dignity, considering what great personages are introduced." According to Bathurst, the play is "historical; but it is chiefly the anecdote of history, not the dignity of it," that Shakespeare presents. The play's strength comes from "passages, where [Shakespeare] lets his mind loose, and follows his fancy and feeling freely . . . and even the verse breaks delightfully out of its trammels." Edward Dowden, on the other hand, saw *Antony and Cleopatra* as anything but "carelessly" made, describing it as "splendid with the colors of Titian and Paul Veronese." In addition, he said that "the characters of the *Antony and Cleopatra* insinuate themselves through the senses, trouble the blood, ensnare the imagination, invade our whole being like color or like music. The figures dilate to proportions greater than human, and are seen through a golden haze of sensuous splendor."

The Danish writer Georg Brandes examined the characters of the play. He wrote that the "great attraction of his masterpiece lies in the unique figure of Cleopatra," but he also noted that Shakespeare "required a throng of personages, and . . . he required a constant coming and going, sending and receiving of messengers, whose communications are awaited with anxiety, heard with bated breath, and not infrequently alter at one blow the situation of the chief characters." According to Brandes, "the greatness of the world-historic drama proceeds from the genius with which [Shakespeare] has entwined the private relations of the two lovers with the course of history and the fate of empires."

1809—August Wilhelm von Schlegel.
From *Lectures on Dramatic Art and Literature*

August Wilhelm von Schlegel (1767-1845) was an influential German critic and poet and a key figure in the German Romantic movement. He translated a number of Shakespeare's plays into German.

Antony and Cleopatra may, in some measure, be considered as a continuation of *Julius Caesar*: the two principal characters of Antony and Augustus are equally sustained in both pieces. *Antony and Cleopatra* is a play of great extent; the progress is less simple than in *Julius Caesar*. The fulness and variety of political and warlike events, to which the union of the three divisions of the Roman world under one master necessarily gave rise, were perhaps too great to admit of being clearly exhibited in one dramatic picture. In this consists the great difficulty of the historical drama:—it must be a crowded extract, and a living development of history;—the difficulty, however, has generally been successfully overcome by Shakspeare. But now many things, which are transacted in the background, are here merely alluded to, in a manner which supposes an intimate acquaintance with the history; but a work of art should contain, within itself, everything necessary for its being fully understood. Many persons of historical importance are merely introduced in passing; the preparatory and concurring circumstances are not sufficiently collected into masses to avoid distracting our attention. The principal personages, however, are most emphatically distinguished by lineament and colouring, and powerfully arrest the imagination. In Antony we observe a mixture of great qualities, weaknesses, and vices; violent ambition and ebullitions of magnanimity; we see him now sinking into luxurious enjoyment and then nobly ashamed of his own aberrations,—manning himself to resolutions not unworthy of himself, which are always shipwrecked against the seductions of an artful woman. It is Hercules in the chains of Omphale, drawn from the fabulous heroic ages into history, and invested with the Roman costume. The seductive arts of Cleopatra are in no respect veiled over; she is an ambiguous being made up of royal pride, female vanity, luxury, inconstancy, and true attachment. Although the mutual passion of herself and Antony is without moral dignity, it still excites our sympathy as an insurmountable fascination:—they seem formed for each other, and Cleopatra is as remarkable for her seductive charms as Antony for the splendour of his deeds. As they die for each other, we forgive them for having lived for each other. The open and lavish character of Antony is admirably contrasted with the heartless littleness of Octavius, whom Shakspeare seems to have completely seen through, without allowing himself to be led astray by the fortune and the fame of Augustus.

1817—William Hazlitt.
From *Characters of Shakespear's Plays*

William Hazlitt (1778-1830) was an English essayist and one of the finest Shakespearean critics of the nineteenth century.

This is a very noble play. Though not in the first class of Shakespeare's productions, it stands next to them, and is, we think, the finest of his historical plays, that is, of those in which he made poetry the organ of history, and assumed a certain tone of character and sentiment, in conformity to known facts, instead of trusting to his observations of general nature or to the unlimited indulgence of his own fancy. What he has added to the history, is upon a par with it. His genius was, as it were, a match for history as well as nature, and could grapple at will with either. This play is full of that pervading comprehensive power by which the poet could always make himself master of time and circumstances. It presents a fine picture of Roman pride and Eastern magnificence: and in the struggle between the two, the empire of the world seems suspended, "like the swan's down-feather,

> That stands upon the swell at full of tide,
> And neither way inclines."

The characters breathe, move, and live. Shakespeare does not stand reasoning on what his characters would do or say, but at once becomes them, and speaks and acts for them. He does not present us with groups of stage-puppets or poetical machines making set speeches on human life, and acting from a calculation of ostensible motives, but he brings living men and women on the scene, who speak and act from real feelings, according to the ebbs and flows of passion, without the least tincture of the pedantry of logic or rhetoric. Nothing is made out by inference and analogy, by climax and antithesis, but everything takes place just as it would have done in reality, according to the occasion.—The character of Cleopatra is a masterpiece. What an extreme contrast it affords to Imogen [in Cymbeline]! One would think it almost impossible for the same person to have drawn both. She is voluptuous, ostentatious, conscious, boastful of her charms, haughty, tyrannical, fickle. The luxurious pomp and gorgeous extravagance of the Egyptian queen are displayed in all their force and lustre, as well as the irregular grandeur of the soul of Mark Antony. Take only the first four lines that they speak as an example of the regal style of love-making.

> *Cleopatra.* If it be love, indeed, tell me how much?
> *Antony.* There's beggary in the love that can be reckon'd.

Cleopatra. I'll set a bourn how far to be belov'd.
Antony. Then must thou needs find out new heav'n, new earth.

The rich and poetical description of her person, beginning:

The barge she sat in, like a burnish'd throne,
Burnt on the water; the poop was beaten gold,
Purple the sails, and so perfumed, that
The winds were love-sick—

seems to prepare the way for, and almost to justify the subsequent infatuation of
Antony when in the sea-fight at Actium, he leaves the battle, and "like a doting
mallard" follows her flying sails.

Few things in Shakespeare (and we know of nothing in any other author like
them) have more of that local truth of imagination and character than the passage
in which Cleopatra is represented conjecturing what were the employments of
Antony in his absence. "He's speaking now, or murmuring—'Where's my serpent
of old Nile?'" Or again, when she says to Antony, after the defeat at Actium,
and his summoning up resolution to risk another fight, "It is my birthday; I
had thought to have held it poor; but since my lord is Antony again, I will be
Cleopatra." Perhaps the finest burst of all is Antony's rage after his final defeat
when he comes in, and surprises the messenger of Caesar kissing her hand—

To let a fellow that will take rewards,
And say, God quit you, be familiar with
My play-fellow, your hand; this kingly seal,
And plighter of high hearts.

It is no wonder that he orders him to be whipped; but his low condition is not
the true reason: there is another feeling which lies deeper, though Antony's
pride would not let him show it, except by his rage; he suspects the fellow to be
Caesar's proxy.

Cleopatra's whole character is the triumph of the voluptuous, of the love of
pleasure and the power of giving it, over every other consideration. Octavia is a
dull foil to her, and Fulvia a shrew and shrill-tongued. What a picture do those
lines give of her—

Age cannot wither her, nor custom stale
Her infinite variety. Other women cloy
The appetites they feed, but she makes hungry
Where most she satisfies.

What a spirit and fire in her conversation with Antony's messenger who brings her the unwelcome news of his marriage with Octavia! How all the pride of beauty and of high rank breaks out in her promised reward to him—

> There's gold, and here
> My bluest veins to kiss!

She had great and unpardonable faults, but the beauty of her death almost redeems them. She learns from the depth of despair the strength of her affections. She keeps her queen-like state in the last disgrace, and her sense of the pleasurable in the last moments of her life. She tastes a luxury in death. After applying the asp, she says with fondness—

> Dost thou not see my baby at my breast,
> That sucks the nurse asleep?
> As sweet as balm, as soft as air, as gentle.
> Oh Antony!

It is worth while to observe that Shakespeare has contrasted the extreme magnificence of the descriptions in this play with pictures of extreme suffering and physical horror, not less striking—partly perhaps to excuse the effeminacy of Mark Antony to whom they are related as having happened, but more to preserve a certain balance of feeling in the mind. Caesar says, hearing of his conduct at the court of Cleopatra,

> Antony,
> Leave thy lascivious wassails. When thou once
> Wert beaten from Mutina, where thou slew'st
> Hirtius and Pansa, consuls, at thy heel
> Did famine follow, whom thou fought'st against,
> Though daintily brought up, with patience more
> Than savages could suffer. Thou did'st drink
> The stale of horses, and the gilded puddle
> Which beast would cough at. Thy palate then did deign
> The roughest berry on the rudest hedge,
> Yea, like the stag, when snow the pasture sheets,
> The barks of trees thou browsed'st. On the Alps,
> It is reported, thou did'st eat strange flesh,
> Which some did die to look on: and all this,
> It wounds thine honour, that I speak it now,
> Was borne so like a soldier, that thy cheek
> So much as lank'd not.

The passage after Antony's defeat by Augustus where he is made to say—

> Yes, yes; he at Philippi kept
> His sword e'en like a dancer; while I struck
> The lean and wrinkled Cassius, and 'twas I
> That the mad Brutus ended,

is one of those fine retrospections which show us the winding and eventful march of human life. The jealous attention which has been paid to the unities both of time and place has taken away the principle of perspective in the drama, and all the interest which objects derive from distance, from contrast, from privation, from change of fortune, from long-cherished passion; and contracts our view of life from a strange and romantic dream, long, obscure, and infinite, into a smartly contested, three hours' inaugural disputation on its merits by the different candidates for theatrical applause.

The latter scenes of *Antony and Cleopatra* are full of the changes of accident and passion. Success and defeat follow one another with startling rapidity. Fortune sits upon her wheel more blind and giddy than usual. This precarious state and the approaching dissolution of his greatness are strikingly displayed in the dialogue between Antony and Eros.

> *Antony.* Eros, thou yet behold'st me?
> *Eros.* Ay, noble lord.
> *Antony.* Sometime we see a cloud that's dragonish,
> A vapor sometime, like a bear or lion,
> A towered citadel, a pendant rock,
> A forked mountain, or blue promontory
> With trees upon't, that nod unto the world
> And mock our eyes with air. Thou hast seen these signs,
> They are black vesper's pageants.
> *Eros.* Ay, my lord.
> *Antony.* That which is now a horse, even with a thought
> The rack dislimns, and makes it indistinct
> As water is in water.
> *Eros.* It does, my lord.
> *Antony.* My good knave, Eros, now thy captain is
> Even such a body, &c.

This is, without doubt, one of the finest pieces of poetry in Shakespeare. The splendor of the imagery, the semblance of reality, the lofty range of picturesque objects hanging over the world, their evanescent nature, the total uncertainty of what is left behind, are just like the moldering schemes of human greatness. It is finer than Cleopatra's passionate lamentation over his fallen grandeur, because it is more dim, unstable, unsubstantial. Antony's headstrong presumption and infatuated determination to yield to Cleopatra's wishes to fight by sea instead of land, meet a merited punishment; and the extravagance of his resolutions, increasing with the desperateness of his circumstances, is well commented upon by Enobarbus.

> I see men's judgments are
> A parcel of their fortunes, and things outward
> Do draw the inward quality after them
> To suffer all alike.

The repentance of Enobarbus after his treachery to his master is the most affecting part of the play. He cannot recover from the blow which Antony's generosity gives him, and he dies broken-hearted "a master-leaver and a fugitive."

Shakespeare's genius has spread over the whole play a richness like the overflowing of the Nile.

1818—Samuel Taylor Coleridge. From *Shakspeare, with Introductory Remarks on Poetry, the Drama, and the Stage*

Samuel Taylor Coleridge (1772–1834) was a great poet and critic and, with William Wordsworth, one of the founders of English Romanticism. In collaboration with Wordsworth, he published *Lyrical Ballads*, which among other pieces contained his enduring poem "The Rime of the Ancient Mariner." His best-known critical work is *Biographia Literaria*.

Shakspeare can be complimented only by comparison with himself: all other eulogies are either heterogeneous, as when they are in reference to Spenser or Milton; or they are flat truisms, as when he is gravely preferred to Corneille, Racine, or even his own immediate successors, Beaumont and Fletcher, Massinger and the rest. The highest praise, or rather form of praise, of this play, which I can offer in my own mind, is the doubt which the perusal always occasions in me, whether the *Antony and Cleopatra* is not, in all exhibitions of a giant power in its strength and vigour of maturity, a formidable rival of *Macbeth, Lear, Hamlet,* and *Othello. Feliciter audax* is the motto for its style comparatively with that of Shakspeare's other works, even as it is the general motto of all his works compared with those of other poets. Be it remembered, too, that this happy valiancy of style is but the representative and result of all the material excellencies so expressed.

This play should be perused in mental contrast with *Romeo and Juliet;*—as the love of passion and appetite opposed to the love of affection and instinct. But the art displayed in the character of Cleopatra is profound; in this, especially, that the sense of criminality in her passion is lessened by our insight into its depth and energy, at the very moment that we cannot but perceive that the passion itself springs out of the habitual craving of a licentious nature, and that it is supported and reinforced by voluntary stimulus and sought-for associations, instead of blossoming out of spontaneous emotion.

Of all Shakspeare's historical plays, *Antony and Cleopatra* is by far the most wonderful. There is not one in which he has followed history so minutely, and yet there are few in which he impresses the notion of angelic strength so much;—perhaps none in which he impresses it more strongly. This is greatly owing to the manner in which the fiery force is sustained throughout, and to the numerous momentary flashes of nature counteracting the historic abstraction. As a wonderful specimen of the way in which Shakspeare lives up to the very end of this play, read the last part of the concluding scene. And if you would feel the judgment as well as the genius of Shakspeare in your heart's core, compare this astonishing drama with Dryden's *All for Love.*

1832—Anna Murphy Brownell Jameson.
From *Shakespeare's Heroines: Characteristics of Women, Moral, Poetical, & Historical*

Anna Murphy Brownell Jameson (1794-1860), born in Dublin, is best remembered for her character studies of Shakespeare's heroines. In addition, she kept a diary of her travels on the Continent as governess to a wealthy family, later published as *The Diary of an Ennuyée* (1826), and wrote *Sacred and Legendary Art* (1848-60).

Great crimes, springing from high passions, grafted on high qualities, are the legitimate source of tragic poetry. But to make the extreme of littleness produce an effect like grandeur—to make the excess of frailty produce an effect like power—to heap up together all that is most unsubstantial, frivolous, vain, contemptible, and variable, till the worthlessness be lost in the magnitude, and a sense of the sublime spring from the very elements of littleness—to do this belonged only to Shakespeare, that worker of miracles. Cleopatra is a brilliant antithesis, a compound of contradictions, of all that we most hate with what we most admire. The whole character is the triumph of the external over the innate; and yet, like one of her country's hieroglyphics, though she presents at first view a splendid and perplexing anomaly, there is deep meaning and wondrous skill in the apparent enigma, when we come to analyse and decipher it. But how are we to arrive at the solution of this glorious riddle, whose dazzling complexity continually mocks and eludes us? What is most astonishing in the character of Cleopatra is its antithetical construction—its *consistent inconsistency,* if I may use such an expression—which renders it quite impossible to reduce it to any elementary principles. It will, perhaps, be found, on the whole, that vanity and the love of power predominate; but I dare not say it is so, for these qualities and a hundred others mingle into each other, and shift, and change, and glance away, like the colors in a peacock's train.

In some others of Shakespeare's female characters, also remarkable for their complexity (Portia and Juliet, for instance), we are struck with the delightful sense of harmony in the midst of contrast, so that the idea of unity and simplicity of effect is produced in the midst of variety; but in Cleopatra it is the absence of unity and simplicity which strikes us; the impression is that of perpetual and irreconcilable contrast. The continual approximation of whatever is most opposite in character, in situation, in sentiment, would be fatiguing, were it not so perfectly natural: the woman herself would be distracting, if she were not so enchanting.

I have not the slightest doubt that Shakespeare's Cleopatra is the real historical Cleopatra—the "rare Egyptian"—individualized and placed before us. Her mental accomplishments, her unequalled grace, her woman's wit and woman's wiles, her irresistible allurements, her starts of irregular grandeur, her bursts of ungovernable temper, her vivacity of imagination, her petulant caprice, her fickleness and her falsehood, her tenderness and her truth, her childish susceptibility to flattery, her magnificent spirit, her royal pride, the gorgeous eastern coloring of the character— all these contradictory elements has Shakespeare seized, mingled them in their extremes and fused them into one brilliant impersonation of classical elegance, Oriental voluptuousness, and gipsy sorcery.

What better proof can we have of the individual truth of the character than the admission that Shakespeare's Cleopatra produces exactly the same effect on us that is recorded of the real Cleopatra? She dazzles our faculties, perplexes our judgment, bewilders and bewitches our fancy; from the beginning to the end of the drama we are conscious of a kind of fascination against which our moral sense rebels, but from which there is no escape. The epithets applied to her perpetually by Antony and others confirm this impression; "enchanting queen!"—"witch"—"spell"—"great fairy"—"cockatrice"—"serpent of old Nile"— "thou grave charm!" are only a few of them: and who does not know by heart the famous quotations in which this Egyptian Circe is described, with all her infinite seductions? . . .

Although Cleopatra talks of dying "after the high Roman fashion," she fears what she most desires, and cannot perform with simplicity what costs her such an effort. That extreme physical cowardice which was so strong a trait in her historical character, which led to the defeat of Actium, which made her delay the execution of a fatal resolve till she had "tried conclusions infinite of *easy* ways to die," Shakespeare has rendered with the finest possible effect, and in a manner which heightens instead of diminishing our respect and interest. Timid by nature, she is courageous by the mere force of will, and she lashes herself up with high-sounding words into a kind of false daring. Her lively imagination suggests every incentive which can spur her on to the deed she has resolved, yet trembles to contemplate. She pictures to herself all the degradations which must attend her captivity: and let it be observed, that those which she anticipates are precisely such as a vain, luxurious, and haughty woman would especially dread, and which only true virtue and magnanimity could despise. Cleopatra could have endured the loss of freedom; but to be led in triumph through the streets of Rome is insufferable. She could stoop to Caesar with dissembling courtesy, and meet duplicity with superior art; but "to be chastised" by the scornful or upbraiding glance of the injured Octavia—"rather a ditch in Egypt!" . . .

She then calls for her diadem, her robes of state, and attires herself as if "again for Cydnus, to meet Mark Antony." Coquette to the last, she must make Death proud to take her, and die, "phoenix-like," as she had lived, with all the pomp of preparation—luxurious in her despair.

. . . The idea of this frail, timid, wayward woman dying with heroism, from the mere force of passion and will, takes us by surprise. The Attic elegance of her mind, her poetical imagination, the pride of beauty and royalty predominating to the last, and the sumptuous and picturesque accompaniments with which she surrounds herself in death, carry to its extreme height that effect of contrast which prevails through her life and character. No arts, no invention, could add to the real circumstances of Cleopatra's closing scene. Shakspeare has shown profound judgment and feeling in adhering closely to the classical authorities; and to say that the language and sentiments worthily fill up the outline is the most magnificent praise that can be given. . . .

1857—Charles Bathurst. From *Remarks on the Differences in Shakespeare's Versification in Different Periods of His Life*

Charles Bathurst attempted to show how the poetry in Shakespeare's plays differed as Shakespeare himself grew older. In particular, he was concerned with "the division of the pauses" in Shakespeare's lines. His thesis was that his later plays, such as *Antony and Cleopatra*, showed a more "interrupted" or broken style of verse.

[*Antony and Cleopatra*] is a far more irregular, varied, play, more, perhaps, than any he has written. It is carelessly written, with no attempt at dignity, considering what great personages are introduced; but with a great deal of nature, spirit, and knowledge of character, in very many parts, and with several most beautiful passages of poetry and imagination; as, for instance, the dream of Cleopatra. It has passages, where he lets his mind loose, and follows his fancy and feeling freely; particularly, perhaps, in the end; and even the verse breaks delightfully out of its trammels, as in the speech about the cloud.

The subject of the play, in fact, was likely often to lead to this looser and softer character; tenderness, even weakness, is its business. It is historical; but it is chiefly the anecdote of history, not the dignity of it. Plutarch's *Lives*, his only authority, is in fact but, in great degree, a collection of anecdotes. But there was no occasion to read Plutarch, to understand the part of Cleopatra. The tenderness of feeling, however, extends itself to other parts than those of the lovers; at least it is most remarkable in the death of Enobarbus—a part which, after the manner of Shakespeare, is made to throw great light on the character of Antony himself, which he meant to elevate as much as possible; notwithstanding his great weakness in all that concerns Cleopatra, and unmistakable misconduct with regard to his wife. He represents him as, what he certainly was not, a man of the most noble and high spirit, capable at times, notwithstanding the luxury he afterwards fell into, of a thoroughly soldier-like life, and full of kind and generous feelings. He seems to delight in supposing the melancholy meditations of a great and active character, when losing his power, and drawing to his end.

The character of Cleopatra is fully like that of a queen, in boldness, pride, command. But not at all otherwise. Her passions are those of a mere ordinary woman, who has no respect for herself. This may have been the case in fact with many queens, in private, because they have less to control them than other people; but it certainly ought not to be so represented. Her love for Antony is much inferior in depth, steadiness, and sincerity to his for her; but this was required by the events of the history. However, Shakespeare has put some very fine things here and there in her speeches, has made her interesting throughout, and winds her up at the last, partly by showing the attachment of her attendants to her, most magnificently.

1875—Edward Dowden.
From *Shakspere: A Critical Study of His Mind and Art*

Edward Dowden (1843-1913) was an Irish critic, university lecturer (Trinity College), and poet. His books of literary criticism include *Shakspere Primer* (1877) and *Studies in Literature* (1878).

The transition from the *Julius Caesar* of Shakespeare to his *Antony and Cleopatra* produces in us the change of pulse and temper experienced in passing from a gallery of antique sculpture to a room splendid with the colors of Titian and Paul Veronese. In the characters of the *Julius Caesar* there is a severity of outline; they impose themselves with strict authority upon the imagination; subordinated to the great spirit of Caesar, the conspirators appear as figures of lifesize, but they impress us as no larger than life. The demand which they make is exact; such and such tribute must be rendered by the soul to each. The characters of the *Antony and Cleopatra* insinuate themselves through the senses, trouble the blood, ensnare the imagination, invade our whole being like color or like music. The figures dilate to proportions greater than human, and are seen through a golden haze of sensuous splendor. *Julius Caesar* and *Antony and Cleopatra* are related as works of art rather by points of contrast than by points of resemblance. In the one an ideal of duty is dominant; the other is a divinisation of pleasure, followed by the remorseless Nemesis of eternal law. Brutus, the Stoic, constant, loyal to his ideas, studious of moral perfection, bent upon gaining self-mastery, unsullied and untarnished to the end, stands over against Antony, swayed hither and thither by appetites, interests, imagination, careless of his own moral being, incapable of self-control, soiled with the stains of passion and decay. And of Cleopatra what shall be said? Is she a creature of the same breed as Cato's daughter, Portia? Does the one word woman include natures so diverse? Or is Cleopatra—Antony's "serpent of old Nile"—no mortal woman, but Lilith who ensnared Adam before the making of Eve? Shakespeare has made the one as truly woman as the other; Portia, the ideal of moral loveliness, heroic and feminine; Cleopatra, the ideal of sensual attractiveness, feminine also:

A bliss in proof, and proved, a very woe;
Before, a joy proposed; behind, a dream

We do not once see the lips of Brutus laid on Portia's lips as seal of perfect union, but we know that their beings and their lives had embraced in flawless confidence, and perfect, mutual service. Antony embracing Cleopatra exclaims,

The nobleness of life
Is to do thus; when such a mutual pair

> And such a twain can do't, in which I bind,
> On pain of punishment, the world to weet
> We stand up peerless.

Yet this "mutual pair," made each to fill the body and soul of the other with voluptuous delight, are made also each for the other's torment. Antony is haunted by suspicion that Cleopatra will betray him; he believes it possible that she could degrade herself to familiarity with Caesar's menials. And Cleopatra is aware that she must weave her snares with endless variety, or Antony will escape.

The spirit of the play, though superficially it appear voluptuous, is essentially severe. That is to say, Shakespeare is faithful to the fact. The fascination exercised by Cleopatra over Antony, and hardly less by Antony over Cleopatra, is not so much that of the senses as of the sensuous imagination. A third of the world is theirs. They have left youth behind with its slight, melodious raptures and despairs. Theirs is the deeper intoxication of middle age, when death has become a reality, when the world is limited and positive, when life is urged to yield up quickly its utmost treasures of delight. What may they not achieve of joy who have power, and beauty, and pomp, and pleasure all their own? How shall they fill every minute of their time with the quintessence of enjoyment and of glory?

> Let Rome in Tiber melt! and the wide arch
> Of the rang'd empire fall! here is my space.

Only *one* thing they had not allowed for,—that over and above power, and beauty, and pleasure, and pomp, there is a certain inevitable fact, a law which cannot be evaded. Pleasure sits enthroned as queen; there is a revel, and the lords of the earth, crowned with roses, dance before her to the sound of lascivious flutes. But presently the scene changes; the hall of revel is transformed to an arena; the dancers are armed gladiators; and as they advance to combat they pay the last homage to their Queen with the words, *Morituri te salutant.*

The pathos of *Antony and Cleopatra* resembles the pathos of *Macbeth.* But Shakespeare like Dante allows the soul of the perjurer and murderer to drop into a lower, blacker, and more lonely circle of Hell than the soul of the man who has sinned through voluptuous self-indulgence. Yet none the less Antony is daily dropping away farther from all that is sound, strong, and enduring. His judgment wanes with his fortune. He challenges to a combat with swords his clear-sighted and unimpassioned rival into whose hands the empire of the world is about to fall. He abandons himself to a senseless exasperation. . . .

Measure things only by the sensuous imagination, and everything in the world of oriental voluptuousness, in which Antony lies bewitched, is great. The passion and the pleasure of the Egyptian queen, and of her paramour, toil after the infinite. The Herculean strength of Antony, the grandeur and prodigal power of his nature, inflate and buoy up the imagination of Cleopatra:

> The demi-Atlas of this earth, the arm
> And burgonet of men.

While he is absent, Cleopatra would, if it were possible, annihilate time,—

> *Charmian.* Why, Madam?
> *Cleopatra.* That I might sleep out this great gap of time,
> My Antony is away.

When Antony dies the only eminent thing in the earth is gone, and an universal flatness, an equality of insignificance remains:

> Young boys and girls
> Are level now with men; the odds is gone,
> And there is nothing left remarkable
> Beneath the visiting moon.

We do not mistake this feeling of Cleopatra towards Antony for love; but he has been for her (who had known Caesar and Pompey), the supreme sensation. She is neither faithful to him nor faithless; in her complex nature, beneath each fold or layer of sincerity, lies one of insincerity, and we cannot tell which is the last and inner-most. Her imagination is stimulated, and nourished by Antony's presence. And he in his turn finds in the beauty and witchcraft of the Egyptian, something no less incommensurable and incomprehensible. Yet no one felt more profoundly than Shakespeare,—as his Sonnets abundantly testify,—that the glory of strength and of beauty is subject to limit and to time. What he would seem to say to us in this play, not in the manner of a doctrinaire or a moralist, but wholly as an artist, is that this sensuous infinite is but a dream, a deceit, a snare. The miserable change comes upon Antony. The remorseless practice of Cleopatra upon his heart has done him to death. And among things which the barren world offers to the Queen she now finds death, a painless death, the least hateful. Shakespeare, in his high impartiality to fact, denies none of the glory of the lust of the eye and the pride of life. He compels us to acknowledge these to the utmost. But he adds that there is another demonstrable fact of the world, which tests the visible pomp of the earth, and the splendor of sensuous passion, and finds them wanting. The glory of the royal festival is not dulled by Shakespeare or diminished; but also he shows us in letters of flame the handwriting upon the wall.

This Shakespeare effects, however, not merely or chiefly by means of a catastrophe. He does not deal in precepts or moral reflections, or practical applications. He is an artist, but an artist who grasps truth largely. The ethical truth lives and breathes in every part of his work as an artist, no less than the truth to things sensible and presentable to the imagination. At every moment in this play we assist at a catastrophe—the decline of a lordly nature. At every moment we are necessarily aware of the gross, the mean, the disorderly womanhood in Cleopatra, no less than of the witchery and wonder which excite, and charm, and subdue. We see her a dissembler, a termagant, a coward; and yet "vilest things become her." The presence of a spirit of *life* in Cleopatra, quick, shifting, multitudinous, incalculable, fascinates the eye, and would, if it could, lull the moral sense to sleep, as the sea does with its endless snakelike motions in the sun and shade. She is a wonder of the world, which we would travel far to look upon. . . .

If we would know how an artist devoted to high moral ideals would treat such a character as that of the fleshy enchantress we have but to turn to the *Samson Agonistes*. Milton exposes Dalila only to drive her explosively from the stage. Shakespeare would have studied her with equal delight and detestation. Yet the severity of Shakespeare, in his own dramatic fashion, is as absolute as that of Milton. Antony is dead. The supreme sensation of Cleopatra's life is ended, and she seems in the first passionate burst of chagrin to have no longer interest in anything but death. By-and-by she is in the presence of Caesar; and hands over to him a document, the "brief of money, plate, and jewels" of which she is possessed. She calls on her treasurer Seleucus to vouch for its accuracy:

> *Cleopatra.*   What have I kept back?
> *Seleucus.* Enough to purchase what you have made known.
> *Caesar.* Nay, blush not, Cleopatra; I approve
> Your wisdom in the deed.

In her despair, while declaring that she will die "in the high Roman fashion," Cleopatra yet clings to her plate and jewels. And the cold approval of Caesar, who never gains the power which passion supplies, nor loses the power which passion withdraws and dissipates, the approval of Caesar is confirmed by the judgment of the spectator. It is right and natural that Cleopatra should love her jewels, and practise a fraud upon her conqueror.

Nor is her death quite in that "high Roman fashion" which she had announced. She dreads physical pain, and is fearful of the ravage which death might commit upon her beauty; under her physician's direction she has "pursued conclusions infinite of easy ways to die." And now to die painlessly is better than to grace the triumph of Octavius. In her death there is something dazzling and splendid, something sensuous, something theatrical, something magnificently coquettish, and nothing stern. Yet Shakespeare does not play the rude moralist; he needs no chorus of Israelite captives to utter invective against this Dalila. Let her possess all her grandeur, and her charm. Shakespeare can show us more excellent things which will make us proof against the fascination of these.

1896—Georg Brandes. "The Dark Lady as a Model— The Fall of the Republic a World-Catastrophe," from *William Shakespeare: A Critical Study*

Georg Brandes (1842–1927) was an important Danish literary critic and critic of Romanticism. He wrote extensively on Shakespeare's plays.

Assuming that it was Shakespeare's design in *Antony and Cleopatra*, as in *King Lear*, to evoke the conception of a world-catastrophe, we see that he could not in this play, as in *Macbeth* or *Othello*, focus the entire action around the leading characters alone. He could not even make the other characters completely subordinate to them; that would have rendered it impossible for him to give the impression of majestic breadth, of an action embracing half of the then known world, which he wanted for the sake of the concluding effect.

He required in the group of figures surrounding Octavius Caesar, and in the groups round Lepidus, Ventidius, and Sextus Pompeius, a counterpoise to Antony's group. He required the placid beauty and Roman rectitude of Octavia as a contrast to the volatile, intoxicating Egyptian. He required Enobarbus to serve as a sort of chorus and introduce an occasional touch of irony amid the high-flown passion of the play. In short, he required a throng of personages, and (in order to make us feel that the action was not taking place in some narrow precinct in a corner of Europe, but upon the stage of the world) he required a constant coming and going, sending and receiving of messengers, whose communications are awaited with anxiety, heard with bated breath, and not infrequently alter at one blow the situation of the chief characters.

The ambition which characterised Antony's past is what determines his relation to this great world; the love which has now taken such entire possession of him determines his relation to the Egyptian queen, and the consequent loss of all that his ambition had won for him. Whilst in a tragedy like Goethe's *Clavigo*, ambition plays the part of the tempter, and love is conceived as the good, the legitimate power, here it is love that is reprehensible, ambition that is proclaimed to be the great man's vocation and duty.

Thus Antony says (i. 2):

These strong Egyptian fetters I must break,
Or lose myself in dotage.

We saw that one element of Shakespeare's artist-nature was of use to him in his modelling of the figure of Antony. He himself had ultimately broken his fetters, or rather life had broken them for him; but as he wrote this great drama, he lived through again those years in which he himself had felt and spoken as he now made Antony feel and speak:

A thousand groans, but thinking on thy face,
One on another's neck, do witness bear,
Thy black is fairest in my judgment's place.
(*Sonnet* cxxxi.)

Day after day that woman now stood before him as his model who had been his life's Cleopatra—she to whom he had written of "lust in action":

Mad in pursuit, and in possession so;
Had, having, and in quest to have, extreme:
A bliss in proof,—and prov'd, a very woe.
(*Sonnet* cxxix.)

He had seen in her an irresistible and degrading Delilah, the Delilah whom De Vigny centuries later anathematised in a famous couplet.[1] He had bewailed, as Antony does now, that his beloved had belonged to many:

If eyes, corrupt by over-partial looks,
Be anchor'd in the bay where all men ride,
. . .
Why should my heart think that a several plot
Which my heart knows the wide world's common place?
(*Sonnet* cxxxvii.)

He had, like Antony, suffered agonies from the coquetry she would lavish on any one she wanted to win. He had then burst forth in complaint, as Antony in the drama breaks out into frenzy:

Tell me thou lov'st elsewhere; but in my sight,
Dear heart, forbear to glance thine eye aside:
What need'st thou wound with cunning, when thy might

Is more than my o'er-pressed defence can 'bide?
(*Sonnet* cxxxix.)

Now he no longer upbraided her; now he crowned her with a queenly diadem, and placed her, living, breathing, and in the largest sense true to nature, on that stage which was his world.

As in *Othello* he had made the lover-hero about as old as he was himself at the time he wrote the play, so now it interested him to represent this stately and splendid lover who was no longer young. In the Sonnets he had already dwelt upon his age. He says, for instance, in Sonnet cxxxviii.:

When my love swears that she is made of truth,
I do believe her, though I know she lies,
That she might think me some untutor'd youth,
Unlearned in the world's false subtleties.
Thus vainly thinking that she thinks me young,
Although she knows my days are past the best,
Simply I credit her false-speaking tongue.

When Antony and Cleopatra perished with each other, she was in her thirty-ninth, he in his fifty-fourth year. She was thus almost three times as old as Juliet, he more than double the age of Romeo. This correspondence with his own age pleases Shakespeare's fancy, and the fact that time has had no power to sear or wither this pair seems to hold them still farther aloof from the ordinary lot of humanity. The traces years have left upon the two have only given them a deeper beauty. All that they themselves in sadness, or others in spite, say to the contrary, signifies nothing. The contrast between their age in years and that which their beauty and passion make for them merely enhances and adds piquancy to the situation. It is in sheer malice that Pompey exclaims (ii. 1):

But all the charms of love,
Salt Cleopatra, soften thy *waned* lip!

This means no more than her own description of herself as "wrinkled." And it is on purpose to give the idea of Antony's age, of which in Plutarch there is no indication, that Shakespeare makes him dwell on the mixed colour of his own hair. He says (iii. 9):

My very hairs do mutiny; for the white
Reprove the brown for rashness, and they them
For fear and doting.

In the moment of despair he uses the expression (iii. 11): "To the boy Caesar send this grizzled head." And again, after the last victory, he recurs to the idea in a tone of triumph. Exultingly he addresses Cleopatra (iv. 8):

> What, girl! though grey
> Do something mingle with our younger brown, yet ha' we
> A brain that nourishes our nerves, and can
> Get goal for goal of youth.

With a sure hand Shakespeare has depicted in Antony the mature man's fear of letting a moment pass unutilised: the vehement desire to enjoy before the hour strikes when all enjoyment must cease. Thus Antony says in one of his first speeches (i. 1):

> Now, for the love of Love and her soft hours . . .
> There's not a minute of our lives should stretch
> Without some pleasure now.

Then he feels the necessity of breaking his bonds. He makes Fulvia's death serve his purpose of gaining Cleopatra's consent to his departure; but even then he is not free. In order to bring out the contrast between Octavius the statesman and Antony the lover, Shakespeare emphasises the fact that Octavius has reports of the political situation brought to him every hour, whilst Antony receives no other daily communication than the regularly arriving letters from Cleopatra which foment the longing that draws him back to Egypt.

As a means of allaying the storm and gaining peace to love his queen at leisure, he agrees to marry his opponent's sister, knowing that, when it suits him, he will neglect and repudiate her. Then vengeance overtakes him for having so contemptuously thrown away the empire over more than a third of the civilised world—vengeance for having said as he embraced Cleopatra (i. 1):

> Let Rome in Tiber melt, and the wide arch
> Of the ranged empire fall! Here is my space.

Rome melts through his fingers. Rome proclaims him a foe to her empire, and declares war against him. And he loses his power, his renown, his whole position, in the defeat which he so contemptibly brings upon himself at Actium. In Cleopatra flight was excusable. Her flight in the drama (which follows Plutarch and tradition) is due to cowardice; in reality it was prompted by tactical, judicious motives. But Antony was in honour bound to stay. He follows her in the tragedy (as in reality) from brainless, contemptible incapacity to remain when she has gone; leaving an army of 112,000 men and a fleet of 450 ships in the lurch, without leader or commander. Nine days did his troops await his return, rejecting every proposal of the enemy, incapable of believing in the desertion and flight of the general they admired and trusted. When at last they could no longer resist the conviction that he had sunk his soldier's honour in shame, they went over to Octavius.

After this everything turns on the mutual relation of Antony and Cleopatra, and Shakespeare has admirably depicted its ecstasies and its revulsions. Never before had they loved each other so wildly and so rapturously. Now it is not only he who openly calls her "Thou day o' the world!" She answers him with the cry, "Lord of lords! O infinite virtue!" (iv. 8)

Yet never before has their mutual distrust been so deep. She, who was at no time really great except in the arts of love and coquetry, has always felt distrustful of him, and yet never distrustful enough; for though she was prepared for a great deal, his marriage with Octavia overwhelmed her. He, knowing her past, knowing how often she has thrown herself away, and understanding her temperament, believes her false to him even when she is innocent, even when, as with Desdemona, only the vaguest of appearances are against her. In the end we see Antony develop into an Othello.

Here and there we come upon something in his character which seems to indicate that Shakespeare had been lately occupied with Macbeth. Cleopatra stimulates Anthony's voluptuousness, his sensuality, as Lady Macbeth spurred on her husband's ambition; and Antony fights his last battle with Macbeth's Berserk fury, facing with savage bravery what he knows to be invincibly superior force. But in his emotional life after the disaster of Actium it is Othello whom he more nearly resembles. He causes Octavius's messenger, Thyreus, to be whipped, simply because Cleopatra at parting has allowed him to kiss her hand. When some of her ships take to flight, he immediately believes in an alliance between her and the enemy, and heaps the coarsest invectives upon her, almost worse than those with which Othello overwhelms Desdemona. And in his monologue (iv. 10) he raves groundlessly like Othello:

Betray'd I am.
O this false soul of Egypt! this grave charm,—
Whose eye beck'd forth my wars, and call'd them home,
Whose bosom was my crownet, my chief end,
Like a right gipsy, hath, at fast and loose,
Beguil'd me to the very heart of loss.

They both, though faithless to the rest of the world, meant to be true to each other, but in the hour of trial they place no trust in each other's faithfulness. And all these strong emotions have shaken Antony's judgment. The braver he becomes in his misfortune, the more incapable is he of seeing things as they really are. Enobarbus closes the third act most felicitously with the words:

> I see still
> A diminution in our captain's brain
> Restores his heart: when valour preys on reason
> It eats the sword it fights with.

To tranquillise Antony's jealous frenzy, Cleopatra, who always finds readiest aid in a lie, sends him the false tidings of her death. In grief over her loss, he falls on his sword and mortally wounds himself. He is carried to her, and dies. She bursts forth:

> Noblest of men, woo't die?
> Hast thou no care of me? shall I abide
> In this dull world, which in thy absence is
> No better than a sty?—O! see, my women,
> The crown o' the earth doth melt.

In Shakespeare, however, her first thought is not of dying herself. She endeavours to come to a compromise with Octavius, hands over to him an inventory of her treasures, and tries to trick him out of the larger half. It is only when she has ascertained that nothing, neither admiration for her beauty nor pity for her misfortunes, moves his cold sagacity, and that he is determined to exhibit her humiliation to the populace of Rome as one of the spectacles of his triumph, that she lets "the worm of Nilus" give her her death.

In these passages the poet has placed Cleopatra's behaviour in a much more unfavourable light than the Greek historian, whom he follows as far as details are concerned; and he has evidently done so wittingly and purposely, in order to complete his home-thrust at the type of woman whose dangerousness he has embodied in her. In Plutarch all these negotiations with Octavius were a feint to deceive the vigilance with which he thought to prevent her from killing herself. Suicide is her one thought, and he has baulked her in her first attempt. She pretends to cling to her treasures only to delude him into the belief that she still clings to life, and her heroic imposture is successful. Shakespeare, for whom she is ever the quintessence of the she-animal in women, disparages her intentionally by suppressing the historical explanation of her behaviour.[2]

The English critic, Arthur Symons, writes: "*Antony and Cleopatra* is the most wonderful, I think, of all Shakespeare's plays, and it is so mainly because the figure of Cleopatra is the most wonderful of Shakespeare's women. And not of Shakespeare's women only, but perhaps the most wonderful of women."

This is carrying enthusiasm almost too far. But thus much is true: the great attraction of his masterpiece lies in the unique figure of Cleopatra, elaborated as it is with all Shakespeare's human experience and artistic enthusiasm. But the greatness of the world-historic drama proceeds from the genius with which he has entwined the private relations of the two lovers with the course of history and the fate of empires. Just as Antony's ruin results from his connection with Cleopatra, so does the fall of the Roman Republic result from the contact of the simple hardihood of the West with the luxury of the East. Antony is Rome, Cleopatra is the Orient. When he perishes, a prey to the voluptuousness of the East, it seems as though Roman greatness and the Roman Republic expired with him.

Not Caesar's ambition, nor Caesar's assassination, but this crumbling to pieces of Roman greatness fourteen years later brings home to us the ultimate fall of the old world-republic, and impresses us with that sense of *universal annihilation* which in this play, as in *King Lear,* Shakespeare aims at begetting.

This is no tragedy of a domestic, limited nature like the conclusion of *Othello;* there is no young Fortinbras here, as in *Hamlet,* giving the promise of brighter and better times to come; the victory of Octavius brings glory to no one and promises nothing. No; the final picture is that which Shakespeare was bent on painting from the moment he felt himself attracted by this great theme—the picture of a world-catastrophe.

NOTES

1. Toujours ce compagnon dont le coeur n'est pas sûr, La Femme—enfant malade et douze fois impur.

2. Goethe has a marked imitation of Shakespeare's Cleopatra in the Adelheid of *Götz von Berlichingen.* And he has placed Weislingen between Adelheid and Maria as Antony stands between Cleopatra and Octavia—bound to the former and marrying the latter.

ANTONY AND CLEOPATRA
IN THE TWENTIETH CENTURY
❧

Had he [Shakespeare] emerged like us from the Second World
War, and had he lived, as we do, through the anxieties caused by
the behavior of the two world powers [the United States and the
Soviet Union] which are holding peace in their hands, I doubt if
he would alter in any way Enobarbus's words when he says about
Antony and Caesar who are now face to face:

Then, world, thou hast a pair of chaps—no more;
And throw between them all the food thou hast,
They'll grind the one the other.
(*Antony and Cleopatra*, III. v. 13–15)
　　　　　　　　　　　　　　　　　　—Jean-Louis Barrault

A reader of nineteenth-century critics on *Antony and Cleopatra* may get the sense
that they were doing their best (and a very good "best" it was) given the decorum
of the time. So many of the principal elements of the play threatened to overwhelm nineteenth-century sensibilities: a voluptuous and criminally seductive
heroine in Cleopatra; a hero, Antony, who was not entirely heroic in the old
Roman sense; the very largeness of the play itself, whose structure appeared to
defy order even if it seemed to be true to history. But the twentieth century was
an era as little defined by decorum as the play itself, and the period produced
great critics who were prepared to analyze all the complex subversions and ethical ambiguities of *Antony and Cleopatra*, unfazed by moral and social restraints.

Writing at the very end of the nineteenth century, George Bernard Shaw set
his own play *Caesar and Cleopatra* against Shakespeare's *Antony and Cleopatra*.
Despite its title, his essay does not quite argue that his play is, in fact, better
than Shakespeare's but instead that Shakespeare, "who knew human weakness so
well" but "never knew human strength," presents a trivial matter in *Antony and
Cleopatra*. Shaw claimed that the play makes "sexual infatuation a tragic theme"
without regard for real "human strength," the kind Shaw said he himself depicted
in his own play.

Although A.C. Bradley wrote about *Antony and Cleopatra* in 1909, he separated the play from *Hamlet*, *Othello*, *King Lear*, and *Macbeth*, which his 1904 lectures established as Shakespeare's canonically supreme tragedies. Continuing in the nineteenth-century tradition of combining story and character analysis with fine scholarship and educated sensitivity, Bradley called Cleopatra one of the three "inexhaustible" characters in Shakespeare, the others being Hamlet and Falstaff. But Bradley concluded that *Antony and Cleopatra*, although magnificent in itself, falls short of the other four great tragedies. He stated that in this play, "tragic emotions" are not "stirred in the fullest possible measure" because "such beauty or nobility of character" is not "displayed as commands unreserved admiration or love." He also claimed that "the forces which move the agents, and the conflict which results from these forces" do not "attain a terrifying and overwhelming power."

G. Wilson Knight's 1931 essay has the stated goal of examining "the more specifically human qualities in *Antony and Cleopatra*." Knight claimed that the realism of the play is just as powerful as its oft-noted magnificence. The combination of "the crude and the ideal" makes this one of Shakespeare's greatest plays. "No play is more true, and, finally, none more beautiful."

Harold C. Goddard, whom Harold Bloom often cites as his favorite American Shakespearean critic, also noted the "harmonious balance" of aspects of the playwright's genius exhibited in this play, though he agreed with Bradley that it was not as great as Shakespeare's four most famous tragedies. Goddard examined the characters of Antony and Cleopatra in depth and was particularly insistent on the importance of Octavius Caesar in the play. He also pointed out parallels between *Antony and Cleopatra* and Shakespeare's other plays, such as *Hamlet* and *King Lear*.

The great Canadian critic Northrop Frye compared the world of *Antony and Cleopatra* to his contemporary world: "*Antony and Cleopatra* is, I think, the play that looks most like the kind of world we seem to be moving into now." Frye also pointed out intriguing connections between this play and *Hamlet* and between the characters of Cleopatra and Falstaff.

The scholar Anne Barton, now a professor at the University of Cambridge, examined the concept of the "divided catastrophe," her term for the procedure by which a play "achieves a tragic climax and then, without warning, presses on beyond it." Barton claims the catastrophe in *Antony and Cleopatra* is split between Acts IV and V. In Act IV, Antony dies memorably in Cleopatra's presence. But after this point, which feels like a true ending, the play carries on for another act to focus on Cleopatra and her own catastrophe. Around the same time, Rosalie L. Colie published an essay exploring the "problem of style" in *Antony and Cleopatra*. According to Colie, "Style of speech necessarily reveals personality, values, and ethics. . . . In the speeches of Antony, Cleopatra, Octavius, Enobarbus, we recognize not just the varying moods of the speakers but their complex inner natures as well."

In 1988 Laura Quinney, now a professor at Brandeis University, published an essay on *Antony and Cleopatra* that Harold Bloom called "a model instance" of contemporary criticism. The essay illuminates, in Bloom's description, "the antithetical languages of intimacy and isolation in the play."

Harold Bloom himself called *Antony and Cleopatra* unique in that "the tragedy's doubleness, equal in both man and woman as it was with *Romeo and Juliet*, takes place between equally titanic personages." His essay goes on to examine what for him is the crucial question of the play: Why are the suicides of both Antony and Cleopatra so moving and even triumphant to the audience?

The twentieth century also witnessed many important stage productions of *Antony and Cleopatra*. In a 1906 production with Sir Herbert Beerbohm Tree and Constance Collier, the emphasis was placed on the grandness of Antony and Cleopatra's sexual passion. The scenes in Rome and of battle were abbreviated, and the entire play was simplified. Cleopatra was played as "dark-skinned, barbaric"; Antony, "fine, masculine, resolute . . . a hero ruined by love." In 1951, Laurence Olivier and Vivien Leigh starred in the play. Unlike the unnamed reviewer of another production a century earlier, who found the play itself of little value, Ivor Brown declared in the *Observer* that "in the last two acts of *Antony and Cleopatra* Shakespeare wrote as never before or after." Of Vivien Leigh's performance he wrote, "She moved me almost beyond endurance." Since then productions of *Antony and Cleopatra* have been offered frequently on the stage and have been filmed for the movies and for television with such notable actors as Peggy Ashcroft, Michael Redgrave, Jonathan Pryce, Charleton Heston, Judi Dench, Anthony Hopkins, Timothy Dalton, and Lynn Redgrave. Shakespeare's play has also served as the basis for a popular film that brought Elizabeth Taylor and Richard Burton together and for an opera by the American composer Samuel Barber ,whose libretto consists only of passages from the play.

1901—George Bernard Shaw. From "Preface: Better than Shakespear?" from *Three Plays for Puritans*

George Bernard Shaw (1856–1950) was a playwright and critic. He often expressed his ambivalence toward Shakespeare. Some of his greatest works include *Saint Joan*, *Pygmalion* (later adapted into the musical play and film *My Fair Lady*), *Man and Superman*, and *Caesar and Cleopatra*, the last of which was published in a volume called *Three Plays for Puritans*. In the preface to the volume, Shaw compares his play with Shakespeare's depictions of the same subject.

As to the other plays in this volume, the application of my title is less obvious, since neither Julius Caesar, Cleopatra, nor Lady Cicely Waynflete [in *Captain Brassbound's Conversion*] have any external political connexion with Puritanism. The very name of Cleopatra suggests at once a tragedy of Circe, with the horrible difference that whereas the ancient myth rightly represents Circe as turning heroes into hogs, the modern romantic convention would represent her as turning hogs into heroes. Shakespear's Antony and Cleopatra must needs be as intolerable to the true Puritan as it is vaguely distressing to the ordinary healthy citizen, because, after giving a faithful picture of the soldier broken down by debauchery, and the typical wanton in whose arms such men perish, Shakespear finally strains all his huge command of rhetoric and stage pathos to give a theatrical sublimity to the wretched end of the business, and to persuade foolish spectators that the world was well lost by the twain. Such falsehood is not to be borne except by the real Cleopatras and Antonys (they are to be found in every public house) who would no doubt be glad enough to be transfigured by some poet as immortal lovers. Woe to the poet who stoops to such folly! The lot of the man who sees life truly and thinks about it romantically is Despair. How well we know the cries of that despair! Vanity of vanities, all is vanity moans the Preacher, when life has at last taught him that Nature will not dance to his moralist-made tunes. Thackeray, scores of centuries later, was still baying the moon in the same terms. Out, out, brief candle! cries Shakespear, in his tragedy of the modern literary man as murderer and witch consulter. Surely the time is past for patience with writers who, having to choose between giving up life in despair and discarding the trumpery moral kitchen scales in which they try to weigh the universe, superstitiously stick to the scales, and spend the rest of the lives they pretend to despise in breaking men's spirits. But even in pessimism there is a choice between intellectual honesty and dishonesty. Hogarth drew the rake and the harlot without glorifying their end. Swift, accepting our system of morals and religion, delivered the inevitable verdict of that system on us through the mouth of the king of Brobdingnag, and described Man as the Yahoo, shocking his superior the horse by his every action. Strindberg, the only genuinely Shakespearean modern dramatist, shews that the female Yahoo, measured by romantic standards, is viler than her male dupe and slave. I respect these resolute tragi-comedians: they are logical and faithful: they force you to face the fact that you must either accept their conclusions as valid (in which case it is cowardly to continue living) or admit that their way of judging conduct is absurd. But when your Shakespears and Thackerays huddle up the matter at the end by killing somebody and covering your eyes with the undertaker's handkerchief, duly onioned with some pathetic phrase, as The flight of angels sing thee to thy rest, or Adsum, or the like, I have no respect for them at all: such maudlin tricks may impose on tea-drunkards, not on me.

Besides, I have a technical objection to making sexual infatuation a tragic theme. Experience proves that it is only effective in the comic spirit. We can bear to see Mrs Quickly pawning her plate for love of Falstaff, but not Antony running away from the battle of Actium for love of Cleopatra. Let realism have its demonstration, comedy its criticism, or even bawdry its horselaugh at the expense of sexual infatuation, if it must; but to ask us to subject our souls to its ruinous glamor, to worship it, deify it, and imply that it alone makes our life worth living, is nothing but folly gone mad erotically—a thing compared to which Falstaff's unbeglamored drinking and drabbing is respectable and right-minded. Whoever, then, expects to find Cleopatra a Circe and Caesar a hog in these pages, had better lay down my book and be spared a disappointment.

In Caesar, I have used another character with which Shakespear has been beforehand. But Shakespear, who knew human weakness so well, never knew human strength of the Caesarian type. His Caesar is an admitted failure: his Lear is a masterpiece. The tragedy of disillusion and doubt, of the agonized struggle for a foothold on the quicksand made by an acute observation striving to verify its vain attribution of morality and respectability to Nature, of the faithless will and the keen eyes that the faithless will is too weak to blind: all this will give you a Hamlet or a Macbeth, and win you great applause from literary gentlemen; but it will not give you a Julius Caesar. Caesar was not in Shakespear, nor in the epoch, now fast waning, which he inaugurated. It cost Shakespear no pang to write Caesar down for the merely technical purpose of writing Brutus up. And what a Brutus! A perfect Girondin, mirrored in Shakespear's art two hundred years before the real thing came to maturity and talked and stalked and had its head duly cut off by the coarser Antonys and Octaviuses of its time, who at least knew the difference between life and rhetoric.

It will be said that these remarks can bear no other construction than an offer of my Caesar to the public as an improvement on Shakespear's. And in fact, that is their precise purport. But here let me give a friendly warning to those scribes who have so often exclaimed against my criticisms of Shakespear as blasphemies against a hitherto unquestioned Perfection and Infallibility. Such criticisms are no more new than the creed of my Diabolonian Puritan or my revival of the humors of Cool as a Cucumber. Too much surprise at them betrays an acquaintance with Shakespear criticism so limited as not to include even the prefaces of Dr Johnson and the utterances of Napoleon. I have merely repeated in the dialect of my own time and in the light of its philosophy what they said in the dialect and light of theirs. Do not be misled by the Shakespear fanciers who, ever since his own time, have delighted in his plays just as they might have delighted in a particular breed of pigeons if they had never learnt to read. His genuine critics, from Ben Jonson to Mr Frank Harris, have always kept as far on this side idolatry as I.

As to our ordinary uncritical citizens, they have been slowly trudging forward these three centuries to the point which Shakespear reached at a bound in Elizabeth's time. Today most of them have arrived there or thereabouts, with the result that his plays are at last beginning to be performed as he wrote them; and the long line of disgraceful farces, melodramas, and stage pageants which actor-managers, from Garrick and Cibber to our own contemporaries, have hacked out of his plays as peasants have hacked huts out of the Coliseum, are beginning to vanish from the stage. It is a significant fact that the mutilators of Shakespear, who never could be persuaded that Shakespear knew his business better than they, have ever been the most fanatical of his worshippers. The late Augustin Daly thought no price too extravagant for an addition to his collection of Shakespear relics; but in arranging Shakespear's plays for the stage, he proceeded on the assumption that Shakespear was a botcher and he an artist. I am far too good a Shakespearean ever to forgive Henry Irving for producing a version of *King Lear* so mutilated that the numerous critics who had never read the play could not follow the story of Gloster. Both these idolators of the Bard must have thought Forbes Robertson mad because he restored Fortinbras to the stage and played as much of Hamlet as there was time for instead of as little. And the instant success of the experiment probably altered their minds no further than to make them think the public mad. Mr Benson actually gives the play complete at two sittings, causing the aforesaid numerous critics to remark with naive surprise that Polonius is a complete and interesting character. It was the age of gross ignorance of Shakespear and incapacity for his works that produced the indiscriminate eulogies with which we are familiar. It was the revival of serious attention to those works that coincided with the movement for giving genuine instead of spurious and silly representations of his plays. So much for Bardolatry!

It does not follow, however, that the right to criticize Shakespear involves the power of writing better plays. And in fact—do not be surprised at my modesty—I do not profess to write better plays. The writing of practicable stage plays does not present an infinite scope to human talent; and the playwrights who magnify its difficulties are humbugs. The summit of their art has been attained again and again. No man will ever write a better tragedy than Lear, a better comedy than Le Festin de Pierre or Peer Gynt, a better opera than Don Giovanni, a better music drama than The Niblung's Ring, or, for the matter of that, better fashionable plays and melodramas than are now being turned out by writers whom nobody dreams of mocking with the word immortal. It is the philosophy, the outlook on life, that changes, not the craft of the playwright. A generation that is thoroughly moralized and patriotized, that conceives virtuous indignation as spiritually nutritious, that murders the murderer and robs the thief, that grovels before all sorts of ideals, social, military, ecclesiastical, royal and divine, may be, from my point of view, steeped in error; but it need not want for as good plays as the hand of man can produce. Only, those plays will be neither written nor relished by men in whose philosophy guilt and innocence, and consequently revenge and idolatry, have no meaning. Such men must rewrite all the old plays in terms of their own philosophy; and that is why, as Stuart-Glennie has pointed out, there can be no new drama without a new philosophy. To which I may add that there can be no Shakespear or Goethe without one either, nor two Shakespears in one philosophic epoch, since, as I have said, the first great comer in that epoch reaps the whole harvest and reduces those who come after to the rank of mere gleaners, or, worse than that, fools who go laboriously through all the motions of the reaper and binder in an empty field. What is the use of writing plays or painting frescoes if you have nothing more to say or shew than was said and shewn by Shakespear, Michael Angelo, and Raphael? If these had not seen things differently, for better or worse, from the dramatic poets of the Townley mysteries, or from Giotto, they could not have produced their works: no, not though their skill of pen and hand had been double what it was. After them there was no need (and *need* alone nerves men to face the persecution in the teeth of which new art is brought to birth) to redo the already done, until in due time, when their philosophy wore itself out, a new race of nineteenth century poets and critics, from Byron to William Morris, began, first to speak coldly of Shakespear and Raphael, and then to rediscover, in the medieval art which these Renascence masters had superseded, certain forgotten elements which were germinating again for the new harvest. What is more, they began to discover that the technical skill of the masters was by no means superlative. Indeed, I defy anyone to prove that the great epoch makers in fine art have owed their position to their technical skill. It is true that when we search for examples of a prodigious command of language and of graphic line, we can think of nobody better than Shakespear and Michael Angelo. But both of them laid their arts waste for centuries by leading later artists to seek greatness in copying their technique. The technique was acquired, refined on, and elaborated over and over again; but the supremacy of the two great exemplars remained undisputed. As a matter of easily observable fact, every generation produces men of extraordinary special faculty, artistic, mathematical and linguistic, who for lack of new ideas, or indeed of any ideas worth mentioning, achieve no distinction outside music halls and class rooms, although they can do things easily that the great epoch makers did clumsily or not at all. The contempt of the academic pedant for the original artist is often founded on a genuine superiority of technical knowledge and aptitude: he is sometimes a better anatomical draughtsman than Raphael, a better hand at triple counterpoint than Beethoven, a better versifier than Byron. Nay, this is true not merely of pedants, but of men who have produced works of art of some note. If technical facility were the secret of greatness in art, Swinburne would be greater than Browning and Byron rolled into one, Stevenson greater than Scott or Dickens, Mendelssohn than Wagner, Maclise than Madox Brown. Besides, new ideas make their technique as water makes its channel; and the technician without ideas is as useless as the canal constructor without water, though he may do very skilfully what the Mississippi does very rudely. To clinch the argument, you have only to observe that the epoch maker himself has generally begun working professionally before his new ideas have mastered him sufficiently, to insist on constant expression by his art. In such cases you are compelled to admit that if he had by chance died earlier, his greatness would have remained unachieved, although his technical qualifications would have been well enough established. The early imitative works of great men are usually conspicuously inferior to the best works of their forerunners. Imagine Wagner dying after composing Rienzi, or Shelley after Zastrozzi! Would any competent critic then have rated Wagner's technical aptitude as high as Rossini's, Spontini's, or Meyerbeer's; or Shelley's as high as Moore's? Turn the problem another way: does anyone suppose that if Shakespear had conceived Goethe's or Ibsen's ideas, he would have expressed them any worse than Goethe or Ibsen? Human faculty being what it is, is it likely that in our time any advance, except in external conditions, will take place in the arts of expression sufficient to enable an author, without making himself ridiculous, to undertake to say what he has to say better than Homer or Shakespear? But the humblest author, and much more a rather arrogant one like myself, may profess to have something to say by this time that neither Homer nor Shakespear said. And the playgoer may reasonably ask to have historical events and persons presented to him in the light of his own time, even though Homer and Shakespear have already shewn them in the light of their time. For example, Homer presented Achilles and Ajax as heroes to the world in the Iliads. In due time came Shakespear, who said, virtually: I really cannot accept this spoilt child and this brawny fool as great men merely because Homer flattered them in playing to the Greek gallery. Consequently we have, in *Troilus and Cressida*, the verdict of Shakespear's epoch (our own) on the pair. This did not in the least involve any pretence on Shakespear's part to be a greater poet than Homer.

When Shakespear in turn came to deal with Henry V and Julius Caesar, he did so according to his own essentially knightly conception of a great statesman-commander. But in the XIX century comes the German historian Mommsen, who also takes Caesar for his hero, and explains the immense difference in scope between the perfect knight Vercingetorix and his great conqueror Julius Caesar. In this country, Carlyle, with his vein of peasant inspiration, apprehended the sort of greatness that places the true hero of history so far beyond the mere *preux chevalier*, whose fanatical personal honor, gallantry, and self-sacrifice are founded on a passion for death born of inability to bear the weight of a life that will not grant ideal conditions to the liver. This one ray of perception became Carlyle's whole stock-in-trade; and it sufficed to make a literary master of him. In due time, when Mommsen is an old man, and Carlyle dead, come I, and dramatize the by-this-time familiar distinction in Arms and the Man, with its comedic conflict between the knightly Bulgarian and the Mommsenite Swiss captain. Whereupon a great many playgoers who have not yet read Cervantes, much less Mommsen and Carlyle, raise a shriek of concern for their knightly ideal as if nobody had ever questioned its sufficiency since the middle ages. Let them thank me for educating them so far. And let them allow me to set forth Caesar in the same modern light, taking the platform from Shakespear as he from Homer, and with no thought of pretending to express the Mommsenite view of Caesar any better than Shakespear expressed a view which was not even Plutarchian, and must, I fear, be referred to the tradition in stage conquerors established by Marlowe's Tamerlane as much as to the chivalrous conception of heroism dramatized in Henry V.

For my own part, I can avouch that such powers of invention, humor and stage ingenuity as I have been able to exercise in Plays Pleasant and Unpleasant, and in these Three Plays for Puritans, availed me not at all until I saw the old facts in a new light. Technically, I do not find myself able to proceed otherwise than as former playwrights have done. True, my plays have the latest mechanical improvements: the action is not carried on by impossible soliloquys and asides; and my people get on and off the stage without requiring four doors to a room which in real life would have only one. But my stories are the old stories; my characters are the familiar harlequin and columbine, clown and pantaloon (note the harlequin's leap in the third act of Caesar and Cleopatra); my stage tricks and suspenses and thrills and jests are the ones in vogue when I was a boy, by which time my grandfather was tired of them. To the young people who make their acquaintance for the first time in my plays, they may be as novel as Cyrano's nose to those who have never seen Punch; whilst to older playgoers the unexpectedness of my attempt to substitute natural history for conventional ethics and romantic logic may so transfigure the eternal stage puppets and their inevitable dilemmas as to make their identification impossible for the moment. If so, so much the better for me: I shall perhaps enjoy a few years of immortality. But the whirligig of time will soon bring my audiences to my own point of view; and then the next Shakespear that comes along will turn these petty tentatives of mine into masterpieces final for their epoch. By that time my twentieth century characteristics will pass unnoticed as a matter of course, whilst the eighteenth century artificiality that marks the work of every literary Irishman of my generation will seem antiquated and silly. It is a dangerous thing to be hailed at once, as a few rash admirers have hailed me, as above all things original: what the world calls originality is only an unaccustomed method of tickling it. Meyerbeer seemed prodigiously original to the Parisians when he first burst on them. Today, he is only the crow who followed Beethoven's plough. I am a crow who have followed many ploughs. No doubt I seem prodigiously clever to those who have never hopped, hungry and curious, across the fields of philosophy, politics, and art. Karl Marx said of Stuart Mill that his eminence was due to the flatness of the surrounding country. In these days of Free Schools, universal reading, cheap newspapers, and the inevitable ensuing demand for notabilities of all sorts, literary, military, political and fashionable, to write paragraphs about, that sort of eminence is within the reach of very moderate ability. Reputations are cheap nowadays. Even were they dear, it would still be impossible for any public-spirited citizen of the world to hope that his reputation might endure; for this would be to hope that the flood of general enlightenment may never rise above his miserable high-watermark. I hate to think that Shakespear has lasted 300 years, though he got no further than Koheleth the Preacher, who died many centuries before him; or that Plato, more than 2000 years old, is still ahead of our voters. We must hurry on: we must get rid of reputations: they are weeds in the soil of ignorance. Cultivate that soil, and they will flower more beautifully, but only as annuals. If this preface will at all help to get rid of mine, the writing of it will have been well worth the pains.

⧗⧗⧗   ⧗⧗⧗   ⧗⧗⧗

1909—A. C. Bradley. From "Shakespeare's *Antony and Cleopatra*," in *Oxford Lectures on Poetry*

A. C. Bradley (1851–1935) was a professor at Oxford and other institutions. His influential book *Shakespearean Tragedy* (1904) was one of the most significant works of Shakespeare criticism of the twentieth century. Bradley also helped to establish Shakespeare as a core subject of study in the emerging university field of English literature.

Coleridge's one page of general criticism on *Antony and Cleopatra* contains some notable remarks. 'Of all Shakespeare's historical plays,' he writes, '*Antony and Cleopatra* is by far the most wonderful. There is not one in which he has followed history so minutely, and yet there are few in which he impresses the notion of angelic strength so much—perhaps none in which he impresses it more strongly. This is greatly owing to the manner in which the fiery force is sustained throughout.' In a later sentence he refers to the play as 'this astonishing drama.' In another he describes the style: '*feliciter audax* is the motto for its style comparatively with that of Shakespeare's other works.' And he translates this motto in the phrase 'happy valiancy of style.'

Coleridge's assertion that in *Antony and Cleopatra* Shakespeare followed history more minutely than in any other play might well be disputed; and his statement about the style of this drama requires some qualification in view of the results of later criticism as to the order of Shakespeare's works. The style is less individual than he imagined. On the whole it is common to the six or seven dramas subsequent to *Macbeth*, though in *Antony and Cleopatra*, probably the earliest of them, its development is not yet complete. And we must add that this style has certain special defects, unmentioned by Coleridge, as well as the quality which he points out in it. But it is true that here that quality is almost continuously present; and in the phrase by which he describes it, as in his other phrases, he has signalised once for all some of the most salient features of the drama.

It is curious to notice, for example, alike in books and in conversation, how often the first epithets used in reference to *Antony and Cleopatra* are 'wonderful' and 'astonishing.' And the main source of the feeling thus expressed seems to be the 'angelic strength' or 'fiery force' of which Coleridge wrote. The first of these two phrases is, I think, the more entirely happy. Except perhaps towards the close, one is not so conscious of fiery force as in certain other tragedies; but one is astonished at the apparent ease with which extraordinary effects are produced, the ease, if I may paraphrase Coleridge, of an angel moving with a wave of the hand that heavy matter which men find so intractable. We feel this sovereign ease in contemplating Shakespeare's picture of the world—a vast canvas, crowded with figures, glowing with colour and a superb animation, reminding one spectator of Paul Veronese and another of Rubens. We feel it again when we observe (as we can even without consulting Plutarch) the nature of the material; how bulky it was, and, in some respects, how undramatic; and how the artist, though he could not treat history like legend or fiction, seems to push whole masses aside, and to shift and refashion the remainder, almost with the air of an architect playing (at times rather carelessly) with a child's bricks. Something similar is felt even in the portrait of Cleopatra. Marvellous as it is, the drawing of it suggests not so much the passionate concentration or fiery force of *Macbeth*, as that sense of effortless and exultant mastery which we feel in the portraits of Mercutio and Falstaff. And surely it is a total mistake to find in this portrait any trace of the distempered mood which disturbs our pleasure in *Troilus and Cressida*. If the sonnets about the dark lady were, as need not be doubted, in some degree autobiographical, Shakespeare may well have used his personal experience both when he drew Cressida and when he drew Cleopatra. And, if he did, the story in the later play was the nearer to his own; for Antony might well have said what Troilus could never say,

When my love swears that she is made of truth,
I do believe her, though I know she lies.

But in the later play, not only is the poet's vision unclouded, but his whole nature, emotional as well as intellectual, is free. The subject no more embitters or seduces him than the ambition of Macbeth. So that here too we feel the angelic strength of which Coleridge speaks. If we quarrelled with the phrase at all, it would be because we fancied we could trace in Shakespeare's attitude something of the irony of superiority; and this may not altogether suit our conception of an angel.

I have still another sentence to quote from Coleridge: 'The highest praise, or rather form of praise, of this play which I can offer in my own mind, is the doubt which the perusal always occasions in me, whether the "Antony and Cleopatra" is not, in all exhibitions of a giant power in its strength and vigour of maturity, a formidable rival of "Macbeth," "Lear," "Hamlet," and "Othello."' Now, unless the clause here about the 'giant power' may be taken to restrict the rivalry to the quality of angelic strength, Coleridge's doubt seems to show a lapse in critical judgment. To regard this tragedy as a rival of the famous four, whether on the stage or in the study, is surely an error. The world certainly has not so regarded it; and, though the world's reasons for its verdicts on works of art may be worth little, its mere verdict is worth much. Here, it seems to me, that verdict must be accepted. One may notice that, in calling *Antony and Cleopatra* wonderful or astonishing, we appear to be thinking first of the artist and his activity, while in the case of the four famous tragedies it is the product of this activity, the thing presented, that first engrosses us. I know that I am stating this difference too sharply, but I believe that it is often felt; and, if this is so, the fact is significant. It implies that, although *Antony and Cleopatra* may be for us as wonderful an achievement as the greatest of Shakespeare's plays, it has not an equal value. Besides, in the attempt to rank it with them there is involved something more, and more important, than an error in valuation. There is a failure to discriminate the peculiar marks of *Antony and Cleopatra* itself, marks which, whether or no it be the equal of the earlier tragedies, make it decidedly different. If I speak first of some of these differences it is because they thus contribute to the individuality of the play, and because they seem often not to be distinctly apprehended in criticism.

1.

Why, let us begin by asking, is *Antony and Cleopatra*, though so wonderful an achievement, a play rarely acted? For a tragedy, it is not painful. Though unfit for children, it cannot be called indecent; some slight omissions, and such a flattening of the heroine's part as might confidently be expected, would leave it perfectly presentable. It is, no doubt, in the third and fourth Acts, very defective in construction. Even on the Elizabethan stage, where scene followed scene without a pause, this must have been felt; and in our theatres it would be felt much more. There, in fact, these two and forty scenes could not possibly be acted as they stand. But defective construction would not distress the bulk of an audience, if the matter presented were that of *Hamlet* or *Othello*, of *Lear* or *Macbeth*. The matter, then, must lack something which is present in those tragedies; and it is mainly owing to this difference in substance that *Antony and Cleopatra* has never attained their popularity either on the stage or off it.

Most of Shakespeare's tragedies are dramatic in a special sense of the word, as well as in its general sense, from beginning to end. The story is not merely exciting and impressive from the movement of conflicting forces towards a terrible issue, but from time to time there come situations and events which, even apart from their bearing on this issue, appeal most powerfully to the dramatic feelings—scenes of action or passion which agitate the audience with alarm, horror, painful expectation, or absorbing sympathies and antipathies. Think of the street fights in *Romeo and Juliet*, the killing of Mercutio and Tybalt, the rapture of the lovers, and their despair when Romeo is banished. Think of the ghost-scenes in the first Act of *Hamlet*, the passion of the early soliloquies, the scene between Hamlet and Ophelia, the play-scene, the sparing of the King at prayer, the killing of Polonius. Is not *Hamlet*, if you choose so to regard it, the best melodrama in the world? Think at your leisure of *Othello, Lear*, and *Macbeth* from the same point of view; but consider here and now even the two tragedies which, as dealing with Roman history, are companions of *Antony and Cleopatra*. Recall in *Julius Caesar* the first suggestion of the murder, the preparation for it in a 'tempest dropping fire,' the murder itself, the speech of Antony over the corpse, and the tumult of the furious crowd; in *Coriolanus* the bloody battles on the stage, the scene in which the hero attains the consulship, the scene of rage in which he is banished. And remember that in each of these seven tragedies the matter referred to is contained in the first three Acts.

In the first three Acts of our play what is there resembling this? Almost nothing. People converse, discuss, accuse one another, excuse themselves, mock, describe, drink together, arrange a marriage, meet and part; but they do not kill, do not even tremble or weep. We see hardly one violent movement; until the battle of Actium is over we witness scarcely any vehement passion; and that battle, as it is a naval action, we do not see. Even later, Enobarbus, when he dies, simply dies; he does not kill himself.[2] We hear wonderful talk; but it is not talk, like that of Macbeth and Lady Macbeth, or that of Othello and Iago, at which we hold our breath. The scenes that we remember first are those that portray Cleopatra; Cleopatra coquetting, tormenting, beguiling her lover to stay; Cleopatra left with her women and longing for him; Cleopatra receiving the news of his marriage; Cleopatra questioning the messenger about Octavia's personal appearance. But this is to say that the scenes we remember first are the least indispensable to the plot. One at least is not essential to it at all. And this, the astonishing scene where she storms at the messenger, strikes him, and draws her dagger on him, is the one passage in the first half of the drama that contains either an explosion of passion or an exciting bodily action. Nor is this all. The first half of the play, though it forebodes tragedy, is not decisively tragic in tone. Certainly the Cleopatra scenes are not so.

We read them, and we should witness them, in delighted wonder and even with amusement. The only scene that can vie with them, that of the revel on

Pompey's ship, though full of menace, is in great part humorous. Enobarbus, in this part of the play, is always humorous. Even later, when the tragic tone is deepening, the whipping of Thyreus, in spite of Antony's rage, moves mirth. A play of which all this can truly be said may well be as masterly as *Othello* or *Macbeth*, and more delightful; but, in the greater part of its course, it cannot possibly excite the same emotions. It makes no attempt to do so; and to regard it as though it made this attempt is to miss its specific character and the intention of its author.

That character depends only in part on Shakespeare's fidelity to his historical authority, a fidelity which, I may remark, is often greatly exaggerated. For Shakespeare did not merely present the story of ten years as though it occupied perhaps one fifth of that time, nor did he merely invent freely, but in critical places he effected startling changes in the order and combination of events. Still it may be said that, dealing with a history so famous, he could not well make the first half of his play very exciting, moving, or tragic. And this is true so far as mere situations and events are concerned. But, if he had chosen, he might easily have heightened the tone and tension in another way. He might have made the story of Antony's attempt to break his bondage, and the story of his relapse, extremely exciting, by portraying with all his force the severity of the struggle and the magnitude of the fatal step.

And the structure of the play might seem at first to suggest this intention. At the opening, Antony is shown almost in the beginning of his infatuation; for Cleopatra is not sure of her power over him, exerts all her fascination to detain him, and plays the part of the innocent victim who has yielded to passion and must now expect to be deserted by her seducer. Alarmed and ashamed at the news of the results of his inaction, he rouses himself, tears himself away, and speeds to Italy. His very coming is enough to frighten Pompey into peace. He reconciles himself with Octavius, and, by his marriage with the good and beautiful Octavia, seems to have knit a bond of lasting amity with her brother, and to have guarded himself against the passion that threatened him with ruin. At this point his power, the world's peace, and his own peace, appear to be secured; his fortune has mounted to its apex. But soon (very much sooner than in Plutarch's story) comes the downward turn or counter-stroke. New causes of offence arise between the brothers-in-law. To remove them Octavia leaves her husband in Athens and hurries to Rome. Immediately Antony returns to Cleopatra and, surrendering himself at once and wholly to her enchantment, is quickly driven to his doom.

Now Shakespeare, I say, with his matchless power of depicting an inward struggle, might have made this story, even where it could not furnish him with thrilling incidents, the source of powerful tragic emotions; and, in doing so, he would have departed from his authority merely in his conception of the hero's character. But he does no such thing till the catastrophe is near. Antony breaks away from Cleopatra without any strenuous conflict. No serious doubt of his return is permitted to agitate us. We are almost assured of it through the impression made on us by Octavius, through occasional glimpses into Antony's mind, through the absence of any doubt in Enobarbus, through scenes in Alexandria which display Cleopatra and display her irresistible. And, finally, the downward turn itself, the fatal step of Antony's return, is shown without the slightest emphasis. Nay, it is not shown, it is only reported; and not a line portrays any inward struggle preceding it. On this side also, then, the drama makes no attempt to rival the other tragedies; and it was essential to its own peculiar character and its most transcendent effects that this attempt should not be made, but that Antony's passion should be represented as a force which he could hardly even desire to resist. By the very scheme of the work, therefore, tragic impressions of any great volume or depth were reserved for the last stage of the conflict; while the main interest, down to the battle of Actium, was directed to matters exceedingly interesting and even, in the wider sense, dramatic, but not overtly either terrible or piteous: on the one hand, to the political aspect of the story; on the other, to the personal causes which helped to make the issue inevitable.

2.

The political situation and its development are simple. The story is taken up almost where it was left, years before, in *Julius Caesar*. There Brutus and Cassius, to prevent the rule of one man, assassinate Caesar. Their purpose is condemned to failure, not merely because they make mistakes, but because that political necessity which Napoleon identified with destiny requires the rule of one man. They spill Caesar's blood, but his spirit walks abroad and turns their swords against their own breasts; and the world is left divided among three men, his friends and his heir. Here *Antony and Cleopatra* takes up the tale; and its business, from this point of view, is to show the reduction of these three to one. That Lepidus will not be this one was clear already in *Julius Caesar*; it must be Octavius or Antony. Both ambitious, they are also men of such opposite tempers that they would scarcely long agree even if they wished to, and even if destiny were not stronger than they. As it is, one of them has fixed his eyes on the end, sacrifices everything for it, uses everything as a means to it. The other, though far the greater soldier and worshipped by his followers, has no such singleness of aim; nor yet is power, however desirable to him, the most desirable thing in the world. At the beginning he is risking it for love; at the end he has lost his half of the world, and lost his life, and Octavius rules alone. Whether Shakespeare had this clearly in his mind is a question neither answerable nor important; this is what came out of his mind.

Shakespeare, I think, took little interest in the character of Octavius, and he has not made it wholly clear. It is not distinct in Plutarch's 'Life of Antony'; and I have not found traces that the poet studied closely the 'Life of Octavius' included in North's volume. To Shakespeare he is one of those men, like Bolingbroke and

Ulysses, who have plenty of 'judgment' and not much 'blood.' Victory in the world, according to the poet, almost always goes to such men; and he makes us respect, fear, and dislike them. His Octavius is very formidable. His cold determination half paralyses Antony; it is so even in *Julius Caesar*. In *Antony and Cleopatra* Octavius is more than once in the wrong; but he never admits it; he silently pushes his rival a step backward; and, when he ceases to fear, he shows contempt. He neither enjoys war nor is great in it; at first, therefore, he is anxious about the power of Pompey, and stands in need of Antony. As soon as Antony's presence has served his turn, and he has patched up a union with him and seen him safely off to Athens, he destroys first Pompey and next Lepidus. Then, dexterously using Antony's faithlessness to Octavia and excesses in the East in order to put himself in the right, he makes for his victim with admirable celerity while he is still drunk with the joy of reunion with Cleopatra. For his ends Octavius is perfectly efficient, but he is so partly from his limitations. One phrase of his is exceedingly characteristic. When Antony in rage and desperation challenges him to single combat, Octavius calls him 'the old ruffian.' There is a horrid aptness in the phrase, but it disgusts us. It is shameful in this boy, as hard and smooth as polished steel, to feel at such a time nothing of the greatness of his victim and the tragedy of his victim's fall. Though the challenge of Antony is absurd, we would give much to see them sword to sword. And when Cleopatra by her death cheats the conqueror of his prize, we feel unmixed delight.

The doubtful point in the character is this. Plutarch says that Octavius was reported to love his sister dearly; and Shakespeare's Octavius several times expresses such love. When, then, he proposed the marriage with Antony (for of course it was he who spoke through Agrippa), was he honest, or was he laying a trap and, in doing so, sacrificing his sister? Did he hope the marriage would really unite him with his brother-in-law; or did he merely mean it to be a source of future differences; or did he calculate that, whether it secured peace or dissension, it would in either case bring him great advantage? Shakespeare, who was quite as intelligent as his readers, must have asked himself some such question; but he may not have cared to answer it even to himself; and, in any case, he has left the actor (at least the actor in days later than his own) to choose an answer. If I were forced to choose, I should take the view that Octavius was, at any rate, not wholly honest; partly because I think it best suits Shakespeare's usual way of conceiving a character of the kind; partly because Plutarch construed in this manner Octavius's behaviour in regard to his sister at a later time, and this hint might naturally influence the poet's way of imagining his earlier action.[3] Though the character of Octavius is neither attractive nor wholly clear, his figure is invested with a certain tragic dignity, because he is felt to be the Man of Destiny, the agent of forces against which the intentions of an individual would avail nothing. He is represented as having himself some feeling of this sort. His lament over Antony, his grief that their stars were irreconcilable, may well be genuine, though we should be surer if it were uttered in soliloquy. His austere words to Octavia again probably speak his true mind:

> Be you not troubled with the time, which drives
> O'er your content these strong necessities;
> But let determined things to destiny
> Hold unbewailed their way.

In any case the feeling of fate comes through to us. It is aided by slight touches of supernatural effect; first in the Soothsayer's warning to Antony that his genius or angel is overpowered whenever he is near Octavius; then in the strangely effective scene where Antony's soldiers, in the night before his last battle, hear music in the air or under the earth:

> 'Tis the god Hercules, whom Antony loved,
> Now leaves him.

And to the influence of this feeling in giving impressiveness to the story is added that of the immense scale and world-wide issue of the conflict. Even the distances traversed by fleets and armies enhance this effect.

And yet there seems to be something half-hearted in Shakespeare's appeal here, something even ironical in his presentation of this conflict. Its external magnitude, like Antony's magnificence in lavishing realms and gathering the kings of the East in his support, fails to uplift or dilate the imagination. The struggle in Lear's little island seems to us to have an infinitely wider scope. It is here that we are sometimes reminded of *Troilus and Cressida*, and the cold and disenchanting light that is there cast on the Trojan War. The spectacle which he portrays leaves Shakespeare quite undazzled; he even makes it appear inwardly small. The lordship of the world, we ask ourselves, what is it worth, and in what spirit do these 'world-sharers' contend for it? They are no champions of their country like Henry V. The conqueror knows not even the glory of battle. Their aims, for all we see, are as personal as if they were captains of banditti; and they are followed merely from self-interest or private attachment. The scene on Pompey's galley is full of this irony. One 'third part of the world' is carried drunk to bed. In the midst of this mock boon-companionship the pirate whispers to his leader to cut first the cable of his ship and then the throats of the two other Emperors; and at the moment we should not greatly care if Pompey took the advice. Later, a short scene, totally useless to the plot and purely satiric in its purport, is slipped in to show how Ventidius fears to pursue his Parthian conquests because it is not safe for Antony's lieutenant to outdo his master.[4] A painful sense of hollowness oppresses us. We know too well what must happen in a world so splendid, so false, and so petty. We turn for relief from the political game to those who are sure to lose it; to those who love some human being better than a prize, to Eros and Charmian and Iras; to Enobarbus, whom the world corrupts, but who has a heart that can break with shame; to the lovers, who seem to us to find in death something better than their victor's life.

This presentation of the outward conflict has two results. First, it blunts our feeling of the greatness of Antony's fall from prosperity. Indeed this feeling, which we might expect to be unusually acute, is hardly so; it is less acute, for example, than the like feeling in the case of Richard II., who loses so much smaller a realm. Our deeper sympathies are focussed rather on Antony's heart, on the inward fall to which the enchantment of passion leads him, and the inward recovery which succeeds it. And the second result is this. The greatness of Antony and Cleopatra in their fall is so much heightened by contrast with the world they lose and the conqueror who wins it, that the positive element in the final tragic impression, the element of reconciliation, is strongly emphasised. The peculiar effect of the drama depends partly, as we have seen, on the absence of decidedly tragic scenes and events in its first half; but it depends quite as much on this emphasis. In any Shakespearean tragedy we watch some elect spirit colliding, partly through its error and defect, with a superhuman power which bears it down; and yet we feel that this spirit, even in the error and defect, rises by its greatness into ideal union with the power that overwhelms it. In some tragedies this latter feeling is relatively weak. In *Antony and Cleopatra* it is unusually strong; stronger, with some readers at least, than the fear and grief and pity with which they contemplate the tragic error and the advance of doom.

3.

The two aspects of the tragedy are presented together in the opening scene. Here is the first. In Cleopatra's palace one friend of Antony is describing to another, just arrived from Rome, the dotage of their great general; and, as the lovers enter, he exclaims:

> Look, where they come:
> Take but good note, and you shall see in him
> The triple pillar of the world transformed
> Into a strumpet's fool: behold and see.

With the next words the other aspect appears:

> *Cleo.* If it be love indeed, tell me how much.
> *Ant.* There's beggary in the love that can be reckoned.
> *Cleo.* I'll set a bourne how far to be beloved.
> *Ant.* Then must thou needs find out new heaven, new earth.

And directly after, when he is provoked by reminders of the news from Rome:

> Let Rome in Tiber melt, and the wide arch
> Of the ranged empire fall! Here is my space.
> Kingdoms are clay: our dungy earth alike
> Feeds beast as man: the nobleness of life
> Is to do thus.

Here is the tragic excess, but with it the tragic greatness, the capacity of finding in something the infinite, and of pursuing it into the jaws of death.

The two aspects are shown here with the exaggeration proper in dramatic characters. Neither the phrase 'a strumpet's fool,' nor the assertion 'the nobleness of life is to do thus,' answers to the total effect of the play. But the truths they exaggerate are equally essential; and the commoner mistake in criticism is to understate the second. It is plain that the love of Antony and Cleopatra is destructive; that in some way it clashes with the nature of things; that, while they are sitting in their paradise like gods, its walls move inward and crush them at last to death. This is no invention of moralising critics; it is in the play; and any one familiar with Shakespeare would expect beforehand to find it there. But then to forget because of it the other side, to deny the name of love to this ruinous passion, to speak as though the lovers had utterly missed the good of life, is to mutilate the tragedy and to ignore a great part of its effect upon us. For we sympathise with them in their passion; we feel in it the infinity there is in man; even while we acquiesce in their defeat we are exulting in their victory; and when they have vanished we say,

> the odds is gone,
> And there is nothing left remarkable
> Beneath the visiting moon.

Though we hear nothing from Shakespeare of the cruelty of Plutarch's Antony, or of the misery caused by his boundless profusion, we do not feel the hero of the tragedy to be a man of the noblest type, like Brutus, Hamlet, or Othello. He seeks power merely for himself, and uses it for his own pleasure. He is in some respects unscrupulous; and, while it would be unjust to regard his marriage exactly as if it were one in private life, we resent his treatment of Octavia, whose character Shakespeare was obliged to leave a mere sketch, lest our feeling for the hero and heroine should be too much chilled. Yet, for all this, we sympathise warmly with Antony, are greatly drawn to him, and are inclined to regard him as a noble nature half spoiled by his time.

It is a large, open, generous, expansive nature, quite free from envy, capable of great magnanimity, even of entire devotion. Antony is unreserved, naturally straightforward, we may almost say simple. He can admit faults, accept advice and even reproof, take a jest against himself with good-humour. He is courteous (to Lepidus, for example, whom Octavius treats with cold contempt); and, though he can be exceedingly dignified, he seems to prefer a blunt though sympathetic plainness, which is one cause of the attachment of his soldiers. He has none of the faults of the brooder, the sentimentalist, or the man of principle; his nature tends to splendid action and lusty enjoyment. But he is neither a mere soldier nor a mere sensualist. He has imagination, the temper of an artist who revels in abundant and rejoicing appetites, feasts his senses on the glow and richness of life, flings himself into its mirth and revelry, yet feels the poetry in all this, and is able also to put it by and be more than content with the hardships of adventure. Such a man could never have sought a crown by a murder like Macbeth's, or, like Brutus, have killed on principle the man who loved him, or have lost the world for a Cressida.

Beside this strain of poetry he has a keen intellect, a swift perception of the lie of things, and much quickness in shaping a course to suit them. In *Julius Caesar* he shows this after the assassination, when he appears as a dexterous politician as well as a warm-hearted friend. He admires what is fine, and can fully appreciate the nobility of Brutus; but he is sure that Brutus's ideas are moonshine, that (as he says in our play) Brutus is mad; and, since his mighty friend, who was incomparably the finest thing in the world, has perished, he sees no reason why the inheritance should not be his own. Full of sorrow, he yet uses his sorrow like an artist to work on others, and greets his success with the glee of a successful adventurer. In the earlier play he proves himself a master of eloquence, and especially of pathos; and he does so again in the later. With a few words about his fall he draws tears from his followers and even from the caustic humorist Enobarbus. Like Richard II., he sees his own fall with the eyes of a poet, but a poet much greater than the young Shakespeare, who could never have written Antony's marvellous speech about the sunset clouds. But we listen to Antony, as we do not to Richard, with entire sympathy, partly because he is never unmanly, partly because he himself is sympathetic and longs for sympathy.

The first of living soldiers, an able politician, a most persuasive orator, Antony nevertheless was not born to rule the world. He enjoys being a great man, but he has not the love of rule for rule's sake. Power for him is chiefly a means to pleasure. The pleasure he wants is so huge that he needs a huge power; but half the world, even a third of it, would suffice. He will not pocket wrongs, but he shows not the slightest wish to get rid of his fellow Triumvirs and reign alone. He never minded being subordinate to Julius Caesar. By women he is not only attracted but governed; from the effect of Cleopatra's taunts we can see that he had been governed by Fulvia. Nor has he either the patience or the steadfastness of a born ruler. He contends fitfully, and is prone to take the step that is easiest at the moment. This is the reason why he consents to marry Octavia. It seems the shortest way out of an awkward situation. He does not intend even to try to be true to her. He will not think of the distant consequences.

A man who loved power as much as thousands of insignificant people love it, would have made a sterner struggle than Antony's against his enchantment. He can hardly be said to struggle at all. He brings himself to leave Cleopatra only because he knows he will return. In every moment of his absence, whether he wake or sleep, a siren music in his blood is singing him back to her; and to this music, however he may be occupied, the soul within his soul leans and listens. The joy of life had always culminated for him in the love of women: he could say 'no' to none of them: of Octavia herself he speaks like a poet. When he meets Cleopatra he finds his Absolute. She satisfies, nay glorifies, his whole being. She intoxicates his senses. Her wiles, her taunts, her furies and meltings, her laughter and tears, bewitch him all alike. She loves what he loves, and she surpasses him. She can drink him to his bed, out-jest his practical jokes, out-act the best actress who ever amused him, out-dazzle his own magnificence. She is his playfellow, and yet a great queen. Angling in the river, playing billiards, flourishing the sword he used at Philippi, hopping forty paces in a public street, she remains an enchantress. Her spirit is made of wind and flame, and the poet in him worships her no less than the man. He is under no illusion about her, knows all her faults, sees through her wiles, believes her capable of betraying him. It makes no difference. She is his heart's desire made perfect. To love her is what he was born for. What have the gods in heaven to say against it? To imagine heaven is to imagine her; to die is to rejoin her. To deny that this is love is the madness of morality. He gives her every atom of his heart.

She destroys him. Shakespeare, availing himself of the historic fact, portrays, on Antony's return to her, the suddenness and the depth of his descent. In spite of his own knowledge, the protests of his captains, the entreaties even of a private soldier, he fights by sea simply and solely because she wishes it. Then in mid-battle, when she flies, he deserts navy and army and his faithful thousands and follows her. 'I never saw an action of such shame,' cries Scarus; and we feel the dishonour of the hero keenly. Then Shakespeare begins to raise him again. First, his own overwhelming sense of shame redeems him. Next, we watch the rage of the dying lion. Then the mere sally before the final defeat—a sally dismissed by Plutarch in three lines—is magnified into a battle, in which Antony displays to us, and himself feels for the last time, the glory of his soldiership. And, throughout, the magnanimity and gentleness which shine through his desperation endear him to us. How beautiful is his affection for his followers and even for his servants, and the devotion they return! How noble his reception of the news that Enobarbus has deserted him! How touchingly significant the refusal of Eros either to kill him or survive him! How pathetic and even sublime the completeness of his love for Cleopatra! His anger is born and dies in an hour. One tear, one kiss, outweighs his ruin. He believes she has sold him to his enemy, yet he kills himself because he hears that she is dead. When, dying, he learns that she has deceived him once more, no thought of reproach crosses his mind: he simply asks to be carried to her. He knows well that she is not capable of dying because he dies, but that does not sting him; when, in his last agony, he calls for wine that he may gain a moment's strength to speak, it is to advise her for the days to come. Shakespeare borrowed from Plutarch the final speech of Antony. It is fine, but it is not miraculous. The miraculous speeches belong only to his own hero:

> I am dying, Egypt, dying; only I here importune death awhile, until Of many thousand kisses the poor last I lay upon thy lips;

or the first words he utters when he hears of Cleopatra's death:

> Unarm, Eros: the long day's task is done, And we must sleep.

If he meant the task of statesman and warrior, that is not what his words mean to us. They remind us of words more familiar and less great—

> No rest but the grave for the pilgrim of love.

And he is more than love's pilgrim; he is love's martyr.

4.

To reserve a fragment of an hour for Cleopatra, if it were not palpably absurd, would seem an insult. If only one could hear her own remarks upon it! But I had to choose between this absurdity and the plan of giving her the whole hour; and to that plan there was one fatal objection. She has been described (by Ten Brink) as a courtesan of genius. So brief a description must needs be incomplete, and Cleopatra never forgets, nor, if we read aright, do we forget, that she is a great queen. Still the phrase is excellent; only a public lecture is no occasion for the full analysis and illustration of the character it describes.

Shakespeare has paid Cleopatra a unique compliment. The hero dies in the fourth Act, and the whole of the fifth is devoted to the heroine.[5] In that Act she becomes unquestionably a tragic character, but, it appears to me, not till then. This, no doubt, is a heresy; but as I cannot help holding it, and as it is connected with the remarks already made on the first half of the play, I will state it more fully. Cleopatra stands in a group with Hamlet and Falstaff. We might join with them Iago if he were not decidedly their inferior in one particular quality. They are inexhaustible. You feel that, if they were alive and you spent your whole life with them, their infinite variety could never be staled by custom; they would continue every day to surprise, perplex, and delight you. Shakespeare has bestowed on each of them, though they differ so much, his own originality, his genius. He has given it most fully to Hamlet, to whom none of the chambers of experience is shut, and perhaps more of it to Cleopatra than to Falstaff. Nevertheless, if we ask whether Cleopatra, in the first four Acts, is a tragic figure like Hamlet, we surely cannot answer 'yes.' Naturally it does not follow that she is a comic figure like Falstaff. This would be absurd; for, even if she were ridiculous like Falstaff, she is not ridiculous to herself; she is no humorist. And yet there is a certain likeness. She shares a weakness with Falstaff—vanity; and when she displays it, as she does quite naïvely (for instance, in the second interview with the Messenger), she does become comic. Again, though like Falstaff she is irresistible and carries us away no less than the people around her, we are secretly aware, in the midst of our delight, that her empire is built on sand. And finally, as his love for the Prince gives dignity and pathos to Falstaff in his overthrow, so what raises Cleopatra at last into pure tragedy is, in part, that which some critics have denied her, her love for Antony.

Many unpleasant things can be said of Cleopatra; and the more that are said the more wonderful she appears. The exercise of sexual attraction is the element of her life; and she has developed nature into a consummate art. When she cannot exert it on the present lover she imagines its effects on him in absence. Longing for the living, she remembers with pride and joy the dead; and the past which the furious Antony holds up to her as a picture of shame is, for her, glory. She cannot see an ambassador, scarcely even a messenger, without desiring to bewitch him. Her mind is saturated with this element. If she is dark, it is because the sun himself has been amorous of her. Even when death is close at hand she imagines his touch as a lover's. She embraces him that she may overtake Iras and gain Antony's first kiss in the other world.

She lives for feeling. Her feelings are, so to speak, sacred, and pain must not come near her. She has tried numberless experiments to discover the easiest way to die. Her body is exquisitely sensitive, and her emotions marvellously swift. They are really so; but she exaggerates them so much, and exhibits them so continually for effect, that some readers fancy them merely feigned. They are all-important, and everybody must attend to them. She announces to her women that she is pale, or sick and sullen; they must lead her to her chamber but must not speak to her. She is as strong and supple as a leopard, can drink down a master of revelry, can raise her lover's helpless heavy body from the ground into her tower with the aid only of two women; yet, when he is sitting apart sunk in shame, she must be supported into his presence, she cannot stand, her head droops, she will die (it is the opinion of Eros) unless he comforts her. When she hears of his marriage and has discharged her rage, she bids her women bear her away; she faints; at least she would faint, but that she remembers various questions she wants put to the Messenger about Octavia. Enobarbus has seen her die twenty times upon far poorer moment than the news that Antony is going to Rome.

Some of her feelings are violent, and, unless for a purpose, she does not dream of restraining them; her sighs and tears are winds and waters, storms and tempests. At times, as when she threatens to give Charmian bloody teeth, or hales the luckless Messenger up and down by the hair, strikes him and draws her knife on him, she resembles (if I dare say it) Doll Tearsheet sublimated. She is a mother; but the threat of Octavius to destroy her children if she takes her own life passes by her like the wind (a point where Shakespeare contradicts Plutarch). She ruins a great man, but shows no sense of the tragedy of his ruin. The anguish of spirit that appears in his language to his servants is beyond her; she has to ask Enobarbus what he means. Can we feel sure that she would not have sacrificed him if she could have saved herself by doing so? It is not even certain that she did not attempt it. Antony himself believes that she did—that the fleet went over to Octavius by her orders. That she and her people deny the charge proves nothing. The best we can say is that, if it were true, Shakespeare would have made that clear. She is willing also to survive her lover. Her first thought, to follow him after the high Roman fashion, is too great for her. She would live on if she could, and would cheat her victor too of the best part of her fortune. The thing that drives her to die is the certainty that she will be carried to Rome to grace his triumph. That alone decides her.[6]

The marvellous thing is that the knowledge of all this makes hardly more difference to us than it did to Antony. It seems to us perfectly natural, nay, in a sense perfectly right, that her lover should be her slave; that her women should adore her and die with her; that Enobarbus, who foresaw what must happen, and who opposes her wishes and braves her anger, should talk of her with rapture and feel no bitterness against her; that Dolabella, after a minute's conversation, should betray to her his master's intention and enable her to frustrate it. And when Octavius shows himself proof against her fascination, instead of admiring him we turn from him with disgust and think him a disgrace to his species. Why? It is not that we consider him bound to fall in love with her. Enobarbus did not; Dolabella did not; we ourselves do not. The feeling she inspires was felt then, and is felt now, by women no less than men, and would have been shared by Octavia herself. Doubtless she wrought magic on the senses, but she had not extraordinary beauty, like Helen's, such beauty as seems divine.[7] Plutarch says so. The man who wrote the sonnets to the dark lady would have known it for himself. He goes out of his way to add to her age, and tells us of her wrinkles and the waning of her lip. But Enobarbus, in his very mockery, calls her a wonderful piece of work. Dolabella interrupts her with the cry, 'Most sovereign creature,' and we echo it. And yet Octavius, face to face with her and listening to her voice, can think only how best to trap her and drag her to public dishonour in the streets of Rome. We forgive him only for his words when he sees her dead:

> She looks like sleep,
> As she would catch another Antony
> In her strong toil of grace.

And the words, I confess, sound to me more like Shakespeare's than his.

That which makes her wonderful and sovereign laughs at definition, but she herself came nearest naming it when, in the final speech (a passage surpassed in poetry, if at all, only by the final speech of Othello), she cries,

I am fire and air; my other elements
I give to baser life.

The fire and air which at death break from union with those other elements, transfigured them during her life, and still convert into engines of enchantment the very things for which she is condemned. I can refer only to one. She loves Antony. We should marvel at her less and love her more if she loved him more—loved him well enough to follow him at once to death; but it is to blunder strangely to doubt that she loved him, or that her glorious description of him (though it was also meant to work on Dolabella) came from her heart. Only the spirit of fire and air within her refuses to be trammelled or extinguished; burns its way through the obstacles of fortune and even through the resistance of her love and grief; and would lead her undaunted to fresh life and the conquest of new worlds. It is this which makes her 'strong toil of grace' unbreakable; speaks in her brows' bent and every tone and movement; glorifies the arts and the rages which in another would merely disgust or amuse us; and, in the final scenes of her life, flames into such brilliance that we watch her entranced as she struggles for freedom, and thrilled with triumph as, conquered, she puts her conqueror to scorn and goes to meet her lover in the splendour that crowned and robed her long ago, when her barge burnt on the water like a burnished throne, and she floated to Cydnus on the enamoured stream to take him captive for ever.[8]

Why is it that, although we close the book in a triumph which is more than reconciliation, this is mingled, as we look back on the story, with a sadness so peculiar, almost the sadness of disenchantment? Is it that, when the glow has faded, Cleopatra's ecstasy comes to appear, I would not say factitious, but an effort strained and prodigious as well as glorious, not, like Othello's last speech, the final expression of character, of thoughts and emotions which have dominated a whole life? Perhaps this is so, but there is something more, something that sounds paradoxical: we are saddened by the very fact that the catastrophe saddens us so little; it pains us that we should feel so much triumph and pleasure. In *Romeo and Juliet, Hamlet, Othello*, though in a sense we accept the deaths of hero and heroine, we feel a keen sorrow. We look back, think how noble or beautiful they were, wish that fate had opposed to them a weaker enemy, dream possibly of the life they might then have led. Here we can hardly do this. With all our admiration and sympathy for the lovers we do not wish them to gain the world. It is better for the world's sake, and not less for their own, that they should fail and die. At the very first they came before us, unlike those others, unlike Coriolanus and even Macbeth, in a glory already tarnished, half-ruined by their past. Indeed one source of strange and most unusual effect in their story is that this marvellous passion comes to adepts in the experience and art of passion, who might be expected to have worn its charm away. Its splendour dazzles us; but, when the splendour vanishes, we do not mourn, as we mourn for the love of Romeo or Othello, that a thing so bright and good should die. And the fact that we mourn so little saddens us.

A comparison of Shakespearean tragedies seems to prove that the tragic emotions are stirred in the fullest possible measure only when such beauty or nobility of character is displayed as commands unreserved admiration or love; or when, in default of this, the forces which move the agents, and the conflict which results from these forces, attain a terrifying and overwhelming power. The four most famous tragedies satisfy one or both of these conditions; *Antony and Cleopatra* though a great tragedy, satisfies neither of them completely. But to say this is not to criticise it. It does not attempt to satisfy these conditions, and then fail in the attempt. It attempts something different, and succeeds as triumphantly as *Othello* itself. In doing so it gives us what no other tragedy can give, and it leaves us, no less than any other, lost in astonishment at the powers which created it.

NOTES

1. As this lecture was composed after the publication of my *Shakespearean Tragedy* I ignored in it, as far as possible, such aspects of the play as were noticed in that book, to the Index of which I may refer the reader.

2. See Note A.

3. 'Now whilest Antonius was busie in this preparation, Octauia his wife, whom he had left at Rome, would needs take sea to come vnto him. Her brother Octauius Caesar was willing vnto it, not for his respect at all (as most authors do report) as for that he might haue an honest colour to make warre with Antonius if he did misuse her, and not esteeme of her as she ought to be.'—*Life of Antony* (North's Translation), sect. 29. The view I take does not, of course, imply that Octavius had no love for his sister.

4. See Note B.

5. The point of this remark is unaffected by the fact that the play is not divided into acts and scenes in the folios.

6. See Note C.

7. See Note D.

8. Of the 'good' heroines, Imogen is the one who has most of this spirit of fire and air; and this (in union, of course, with other qualities) is perhaps the ultimate reason why for so many readers she is, what Mr. Swinburne calls her, 'the woman above all Shakespeare's women.'

NOTE A. We are to understand, surely, that Enobarbus dies of 'thought' (melancholy or grief), and has no need to seek a 'swifter mean.' Cf. IV. vi. 34 *seq.*, with the death-scene and his address there to the moon as the 'sovereign mistress of true melancholy' (IV. ix.). Cf. also III. xiii., where, to Cleopatra's question after Actium, 'What shall we do, Enobarbus?' he answers, 'Think, and die.'

The character of Enobarbus is practically an invention of Shakespeare's. The death-scene, I may add, is one of the many passages which prove that he often wrote what pleased his imagination but would lose half its effect in the theatre. The darkness and moonlight could not be represented on a public stage in his time.

NOTE B. The scene is the first of the third Act. Here Ventidius says:

> Caesar and Antony have ever won
> More in their officer than person: Sossius,
> One of my place in Syria, his lieutenant,
> For quick accumulation of renown,
> Which he achieved by the minute, lost his favour.

Plutarch (North, sec. 19) says that 'Sossius, one of Antonius' lieutenants in Syria, did notable good service,' but I cannot find in him the further statement that Sossius lost Antony's favour. I presume it is Shakespeare's invention, but I call attention to it on the bare chance that it may be found elsewhere than in Plutarch, when it would point to Shakespeare's use of a second authority.

NOTE C. Since this lecture was published (*Quarterly Review*, April, 1906) two notable editions of *Antony and Cleopatra* have been produced. Nothing recently written on Shakespeare, I venture to say, shows more thorough scholarship or better judgment than Mr. Case's edition in the Arden series; and Dr. Furness has added to the immense debt which students of Shakespeare owe to him, and (if that is possible) to the admiration and respect with which they regard him, by the appearance of *Antony and Cleopatra* in his New Variorum edition.

On one question about Cleopatra both editors, Mr. Case more tentatively and Dr. Furness very decidedly, dissent from the interpretation given in the last pages of my lecture. The question is how we are to understand the fact that, although on Antony's death Cleopatra expresses her intention of following him, she does not carry out this intention until she has satisfied herself that Octavius means to carry her to Rome to grace his triumph. Though I do not profess to feel certain that my interpretation is right, it still seems to me a good deal the most probable, and therefore I have not altered what I wrote. But my object here is not to defend my view or to criticise other views, but merely to call attention to the discussion of the subject in Mr. Case's Introduction and Dr. Furness's Preface.

NOTE D. Shakespeare, it seems clear, imagined Cleopatra as a gipsy. And this, I would suggest, may be the explanation of a word which has caused much difficulty. Antony, when 'all is lost,' exclaims (IV. x. 38):

> O this false soul of Egypt! this grave charm,—
> Whose eye beck'd forth my wars, and call'd them home,
> Whose bosom was my crownet, my chief end,—
> Like a right gipsy, hath, at fast and loose,
> Beguil'd me to the very heart of loss.

Pope changed 'grave' in the first line into 'gay.' Others conjecture 'great' and 'grand.' Steevens says that 'grave' means 'deadly,' and that the word 'is often used by Chapman' thus; and one of his two quotations supports his statement; but certainly in Shakespeare the word does not elsewhere bear this sense. It could mean 'majestic,' as Johnson takes it here. But why should it not have its usual meaning? Cleopatra, we know, was a being of 'infinite variety,' and her eyes may sometimes have had, like those of some gipsies, a mysterious gravity or solemnity which would exert a spell more potent than her gaiety. Their colour, presumably, was what is called 'black'; but surely they were not, like those of Tennyson's Cleopatra, '*bold* black eyes.' Readers interested in seeing what criticism is capable of may like to know that it has been proposed to read, for the first line of the quotation above, 'O this false fowl of Egypt! haggard charmer.' [Though I have not cancelled this note I have modified some phrases in it, as I have not much confidence in my suggestion, and am inclined to think that Steevens was right.]

1931—G. Wilson Knight. "The Diadem of Love: An Essay on *Antony and Cleopatra*," from *The Imperial Theme: Further Interpretations of Shakespeare's Tragedies Including the Roman Plays*

G. Wilson Knight (1875-1965) was professor of English at Leeds University and also taught at the University of Toronto. At both universities he produced and acted in Shakespeare plays. In addition, Knight wrote plays for the British stage and television. His critical books include *The Wheel of Fire*, *Shakespearean Production*, and *Lord Byron: Christian Virtues*.

I

In this essay I shall observe the more specifically human qualities in *Antony and Cleopatra*. I have indicated something of the visionary brilliance and sweeping scope of our imagery, wherein man is all but deified through love. This transcendental and ethereal humanism is primary: all else works within it. But there is a stern realism too. *Antony and Cleopatra* is fired by an intenser realism than any play from *Hamlet* to *Timon of Athens*. There is pain, failure, hate, and evil. The poet never shirks the more sordid aspects of things divine. The play's visionary transcendence marks not a severance from reality but a consummation of it. It neglects nothing, and its prevailing optimism is due to emphasis rather than selection. The lovers are old, their passion often called 'lust'. Antony's armour is shown as 'bruised pieces' (IV. xii. 42). Those primary elements of evil and hate turbulent throughout the sombre plays are present here: but they are resolved constituent to a wider harmony, a less partial view. Those were provisional plays: this is complete and perfect. Those earlier themes—death, unfaithfulness, loathing, hatred, and self-begotten evil: they are here too, transmuted to something rich and strange, blending their wild notes in the full chorus of sweeter melodies. There we lived an earth-life canopied by sombre clouds: the leaden hopelessness of *Lear*, the 'sterile promontory' and forbidding gloom of *Hamlet*, the black minatory rack and forked flashing Satanism of *Macbeth*. Here, though our vision often glimpses that shadowed territory, our sight bends oftener to the clouds' reverse, their silver and gold lining, their ethereal and shimmering floor. In *Pericles* we tread that insubstantial gold.

Now in *Antony and Cleopatra* no persons are bad. There is no one exponent of any pure negation: no Ghost, no Weird Sisters, no Thersites, Iago, Edmund, nor Apemantus. In no play is the moral outlook so irrelevant as a means to distinguish the persons: it is rather an impossibility, has no meaning. Analysis reveals that all the chief persons reflect identical spiritual rhythms: from positive to negative, negative to positive. Personification is thus levelled under a single ethical colouring: so that there are no ethical distinctions—not even the most purely artistic—between the chief persons. We watch as though from the turrets of infinity, whence the ethical is found unreal and beauty alone survives. Though the individual himself shows a systole and diastole of 'good', yet, since all the primary persons equally share this ebb and flow, it is clearly impossible to condemn any one person as 'bad'. Rather we must watch these varying rhythms and expect to find their significance: which will be similar in all the persons. Our negation here is disloyalty; our excellence, loyalty, with striking examples of each: but often conflicting loyalties render our impressions very complex. Here is an example:

Antony. I did not think to draw my sword 'gainst Pompey;
For he hath laid strange courtesies and great
Of late upon me: I must thank him only,
Lest my remembrance suffer ill report;
At heel of that, defy him. (II. ii. 160)

Every one here is friendly at heart: circumstances force friends and lovers apart. But there is no ill will. Now Antony's problem is acute. It is the same with Octavia:

. . . A more unhappy lady,
If this division chance, ne'er stood between,
Praying for both parts:
The good gods will mock me presently,
When I shall pray, 'O, bless my lord and husband!'
Undo that prayer, by crying out as loud,
'O, bless my brother!' Husband win, win brother,
Prays, and destroys the prayer; no midway
'Twixt these extremes at all. (III. iv. 12)

Loyalty is our theme: but loyalty is not shown as easy. Often the persons fall
from faith or love, but they fall to rise again. There is a strong predominance of
the positive essences in each: they are all, at the last, true to their deepest loyalty.
Therefore the play of action leaves scant feeling of victorious evil. Evil—here, of
course, disloyalty—is ever melted in the prevailing delight. In so far as the play
reflects human affairs, the problems of mortality are answered and the questing
mind is at peace.

The first effect to be noticed in these persons is a certain strange—the
word is apt, the idea of 'strangeness' being frequent in the play—a strange see-
saw motion of the spirit, an oscillating tendency, back and forth; a 'varying'.
This appears in Antony's wavering between the twin loyalties at Rome and
Alexandria; in Cleopatra's hesitation at the end between Antony and Caesar;
in Antony's consequent swift changes from love to loathing. The persons seem
uneasily balanced, swaying, first one side, then the other. It was the same with
Hamlet: like him, they each contain the dual principles, positive and negative,
locked in a single personality. With *Hamlet*, this incertitude was the controlling
force of the play: his world wavered with the oscillation of his mind. Here the
whole is not unsteadied by those actions which compose it: there is a constant
sense of surety and safety, a motion within stillness, temporal successions
building a strange eternity. The technique, as in *Lear*, is massively spatialized.
But in *Lear* the sense of conflict, the opposing parties in the dramatis personae,
the conflicting assurances in Lear's mind; and, again, the stark contrast between
Lear's reunion with Cordelia and her brutal death—all these forbid quite that
harmonious stillness, as of a silence holding all sounds in vassalage, which we find
here. Here there are changes, but no proper conflicts; the opposing armies are led
by staunch friends, Antony and Caesar, forced only by circumstance to military
rivalry. The root antagonists of the play are the two supreme Shakespearian
values—War or Empire, and Love: there is no question of any ultimate denial or
cynicism. All wide antinomies are melted, fused in unity. In *Lear* there is a double
climax: Lear's reunion with Cordelia in love, next her death and his. Here these
two realities are always synchronized. Eros, Iras, Charmian, Enobarbus, Antony
and Cleopatra—all die at the height of love or loyalty: death and love blend in
each. All dualisms here are less vital than the unities they build. I will now notice
certain such dualisms, clear enough when isolated, in the more purely subsidiary
persons: and from them pass to Antony and Cleopatra themselves.

Pompey, Caesar, and Antony draw lots as to who shall feast the others to
celebrate their amity. A feast is held on Pompey's galley, off Misenum. Pompey is
thus the host. During the revelry, Menas draws him aside, suggests that the cable
be cut, the ship set adrift, and the guests slaughtered at sea: then Pompey will be
'lord of the whole world' (II. vii. 67). Here is Pompey's reply:

> Ah, this thou shouldst have done,
> And not have spoke on 't! In me 'tis villainy;

> In thee 't had been good service. Thou must know,
> 'Tis not my profit that does lead mine honour;
> Mine honour, it. Repent that e'er thy tongue
> Hath so betray'd thine act: being done unknown
> I should have found it afterwards well done;
> But must condemn it now. Desist, and drink. (II. vii. 79)

This is a curious blending of sophistry and honour; of frank nobility and ignoble treachery. Treachery is very evident in the play, and Pompey's fall from hospitality and honour—in so far as this speech lowers him to our eyes—is a reflection of other similar falls. The movement is typical. Notice, too, the stress laid on personal loyalty: in Menas this act would have been 'good service'. This, too, is typical. There is a strong feeling throughout that loyalty to an individual may outweigh common sense, abstract virtue, honour: the human element, we must remember, being strongly idealized, more potent than all less concrete incentives. Abstract virtue has much less autonomy here: the significant choice is between one loyalty and another, or loyalty and treachery. An odd sort of treachery occurs naturally. Pompey with a curious readiness is here all but willing to slip the cable of his new-trothed pact: there is no strong evil intent, nor any burning ambition—just a sudden absence of loyalty. Another example occurs in Caesar's conduct at the end. His treachery towards Lepidus is suggested earlier (III. v). Hearing of Antony's death, his response is noble, generous and, it would seem, profound:

>   O Antony!
> I have follow'd thee to this; but we do lance
> Diseases in our bodies: I must perforce
> Have shown to thee such a declining day,
> Or look on thine; we could not stall together
> In the whole world: but yet let me lament,
> With tears as sovereign as the blood of hearts,
> That thou, my brother, my competitor
> In top of all design, my mate in empire,
> Friend and companion in the front of war,
> The arm of mine own body, and the heart
> Where mine his thoughts did kindle,—that our stars,
> Unreconciliable, should divide
> Our equalness to this. (V. i. 35)

At this point a messenger comes from Cleopatra, asking Caesar his intents towards her. He replies:

>   Bid her have good heart:
> She soon shall know of us, by some of ours,

> How honourable and how kindly we
> Determine for her; for Caesar cannot live
> To be ungentle. (V. i. 56)[1]

The messenger is dismissed, and he continues:

> Come hither, Proculeius. Go and say,
> We purpose her no shame: give her what comforts
> The quality of her passion shall require,
> Lest, to her greatness, by some mortal stroke,
> She do defeat us; for her life in Rome
> Would be eternal in our triumph ... (V. i. 61)

Then he seems somewhat ashamed:

> Go with me to my tent; where you shall see
> How hardly I was drawn into this war;
> How calm and gentle I proceeded still
> In all my writings: go with me, and see
> What I can show in this. (V. i. 73)

Was Caesar's first flood of sentiment insincere? I do not think so. We are constantly shown a sincere emotion suddenly giving place to an ignominious and selfish policy. Pompey's troth-plight was sincere: but he could have wished his followers to smirch it with treachery. Both Caesar and Pompey have a streak of the *Macbeth*-evil. Pompey 'would not play false and yet would wrongly win', and Caesar 'makes his face a vizard to his heart, disguising what it is'. The *Macbeth*-evil, once titanic and overpowering, is here a minor element: a sinister ripple, indicative of potential black typhoon, on the smooth heaving ocean of this play's resplendent humanism. The evil here, however, exercises no continual power over the personality which is its channel: it comes by fits and starts, intermittent. Events always render it ineffective. Menas' treachery does not materialize, Caesar's plans for Cleopatra are short-circuited by her death. At the end, Caesar's nobler quality is forced into prominence:

> Bravest at the last,
> She levell'd at our purposes, and, being royal,
> Took her own way. (V. ii. 338)

This is more typical: but the other is present. There is a dark unvalued strain of dross which curiously interlines the rich one of nobility, bounty, and loyalty.

We meet it again in Enobarbus. Through the early acts he is very lovable, faithful to Antony, his caustic and illuminating commentary never quite hiding his warmth of heart. Often he is a chorus to the action: from time to time he voices that common-sense wisdom which is usually forgotten in the visionary brilliance. He both favours and criticizes Antony's reckless love. He, too, wavers, like the others. He can cry:

> Bring in the banquet quickly; wine enough
> Cleopatra's health to drink. (I. ii. 11)

But he can also advise Antony:

> Under a compelling occasion, let women die: it were pity to cast them away for nothing; though, between them and a great cause, they should be esteem'd nothing. (I. ii. 146)

Yet again, soon after, he defends her:

> *Antony.* She is cunning past man's thought.
> *Enobarbus.* Alack, sir, no; her passions are made of nothing but the finest part of pure love . . . (I. ii. 156)

She is 'a wonderful piece of work, which not to have been blest withal would have discredited your travel' (I. ii. 164). He even persuades Antony that

> . . . the business you have broached here cannot be without you;
> especially that of Cleopatra's, which wholly depends on your abode.
> (I. ii. 185)

Notice the contrasts—between 'women' and 'a great cause'; or the 'business' of state (I. ii. 183) and the 'business' referred to by Enobarbus, the business of love. The conflicting calls of these two are at the heart both of this play and *Coriolanus.* The values of War or Empire and Love are ever twin supremities in Shakespeare; more crudely, we can name them 'efficiency' and 'sentiment'; more nobly, the great spiritual heritages of West and East. So apt in this play is Charmian's cry: 'O Eastern Star!'—the star of the eternal feminine burning through mists of masculine ambition, unfaith, doubt: to this star our study of Shakespeare's tragedies leads us. Enobarbus thus early reflects our wavering antagonism. In II. ii. he speaks his fine descriptions of Cleopatra's magic fascination; but later he sternly opposes Antony's rashness. He is the spokesman of enlightened common sense, both appreciative and critical. Often he sees the truth whilst his superiors blunder at cross-purposes. The Triumvirs forget private quarrels to unite against Pompey:

> *Enobarbus.* Or, if you borrow one another's love for the instant, you may, when you hear no more words of Pompey, return it again: you shall have time to wrangle in when you have nothing else to do.
> *Antony.* Thou art a soldier only: speak no more.
> *Enobarbus.* That truth should be silent I had almost forgot.
> *Antony.* You wrong this presence; therefore speak no more.
> *Enobarbus.* Go to, then; your considerate stone. (II. ii. 103)

Later, when Antony and Caesar are opposed, he urges strongly that Cleopatra should not take part in the war:

> Your presence needs must puzzle Antony;
> Take from his heart, take from his brain, from 's time,
> What should not then be spar'd. (III. vii. 11)

He insists with vehemence that Antony should fight by land, not by sea. His warnings are proved wise by the event. The sea-fight is a disaster. Cleopatra flies, Antony follows. His soldier's heart is disgusted:

> Mine eyes did sicken at the sight, and could not
> Endure a further view. (III. viii. 26)

Though Antony's cause is hopeless, he at first remains loyal. 'Six kings' show Canidius the way of yielding (III. viii. 43). But Enobarbus recognizes that loyalty may be called to rule common sense:

> Mine honesty and I begin to square.
> The loyalty well held to fools does make
> Our faith mere folly: yet he that can endure
> To follow with allegiance a fall'n lord
> Does conquer him that did his master conquer,
> And earns a place i' the story. (III. xi. 41)

He remains loyal while he can feel the glamour of Antony's love. Always he has been sensitive to Cleopatra's rich fascination. He will die with his master in such a cause. But, when he sees Cleopatra herself descend to treacherous betrayal—then, it is as though our whole fabric of love's vision is smirched, blackened: we, and Enobarbus, feel it:

> Sir, sir, thou art so leaky,
> That we must leave thee to thy sinking, for
> Thy dearest quit thee. (III. xi. 63)

He tells Antony of her betrayal. Antony rages at her—then accepts her excuses, recaptures his hopes, becomes recklessly valorous and merry. Enobarbus, not so easily satisfied, now knowing love's ship to be unseaworthy and not trusting Antony's rash optimism, finds the situation intolerable. Cleopatra is treacherous, Antony a fool. He has all reason on his side. Antony is 'frighted out of fear' (III. xiii. 196):

> . . . and I see still,
> A diminution in our captain's brain
> Restores his heart: when valour preys on reason,
> It eats the sword it fights with. I will seek
> Some way to leave him. (III. xi. 197)

Enobarbus' desertion is more than a personal disloyalty. It is a symbol of the protagonists' tottering romance. While Antony's love-cause is intact, Enobarbus would 'earn a place in the story': now that storied romance bids fair to be a farce. He believes the evidence of his eyes, and it is hard to blame him. Here the rightness of his course depends largely on whether his judgement of Cleopatra's integrity is sound. But there is no doubt of her treachery: he is emotionally excused. Moreover, Antony's rash conduct, kissing away all chances of success for the sake of an unprincipled and disloyal woman, will ruin not only himself but his followers. What duty binds a follower to a madman? He is rationally excused. But events, as always in this play, press Enobarbus on to realization of his true self. He deserts. He finds deserters coldly received by Caesar. Alexas was hanged. (IV. vi. 16). Canidius and others have 'no honourable trust' (IV. vi. 18). Now he knows his fault:

> I have done ill;
> Of which I do accuse myself so sorely,
> That I will joy no more. (IV. vi. 18)

A soldier brings news that Antony has sent his treasure after him with 'his bounty overplus' (IV. vi. 22). Now knowledge of his baseness inrushes, and he shivers in naked shame:

> I am alone the villain of the earth,
> And feel I am so most. O Antony,

Thou mine of bounty, how would'st thou have paid
My better service, when my turpitude
Thou dost so crown with gold! This blows my heart:
If swift thought break it not, a swifter mean
Shall outstrike thought: but thought will do it, I feel.
I fight against thee! No: I will go seek
Some ditch wherein to die; the foul'st best fits
My latter part of life. (IV. vi. 30)

Too late he finds the worth of common sense and reason in a world so ruled by
the diademed principle of love. Outward events urge him thus to knowledge of
himself. Now he cannot understand his baseness—it is as a madness. Loyalty
returns, a thousandfold more potent for his renegade act. Alone the villain of the
earth, he speaks confession to the watery eye of heaven's moonlight, opening his
soul to the infinite spaces, unburdening the infinity of his sorrow:

Enobarbus. Be witness to me, O thou blessed moon,
When men revolted shall upon record
Bear hateful memory, poor Enobarbus did
Before thy face repent!
First Soldier. Enobarbus!
Second Soldier. Peace!
Hark further.
Enobarbus. O sovereign mistress of true melancholy,
The poisonous damp of night disponge upon me,
That life, a very rebel to my will,
May hang no longer on me: throw my heart
Against the flint and hardness of my fault;
Which, being dried with grief, will break to powder,
And finish all foul thoughts. O Antony,
Nobler than my revolt is infamous,
Forgive me in thine own particular;
But let the world rank me in register
A master-leaver and a fugitive:
O Antony! O Antony! (IV. ix. 7)

Enobarbus has throughout been a common-sense commentary on the action:
this is the action's commentary on common sense. Moreover, this story of
Enobarbus exactly reflects our primary strands in the play, the stories of Antony
and Cleopatra; it is therefore most valuable to our general understanding.
Enobarbus wavers between personal loyalty and reason; at a crucial moment
takes the path dictated by his puny wisdom; is next wrenched back by events and

by his own heart to a sudden and shattering realization that all expediency is dust and ashes beside the living flame of his love. He cannot fight against the universe. The whole universe ranges itself against his turpitude, in panoply of that moon and glimmering dark in which his soul repents. Now his only life is in death. Death is synchronized with uttermost loyalty. This is the way our joyous universe makes music from the wilful unfaith and wayward purposes of man. There is an unseen power at work forcing each in his own despite to realize a consummate beauty in life and in death, ever pressing the richest liquid from the vines of his soul. Each thus dies for love or loyalty—Eros, who slays himself to 'escape the sorrow of Antony's death' (IV. xii. 95), Enobarbus, Iras, Charmian, and the two protagonists themselves. But there is no fall to death. Death is a rising. We watch a crescendo of the soul to death, itself the aim, the canopy, climacteric, and crown of life. In Enobarbus, in Antony, in Cleopatra, the same theme rings out: a wavering, a failing of trust in love's unreason, a swift and beauteous recovery in death. Each life-story is as a wild twang of harp-like music, whose ringing and swiftening vibrations rise, sweeping ethereally beyond sound.

II

This wavering, this ebbing and flowing of love's vision is apparent in Antony. It is an all-important element in the play, and is reflected in typical passages. There is the curious image:

> This common body,
> Like to a vagabond flag upon the stream,
> Goes to and back, lackeying the varying tide,
> To rot itself with motion. (I. iv. 44)

Again,

> . . . the swan's down-feather,
> That stands upon the swell at full of tide,
> And neither way inclines. (III. ii. 48)

And observe Cleopatra's

> O sun,
> Burn the great sphere thou movest in! darkling stand
> The varying shore o' the world. (IV. xiii. 9)

'Varying' again: either because of the alternation of light and dark, or the ebb and flow of ocean whose ceaseless interaction with earth is in Shakespeare a typical image of temporal change. Antony is always varying. First we find him swearing

an heroic love for Cleopatra compared with which 'kingdoms are clay' (I. i. 35).
A messenger from Rome reminds him of other ties, and he changes to:

> These strong Egyptian fetters I must break,
> Or lose myself in dotage. (I. ii. 125)

Fulvia's death is reported. Like Enobarbus, after his desertion, Antony finds the
event has a quite different taste from its pre-imagined quality:

> There's a great spirit gone! Thus did I desire it:
> What our contempt doth often hurl from us,
> We wish it ours again; the present pleasure,
> By revolution lowering, does become
> The opposite of itself: she's good, being gone;
> The hand could pluck her back that shoved her on. (I. ii. 131)

The same thought is echoed by Caesar:

> It hath been taught us from the primal state,
> That he which is was wish'd until he were;
> And the ebb'd man, ne'er lov'd till ne'er worth love,
> Comes dear'd by being lack'd. (I. iv. 41)

And Agrippa:

> strange it is
> That nature must compel us to lament
> Our most persisted deeds. (V. i. 28)

There is continually this wavering, ebb and flow, of the spirit, a shifting, varying
psychology. It recurs with great force later: the death of Fulvia forecasts the
reported death of Cleopatra in Act IV, the same rhythm of a sudden regret at
the impact of loss is apparent to both. Such reversals occur throughout. On
receipt of this Rome-news Antony swerves from reverberating protestation of
his love to criticism of Cleopatra. 'She is cunning past man's thought' (I. ii. 155).
Cleopatra taxes him with inconstancy; but he leaves for Rome, still assuring her
of his love:

> ... I go from hence
> Thy soldier, servant; making peace or war
> As thou affect'st. (I. iii. 69)

Yet, once away from Cleopatra, he is less governed by her magic. At Rome he is offered Caesar's sister, Octavia, to be his wife. Policy advises it. He accepts quite readily. He slips easily and naturally into the contract with a curious perversity. And all the time we endorse Enobarbus' prophecy:

> *Maecenas.* Now Antony must leave her utterly.
> *Enobarbus.* Never; he will not . . . (II. ii. 241)

An invisible bond binds the protagonists, heart to heart. Though Antony may not always know it—albeit, however, he soon realizes that 'i' the East my pleasure lies' (II. iii. 40)—it is true and clear to us as to Enobarbus. The strongest thing in Antony is his love for Cleopatra; The strongest thing in Enobarbus his loyalty to Antony. Both try to break free from themselves. They can no more do it with any permanence than a man can upspring from the earth whose centre draws his weight.[2] Antony speaks, perhaps at the time sincerely, to Octavia:

> My Octavia,
> Read not my blemishes in the world's report:
> I have not kept my square; but that to come
> Shall all be done by the rule. Good-night, dear lady. (II. iii. 4)

But his burning passion for Cleopatra remembered, the contrast is pitiful. The marriage only widens the split between Antony and Caesar. The interplay of human intention, action, and event is ever strange here; yet again resulting finally always in a strange and unforeseen beauty. Enobarbus sees clearly the probable future: he knows Antony better than he knows himself:

> . . . He will to his Egyptian dish again: then shall the sighs of Octavia
> blow the fire up in Caesar; and, as I said before, that which is the
> strength of their amity shall prove the immediate author of their
> variance. (II. vi. 134)

We cannot analyse the exact responsibility for the breach when it occurs. Each blames the other: which refusal to allot explicit blame is throughout a quality in this play. Such realism is vital: real life witnesses the same futility of surface 'causes', the same complexity of inimical loyalties and loves, the meaningless ineptitude of 'rights' and 'wrongs'. The deep things have their way, and appearances are froth. One thing is clear: Antony returns to Cleopatra. And that is natural and necessary.

From now on, Antony and Caesar oppose each other. Now Antony's swift oscillations from despair to reckless courage, from loathing to love of Cleopatra,

are emphasized. He insists on fighting at sea. He leaves the battle to follow
Cleopatra's flying ship. Shame engulfs him:

> Hark! the land bids me tread no more upon't;
> It is asham'd to bear me! Friends, come hither:
> I am so lated in the world, that I
> Have lost my way for ever. (III. ix. 1)

He is 'unqualitied with very shame' (III. xi. 44). Cleopatra is grieved, did not
guess he would follow:

> Egypt, thou knew'st too well
> My heart was to thy rudder tied by the strings,
> And thou shouldst tow me after: o'er my spirit
> Thy full supremacy thou knew'st, and that
> Thy beck might from the bidding of the gods
> Command me. (III. ix. 56)

He struggles vainly against this unresisted power bearing him toward his
destiny. Antony loses his wisdom, challenges Caesar to single fight. He is jovial,
melancholy, reckless by turns. The fleeting insubstantiality of psychic modes
is vivid: shifting, dissolving, reforming essences, and nothing permanent save
Antony's preoccupation with Cleopatra, either in love or loathing. For now he
finds Cleopatra making private terms with Thyreus, Caesar's envoy. He is as a
wild beast in his fury:

> Approach, there! Ah, you kite! Now, gods and devils!
> Authority melts from me: of late, when I cried Ho!'
> Like boys unto a muss, kings would start forth,
> And cry 'Your will?' Have you no ears? I am
> Antony yet. (III. xi. 89)

He abuses Cleopatra violently:

> You have been a boggler ever:
> But when we in our viciousness grow hard—
> O misery on't!—the wise gods seel our eyes;
> In our own filth drop our clear judgements; make us
> Adore our errors; laugh at us, while we strut
> To our confusion. (III. xi. 110)

This is how Antony sees his love: filth, vice, error. We remember:

> Kingdoms are clay: our dungy earth alike
> Feeds beast as man: the nobleness of life
> Is to do thus . . . (I. i. 35)

What has happened? Which is it to be, filth or all the stars of a new heaven ablaze with uncomprehended glory? So swift our interspaced modes of consciousness succeed, so sure they exclude each other. Like Hamlet, Troilus, Othello, Lear, and Timon, Antony is brought to the extreme test. This is the thing which makes Hamlet cry: 'I loved you not'; which wrenched from Troilus the distraught agony of, 'This is and is not Cressid'; which turned the Othello-music to 'Goats and monkeys!' So, too, Lear was transfixed by an unbearable knowledge, the rending tear of his heart's fabric—'Your old kind father, whose fond heart gave all . . .' This it is which attains what grandeur it may in Timon's universal anathema of hate:

> Hate all, curse all, show charity to none.

Not individual persons—no, nor 'dramatic situations'—are here at stake. Heaven and Hell are playing for the validity of the romantic vision. Is that vision true, or is it false? In this resplendent universe will Antony succeed where others fail—yes, in the face of such steel-cold treachery in love's perfected embodiment, Cleopatra, Eastern Star of Love? Now Antony's imperial palace of romance melts, insubstantial, a delusion and a cheat: and the austere Caesar and wronged Octavia look down from their ice-heaven of reason, condemning, scorning. The world may be well lost for love: but for this? Enobarbus' loyalty breaks. Antony's abuse is hideous. Now Cleopatra is a 'morsel Cold upon dead Caesar's trencher', a 'fragment of Cneius Pompey's' (III. xi. 117). He disgraces her in brutal words, flings on her memory of lustful intemperance. Cleopatra, 'our terrene moon', is 'eclipsed', portending Antony's fall (iii. xi. 153). The word is apt. The shadow passes. Antony is 'satisfied' by Cleopatra's answer. Now he is 'brave' again:

> *Cleopatra.* That's my brave lord!
> *Antony.* I will be treble-sinew'd, hearted, breathed,
> And fight maliciously: for when mine hours
> Were nice and lucky, men did ransom lives
> Of me for jests; but now I'll set my teeth,
> And send to darkness all that stop me. Come,
> Let's have one other gaudy night: call to me

All my sad captains; fill our bowls once more;
Let's mock the midnight bell.
Cleopatra. It is my birth-day:
I had thought to have held it poor; but, since my lord
Is Antony again, I will be Cleopatra. (III. xi. 177)

The contrast is violent: there is a sudden change of consciousness in Antony. The lustful faults for which he blamed Cleopatra were known to him before: facts are not here so significant as Antony's attitude towards them. Love floods again in his heart: perhaps he willingly deceives himself that Cleopatra was not sincere to her betrayal. This swift oscillation of the spirit from positive to negative and back again is markedly emphasized toward the end of Antony's story.

Next Antony bids his servants farewell:

Antony. Give me thy hand,
Thou hast been rightly honest;—so hast thou;
Thou,—and thou,—and thou:—you have served me well,
And kings have been your fellows.
Cleopatra. What means this?
Enobarbus. 'Tis one of those odd tricks which sorrow shoots
Out of the mind. (IV. ii. 10)

'Odd': throughout the play we meet a strange beauty, in tragedy as in mirth or love. This is a new facet of Antony—Antony generous and warm-hearted to his followers. In this scene—and at other instances of his 'bounty'—we are irresistibly reminded of Timon and his servants. Both heroes are given a setting of rich magnificence and Oriental display, apt frame to their rich nobility of soul, their generosity and bounty: both enjoy the feasting and the music, both are dedicate alike to love. Antony continues to expand this farewell:

Cleopatra. What does he mean?
Enobarbus. To make his followers weep. (IV. ii. 23)

Antony continues. Enobarbus interrupts, urges that the others weep and he is himself 'onion-eyed', that Antony is transforming them to women. Antony recovers himself.

Ho, ho, ho!
Now the witch take me, if I meant it thus!
Grace grow where those drops fall! My hearty friends,

You take me in too dolorous a sense;
For I spake to you for your comfort; did desire you
To burn this night with torches: know, my hearts,
I hope well of to-morrow; and will lead you
Where rather I'll expect victorious life
Than death and honour. Let's to supper, come,
And drown consideration. (IV. ii. 36)

Again, we are sensible of a wavering, a tremulous rise and fall, like a boat tossing idly on a vast sea: the deep current of that sea bears Antony on.

Next we rise to a high pinnacle of triumphant love. For the first time we meet the two great values, Love and War, perfectly blended in two personalities and one victorious event. Cleopatra buckles on Antony's armour, and he returns in triumph, his warrior-strength and love-ardour at their meridian of glory. At the start, before the battle, he is a little dashed by news of Enobarbus' desertion:

Say that I wish he never more find cause
To change a master. O, my fortunes have
Corrupted honest men! Dispatch.—Enobarbus! (IV. v. 15)

Then he returns miraculous in strength, Herculean in love and war:

We have beat him to his camp: run one before,
And let the queen know of our gests. To-morrow,
Before the sun shall see 's, we'll spill the blood
That has to-day escap'd. (IV. viii. 1)

He clasps Cleopatra to him, adoration of her and pride in his victory blended in a noble phrase:

Antony. . . . O thou day o' the world,
Chain mine arm'd neck; leap thou, attire and all,
Through proof of harness to my heart, and there
Ride on the pants triumphing!
Cleopatra. Lord of lords!
O infinite virtue, comest thou smiling from
The world's great snare uncaught?
Antony. My nightingale,
We have beat them to their beds. What, girl! though grey
Do something mingle with our younger brown, yet ha' we

A brain that nourishes our nerves, and can
Get goal for goal of youth. (IV. viii. 13)

Antony's 'brain' or spirit is young, his body old. Throughout we have this contrast:
spiritual romance, material realism. Both Antony and Cleopatra are old. Notice,
too, the curious game-metaphor 'goal'. So love's victory in arms is to be celebrated
right nobly, in triumphal and processional magnificence:

　　　Give me thy hand:
Through Alexandria make a jolly march;
Bear our hack'd targets like the men that owe them:
Had our great palace the capacity
To camp this host, we all would sup together,
And drink carouses to the next day's fate,
Which promises royal peril. Trumpeters,
With brazen din blast you the city's ear;
Make mingle with our rattling tabourines;
That heaven and earth may strike their sounds together,
Applauding our approach. (IV. viii. 29)

So high exultation rides on the crest of this wave of victory. But now our
oscillation is both fast and violent. An *Othello*-image is apt—from a scene where
warriorship and love are mated for a short while finely as in this scene of *Antony
and Cleopatra*:

And let the labouring bark climb hills of seas
Olympus-high, and duck again as low
As hell's from heaven. (*Othello*, II. i. 189)

One such movement of the spirit is the whole drama of *Othello, Lear, Timon*. It
is but an event within the many other waverings and wide visionary spaces of
our present paradise: but the analogy is important. The coarse agonies of those
sombre plays are being ground into rich flour in this whirring, spindling, soft-
voiced, unerring mechanism that tops the tortured progress of Shakespearian
tragedy: here those agonies will be resolved, melted in the one 'heavenly mingle'
of our new vision. So again Antony's love and hope sink low. No longer drunk
with success, cold fears besiege him intermittently:

　　　Antony
Is valiant, and dejected; and, by starts,
His fretted fortunes give him hope, and fear,
Of what he has, and has not. (IV. x. 19)

Again, there is failure by sea: now again Cleopatra is suspect—she is 'foul Egyptian' (IV. x. 23), and 'triple-turn'd whore' (IV. x. 26). He will have it she has sold him to Caesar:

> Betray'd I am:
> O this false soul of Egypt! this grave charm,—
> Whose eye beck'd forth my wars, and call'd them home;
> Whose bosom was my crownet, my chief end,—
> Like a right gipsy, hath, at fast and loose,
> Beguil'd me to the very heart of loss. (IV. x. 37)

Cleopatra enters, and he hurls the vilest abuse at her. He would have Caesar disgrace her:

> . . . Let him take thee,
> And hoist thee up to the shouting plebeians:
> Follow his chariot, like the greatest spot
> Of all thy sex; most monster-like, be shown
> For poor'st diminutives, for dolts; and let
> Patient Octavia plough thy visage up
> With her prepared nails. (IV. x. 46)

He drives her from him; then swears she shall die. His love-vision is now bright or dimmed according as he prospers in fight. This is only superficially irrational. Beneath all superficies and outward varying shows, the theme of these love-tragedies is one: the failure of love—the fact that it is here a sea-failure is significant—to assert its royalty in the temporal scheme. Therefore it is often associated with war, a symbolic value of practical efficiency. When Love and War embrace harmonious, as in *Othello* or our recent scene here, then Feminine and Masculine, East and West, are blended in a universal concord. But in so far as love and world-success are antagonistic, love has failed, and meets condemnation. Wherever or however it be condemned matters little: justly, for unfaith, in *Troilus*; unjustly in *Othello*; for lack of generosity in *Timon*, of sentiment in *Lear*—these differences are surface deep. All we know is that twice, in *Othello* and here, love and world-victory are seen together. It is the destruction of that unity which maddens Antony: he is metaphysically justified, even without our memory of Cleopatra's former attempt at betrayal. So she must die, like Desdemona, lest love's false gilding 'betray more men' in a world that denies the validity of the romantic vision:

> The witch shall die:
> To the young Roman boy she hath sold me, and I fall
> Under this plot; she dies for 't. (IV. x. 60)

If this play is to solve our earlier dualisms, it yet shirks nothing of their essence.

Now at the extremity of despair, Antony sees himself a shifting, unreal substance, forming, dissolving; purposeless and derelict. He is like the phantasmagoria of sunset skies, whose essence is mutability:

> That which is now a horse, even with a thought
> The rack dislimns, and makes it indistinct
> As water is in water. (IV. xii. 9)

The liquidity of 'life' is to melt within the elemental liquidity of 'death'. This is now Antony:

> My good knave Eros, now thy captain is
> Even such a body: here I am Antony;
> Yet cannot hold this visible shape, my knave. (IV. xii. 12)

Death is visaged as the dissolution of life, mutation whose artistry is strange and mysterious as the multiform pencillings of a vesper heaven. In this life-vision death is not, even at the depth of despair, quite like the 'nothing' of earlier plays: rather a change of mode, a breath scattering and dissolving the wisp of smoke that for a short while claimed individual form and direction. Antony's experiences have ever wavered, unsteady. Now he would end these swift changes from unreality to unreality by the last alternation from the flux of life to the flux of death.

At this point Mardian enters, reporting Cleopatra's supposed death:

> . . . the last she spake
> Was 'Antony! most noble Antony!'
> Then in the midst a tearing groan did break
> The name of Antony; it was divided
> Between her heart and lips: she render'd life
> Thy name so buried in her. (IV. xii. 29)

We have just been shot to the lowest depths of despair: love's failure has made Antony's purposes a mockery, his defeat a shame unexcused, his life a vapid and lunatic thing of hazy incertitude. There was only death, itself vaporous as life. Heaven and Hell gamble for man's Love. Antony's soul has been tossed and rocked, first heaven-high, then to tartarean depths. Now, when all seems lost, Heaven plays its final card, the single ace of Cleopatra's death:

> *Antony.* Dead then?
> *Mardian.* Dead. (IV. xii. 34)

This is one of the strangest, simplest, most beautiful and most transparent dramatic movements in Shakespeare. There is no flight more swift or sure. This is our last violent alternation. The sun swims back on a blackened universe, Life's sun itself more radiant in panoply of Death, no longer life's antagonist, but rather its robe, its sceptre, and its crown. For now death is no vain dissolution, but charged with an almighty significance. There is no rational sequence, the swelling flood of love's vision has no shallow 'reason' any more than Antony's loathing could defend itself in terms of sharp logic. At this news his anger is not denied, its 'causes' are no less real than before, nor is Cleopatra excused of treachery. His anger, its reasons, still exist: but they are straightway as a raindrop fallen in the ocean of his love, lost therein, meaningless; love's ocean-infinity mingling now with the infinity of Cleopatra's death. The symbol of love, itself infinite, has taken infinity as its territory. In terms of that eternity Love, not War, emerges victor: therefore—

> Unarm, Eros; the long day's task is done,
> And we must sleep. (IV. xii. 35)

Two things agonized Hamlet: faithlessness and death. Here they cancel out, like a fractional calculation, and instead of a baffling complex of figures we are left 1/1, itself unity. We are thus beyond all provisional negations; 'infinity' even is inept. We face rather a simple and positive unity, resultant from a calculation in terms of minus quantities. Even our old positive good, 'War', becomes meaningless now. Antony throws off his armour. He knows, like Enobarbus, his purpose, his direction. All else was froth, now the deep surges claim their own:

> Off, pluck off:
> The seven-fold shield of Ajax cannot keep
> The battery from my heart O, cleave, my sides!
> Heart, once be stronger than thy continent,
> Crack thy frail case! Apace, Eros, apace.
> No, more a soldier: bruised pieces, go;
> You have been nobly borne. From me awhile.
> I will o'ertake thee, Cleopatra, and
> Weep for my pardon. So it must be, for now
> All length is torture: since the torch is out,
> Lie down, and stray no farther: now all labour
> Mars what it does; yea, very force entangles
> Itself with strength: seal then, and all is done.
> Eros!—I come, my queen:—Eros!—Stay for me:
> Where souls do couch on flowers, we'll hand in hand,
> And with our sprightly port make the ghosts gaze:

> Dido and her Aeneas shall want troops,
> And all the haunt be ours . . . (IV. xii. 37)

Dido and Aeneas are apt here. The Vergilian hero sacrificed love for empire; the Shakespearian, empire for love. This is the dying of our practical value War, or Empire, the ascent of the immortal value, Love. War, so bright-honoured in terms of time, holds less prestige in that eternity to which Love steps as into the element for which it is born, as the cygnet takes to the waters with untutored ease. And Antony's vision is now a vision of eternity. Recently he would slay Cleopatra: then one brief facet, one little segment, one hour of her, was in his consciousness. Now death silhouettes both her personality and his warrior-story in perfect completion; but against its darkness she is lit by the greater light.

> Since Cleopatra died,
> I have lived in such dishonour, that the gods
> Detest my baseness. (IV. xii. 55)

Here love, not empire or warriorship, has the monopoly of 'honour'. Only in death is the finite thing complete. Nor is this death an ending. It rather circumferences and silhouettes its theme, throwing out the whole loved essence in a bold and rounded perfection. And it is more—its mystery casts a new glamour, so that our central figure is not bounded by a rigid line, but rather mingles with the surrounding unknown, every contour blended with its setting, like the magic nimbus which haloes the fine word of poetry, or the bright-haired sun-corona flashing its brilliance to melt in heaven's blue. This is the mating of finite and infinite in death: good and ill, ugly and beautiful, blending in the one perfection. All length, all temporal duration, is now 'torture'. Blind 'force' of earthly life is entangled with the mastering and purposeful 'strength' of eternity, itself visioned as a brighter life, the prize of love; no shadowed Hades, but a mode whose grand Elysium transcends the flowery foisons of our little O, the earth. Now death is Antony's bride:

> I will be
> A bridegroom in my death, and run into 't
> As to a lover's bed. (IV. xii. 99)

Death and love become identical.

I have stressed the alternating movements in Pompey and Caesar, where they are less distinct; and in Enobarbus and Antony where they are extremely vivid. Antony and Enobarbus both show a wavering and interchange of consciousness, the sweep of their oscillations getting wider and faster till the final equating of death with loyalty or love. This death is no cadence: death is rather the meridian of that embracing unknown which holds 'time' and 'eternity' as twin quadrants of its arching glory. Life is here deserted for love, itself 'Time's best jewel' (Sonnet LXV), and, since that love is now equated with death, life—or all that is most significant in life—and death are mated. This blending, interfusing, of life and death is echoed often before, the climax sending back reverberations, rippling movements of casual speech, into the preluding acts. Note Enobarbus' words on Cleopatra:

> . . . I do think there is mettle in death, which commits some loving act
> upon her, she hath such a celerity in dying. (I. ii. 152)

Antony spoke truer than he knew when he referred to making death 'love' him (III. xi. 193); or when he said that in the next day's fight, he would rather expect 'victorious life than death and honour' (IV. ii. 43). I have already observed how Antony's reception of the news of Fulvia's death exactly prefigures the later announcement of Cleopatra's:

> . . . she's good, being gone;
> The hand could pluck her back that shov'd her on. (I. ii. 135)

A pale reflex of the later movement; but a neat comment on the 'varying' psychology I have noticed. I noted, too, another such comment:

> . . . the ebb'd man, ne'er lov'd till ne'er worth love,
> Comes dear'd by being lack'd. (I. iv. 43)

When Antony tells Enobarbus of Fulvia's death, the resemblance to the later report of Cleopatra's is especially clear: the word 'dead' sounding with a leaden simplicity similar in both.

> *Antony.* Fulvia is dead.
> *Enobarbus.* Sir?
> *Antony.* Fulvia is dead.
> *Enobarbus.* Fulvia!
> *Antony.* Dead. (I. ii. 167)

The theme of death's sudden revelation is thus recurrent. Another early passage curiously forecasts the triple association of death, love, and life which forms the climacteric of Enobarbus', Antony's, and Cleopatra's stories. Cleopatra speaks:

> . . . and great *Pompey*
> Would stand and make his eyes grow in my brow;

There would he anchor his aspect and die
With looking on his life. (I. v. 31)

Here life and love blend in a kind of death; and in the later action love and
death blend in a kind of life. Death and Antony are, towards the end, lovers;
for death is kind in this play, a positive, not a negative, reality: death 'enlarges'
life's 'confine' (III. v. 13). But it should also be observed that Antony, finding
Cleopatra still alive, knowing he is to leave, not meet her, reverts to troubled
retrospect of his end, asking Cleopatra to think of him as when he was the
greatest prince of the world (IV. xiii. 54). We can yet see his end as a 'miserable
change' (IV. xiii. 51) in terms of temporal affairs, the while he is lifted up to
the waiting arms of love. The more perfect and joyful blending of death with
love is left for Cleopatra.

The oscillation we have observed is no dynamic antagonism: there are not two
hostile elements coexistent yet incompatible as in *Troilus, Macbeth, Lear*. It more
nearly resembles the swift single alternations of *Othello* and *Timon*: yet here there
is a continual, less irrevocable, succession, almost placid in its gentle varying.
The *Macbeth* or *Lear* modes might be compared to the atom with its opposing
protonic elements, negative and positive. Recently it has been suggested that
this is a false analysis: that the atom is the ultimate unit, itself varying between
positive and negative, alternately charged with interchanging significance. Though
this appears a provisional and not quite satisfying statement, yet it exactly reflects
the mature humanism of *Antony and Cleopatra*: it is in this sense that our play
presents a unity in place of the former dualisms. Moreover, these alternations
result in an awareness of timelessness. The persons throughout: endure the
present mode without vivid reference to past or future: the cloud passes, leaving
no shadow on the sun it eclipsed. The recollection of past incompatibility with
the present mood appears to be at the root of all psychic conflict. Here there is
no such conflict, quite: the persons submit first to one, then the other, mode.
There is an ebb and flow, a systole and diastole, of positive vision. There is no
clear time-continuum of cause and effect: all 'causes' are surface deep, sometimes
perhaps non-existent, certainly non-evident. Here the sombre or treacherous
or distrustful mood falls, like Keats's melancholy, 'sudden from heaven, like an
angry cloud': causeless, self-begotten, mysterious. It was similar with Hamlet. It
is so in our own lives. Both *Antony and Cleopatra* and *Hamlet* present in this way
a more vital realism by which other plays appear artificial. Here there is little
significant feeling of any time-succession, the events are otherwise related and
woven. This is clear also in the death-theme; a timeless instant of death and love
synchronized opening vistas eternal. By synchronizing death, the most absolute
of all negations, with the positive aspect of life, love, we are left with a sense of
peace and happiness, an apprehension of pure immortality. Later I shall revert
to this timeless quality, noting the massively spatialized technique of the whole.

I shall next attempt analysis of Shakespeare's most amazing and dazzling single personification.

III

Cleopatra is baffling in the remarkable combination of diversity and unity. She has, far more than Hamlet, all qualities potential in her. All colours blend in a rich fascination, a single impact, a myriad tints: like some sky-rainbow of humanity she circles the solid humanism of former plays, containing all their essences, but, in sweeping curves of the spirit, outdistancing their varied experiences with ethereal compass. She is by turns proud and humble, a raging tigress and a demure girl; utterly deceitful, she is yet faithful to death, compact of highest regality, she is skittish as a shop girl on a bank-holiday; expressly feminine, she loves to engage in war; all woman's gentleness is hers, yet she shows the most callous and inhuman cruelty. Finally, though she is woman's loveliness incarnate, beauty enthroned beyond the shores of time, set above the rugged map of imperial splendour and down—watching the fighting princes below—herself the only prize of valour, another Helen of Troy, fit to glorify a Caesar's triumph with 'eternal' (V. i. 66) splendour, or crown an Antony with immortality, with all this there is in her a streak of mysterious and obscene evil. She is at once Rosalind, Beatrice, Ophelia, Gertrude, Cressid, Desdemona, Cordelia, and Lady Macbeth. Moreover, since the Antony-theme clearly reflects the essence of the former Shakespearian love and hate antagonisms, it will appear that *Antony and Cleopatra*, among its other amazing subtleties, contains the main elements of the sombre plays: not, as elsewhere, presented as negations, but viewed from the reverse, all fused and united in a single vision of universal and positive assertion, all equally blended in a finely-wrought, harmonious, complexity.

Cleopatra's first words are expressly feminine in their desire to hear love's accents reiterated:

If it be love indeed, tell me how much. (I. i. 14)

She urges Antony to hear the messengers from Rome. In a mingle of jealousy and mockery, perhaps meaning to sound his faith and play on his affections, she calls to mind the precariousness of their love, the Roman turbulences that may threaten their paradisal Egyptian dream:

Cleopatra. Nay, hear them, Antony:
Fulvia perchance is angry; or, who knows
If the scarce-bearded Caesar have not sent
His powerful mandate to you, 'Do this, or this;
Take in that kingdom and enfranchise that;
Perform't, or else we damn thee.'

Antony. How, my love!
Cleopatra. Perchance! nay, and most like:
You must not stay here longer, your dismission
Is come from Caesar; therefore hear it, Antony.
Where's Fulvia's process? Caesar's I would say? both?[3]
Call in the messengers. As I am Egypt's queen,
Thou blushest, Antony; and that blood of thine
Is Caesar's homager: else so thy cheek pays shame
When shrill-tongued Fulvia scolds. (I. i. 19)

She gets her desire: a noble apostrophe to their love. Yet she is not satisfied. Intuitively, she fears Rome:

Excellent falsehood!
Why did he marry Fulvia, and not love her?
I'll seem the fool I am not; Antony
Will be himself. (I. i. 40)

Antony will not attend to Rome—he, luxuriating in love's 'soft hours' (I. i. 44), would continue nothing but 'sport' (I. i. 47). Cleopatra is insistent, she would 'hear the ambassadors' (I. i. 48). She senses danger and cannot rest. Antony brushes her mood aside:

Fie, wrangling queen!
Whom every thing becomes, to chide, to laugh,
To weep; whose every passion fully strives
To make itself, in thee, fair and admir'd!
No messenger, but thine; and all alone
To-night we'll wander through the streets, and note
The qualities of people. Come, my queen;
Last night you did desire it. (I. i. 55)

The spectroscopic variety of Cleopatra is thus early observed. Next we find her anxiously searching for Antony, afraid:

He was dispos'd to mirth; but on the sudden
A Roman thought hath struck him. (I. ii. 90)

Yet, on hearing of his approach, the searcher would hide: she is like a wild animal suddenly scenting danger. Now throughout we must be ready to observe two things: her ability to act any part to gain or retain hold over Antony's heart; and the deep sincerity of love beneath these surface insincerities. With exquisite subtleties she plays on Antony's affection when she can win, but changes her tactics as soon as her power appears to be failing. Her integrity is questioned by Enobarbus:

> ... Cleopatra, catching but the least noise of this, dies instantly; I have seen her die twenty times upon far poorer moment. (I. ii. 149)

But when Antony bitterly admits her 'cunning', he continues:

> Alack, sir, no; her passions are made of nothing but the finest part of pure love: we cannot call her winds and waters sighs and tears; they are greater storms and tempests than almanacs can report: this cannot be cunning in her; if it be, she makes a shower as well as Jove. (I. ii. 156)

So closely is play-acting woven into her love. She is a mixture of truth and falsehood, and the complexity is often baffling: passion and premeditation are curiously entwined in her. She is an adept in love's cunning, and so she tells Alexas:

> See where he is, who's with him, what he does:
> I did not send you: if you find him sad,
> Say I am dancing; if in mirth, report
> That I am sudden sick: quick, and return. (I. iii. 2)

When Charmian advises her rather to 'give him way, cross him in nothing,' she answers:

> Thou teachest like a fool; the way to lose him. (I. iii. 10)

It is all thought out, carefully planned.

There follows the important scene of Antony's farewell to her. Cleopatra's changes throughout are very significant. First she pretends to be ill, asks Charmian to help her away, tells Antony to stand far off. Then, in withering scorn, she speaks:

> *Cleopatra.* I know, by that same eye, there's some good news.
> What says the married woman? You may go:
> Would she had never given you leave to come!
> Let her not say 'tis I that keep you here:
> I have no power upon you; hers you are.
> *Antony.* The gods best know,—
> *Cleopatra.* O, never was there queen

> So mightily betray'd! yet at the first
> I saw the treasons planted.
> *Antony.* Cleopatra,—
> *Cleopatra.* Why should I think you can be mine and true,
> Though you in swearing shake the throned gods,
> Who have been false to Fulvia? Riotous madness,
> To be entangled with those mouth-made vows,
> Which break themselves in swearing. (I. iii. 19)

She continues to taunt him: tells him to go, if so he will, without patching excuses. Then she flings down the noble petulances of her love:

> Nay, pray you, seek no colour for your going,
> But bid farewell, and go: when you sued staying,
> Then was the time for words: no going then;
> Eternity was in our lips and eyes,
> Bliss in our brows' bent; none our parts so poor,
> But was a race of heaven: they are so still,
> Or thou, the greatest soldier in the world,
> Art turn'd the greatest liar. (I. iii. 32)

Then again—

> I would I had thy inches; thou shouldst know
> There were a heart in Egypt. (I. iii. 40)

Antony at last tries to stem the liquid fire of her thwarted passion inblazing at his readiness to leave her. Hearing of Fulvia's death, she bitterly reproaches him for lacking proper sorrow: so will her own death be received. She is unfair, quite irrational, typically feminine. But all these shows are projections of one central reality: her burning passion, fierce tigress-love, for Antony. Now Antony protests his love's integrity: he goes to make war in her name, her knight. His words are a little facile and perfunctory. Still, the delicious assurance draws from her:

> Cut my lace, Charmian, come;
> But let it be: I am quickly ill, and well,
> So Antony loves. (I. iii. 71)

Love is ever the pivot of her gyrating personality, the light which illumes the phantasmagoria of her shifting moods. Again Antony assures her that his love is firm. Now again she taunts him, less bitterly; rather with a touch of satiric playfulness, bids him to weep and play one scene 'of excellent dissembling'

(I. iii. 79). Antony's patience begins to fail: he has done all that could possibly be required by way of masculine adoration. She has not responded by submitting to his wider duties:

> *Antony.* You'll heat my blood: no more.
> *Cleopatra.* You can do better yet; but this is meetly.
> *Antony.* Now, by my sword,—
> *Cleopatra.* And target. Still he mends;
> But this is not the best. Look, prithee, Charmian,
> How this Herculean Roman does become
> The carriage of his chafe. (I. iii. 80)

Envenomed anger is dissolved by a moment of love satisfied—'I am quickly ill, and well, so Antony loves'—and is solidified again to half-playful mockery, which then alters gradually to this laughing Rosalind love: an exquisite gradation, like an April sun from out showery clouds, an unanalysable movement like the meltings of sunset. For now, partly due to Antony's rising impatience, partly as though these surface impersonations can no longer mask her passion's simplicity, she breaks down in the jewelled statement of their love, a sweet finality beyond words:

> Courteous lord, one word.
> Sir, you and I must part, but that's not it:
> Sir, you and I have lov'd, but there's not it;
> That you know well: something it is I would,
> O, my oblivion is a very Antony,
> And I am all forgotten. (I. iii. 86)

We remember Enobarbus' apt phrase: 'her passions are made of nothing but the finest part of pure love' (I. ii. 151). It is seen true in this sudden abandon, a roseate sincerity swiftly unfurled, the flower to which her other moods are as unopened buds. As he reproaches her with 'idleness', she answers:

> 'Tis sweating labour
> To bear such idleness so near the heart
> As Cleopatra this. (I. iii. 93)

But now she is gentle, plays properly woman's part of relinquishing her man to his duty:

> But, sir, forgive me;
> Since my becomings kill me, when they do not
> Eye well to you: your honour calls you hence;

Therefore be deaf to my unpitied folly,
And all the gods go with you! upon your sword
Sit laurel victory! and smooth success
Be strew'd before your feet! (I. iii. 95)

Cleopatra angles for her Antony; giving out when necessary, drawing in when possible. She would draw him to her bosom from that world of stern action which is his sphere. She is typical of woman trying to hold man from other interests, other calls. Throughout this scene it will be observed that she is the primary force in their love, its origin and strength, while he is perfunctory, hasty, anxious to be gone:

Let us go. Come;
Our separation so abides, and flies,
That thou, residing here, go'st yet with me,
And I, hence fleeting, here remain with thee.
Away! (I. iii. 101)

A usual Shakespearian love-thought: but not elsewhere presented so casually. Cleopatra fights for his love. But she knows the limitations of her magic, works within them, employing a conscious artistry to serve her instinctive passion. Always, however, till near the play's end, we must observe that love is the only root of her actions. She is thus undivided, a trader in love alone: whereas Antony serves two gods: 'love' and 'honour'.

Now Antony is gone and she is alone with her girls. But she is still all in Antony; would drink mandragora to sleep out the 'great gap of time' which is Antony's absence (I. v. 5). Every moment is weighted with love's memory:

O Charmian,
Where think'st thou he is now? Stands he, or sits he?
Or does he walk? or is he on his horse?
O happy horse, to bear the weight of Antony!
Do bravely, horse! far wot'st thou whom thou movest?
The demi-Atlas of this earth, the arm
And burgonet of men. He's speaking now,
Or murmuring 'Where's my serpent of old Nile?'
For so he calls me: now I feed myself
With most delicious poison . . . (I. v. 18)

Alexas enters, brings news of Antony. He presents to her an 'orient pearl', kissed by Antony, an ambassador of love. He repeats Antony's reverberating message:

'Good friend', quoth he,
'Say, the firm Roman to great Egypt sends

This treasure of an oyster; at whose foot,
To mend the petty present, I will piece
Her opulent throne with kingdoms; all the east,
Say thou, shall call her mistress.' (I. v. 42)

Such is the imperial glory of our love-theme: for our material splendour is generally, as here, but the suits and trappings to a spirit-passion out scintillating the diadems of empire. But Cleopatra takes no note of resounding phrases. Kingdoms are clay. She would hear rather of her Antony alone:

Cleopatra. What, was he sad or merry?
Alexas. Like to the time o' the year between the extremes
Of hot and cold; he was nor sad nor merry.
Cleopatra. O well-divided disposition! Note him,
Note him, good Charmian, 'tis the man; but note him
He was not sad, for he would shine on those
That make their looks by his; he was not merry,
Which seem'd to tell them his remembrance lay
In Egypt with his joy; but between both:
O heavenly mingle! Be'st thou sad or merry,
The violence of either thee becomes,
So does it no man else. (I. v. 50)

Cleopatra's world, despite her queenship, is a woman's world: her mental horizon close bounded by love's infinity. So she sends messengers daily to Antony. Alexas met no less than twenty. Antony blazes in her thought, hour by hour. Nor even music relieves her longing. Like Orsino, she would bid music, love's solace and companion, assuage her loneliness:

Cleopatra. Give me some music; music, moody food
Of us that trade in love.
Attendant. The music, ho!
Cleopatra. Let it alone . . . (II. v. 1)

Cleopatra 'trades in love'; so beauty ever lives by absorbing strength, woman by allure of man. The phrase does not apply to Cleopatra alone, nor even to a feminine type: it goes deeper, and to misread it is to forgo the fine scope of our vision. Cleopatra is not one, but all, woman, waiting for man. She is another Dido, as Vergil writes down the story; or as Milton's Eve—'He for God only, she for God in him'. She waits with her girls for Antony. They generously humour her restlessness. Poor Charmian's arm is sore with billiards (II. v. 4). Cleopatra and her girls at Alexandria are as the Eternal Femininity waiting for Man. A certain eternity broods over this still, languorous Alexandria. The wars of Caesar and Antony seem a little childish by these deeps of love: what, to Cleopatra, are the empires of Antony's promise, to the look of his eye, his joy or sorrow, his divine humanity? So Cleopatra, her maids, her eunuch Mardian, talk and think of Antony, play billiards, go fishing: a life still as a windless sea, bronzed tropically by heaven's wide arch of melting flame; a life of ease, but charged to breaking with love's burning weight. And again, this silent Alexandria is a place of eternal peace, calling man back to rest among its olives from the heat and dust of battering days. All here is translucent and bright, pure as the Nile waters:

> . . . we'll to the river: there,
> My music playing far off, I will betray
> Tawny-finn'd fishes. . . (II. v. 10)

Cleopatra is incarnate queen of music and romance; her Alexandria eternity inspaced on earth.

But there is merriment here, in this eternity. It holds no chill solemnity. Charmian recalls how she once made sport of Antony's 'fervency' and warrior-prowess:

> *Charmian.* 'Twas merry when
> You wager'd on your angling; when your diver
> Did hang a salt-fish on his hook, which he
> With fervency drew up.
> *Cleopatra.* That time,—O times!—
> I laugh'd him out of patience; and that night
> I laugh'd him into patience: and next morn,
> Ere the ninth hour, I drunk him to his bed;
> Then put my tires and mantles on him, whilst
> I wore his sword Philippan. (II. v. 15)

So much for masculine 'fervency'. Alexandria is a paradise of feast, fun, and love. This is a myriad-qualitied heaven: a warrior's Valhalla, but also a paradise brimming with the merriment of Shakespeare's own Beatrice, and the mystic wells of romantic light that gleam in Dante's. Alexandria calls Antony from imperial turbulence, would have him relinquish the childish all-too-serious quarrels of Rome and join in the glinting laughter of love. Why must he take things so deadly earnest? Cleopatra, woman-like, cannot admit an Antony's ambitions as all-worthy, would laugh at them: watches them, as Asia diademed with ages of spiritual insight might tolerantly watch Europe proudly flaunting her war-dinted and plated helmet to the skies. Cleopatra is 'riggish' (II. ii. 245); Enobarbus once saw her 'hop forty paces through the public street' (II. ii. 234). Sportiveness is strong in Antony's and Cleopatra's love. To this happy paradise she would recall him.

But she is a very tigress in wrath. A messenger brings news of Antony's marriage. She strikes him, again and again:

> What say you? Hence,
> Horrible villain! or I'll spurn thine eyes
> Like balls before me; I'll unhair thy head:
> Thou shalt be whipp'd with wire, and stew'd in brine,
> Smarting in lingering pickle. (II. v. 62)

Next she draws a knife and all but slays him. She is merciless, a Jezebel of wrath. She dismisses him at last, is 'faint', and through her tigress-wrath we again see the purely feminine weakness and love:

> Lead me from hence;
> I faint: O Iras, Charmian! 'tis no matter.
> Go to the fellow, good Alexis; bid him
> Report the feature of Octavia, her years,
> Her inclination, let him not leave out
> The colour of her hair: bring me word quickly.
> Let him for ever go:—let him not—Charmian,
> Though he be painted one way like a Gorgon,
> The other way's a Mars. Bid you Alexis
> Bring me word how tall she is. Pity me, Charmian,
> But do not speak to me. Lead me to my chamber. (II. v. 109)

Cleopatra is a match for the Roman Empire, yet weak as a child. Later she sends for the messenger, again questions him minutely, with a finely feminine inquisitiveness about her rival. The messenger is tactful.

> *Cleopatra.* Is she as tall as me?
> *Messenger.* She is not, madam.
> *Cleopatra.* Did'st hear her speak? is she shrill-tongued or low?
> *Messenger.* Madam, I heard her speak; she is low-voiced.
> *Cleopatra.* That's not so good: he cannot like her long.
> *Charmian.* Like her! O Isis! 'tis impossible.
> *Cleopatra.* I think so, Charmian: dull of tongue, and dwarfish! (III. iii. 14)

Cleopatra continues by a suggested comparison of her own 'majesty' with Octavia's bearing:

> *Cleopatra.* What majesty is in her gait? Remember,
> If e'er thou look'dst on majesty.

Messenger. She creeps:
Her motion and her station are as one;
She shows a body rather than a life,
A statue than a breather. (III. iii. 20)

So finely is the contrast pointed. Octavia's whiteness is as paste, or deathly alabaster, compared with Cleopatra's vital sun whose single fire is blent of all passion's varying colours, shifting, opalescent, dazzling. Cleopatra is all womanly things, good or evil. There is danger in her, danger and violence, as in her reception of the messenger, in her desire to distract Antony from all things but herself. She has a serpent's grace, a serpent's attraction, dangerous as Eve, serpent-beguiled. She is well-named 'The Serpent of Old Nile'. Sometimes her love appears violent and selfish and almost evil; at others, it is pure and innocent as the frosty light of a Christmas star. She is one way a Medusa, the other a Madonna of serenity and peace. Now she is reassured by the messenger's details. She cannot fear this puppet, Octavia. She praises the messenger's insight and judgement. She continues:

Cleopatra. Guess at her years, I prithee.
Messenger. Madam,
She was a widow,—
Cleopatra. Widow! Charmian, hark.
Messenger. And I do think she's thirty.
Cleopatra. Bear'st thou her face in mind? is't long or round?
Messenger. Round even to faultiness.
Cleopatra. For the most part, too, they are foolish that are so.
Her hair, what colour?
Messenger. Brown, madam: and her forehead
As low as she would wish it. (III. iii. 29)

Now she asks the messenger not 'to take her former harshness ill'; she regrets that she so 'harried' him; agrees he is a 'proper' man. Her opinion of him varies according to the news he brings. She is not fair. She does not control and unify her impressions by any cool reason. She is a sapling swaying to every breath of her passionate desires. But those passions harp so fine a natural music as they pass, that there is no incongruity, no lack of beauty: rather an ever-harmonized music of passionate discords.

When Caesar and Antony oppose each other in the third act, Cleopatra assumes another role. Now she is an Amazon. Like Desdemona she will not be 'a moth of peace' when her lord goes to fight. Though Enobarbus strongly attempts dissuasion, she is angered:

Sink Rome, and their tongues rot
That speak against us! A charge we bear i' the war,

And, as the president of my kingdom, will
Appear there for a man. Speak not against it;
I will not stay behind. (III. vii. 16)

Now she would be a proper general, practical and efficient as any man, a veritable
St. Joan. When Antony is amazed at Caesar's sudden proximity, she is incisively
critical:

Celerity is never more admir'd
Than by the negligent. (III. vii. 25)

Now she boasts, prideful of her navy. There is really no limit to her repertory. But
the feminine basis of her varying shows is never long forgotten. Here, as usual,
it reswims into our vision, asserts itself. Always this is our unifying principle
in analysis: every strong passion and violent assertion, with a varying, see-saw
motion, returns, as with Lady Macbeth, to pure femininity. We noticed this
rhythm in Act I; it was vivid in her meeting with the messenger. So, now, her
Amazon courage melts into a woman's fear. She would aspire to man's courage,
she would have Antony all hers: if he cannot leave the world of turbulence for the
crowned peace of love, then she, queen of love, will share this action with him. So
her woman's heart ruins his manhood. He follows her flying sails.

The interplay of the sexes, their respective weaknesses and strengths, is always
finely pictured. The play throughout shows not only the blending of sex, but also
its necessary antagonism and mutual hindrance. Antony never quite forgets his
soldiering till the end: he and Cleopatra never blend perfectly till death. The
theme of the action is thus the antagonism of those values, the masculine and the
feminine, which we have observed already: War, or Empire, and Love. Both these
high Shakespearian values, positive and rich in romantic colour and suggestion,
contend together; and their contest is as the impact of angelic forces. Not Caesar
against Antony, rather Antony the soldier against Antony the lover. Here the
love-value finally wins—indeed, one short scene (III. i.) exists partly (not wholly)
to show a strain of ugly self-glorification, Coriolanus-wise, in our Antony's
soldiership, decreasing its worth in comparison with his adoration of Cleopatra.
Now the wrench apart, and blending, of these elements is the repulsion and
attraction of sex. Nor any theme outspaces this. For, in a final judgement, our
story is the story of the universal differentiation, the separation and multiplicity,
the retraction to unity; the ebbing and flowing of God Himself into His universe.
But, whereas in *Timon* after the agony of differentiation unity is reached by utter
severance, here it will be attained by sex with sex blending, and death blent with
life. Death and Life are the sexes of the absolute: Death, the feminine, calls back
the adventurer, Life, to her bosom. So Cleopatra awaits Antony; and so Antony
finally dies into the arms of Cleopatra's love. And this sudden raising of our
protagonists' love and death story into so universal and titanic a meaning is no

extravagance in a play where all elements are ever seen to blend and mingle in a fruitful matrimony, where man himself in love is drawn as a colossus overtopping the spheres of heaven. For, in the meanest and smallest atom the eternal systole and diastole is at work; and this play shows us that same seesaw alternation, that waking and sleeping of vision, that pulsing of eternity, pumping life-blood into the tingling veins of time.

After her fatal action and Antony's shameful retrograde captaincy, Cleopatra is all repentance, distracted, asking pardon:

> O my lord, my lord,
> Forgive my fearful sails! I little thought
> You would have follow'd. (III. ix. 54)

Now she is femininely weak, all bowed to man's strength which that weakness has ruined. But next there is Caesar's offer of peace if Antony be delivered, followed by Antony's challenge to single combat. Thyreus attends Cleopatra alone, and personally offers her safety and protection, if she will betray Antony's cause. He gives her every chance to do so easily:

> *Thyreus.* He knows that you embrace not Antony
> As you did love, but as you fear'd him.
> *Cleopatra.* O!
> *Thyreus.* The scars upon your honour, therefore, he
> Does pity, as constrained blemishes,
> Not as deserved.
> *Cleopatra.* He is a god, and knows
> What is most right: mine honour was not yielded,
> But conquer'd merely. (III. xi. 56)

This is truly a pivot moment, not only of this play, but of the whole sequence of Shakespeare's later visions. Love is at stake. On Cleopatra depends the integrity to Love's cause of Antony, Enobarbus, Iras, Charmian—and Caesar, too, who must laugh to see Antony's prostitute queen desert him. Octavia and all Rome will scorn this love-madness of a once noble soldier, now gipsy-betrayed. She is another Delilah to his Samson, man again is betrayed by woman's cheating lure. Cleopatra is clearly the origin of our love-vision, all other loves and allegiances depend on her integrity; she is Queen of Love, Alexandria Love's palace home. Moreover, where Ophelia, Desdemona, Cressid, Cordelia, all failed through a certain weakness intrinsic to their limited personalities, here, in the infinite love-spaces of our present play, in Cleopatra's infinity, we might expect success. Those heroines we pitied, or, if we loved, then, with our Cleopatra now known, we realize we loved them but in 'our salad days', when 'green in judgement' (I. v. 73). Cleopatra's rich profusion and 'infinite variety' makes them cloy to our taste: they are all merest Octavias beside her. For Cleopatra is all womankind, therefore all romantic vision, the origin of love, the origin of life. The universe is compacted embryonic in the womb of her divine and unlimited femininity. If she fails, it is as though the origin of life itself were poisoned at its source. With an inscrutably evil callousness Cleopatra now proceeds to fail:

> Most kind messenger,
> Say to great Caesar this: in deputation
> I kiss his conquering hand: tell him, I am prompt
> To lay my crown at's feet, and there to kneel:
> Tell him, from his all-obeying breath I hear
> The doom of Egypt. (III. xi. 73)

The Serpent of old Nile. This is the primal Eve in Cleopatra. It is a serpentine evil, an utterly selfish streak of bottomless evil. She will try to win Octavius. She even takes pleasure in reminding the messenger of her other conquests, how great Julius Caesar loved her:

> Your Caesar's father oft,
> When he hath mus'd of taking kingdoms in,
> Bestow'd his lips on that unworthy place,
> As it rain'd kisses. (III. xi. 82)

Pompey (I. v. 31), Julius Caesar, Antony—and now, perhaps, Octavius. The murmured remembrance is sweet to her. Antony is put aside. 'Policy' wins, unutterable baseness, love's ripening apple worm-eaten at the core.

Antony enters: Enobarbus had left to tell him of Cleopatra's treachery. He directs his fury first on Thyreus, then on Cleopatra. He abuses her with all possible foul invectives. His ideal is now filth, his loathing knows no limit. It is the old story of Hate from *Hamlet* to *Timon*. Cleopatra for long can get no word in to stem the torrential abuse. At last:

> *Cleopatra.* Not know me yet?
> *Antony.* Cold-hearted toward me?
> *Cleopatra.* Ah, dear, if I be so,
> From my cold heart let heaven engender hail,
> And poison it in the source; and the first stone
> Drop in my neck: as it determines, so
> Dissolve my life! (III. xi. 157)

Are we to accept this excuse? It is all we get. Antony is 'satisfied'. It is as though her fascination wins us to a changed outlook, willing to question no further. Perhaps Cleopatra has persuaded herself even that she was not dallying with treachery. Antony recovers his spirits. All is now again new-born hope, splendid and festive. Again our rocking motion swings back on to our vision the positive essences, love, hope, ardour:

> It is my birth-day:
> I had thought to have held it poor; but, since my lord
> Is Antony again, I will be Cleopatra, (III. xi. 185)

The eclipsing of our 'terrene moon' (III. xi. 153), Cleopatra, is past. Again she shines refulgent.

Next day, before the battle, she is Antony's faithful woman, solicitous for his health and comfort. She would have him 'sleep a little' first (IV. iv. i). Then, since he will arm straightway, she would help:

> Nay, I'll help too.
> What's this for? (IV. iv. 5)

Now Samson's Delilah has become an Andromache, bidding her Hector to battle. Antony laughingly praises her:

> Thou fumblest, Eros; and my queen's a squire
> More tight at this than thou. (IV. iv. 14)

Here love and warriorship blend finely, each gilded by the other. The rigid dualisms of the sombre plays crossed at right angles, making each a crucifix of torture. Here there is no such pain. The two supreme values are like lines intersecting and gently diverging at acute angles. Here is the point of intersection, the highest point of pure life-joy reached in the play, love and warrior-strength blended:

> O love,
> That thou couldst see my wars to-day, and knew'st
> The royal occupation I thou shouldst see
> A workman in't. (IV. iv. 15)

He returns, victor. Cleopatra's phrase of love floods out in:

> Lord of lords!
> O infinite virtue, comest thou smiling from
> The world's great snare uncaught? (IV. viii. 16)

But there is next more failure at sea. Antony believes Cleopatra has betrayed him, the universe is again blackened, love's lamp-flame oil and smoke malodorous. Antony is mad as a trapped animal, swears she must die. Cleopatra is baffled:

> O, he is more mad
> Than Telamon for his shield . . . (IV. xi. 1)

Her cunning comes to aid her:

> To the monument!
> Mardian, go tell him I have slain myself;
> Say, that the last I spoke was 'Antony',
> And word it, prithee, piteously: hence, Mardian,
> And bring me how he takes my death . . . (IV. xi. 6)

Now she hears he is dying, and her tragic passion is richly inwrought:

> All strange and terrible events are welcome,
> But comforts we despise; our size of sorrow,
> Proportion'd to our cause, must be as great
> As that which makes it. (IV. xiii. 3)

And, as Antony is carried to her:

> O sun,
> Burn the great sphere thou movest in! darkling stand
> The varying shore o' the world. O Antony,
> Antony, Antony! Help, Charmian, help, Iras, help;
> Help, friends below; let's draw him hither. (IV. xiii. 9)

She is strangely efficient and practical as she gives direction for lifting Antony up to the monument; and withal still more strangely cheerful, as though this snow-crest of tragedy catches a glittering brilliance of delicate merriment from a source unseen:

> Here's sport indeed! How heavy weighs my lord!
> Our strength is all gone into heaviness,
> That makes the weight: had I great Juno's power,
> The strong-wing'd Mercury should fetch thee up,
> And set thee by Jove's side. Yet come a little,—
> Wishers were ever fools,—O, come, come, come;
> And welcome, welcome! die where thou hast lived:

Quicken with kissing: had my lips that power,
Thus would I wear them out. (IV. xiii. 32)

Death is showered with love's quickening kisses. So she abandons herself to love,
and then anger:

. . . let me rail so high,
That the false housewife Fortune break her wheel,
Provok'd by my offence. (IV. xiii. 43)

When he dies, the world is 'no better than a sty' (IV. xiii. 62):

. . . young boys and girls
Are level now with men; the odds is gone,
And there is nothing left remarkable
Beneath the visiting moon. (IV. xiii. 65)

Love gone, the world is now a barren promontory extending its naked
irrelevances to a staring moon. At the climax of grief she faints. When she revives
there are swift changes in her passionate words. First, we are drawn to observe
that primary element of pure femininity, something not unlike the weakness of
Lady Macbeth:

No more, but e'en a woman, and commanded
By such poor passion as the maid that milks
And does the meanest chares. (IV. xiii. 72)

In an ecstasy of wrath she next opposes her regality to heaven:

It were for me
To throw my sceptre at the injurious gods;
To tell them that this world did equal theirs
Till they had stol'n our jewel. (IV. xiii. 75)

But she recognizes the futility and puerility of all passion: now death only makes
meaning to her, it alone has positive significance. Throughout this scene her
passion sings so sweet its varying melodies that we find her supreme in sorrow
as in 'love' or 'sport':

All's but naught;
Patience is sottish, and impatience does
Become a dog that's mad: then is it sin

To rush into the secret house of death,
Ere death dare come to us? (IV. xiii. 78)

Suddenly she is strangely bright-hearted, an April brilliance smiling through tears and cloud. Throughout we note how merriment is here a ripple on the tragic waters, ruffling their sombre deeps to reflect sun-ward a myriad laughters:

> How do you, women?
> What, what! good cheer! Why, how now, Charmian!
> My noble girls! Ah, women, women, look,
> Our lamp is spent, it's out! Good sirs, take heart:
> We'll bury him; and then, what's brave, what's noble,
> Let's do it after the high Roman fashion,
> And make death proud to take us. (IV. xiii. 82)

There is an exquisite variety in her glinting, shifting, evanescent moods of passion; aglow with the pulsing blood of her radiant femininity, compact of meekness and infinite pride, of strength and weakness intertwined. Throughout this scene there has, too, been a strange serenity refusing all black Satanic effects, a strength of wing on which the Ariel spirit of try towers above tragedy, its eagle-eyes up-raised. So Cleopatra is strange to us, pure woman as she is, like some foreign bird of similar form to ours, yet surpassing them in its rich variance of plumage; most surely of our world, most strangely different; most radiant and peaceful even at the climacteric of grief.

On casting retrospect over Cleopatra's tale we are struck by her variety. It surpasses that of any other Shakespearian person. In this way she is all womankind, rather than a single woman: or again, we may say she is universal in the sense that any one person, or, indeed, any one object of any sort, becomes a symbol of universal meaning and content if properly understood. And Cleopatra's 'variety' is so vividly depicted that it is easy to understand. Her two primary qualities are: (i) the essential femininity we have continually observed, and (ii) her profuse variety of psychic modes: which two are clearly one, since a profound and comprehensive delineation of essential woman is necessarily very varied, and built of contradictions. Our analyses have without straining made reference, not only to Shakespeare's previous heroines, but to Eve, Jezebel, Helen of Troy, Amazons, St. Joan, Dido, Delilah, Andromache, Dante's Beatrice, Medusa, the Madonna. All women of legend or literature combine to make our Cleopatra. She is a silk shot with dazzling, shifting, colours. The same is true of the play as an artistic whole. She, more than any other, is the play. Hence the femininity in the vowel-sounds and the style generally, which I have noted already, and its shifting, dazzling, opalescent interplay of imagery. Now it will be clear that Cleopatra is the divinity of this play in the sense that Desdemona is the divinity of *Othello*. Her transcendent divinity and beauty are stressed in Enobarbus' description of her in her barge. The sombre plays all revolved on such ideals: Hamlet's father, Isabella, Helen of Troy (in *Troilus*), Desdemona, Duncan and the English King in *Macbeth*, Cordelia, Timon himself: all are at some time vividly idealized, all but equated with divinity. Such divinity was ever divine by nature of a certain limited perfection, a certain limited beauty. Cleopatra is divine by nature of her divine variety and profusion. Queen of romance, she is yet, like Antony, old: 'wrinkled deep in time'. The contrast is the same as that between the two theological conceptions of a God containing all qualities good and evil, and a God partial and exclusive: God the Father, and God the Son. The same contrast is reflected in the ethic of the Duke in *Measure for Measure*, who knows both good and evil within himself, and that of Angelo who prides himself on a false, because exclusive, sanctity. Here Cleopatra has beside her Octavia to point the same contrast: and Octavia is a thing of cardboard in this comparison. Now since Cleopatra is so comprehensively conceived, it will be clear that the streak of serpentine evil in her is part of her complex fascination: and, though real and as truly part of her as any other quality, it will be found to melt into her whole personality, enriching rather than limiting her more positive attractions. A limited perfection is sand on which to build: thus Isabella was exposed to shame, her very virtue turned against her when it claimed all-importance. Troilus could not accept Cressid's faithlessness as hers; Desdemona's purity could not save her in a world where an Iago exists. In Cleopatra we find a personification blent of 'good' and 'evil', a Cordelia with a streak of Lady Macbeth. The perfection flowers from totality, not exclusion. From any limited view, her treachery is nauseating; but, from the view of eternity, the whole and all its parts observed, the 'evil' is seen otherwise, as part of a wider pattern. This is why Antony, when his anger is thrown suddenly into relation with death's eternity, so completely alters: his rage abates, its 'reason' now meaningless. Enobarbus speaks truth of Cleopatra:

> Age cannot wither her, nor custom stale
> Her infinite variety: other women cloy
> The appetites they feed; but she makes hungry
> Where most she satisfies: for vilest things
> Become themselves in her; that the holy priests
> Bless her when she is riggish. (II. ii. 240)

Her power to assimilate all qualities and gild them with the alchemy of her rich personality was observed, too, by Antony. She is one

> Whom every thing becomes, to chide, to laugh,
> To weep; whose every passion fully strives
> To make itself, in thee, fair and admir'd! (I. i. 49)

She is, indeed, 'a most triumphant lady' (II. ii. 193): and she triumphs where others failed. I conclude, therefore, that the Cleopatra-vision, without shirking the problems of the sombre plays, yet answers them imaginatively. It remains to indicate how this completer creation, Cleopatra, proceeds through the final scenes to vindicate this statement, and assert the rights of her 'infinite variety' to that imperial diadem of love denied by the poet to other more limited and therefore less perfect divinities. Cleopatra excels by virtue of her psychic infinity, which necessarily includes evil: she wins by her very capacity to fail, and, herself infinite, steps the more naturally to the infinities of death.

So our final act here is as the crest not only of this play but of the whole Shakespearian progress. All this consummate artistry has been lavished on Cleopatra that she may assert the power of love to enclose not only life, but death, in its vision. Her Antony dead, she faces Caesar and his powers alone. She has determined on the 'better life' of death:

> My desolation does begin to make
> A better life. 'Tis paltry to be Caesar;
> Not being Fortune, he's but Fortune's knave,
> A minister of her will: and it is great
> To do that thing that ends all other deeds;
> Which shackles accidents and bolts up change;
> Which sleeps, and never palates more the dung,
> The beggar's nurse and Caesar's. (V. ii. 1)

'Death' is not here even named. It is 'a better life', 'that thing. . . .' Here, where we are directly to catch some awareness of 'death's' mystery, the word itself, with its sombre associations, inevitably blurs somewhat our vision. The root idea of this pregnant passage is the sharp juxtaposition of 'time' and 'eternity'. Caesar, with his worldly success, is 'paltry', tossed hither and thither on the rough flux of 'fortune': so much for world-success. For Cleopatra there is 'that thing', the ender of all other deeds. First we are pointed to its 'ending'—the death of Lear. And we are shown its essential 'greatness' or grandeur, its aesthetic appeal: so, too, in *Lear* death, by its majestic and grand impact, left us with a sense of peace. Next we see how it is master of 'accidents' and 'change', that is, time. Eternity nullifies time at one stroke, prisons it, renders it harmless; that thief 'injurious time', thing of 'robber's haste', ever ready to 'cram his rich thievery up' and escape with it (*Troilus*, IV. iv. 44). So far we have noted death's effect from the side of life: now we pass to its own essential sovereignty. First, it is like sleep; second, it tastes no longer that 'dungy earth' (I. i. 35) which is unworthy of its child; finally, it is nurse alike to Caesar in his glory and the beggar in his penury—a kindly presence, dear nurse to life, eternity calling back the child of time to its bosom. We have passed from its aesthetic appeal to a quick and tight analysis of its apparent effects, and finally we contemplate its more personal, moral, attitude to man: that of a nurse to a child. Is this 'death'? What is the 'death' of *Antony and Cleopatra*? Not that the word itself is elsewhere absent: but it is continually welcomed—as something of positive worth and sweet nourishing delight, like love:

> Where art thou, death?
> Come hither, come! come, come, and take a queen
> Worth many babes and beggars! (V. ii. 46)

So cries Cleopatra when she is surrounded by enemies. They have taken the dagger from her hand, and she has been derived even of death 'that rids our dogs from languish' (V. ii. 42). Proculeius has falsely promised her Caesar's 'grace', but she does not believe him. In torrential passion she swears she will some way die. She will 'eat no meat', nor drink, nor sleep (V. ii. 49–51). She will not go as a prize to Rome:

> Rather a ditch in Egypt
> Be gentle grave unto me! rather on Nilus' mud
> Lay me stark naked, and let the water-flies
> Blow me into abhorring! rather make
> My country's high pyramides my gibbet,
> And hang me up in chains! (V. ii. 57)

Her changes are again swift. All this follows closely after her regal reception of Caesar's embassy:

> If your master
> Would have a queen his beggar, you must tell him,
> That majesty, to keep decorum, must
> No less beg than a kingdom: if he please
> To give me conquer'd Egypt for my son,
> He gives me so much of mine own, as I
> Will kneel to him with thanks. (V. ii. 15)

But now she is wild, entrapped. All the message she will send to Caesar is

> Say, I would die. (V. ii. 70)

Proculeius leaves her with Dolabella. She recounts now her dream of Antony.

Out of her varying moods, passions, experiences, one fact emerges: her serene love of Antony. This, among all else fleeting, is, ultimately, changeless and still, the centre and circumference of her personality, of the play. Here she is tranced by a breathless tranquillity as she rehearses her marvellous dream. She, who is herself all things potential, knows Antony now as all things accomplished. In death, by love, transfigured, he is the universe and more:

> His face was as the heavens; and therein stuck
> A sun and moon, which kept their course, and lighted
> The little O, the earth. (V. ii. 79)

Cleopatra, in splendour of love's imaginings, holds earth and its sun, heaven and all eternities in her gaze. So image succeeds image in placid miraculous succession, wondrous. And Cleopatra is tipped with orient fire, the mouthpiece of a revelation beyond earthly sight:

> His legs bestrid the ocean: his rear'd arm
> Crested the world . . . (V. ii. 82)

In this blazing love-sight, Cleopatra, herself infinite woman, is being mated to the infinity of Antony dead. They, who were not married in life, will find their bridal in death. As a butterfly from its chrysalis she slowly wakes, and is spreading roseate wings to the dawn. But first Caesar comes to her, delays her flight.

A curious dialogue follows. There is a long and elaborate fencing of insincerities, Cleopatra all humility, Caesar all generous bounty: neither is honest. Caesar means to add Cleopatra to his trophies of victory. Cleopatra knows well his purposes, forewarned by Dolabella, but she is trying her last hope: she would fascinate him, add him to her triumphs of love. Caesar deceives her, she deceives him, especially in her proffer of an inventory of her wealth, its falsity disclosed by her servant, Seleucus. Once again her wrath burns at Seleucus' betrayal, at the end dying down to womanly pathos:

> Prithee, go hence;
> Or I shall show the cinders of my spirits
> Through the ashes of my chance: wert thou a man,
> Thou would'st have mercy on me. (V. ii. 172)

Now all hope of Caesar's favour is dispelled. Both played with the other, played for a rich prize. Caesar for Cleopatra, a jewel in the crown of his triumph, Cleopatra for Caesar's love, another fine emerald to set beside those other victories, Pompey, Julius Caesar and Antony.

So, even at this last moment, the Serpent of old Nile pursues a wavering course. That she sincerely tries to ensnare Caesar is evident enough from her deceit regarding the treasure. But circumstances force her on, as ever in this play, to the final immolation on love's altar. She fails with Caesar, and knows it:

> *Cleopatra.* He words me, girls, he words me, that I should not
> Be noble to myself: but, hark thee, Charmian.
> *Iras.* Finish, good lady, the bright day is done,
> And we are for the dark. (V. ii. 191)

Cleopatra is to be 'noble to herself': in their death for love, Eros, Enobarbus, and Antony, too, are noble to that which is most stalwart and irresistible in themselves. Now Cleopatra is steadfast in her course of dying. She will not go to Rome to have Antony 'brought drunken forth', before her, or to see

> Some squeaking Cleopatra boy my greatness
> I' the posture of a whore. (V. ii. 220)

Rather she will 'fool their preparation' and 'conquer their most absurd intents' (V. ii. 2–25). She now speaks from heights overtopping the childish glorification of empire. She has the dignity of a Clytemnestra—but set, not on murder, but self-immolation. Though compact of variety and waverings, she assumes a steadily increasing grandeur of immobility. She is again in the still consciousness of her dream: her 'variety' is now 'infinity', and infinity means death and love, Antony and all the stars sun-blazing to make of one night's darkness a myriad brilliant days. So she will deck herself for the bridal morning of death:

> Now, Charmian!
> Show me, my women, like a queen: go fetch
> My best attires: I am again for Cydnus,
> To meet Mark Antony: sirrah Iras, go.
> Now, noble Charmian, we'll despatch indeed;
> And, when thou hast done this chare, I'll give thee leave
> To play till doomsday. Bring our crown and all. (V. ii. 226)

Iras and Charmian have throughout been supporters of Cleopatra's love, waiting with her for Antony, recalling old merriment in the empty days of Antony's absence, now urging Cleopatra to step to Antony, to 'finish' and set out 'for the dark'. They are faithful to love's cause always. Now at last Cleopatra is raised beyond wavering, beyond incertitude. She hears that a 'rural fellow' is at hand with figs:

> *Cleopatra.* Let him come in. What poor an instrument
> May do a noble deed! he brings me liberty.

My resolution's placed, and I have nothing
Of woman in me: now from head to foot
I am marble-constant; now the fleeting moon
No planet is of mine. (V. ii. 236)

Death is 'liberty'; it 'enlarges' the 'confine' (III. v. 13) of even her infinity.
Cleopatra's pulsing variety begins to show a marble stillness; and, after our long
pageantry of empire, it rests with a 'rural fellow' to bring Cleopatra the key to a
wider empire, to speak her sailing orders as she puts out on the brighter seas of
death. This short dialogue is important.

First, the clown in blundering Shakespearian rusticity emphasizes again that
quality of our death theme here that I have so stressed:

Cleopatra. Hast thou the pretty worm of Nilus there, That kills and pains
not?
Clown. Truly, I have him: but I would not be the party that should desire
you to touch him, for his biting is immortal; those that do die of it do
seldom or never recover. (V. ii. 243)

'His biting is immortal': so, too, Cleopatra echoes the word shortly after, she
has 'immortal longings' in her. Now the clown, rude instrument of truth,
proceeds to speak of the most profound difficulty in our understanding of
Cleopatra, this play, or, indeed, the whole Shakespearian sequence. Within
Cleopatra there is, as I have noticed, a vein of pure evil; necessary in so
rich a feminine creation. This is the evil of Lady Macbeth, or Eve.[4] In the
Shakespearian and Biblical visions of the birth of evil, man is influenced
through woman by a supernatural evil: so Satan tempts Eve, and the Weird
Sisters, themselves feminine, tempt Macbeth, but succeed rather through Lady
Macbeth who herself, after reading of their prophecy, addresses satanic prayer
to the 'powers that tend on mortal thoughts'. At the root of the Shakespearian
agony seems ever a dark feminine evil. It is, less strongly, apparent in
Gertrude and Cressid, where it is little more than weakness, and in Goneril
and Regan, where it is somewhat colourless. Perhaps it is even more ultimate
than masculine cynicism—as to Hamlet, Iago, Apemantus—since it so often
appears to precede and condition such cynicism. In Shakespeare woman is
both the divine ideal and the origin of evil: because she is more eternal than
man, more mysterious, the mysterious origin of life. On that dualism the past
agonies revolve. Woman, rather than man, is the creative essence, the one
harmony, from which man is separated, to which he aspires. On her ultimate
serenity and sweetness, not denying but over-swamping her evil, depends
the sanity of religion, and the universal beauty. And at this last moment
the clown slowly, incisively, speaks, acts as the embassy of the heavenly

spheres which ask now from Cleopatra a music to rise and mingle with their own:

> *Cleopatra.* Rememberest thou any that have died on 't?
> *Clown.* Very many, men and women too. I heard of one of them no
> longer than yesterday: a very honest woman, but something given to lie;
> as a woman should not do, but in the way of honesty: how she died of
> the biting of it, what pain she felt: truly, she makes a very good report o'
> the worm; but he that will believe all that they say, shall never be saved
> by half that they do ... (V. ii. 249)

Two thoughts are apparent: (i) the dishonesty of woman, and (ii) the queer 'report'—as though still living—of a dead woman on her own death. But the ultimate purpose of this dialogue is more exactly stated a little later. Here clearly is expressed the twin potentialities of woman: the divine and the satanic— Desdemona and Lady Macbeth—two qualities which, as we have seen, blend in Cleopatra. Thus up to our very last moment the dualism is emphasized:

> *Cleopatra.* Will it eat me?
> *Clown.* You must not think I am so simple but I know the devil himself
> will not eat a woman: I know that a woman is a dish for the gods, if the
> devil dress her not. But, truly, these same whoreson devils do the gods
> great harm in their women; for in every ten that they make, the devils
> mar five.
> *Cleopatra.* Well, get thee gone; farewell.
> *Clown.* Yes, forsooth: I wish you joy o' the worm. (V. ii. 272)

That speech is not 'comic relief': the clown fixes his gaze on Cleopatra, drives in word on word into her heart, warning her. Now, at the last, we are to watch the long issue decided. That dialogue limns it clear for us, exact. We knew it, from other plays, and remember. And it is well that the champion of the divinely feminine is no pulseless abstraction to lie like Desdemona unjustified in death and pitiable, but rather a Cleopatra blended of all varieties: eternal woman, strong in all womanly passion, all evil and love intrinsicate. Cleopatra has ruined Antony; it is left to her to justify Antony's sacrifice to love. We shall see whether the orient star of woman's divinity, so long questioned, is a cheat, whether it, so oft the origin of evil, will here accomplish a triumph proportional to all past burdens of shame; whether the Arabian perfume of a Cleopatra's death can at last sweeten to all eternity the nightmare agony of that other blood-stained hand; whether the romantic vision, which sees through 'evil' appearance into the blazing heart alone, is a deception, an Octavia more blest than Cleopatra. In Cleopatra's death is involved no single event only, but rather the justification of that starry hope beyond good or evil, that vision which is poetry in all its guiltless profusion, that trust that unity, not duality, is hearted in the universal breast; that all things blend into a single glory in the universal Cleopatra.

At this point Cleopatra becomes love absolute and incarnate. Caesar, not being Fortune, is only 'Fortune's knave' (V. ii. 3). With love it is different. The perfect lover becomes love. Nor is there any contrast here between temporal failure and love as with Antony. Cleopatra melts naturally into love's eternity. Therefore the poet, ascending to this point, flings out the death of Cleopatra across the page like an upward tongue of fire, and earth-bound tragedy, so long our occupation, now lifts its wings and first takes the airs of immortality:

> *Re-enter Iras with a robe, crown, &c.*
> *Cleopatra.* Give me my robe, put on my crown; I have
> Immortal longings in me: now no more
> The juice of Egypt's grape shall moist this lip:
> Yare, yare, good Iras; quick. Methinks I hear
> Antony call; I see him rouse himself
> To praise my noble act; I hear him mock
> The luck of Caesar, which the gods give men
> To excuse their after wrath: husband, I come:
> Now to that name my courage prove my title!
> I am fire and air; my other elements
> I give to baser life. So; have you done?
> Come then, and take the last warmth of my lips.
> Farewell, kind Charmian; Iras, long farewell.
> Have I the aspic in my lips? Dost fall?
> If thou and nature can so gently part,
> The stroke of death is as a lover's pinch,
> Which hurts, and is desir'd. Dost thou lie still?
> If thus thou vanishest, thou tell'st the world
> It is not worth leave-taking.
> *Charmian.* Dissolve, thick cloud, and rain; that I may say
> The gods themselves do weep!
> *Cleopatra.* This proves me base:
> If she first meet the curled Antony,
> He'll make demand of her, and spend that kiss
> Which is my heaven to have. Come, thou mortal wretch,
> With thy sharp teeth this knot intrinsicate
> Of life at once untie: poor venomous fool,
> Be angry, and dispatch. O, could'st thou speak,
> That I might hear thee call great Caesar ass
> Unpolicied!

Charmian. O eastern star!
Cleopatra. Peace, peace!
Dost thou not see my baby at my breast,
That sucks the nurse asleep?
Charmian. O, break! O, break!
Cleopatra. As sweet as balm, as soft as air, as gentle,—
O Antony!—Nay, I will take thee too:
What should I stay—
Charmian. In this vile world? So, fare thee well.
Now boast thee, death, in thy possession lies
A lass unparallel'd. Downy windows, close;
And golden Phoebus never be beheld
Of eyes again so royal! Your crown's awry;
I'll mend it, and then play. (V. ii. 283)

Even death is 'play'. The guard rushes in, and Charmian applies an asp to
herself:

First Guard. Where is the queen?
Charmian. Speak softly, wake her not.
First Guard. Caesar hath sent—
Charmian. Too slow a messenger.
O, come apace, dispatch! I partly feel thee. (V. ii. 322)

Asked if this act is well done, Charmian answers:

It is well done and fitting for a princess:
Descended of so many royal kings. (V. ii. 329)

Then she, too, falls. As the guard tells Caesar:

I found her trimming up the diadem
On her dead mistress; tremblingly she stood
And on the sudden dropp'd. (V. ii. 345)

So Cleopatra is attended in death by her girls, Iras and Charmian. Throughout
this scene there is insistence on the crowned regality of Cleopatra's death; its
softness, gentleness; its positive nature, loosing life's complex knot; on the
absurdity of temporal things—an 'ass unpolicied'; on the ascension from 'baser
elements' to air and fire; on life, the 'baby', and the star of dawn; above all, on
Antony—for 'death' and Antony are one. This is the love intercourse of life and
death.

We are reminded throughout of humanity's spiritual wavering, a torch-like flame flickering, buffeted in the winds of time; extinguished, it would seem, one moment, then again bright-flaring. At the death-moments of the chief persons it burns with a steady brilliance. There is a graded ascent: the death in bitter remorse of Enobarbus; the twining of tragedy with love at the death of Antony; and now, our final resplendent vision. Here the bright palace of love falls; like a falling star, its lambent arrow-flame shooting whitely through the night. Cleopatra, Queen of Love's Eternity, has been attended throughout by her girls, Iras, Charmian, twin pillars of this palatial love, Cleopatra. We have seen them with her, stilly waiting at Alexandria, beyond the turbulence of imperial contest, eternal feminine beauty outwatching the glories of time. Iras and Charmian stabilize and solidify the marbled theme of Love above the flux of change. But now Cleopatra dies, diademed imperially with the crown of Life, to meet her Antony, attended by her girls, whose dying with her, before and after, makes a silent melodic succession, a triple cadence, one death on either side her death, harbinger and escort of her approach.[5] The marble palace of Love falls, piece by piece, dissolves, a visionary Taj Mahal, its fabric melting in the Phoenix fire of its own immortal beauty. Thus an unearthly glory is snatched from heaven, Promethean blaze, to light on Iras, Cleopatra, Charmian in their dying: like the sudden gilding by a horizontal sunset of a myriad pools on sand, before unnoticed, now gold beside a golden sea, till all is alive with fire, and earth itself unplaneted, a burning, tranquil star.

Caesar, symbol of temporal sway, of Western power, stands dazed by this Orient beauty in death. He has wavered between admiration and despisal of love's disciple Antony. He has himself resisted Cleopatra. But there is to be no dissentient voice in our final massive unity. He, like the rest, bows finally to love. Cleopatra, who could not win him in life, wins him in her death. Dazedly he looks on her, crowned and robed for another Cydnus:

> . . . she looks like sleep,
> As she would catch another Antony
> In her strong toil of grace. (V. ii. 349)

Again events have so fashioned his course that, reft of all hope of an ignoble desecration of Cleopatra's majesty to swell his triumph, himself he speaks the last epitome of her, and Antony's, glory:

> Take up her bed;
> And bear her women from the monument:
> She shall be buried by her Antony:
> No grave upon the earth shall dip in it
> A pair so famous. High events as these

> Strike those that make them; and their story
> No less in pity than his glory which
> Brought them to be lamented. (V. ii. 359)

Here, where all dualisms are blended, the intrinsic unity of tragic peace is thus set down for us by the poet. High events strike those that make them: the positive purpose of the event is conditioned by the death of the protagonist. That is why here, as never elsewhere in Shakespeare, there is finally no suggestion of tragic pain, so that we freely and joyfully

> let determin'd things to destiny
> Hold unbewail'd their way. (III. vi. 84)

Destiny is here kind: it ever wrenches man from his perversity, forces him, in his own despite, to reach his heritage of love's immortality. So Antony 'dies' where only he has 'lived'—in Cleopatra's arms (IV. xiii. 37). The spirit of man is each a string vibrating to the sweeping arm of an unseen eternity.

IV

I have concentrated on the human element in this essay, tracing the stories of individual persons. But they, like our former strands of imagery, are only provisionally to be abstracted. The play, as a whole, is to be understood only by these various approaches assimilated in a single vision. A comprehensive view shows it to be amazingly constructed, with so infinite a care that, though we are concerned largely with an historical tale, yet we have a vision far transcending the narration of any single series of events. The technique of scene arrangement is especially noteworthy. There are no long dramatic movements. The massively expanded and spatialized technique forbids any prolonged single swirl of passion. The most powerful emotional movements are all compressed, both by the 'wavering' psychology which presents alternation rather than development, and by the scene variation. This variation of scene applies a break to the action. The vision is diffused over a very wide space, so that the short scenes, with the vast distances between their locations, convey not only an impression of empire, but a still more powerful impression of space as opposed to time. They tend to crush time, to render it subordinate to simultaneity, which eternity envelopes, and encloses the action like a moveless sphere englobing an oiled mechanism smoothly working within.

And this element of stillness is to be related especially to the love-element, as the movement and the action are related to the war-theme. Love is omnipresent universally in our numerous images of element mated with element, the sun fecundating the Nile basin, cloud-forms dissolved in the air, the melting, blending, mingling; and in the sexual conversation of Cleopatra's retainers.

Love is imperial over empires. All the persons tend to cohere, to make peaceful societies, as when Antony cements his friendship with Caesar by marriage, or the triumvirs celebrate their new amity with Pompey by feasting and music. This is the natural tendency, only disturbed by the wavering, the alternations, in the persons, perversely spoiling happiness. This love-eternity stilly overwatches the flux of time, its action and imagery interpenetrate the whole action. And Antony alternates from one to the other, between the eternity of love and the temporal glories of empire. Hence the stillness of Cleopatra's palace at Alexandria. It is static, in a world of movement, waiting. Though the action be far-flung we are never left to forget that Cleopatra and her girls hold the destinies of the empire in their eyes. Alexandria encloses the action, frames it: our first and last scenes are necessarily laid there. Moreover, this motionless quality related to action's movement is finely developed in Acts II and III. In II. v. Cleopatra hears of Antony's marriage and drives the messenger from her. The following scenes are at Misenum, Pompey's galley, Syria, Rome. In III. iii we are again at Alexandria. Cleopatra is sending for the messenger she has just dismissed. Hardly any time has elapsed. A few minutes at Alexandria enclose—it is logically impossible since Caesar and Antony appear in three of the interposed scenes—a vast and varied stream of action in the outer world. Therefore we have an impression of stillness over-watching motion, eternity outstaring time; and so our total effect is one of Love at the start supreme, Antony and Cleopatra together at Alexandria; next, that love inter-threads, encloses, watches and waits for the protagonists of empire; lastly, draws them back within its own quality, as Caesar follows Antony to Egypt and Cleopatra at the end. To understand the play aright we must be prepared to see Antony, as a very human lover, Cleopatra as love itself. Hence the exquisite contrast of Antony's death, its quality of tragedy and failure, subtly differentiated from Cleopatra's dissolving immortality. So we watch love calling man to her bosom; and death, gentle and soft as a nurse's love, drawing the wanderers, life, and last love itself, back to its peace. Accordingly our love-theme, which ranges equally through all the natural imagery, is shown as a force not to be denied, more potent than kings, controlling their actions by its own passivity. We watch the dualism of East and West, spirit and action, death and life: and all are finally blended in love. And it must be remembered that Eastern splendour is closely associated in Shakespeare with love's ideal, which ideal is often imaged as set beyond a sea: hence the consummate symbolic accuracy of Cleopatra, Love's Queen, at Egypt, contrasted with Caesar, empire-symbol, at Rome. Between these two Antony wavers. His final surrender to love and death completes the pattern of his story. Time is annulled. At his dying, 'the star is fall'n' and 'time is at his period' (IV. xii. 106).

But, though East and West—I use the terms purely to assist my present attempt—eternity and time, feminine love and masculine warriorship, are opposing values here, there is no strong dualism. The final effect is a blending, a melting, with a victory for the finer, over the cruder, ideal. And this points us to a final statement about the play. I have noticed that the varying psychology of the play is true to human normality in a way that the cataclysmic psychic eruptions in *Macbeth*, *Lear*, and *Timon* are not: since our life is usually a sequence of such alternations, such systole and diastole of vision. And yet in no former play is humanity so finely idealized. I have also remarked that, though the poet here uses very sensuous and emotional, even coarse, essences, yet the result is not exactly sensuous or emotional: all is constricted, rarefied by a fine control, a sifting of any but the purest gold-dust of vision. The play presents opposing aspects of its love-theme: the crude and the ideal. Moreover, the lovers are old, Cleopatra 'wrinkled' (I. v. 29), Antony's head is 'grizzled' (III. xi. 17). There is no excess of physical beauty, as in *Romeo and Juliet*. There is a violent, sometimes a harsh, realism in *Antony and Cleopatra*. Human love is battered, weary, yet divine. These opposing aspects we view alternately. It is the opposition of our own lives. No play is more true, and, finally, none more beautiful. It is written from a height overlooking every essence which is employed: it is not only a vision, but a vision understood, and continually interpreting itself. It relates to *Romeo and Juliet* exactly as *The Tempest* relates to *A Midsummer Night's Dream*. Every negation in the play is subservient to the total unity. I have also noticed the peacefulness, and merriment even, which here accompanies tragedy. So that we find a rarefied, unemotional, and happy vision of essences coarsely material, immoral—remembering Antony's unfaithfulness to Fulvia and Octavia—passionate, and tragic; one in which humanity seems at once more tragically real and more divinely ideal than elsewhere; something beside which the dualistic modes of the sombre tragedies appear not only as morbid, but essentially partial and provisional; which, as nearly as any work in literature, solves by direct and truthful life-presentation and immediate understanding, that is, without resorting to 'myth', the dualisms of love and evil, life and death; which more perfectly than any other work of literature blends a myriad diversities of person, place, image, and thought, in a single and harmonious oneness. I conclude that *Antony and Cleopatra* is a dramatic microcosm of human, and other, life viewed from within the altitudes of conscious Divinity; that we have here our most perfect statement of the real; that, whereas the sombre plays are aspects of 'appearance', in *Antony and Cleopatra* we touch the Absolute.

Additional Note, 1951: There is no doubt that the phrase 'terrene moon' (at III. xi. 153) applies directly to Cleopatra. See my letter in *The Times Literary Supplement*, 14 July, 1950.

    1965: Before my own essay in 1931 J. Middleton Murry had already in 'The Nature of Poetry' (*Discoveries*, 1924) observed briefly the themes of dying for loyalty and of death as a sweetness in *Antony and Cleopatra*, and also the play's prevailing calm. There was, too, an early phrase of his about 'dying into love' which I cannot trace. See above, pp. vi, 264–6; also p. 341 note, below.

Murry's *Shakespeare* appeared much later, in 1936. I have described my literary relations with Middleton Murry in *Of Books and Humankind* (Essays presented to Bonamy Dobrie, ed. John Butt, 1964).

NOTES

1. The Folio reading is '. . . Caesar cannot leave to be ungentle'. Dr. S. A. Tannenbaum defends this as a blunder of Caesar's intended by Shakespeare. See *Shakespeare Studies*, No. 1, *Slips of the Tongue in Shakespeare*, New York, 1930.

2. Compare *Romeo and Juliet*, II. i. 1:

> Can I go forward when my heart is here?
> Turn back, dull earth, and find thy centre out.

3. Again, Dr. Tannenbaum suggests as a better punctuation:

> 'Where's Fulvia's process? "Caesar's" I would say!—Both?'

which seems an improvement. See *Slips of the Tongue in Shakespeare*, as quoted in my former note.

4. I find Mgr. Kolbe also compares Lady Macbeth with Eve: 'We no more shrink from Lady Macbeth than we do from our first mother Eve.' I think this comparison—to which mine may be partly indebted—important.

5. We find an imaginative parallel in the Crucifixion.

1951—Harold C. Goddard. "Antony and Cleopatra," from *The Meaning of Shakespeare*

Harold C. Goddard (1878-1950) was head of the English department at Swarthmore College. *The Meaning of Shakespeare*, a collection of his essays published after his death, is one of the most important twentieth-century books on Shakespeare's plays.

I

If one were asked to select the play of Shakespeare's that best represents all aspects of his genius and preserves the most harmonious balance among them, *Antony and Cleopatra* would be the inevitable choice. Here history, comedy, and tragedy are chemically combined; here the scope of the drama is world-wide; here sprawling and recalcitrant material is integrated with a constructive art that only many rereadings permit one to appreciate; here all the important characters of a huge cast are distinctly individualized, the central figures ranking among

Shakespeare's masterpieces; here the humor is so inherent that we do not think of it and could not conceivably speak of it as comic relief; here poetry of the highest order remains continually in keeping with the immense variety of scene and subject; here, finally, a conclusion that borrows touches from the death scenes of *Romeo and Juliet*, *Hamlet*, *Othello*, and *King Lear* blends them into what is in some respects the most complex, sustained, and magnificent piece of musical orchestration to be found anywhere in Shakespeare.

And yet, as Bradley has pointed out, this play can never compete with the four most famous Tragedies for the affections of readers. The chief reason for this seems to be that Antony and Cleopatra, compared with Shakespeare's other heroes and heroines, even the Macbeths, are a pair soiled and stained by long submersion in the world. Yet the peculiar effect at which Shakespeare was aiming in this instance is dependent on that very fact. As far back as *Richard III* Shakespeare had intimated that love is the natural first choice of all mankind, but that, defeated in love, the "strong" nature will turn next to power.

And therefore, since I cannot prove a lover . . .
I am determined

not "to prove a villain," as Richard had too crudely phrased it, but to get power without end. So analyzed, the thirst for power is a sort of revenge on life for the loss of love. To put love above any form of merely mundane achievement accords with the normal instincts of youthful human nature. When even maturity rates it first, its supremacy is asserted as it were a fortiori. Love, it is true, has usually lost some of its pristine quality when it appears late or in natures already tarnished with carnality, but its miraculousness may on that account actually be enhanced. All of which will appear impertinent to those who think that this play has to do with lust and not at all with love.

II

If the distinction is not held too rigidly nor pressed too far, it is interesting to think of Shakespeare's chief works as either love dramas or power dramas, or a combination of the two. In his Histories, the poet handles the power problem primarily, the love interest being decidedly incidental. In the Comedies it is the other way around, overwhelmingly in the lighter ones, distinctly in the graver ones, except in *Troilus and Cressida*—hardly comedy at all—where without full integration something like a balance is maintained. In the Tragedies both interests are important, but *Othello* is decidedly a love drama and *Macbeth* as clearly a power drama, while in *Hamlet* and *King Lear* the two interests often alternate rather than blend. *Antony and Cleopatra* is the one play of the author's in which they are completely fused.

Where criticism has most often fallen short, in my judgment, in dealing with this play has been in its failure to stress sufficiently the role of Octavius Caesar.

Octavius is the indispensable background against which Antony and Cleopatra must be seen and in contrast with which they take on their significance, for before the play is over Octavius has become practically a synonym for the Roman Empire. From this angle it might be said to be a study in the power of personality versus the impersonality of power. Antony and Cleopatra are two of the most vivid and most vital personalities Shakespeare ever drew. Octavius, save for a few moments when the man God intended him to be shines through, has no personality in any proper sense. He has sacrificed it to the place and position he holds and has identified himself with the power they afford him. It is as if he had extended himself so widely over his empire that there is nothing of himself left to reside within himself. It is precisely to emphasize that fact that the play is so spread out in space. Its geographical ramifications leave us with the feeling that this "universal landlord" in asserting his sway must have stretched himself very thin. The impression he produces on us, except in the rare moments mentioned, is one of coldness, of nullity, of death. And the impression is the stronger because of his many virtues. He is no villain like Richard III nor a man maddened by ambition like Macbeth. He is cold, like Iago, but instead of taking delight in the evil he does, he doesn't even know that it is evil. For aught he is aware of to the contrary he might be the noblest Roman of them all. He has intelligence, but not enough to have understood what Samuel Butler meant when he said "As we should not do evil that good may come, so we should not do good that evil may come." He might have smiled if he had heard the epigram, but would never have dreamed that it had any application to himself.

But trust Shakespeare not to let Octavius degenerate into a mere personification of power in the abstract. He keeps him human by a number of little touches. By convincing us of the sincerity of his love for his sister he multiplies many times the ignominy of his sacrifice of her to his career.

> No, my most wrong'd sister,

he tells her, speaking of Antony, on her return to Rome after her marriage,

> Cleopatra
> Hath nodded him to her. He hath given his empire
> Up to a whore.

He does not ask whether it is worse to give up one's empire to a whore or to give up one's sister to an empire. Yet it is in the same scene that he speaks those ringing stoic words:

> Cheer your heart.
> Be you not troubled with the time, which drives
> O'er your content these strong necessities;

But let determin'd things to destiny
Hold unbewail'd their way.

But such lines are exceptional and serve only to intensify by contrast his general effect on us, which is just the opposite of what we remarked in connection with Cordelia in *King Lear*. Cordelia is felt even when she is not present. Octavius is not felt even when he is. The negativeness of the impression in the face of the power he represents is the paradox—and the point. Who can doubt that it was intentionally contrived? And so, when we find Bradley writing, "Shakespeare, I think, took little interest in the character of Octavius," we can agree if he meant that Octavius was not the sort of man to excite the sympathy or admiration of Shakespeare, but we have to dissent completely if he means that the poet took little interest in depicting him. How could he have failed to take the deepest interest? From Richard III and Cardinal Pandulph and Henry IV on, Shakespeare's plays contain portrait after portrait of King Lear's "great ones" who ebb and flow by the moon. But judged in terms of territorial dominion securely held, Octavius Caesar is the greatest of the great. He actually attained the summit up the slippery slopes toward which so many other Shakespearean thirsters after power struggled—only to fall. Octavius did not fall, and the play leaves him in possession of pretty much all the known world. But what of it—the poet compels us to ask—if in the process he has lost his own soul? "How Shakespeare hated people who have no joy!" I heard a young reader of the play remark in connection with Octavius. His verb was too strong, but his insight was right. "How intolerable people are sometimes," says Chekhov, "who are satisfied and successful in everything." It is this capacity in Octavius Caesar to be successful in everything that drives both Antony and Cleopatra to fury. Antony perceives truly that it is Caesar's fortune, not Caesar, the empire that backs him, not the man, that he is up against. The very greatness of the forces on which he relies is a measure of their agent's littleness:

　　　　His coin, ships, legions,
May be a coward's; whose ministers would prevail
Under the service of a child as soon
As i' the command of Caesar. I dare him therefore
To lay his gay comparisons apart
And answer me declin'd, sword against sword,
Ourselves alone. I'll write it. Follow me.

Antony would challenge Caesar to a duel—and nothing would delight us more, as spectators, than to witness a personal encounter between the great warrior and the man who was once practically on his knees to him when he needed his help in conquering Pompey. But that time is past, and Enobarbus punctures Antony's foolish proposal in one of the wisest speeches in the play:

> Yes, like enough high-battl'd Caesar will
> Unstate his happiness and be stag'd to the show
> Against a sworder! I see men's judgements are
> A parcel of their fortunes, and things outward,
> Do draw the inward quality after them,
> To suffer all alike.

III

Nowhere in the drama, except at the very end, is the ridicule of worldly power more concentrated and effective than in the scene on Pompey's galley that concludes the second act. The situation is a counterpart of the one in *Julius Caesar* where we see the triumvirs seated around a table at a banquet of blood. Here they are again at a banquet, but this time, though it is there, they are unaware of the blood. Language fails in any attempt to characterize this incomparable scene. It is a fresh version of the skeleton at the feast. It is as perfect a fusion of burlesque and political wisdom as is to be found outside of Aristophanes, and yet, by a hair line, not burlesque. It is close to Shakespeare's last word on all the brands of intoxication. It is the spirit of tragedy masquerading as farce, the chariot of comedy driven by death. It is anything you please that is consummate.

In the preceding scene Pompey, relic of republican Rome, as someone has called him, talks loftily of Brutus and Cassius and of his purpose to be the avenger of his father; but by a slip in one of his tenses when he speaks of his navy

> with which I *meant*
> To scourge the ingratitude that despiteful Rome
> Cast on my noble father,

he gives away the fact that his purpose is already a thing of the past, and in the face of the "offers" of the triumvirate and the frank attitude of Antony, his defiance quickly melts into compliance. It ends by his inviting his new friends to a feast, and we are reminded of Enobarbus' reference to "thieves kissing." The scene shifts and we are on Pompey's galley.

"Music," the stage direction reads. "*Enter two or three* SERVANTS *with a banquet*." The music, in the circumstances, may be supposed to symbolize harmony, and as for "two or three servants," though only two speak, it surely should be three, for the whole point is that here is a little triumvirate in the world of servants to put in comparison with the Big Triumvirate that is about to enter. Comedy, from the beginning down to Bernard Shaw, has delighted in the servant who is superior to his master. It remained for Shakespeare to suggest that if the Roman Empire had to put itself in the hands of three men it might better have selected the servants who open the scene, one of whom in particular seems to be a man of high intelligence and moral perception. "To be called into a huge sphere, and not to be seen to move in't," he says, "are the holes where eyes should be, which pitifully disaster the cheeks." The remark was made of Lepidus, but, in view of what is to follow, it seems of wider application.

A sennet sounds, and the three owners of the earth enter. They are all drunk. Or at least Lepidus and Antony are, and even the cautious Caesar, before the scene is over, finds that his tongue "splits what it speaks." They are drunk in character, of course. Lepidus is maudlin- and stupid-drunk. "I am not so well as I should be, but I'll ne'er out." And he does indeed have to be carried out a little later. Antony is witty- or silly-drunk—or, if you will, a mixture of the two. His account, for Lepidus, of the character of the crocodile achieves a wisdom-in-inanity that reminds one of the wisdom-in-insanity of Lear. To Caesar, as we should expect, the revelry is distasteful. He grows cold and circumspect. He would not be a spoil-sport, but he does not intend to be taken off guard. He speaks only four times, and three of those four speeches are in deprecation of the proceedings:

> It's monstrous labour, when I wash my brain,
> And it grows fouler. . . .
> . . . I had rather fast from all four days
> Than drink so much in one. . . .
> What would you more? . . .
> . . . . . . our graver business
> Frowns at this levity. . . .
> . . . . . . the wild disguise hath almost
> Antick'd us all.

It is a side-splitting or a sorry spectacle according to taste when Enobarbus makes all those still capable of standing join hands and dance a drunken song. The seeming harmony is in inverse ratio to the real. Here is comedy at its acme, politics become visible.

If this be drunkenness, what is sobriety?

For full measure, Shakespeare gives us a sample of that too. One man, Menas, a "pirate" friend of Pompey's, has deliberately kept himself "from the cup," and, in the midst of the frolic, whispers in Pompey's ear the suggestion that they cut the cable, and then the throats of the triumvirs. Whereupon the world will be Pompey's. This is a sober proposal. Pompey replies in effect: O good Menas! but you should have done it first and told me afterward,

> In me 'tis villany;
> In thee 't had been good service.

After which, Pompey's talk about his "honour" coming before his "profit" sounds hollow, and we see it was fear, not moral scruples, that withheld him. What a situation! Here Shakespeare is plainly paying his compliments to the fatuousness of a humanity that can delegate all its power to three drunken men on a boat—let its destiny depend on the slender string of a galley's cable and the still slenderer string of one weak man's "honour."

There's a strong fellow, Menas,

says Enobarbus, pointing to the man who is carrying out the dead-drunk Lepidus.

> *Men.*: Why?
> *Eno.*: A'bears the third part of the world, man; see'st not?
> *Men.*: The third part, then, is drunk; would it were all,
> That it might go on wheels!

Power tends to go on concentrating. Lepidus was included in the triumvirate in the first place only in order to make the arrangement look more respectable. Three is a less autocratic number than two or one. But except numerically Lepidus has been a cipher from the start. And Antony is a vanishing fraction.

"We are three of them," says Trinculo in *The Tempest*; "if the other two be brained like us, the state totters." It is the perfect comment on this scene and the political moral of the play, for the three triumvirs are drunk throughout most of the drama in another sense: Lepidus with flattery and fawning; Antony with infatuation; Caesar with thirst for power. And when, at the end of the banquet, Menas, the pirate and would-be cutter of the cable, calls for drums, flutes, and trumpets to "bid a loud farewell to these great fellows" we are again reminded that through all the revelry death has been present, has even drawn his sword, though for the moment he decided to lay it aside.

IV

The same satire on power that is so evident in the galley scene appears more subtly throughout most of the play. Only "satire" is the wrong word. Satire is a conscious intellectual weapon wielded by the author. Shakespeare is above that. What he does is to turn their metaphors against these pretenders to worldly might until their own words fairly wink and whisper in mockery of them.

Recognizing the difficulty of friendship with Antony, Octavius declares,

> Yet if I knew
> What hoop should hold us stanch, from edge to edge
> O' the world I would pursue it.

As if the two were to be held together as a keg of liquor is—as indeed they were for a moment on Pompey's galley! Whereupon Agrippa, put up to it doubtless by Caesar, suggests that Octavia might well serve as this hoop, though of course he does not state it quite so baldly. But what power have you, Agrippa, Antony asks, to bring your suggestion to fruition?

> The power of Caesar, and
> His power unto Octavia,

Caesar himself interjects, and at that the "brothers" clasp hands as he seals the bargain:

> A sister I bequeath you (whom no brother
> Did ever love so dearly). Let her live
> To join our kingdoms (and our hearts),

while Lepidus, like a smirking justice-of-the-peace, puts an "amen" to the ridiculous ceremony. Octavius' legal figure ("bequeath") gives away the truth about this brother who thus disposes of his sister as if she were a feudal chattel, and justifies, as does the outcome, the liberty I have taken with the punctuation to distinguish the sincere from the insincere Caesar. That he himself has forebodings about that outcome is shown on his parting with his sister. "Most noble Antony," he says,

> Let not the piece of virtue which is set
> Betwixt us as the cement of our love,
> To keep it builded, be the ram to batter
> The fortress of it.

Octavia as cement is after all not much better than Octavia as battering ram. And the love of Antony and Caesar as a fortress is even more confusing. Octavius may exact the submission of kings and kingdoms, but his own imagination seems to be in a state of chronic rebellion. As an instrument of unconscious confession, however, it is perfect.

This same treachery of the metaphor extends to Octavius' friends. Thyreus, seeking to seduce Cleopatra from Antony to Caesar, declares,

> it would warm his spirits
> To hear from me you had left Antony
> And put yourself under his shroud,
> The universal landlord.

Landlord! That is the unkindest cut of all. And shroud! Thyreus of course means protection. But who can doubt what Shakespeare meant? There in perhaps the grimmest pun in the play he announces once for all that domination of the earth is death. The delusions to which it leads Octavius himself packs into the colossal irony of that mocking line:

> The time of universal peace is near.

But all these devices, bold and subtle, for wrecking Caesar in our estimations are as nothing beside Cleopatra's savage contempt for his power, and fierce derision of it. "'Tis paltry to be Caesar." The First Triumvir is "Fortune's knave" to her, "ass unpolicied," and his precious empire a dicer's paradise:

> The luck of Caesar, which the gods give men
> To excuse their after wrath.

This is no mere rationalization. Cleopatra is dying. The moment invests her words with something of the doom of those very gods.

V

And now, over against this Octavius who becomes more and more identified with Rome and rules by that impersonality of power for which the empire stands, Shakespeare puts Antony and Cleopatra—or perhaps we should say Cleopatra, and Antony in so far as he comes under her influence—who at their best, and even sometimes at less than their best, represent the power of personality to exact free obedience by what it is. The play has hardly opened when Antony, in the name of love and with a music that is unanswerable, hurls defiance once for all in the face of space and power:

> Let Rome in Tiber melt, and the wide arch
> Of the rang'd empire fall! Here is my space.
> Kingdoms are clay; our dungy earth alike
> Feeds beast as man; the nobleness of life
> Is to do thus. (*Embracing*)

The word "love" as it is commonly used in English is forced to cover a hundred shades of emotion from the highest spiritual and mystical feelings known to man down not only to sexual passion but to the basest perversions of it. It embraces literally both heaven and hell. The word means nothing until we know the context in which it is used. Yet its very confusion serves to convey the completeness with which man's loftiest and lowest experiences are entangled.

"God and the devil are fighting there and the battlefield is the heart of man." That great sentence of Dostoevsky's—in the mouth of Dmitri Karamazov—was spoken of beauty. It might equally well have been said of "love." And *Antony and Cleopatra* might have been written to confirm and amplify it.

Let us grant that the mutual attraction of Antony and Cleopatra at the opening of the play is not love in any very lofty sense; allow even that it may be an illusion. At least it is not a delusion as lust for power is, and illusions, as Emerson bids us remember, often have a habit of pointing to or even turning out to be the truth.

> There's not a minute of our lives should stretch
> Without some pleasure now.

Is this the gospel of self-indulgence or that pursuit of happiness that philosophy has so often declared to be the purpose of life? Is it a mere urge to squander vitality or a longing to embrace and comprehend existence? In this pair it appears to be the strangest mixture of the two. No one can deny, at any rate, that both Antony and Cleopatra are filled with a passionate thirst for life. They are afraid to lose one instant of it. They want to try it out in all its multifarious variety.

> But that your royalty
> Holds idleness your subject, I should take you
> For idleness itself,

says Antony, appearing to deny this hunger for experience on Cleopatra's part. But there is no contradiction. In her the categories of Idleness and Activity are transcended. The worst the play records of this pair is a debasement and waste of life, not a perversion of it as is the pursuit of power. To test all the potentialities of human emotion is at any rate a nobler thing than to collect kingdoms. In comparison, Octavius impresses us as an adolescent who has never outgrown the stage of playing with toy soldiers.

But Antony too, it will be said, was a seeker after power. He also was a world-sharer. True, and it was perhaps to show how far the poison of success could infect him that Shakespeare inserted that otherwise superfluous scene that opens Act III in which Ventidius is careful to give Antony credit for military triumphs with which personally he had nothing to do. But compared with Octavius, Antony never put his whole heart into conquest and government, and the Soothsayer is right in divining that the geniuses of the two men are antipodal. The spirit that keeps Antony is a celestial one. Only in the presence of Octavius' power-demon does it wilt into fear. Had he been an unreserved worshiper of power this "greatest soldier of the world" whose "soldiership is twice the other twain" would have eliminated his final competitor instead of being eliminated by him. Who can doubt it? But Antony was interested in something beside ruling others, and the difference between him and Octavius comes down in the end to one more instance of Shakespeare's old contrast between man and king, in this case man and emperor.

At heart Antony was no more interested in governing than was Hamlet, of whom indeed he is another fragment, one of the biggest. One is willing to wager that the passage of self-analysis in which Antony likens himself to the dissolving clouds and colors in the sky comes close to what Shakespeare in some moods thought of himself. It ties Antony indissolubly to the cloud passages in *Hamlet* and *The Tempest*, and shows the Hamletian powers of introspection that lay within a man whose active life had left them half-repressed. He embodies many of the paradoxes of the Prince of Denmark: strength and weakness, courage and irresolution, masterful manhood and feminine sensibility. He was passionate, rash, and self-indulgent. But he had compensating virtues. He was a military genius who saw beyond war, a ruler who had no craving to dominate, a conqueror to whom kings had been servants who treated his own servants as kings. He was neither resentful nor revengeful. He could admit his faults without false modesty. Such a combination of traits is irresistible. Enobarbus dies of a broken heart because, after long loyalty, he has at last deserted his declining master.[1] Eros—who had agreed to take, whenever he should demand it, the life of this man who had given him his freedom—kills himself rather than keep his promise. Even Octavius is genuinely moved at the news of Antony's end, and when Agrippa declares,

> A rarer spirit never
> Did steer humanity,

we pardon the exaggeration and for a moment almost believe it.

And so when this Herculean Roman turns from the conquest of the world to the conquest of the most complex and in many respects the most astonishing woman Shakespeare ever created, this woman to whom Julius Caesar and Pompey succumbed but against whose seductiveness Octavius Caesar appears proof, we cannot accept it as a mere act of dereliction, nor even as a descent. Rather, we see here the whole purpose and scheme of the play for the first time. It is the conquest of the earth versus the conquest of Earth. For Cleopatra is Earth.

It is no mere caprice that leads Antony to call her Egypt. Whatever she may be as an individual human being, she is also Woman in her infinite variety. And Woman is the Earth, as various in her different moods as the landscape under changing effects of light and shadow, sun and rain. "We cannot call her winds and waters sighs and tears; they are greater storms and tempests than almanacs can report." Cleopatra has all the moral neutrality of nature. There she is, like the soil, equally ready to produce the most noxious weed or the rarest flower. Will this Serpent of old Nile drag Antony down and strangle him in sensuality or will he lift her up to the level of his own guardian angel, who, as the Soothsayer has divined, is "noble, courageous, high, unmatchable"? That is the question. And, generalized, it is the question of questions for humanity itself, compared with which the conquests and reconquests of the earth that have gone on throughout history, doing and undoing themselves like so much weather, are of no interest whatever, not worth remembering, nothing. Until Cleopatra sends the lying message to Antony that she is dead, it looks as if she were to be his Dark Lady and he her victim. And then something else happens.

VI

It is not by chance that Shakespeare puts the description of the meeting of Antony and Cleopatra at Cydnus right after the account of the selling of his sister by Octavius to Antony. Caesar issues his orders and Octavia obeys. Cleopatra does not have to issue orders. The winds fall in love with the very sails of the barge she sits in. The water is amorous of its oars and follows faster. Boys and maids, like Cupids and Nereides, fan and tend her. The city pours out its multitudes to behold her. But for the gap it would have left in nature, the air itself would have gone to gaze on her.

> I saw her once,

says Enobarbus,

> Hop forty paces through the public street;
> And having lost her breath, she spoke, and panted,
> That she did make defect perfection
> And, breathless, power breathe forth.

Here is power of another species than power military or political. Cleopatra's beauty may have been more the Dionysian beauty of vitality than the Apollonian beauty of form, but whatever it was it justifies Keats's dictum:

> 'tis the eternal law
> That first in beauty should be first in might.

And yet the magnetism that emanates from her at her first meeting with Antony at Cydnus is mere witchcraft and magic compared with the authentic "fire and air" that descends on her before her second immortal meeting with him at the end.

It is this magic and witchcraft that captivate Antony in the first place.

> I must from this enchanting queen break off.

The adjective shows that it is with the semi-mythological Cleopatra, the ancestral image of Woman she evokes within him, the gypsy, Egypt, the Serpent of old Nile, that he is in love. The fascination is mutual, and she in turn endows him with superhuman attributes. He is anything to her from the demi-Atlas of the Earth to Mars. The tradition that Antony was descended from Hercules, son of Zeus, abets this cosmic overvaluation of the human being, as does, for him, her assumption of the role of the goddess Isis. In so far as these things amount to a conscious affectation or attribution of divinity—and, even more, a willingness to make political use of them—they degrade the pair deeply in our estimations, proving them victims not only of infatuation with each other but of a self-infatuation far less excusable. But infatuation, analyzed, generally turns out to be more a failure to locate the origin of compelling forces from underneath or from overhead than mere vanity, folly, or egotism in the usual sense. "No man," says Robert Henri, "ever overappreciated a human being." And so when Cleopatra, about to part from Antony, exclaims,

> Eternity was in our lips and eyes,
> Bliss in our brows bent; none our parts so poor
> But was a race of heaven,

it strikes us less as affectation of divinity than as genuine perception of the divine element in love-insight into the heart of something which their wildest words about each other are abortive or rapturous attempts to express. In such poetry as Cleopatra attains in those three lines the illusion becomes almost indistinguishable from the truth.

Far more subtly than in the case of Cleopatra and earth, Shakespeare suggests correspondingly that Antony is like the sun. Not until near the end does this analogy shine forth so clearly that we know the author must have intended it. But looking back we can see that he has insinuated it from the beginning. Granted that if Antony is the sun he is an intermittent and often obscured luminary, uncertain of his course across the heavens and subject to frequent total eclipse or worse, as when he orders Caesar's emissary whipped and sends word that, if Caesar does not like it, he may "whip, or hang, or torture" an enfranchised bondman of Antony's in requital. But these things strike us as mere aberrations of that real Antony in whose presence alone Cleopatra germinates and blossoms and matures into her full self as does the earth under the sun. Antony's power to attract and hold men in his sphere is sun-like also, as is the bounty he dispenses as freely and widely in his degree as the sun does his warmth. It was Eros who referred to his face as

> that noble countenance
> Wherein the worship of the whole world lies.

Yet this is a sun that, reversing all known laws of heavenly bodies, when the planet he should illuminate and hold in her course flies off at a tangent at the Battle of Actium, follows ignominiously after her. What wonder that he cries, when he realizes what he has done:

> Hark! the land bids me tread no more upon't!
> It is asham'd to bear me. . . .
> *Cleo.*: O, my lord, my lord,
> Forgive my fearful sails! I little thought
> You would have follow'd.
> *Ant.*: Egypt, thou knew'st too well
> My heart was to thy rudder tied by the strings,
> And thou shouldst tow me after. O'er my spirit
> Thy full supremacy thou knew'st, and that
> Thy beck might from the bidding of the gods
> Command me.

But the shame is not the whole story. Even here Shakespeare seems less interested in the outcome of the Battle of Actium than in the nature of that force that at the height of the action can obliterate utterly in the mind of this greatest soldier of the world all thought of military conquest and glory, all concern for what the world will think of his disgrace. Here is a mystery indeed. In the Battle of Actium, war and love—or at least war and something akin to love—grapple, and war wins. Yet does it win? To deepen the enigma the poet proceeds to show that it is precisely out of the dishonor and defeat that the spiritual triumph emerges which is always found at the heart of the highest tragedy. More and more as it nears its end, *Antony and Cleopatra* seems to recede from mere history into myth, or, if you will, to open out and mount above history into a cosmic sunset of imagination.

Sunset is the inevitable figure, and Antony himself gives us the cue for it in the superlative passage in which he compares himself with black vesper's pageants.

But even before this, Shakespeare has given our imaginations a hint of the element into which the action is to pass when it rises above earth. In a little scene that reminds one of nothing so much as the opening of *Hamlet*, a group of soldiers discuss rumors of strange happenings about the streets. Suddenly mysterious music is heard. Where is it? "Under the earth," says one.

> 'Tis the god Hercules, whom Antony lov'd,
> Now leaves him,

says another. But still another one (of rarer sensibility than the others, we cannot but believe) locates the sound in the air. It is a premonition of the transubstantiation that is to overtake Antony in defeat. In defeat he puts off the strength and renown that are like those of his mythical ancestor, and with them, by implication, his spurious claim to divinity through descent from the gods, putting on, in exchange, the true divinity of his own guardian angel who, as the Soothsayer foresaw, is the enemy and the opposite of the demon of power. Antony's metaphor of the sunset is but a confirmation of this scene, adding, however, the element of fire to the element of air.

The marks of a sunset are beauty and insubstantiality—a splendor that makes whatever it touches more real than earth, a transiency that makes it seem less than a dream. It is all in the evanescence and dissolution of the shapes and colors in the sky that Antony sees the likeness to himself:

> Here I am Antony;
> Yet cannot hold this visible shape.

But we see more than that. Only when the sun nears or goes under the horizon do men catch a glimpse reflected on the clouds of what they dared not gaze on directly when it was overhead. The sun, when it goes down, has an alchemic power to transmute the material world into its own substance.[2] It is the same with a great man when he dies. The world in which he had lived is lit up with his afterglow; the common scene where he once walked seems changed into a vision. This is the miracle that Antony, dead, performs on Cleopatra. His devotion to her, even unto death, is what does it, bringing to the surface at last a Cleopatra that his love has long been shaping underneath. In this revolution of everything, Cleopatra the enchantress disappears forever—except in so far as she survives as the willing servant of the new Cleopatra that takes her place. So fully does this new Cleopatra realize the splendor of Antony at death that her memory of him transforms what little of life is left for her on earth into heaven. She enters heaven, as it were, in advance. And we enter it with her.

VII

Incredibly, many readers and critics find in the conclusion of *Antony and Cleopatra* only the old Cleopatra, thinking at bottom just of herself, bent above all things on saving herself from being shown in Caesar's triumph. That the old Cleopatra, bent on precisely this end and with every histrionic device still at her command, is still present cannot indeed be questioned. But that she is now the only or the predominant Cleopatra everything in the text converges to deny. What has happened is that a new Cleopatra is now using the old Cleopatra as her instrument. It is the new one who issues the orders. It is the old one who obeys.

When Cleopatra, frightened by Antony's reaction to his belief that she has betrayed him and caused the surrender of his fleet, sends word to him that she is dead, it is the culmination of Cleopatra the actress and deceiver, of the woman who will go to any extreme to attain her end. Little does she realize at the moment—though soon afterward she has a premonition of what she has done—that by her lie she has thrust a sword into the man she loves and who loves her even unto death, as certainly as if she had done it with her own hand. But from the moment when the dying Antony is lifted into her monument and she finds no word of reproach on his lips for what she has done, scales seem to drop from her eyes, and never from then on does she waver in her undeviating resolution to join him in death. What looks like hesitation and toying with the thought of life is but deception utilized with the highest art to make certain that her determination to die is not thwarted. The fact is that the new Cleopatra, with all the histrionic devices of the old Cleopatra at her command, acts so consummately in these last hours of her life that she deceives not only Octavius Caesar but full half the readers of the play. She stages a mousetrap beside which Hamlet's seems melodramatic and crude, enacts its main role herself, and, unlike the Prince of Denmark, keeps her artistic integrity by never for a second revealing in advance what its purpose is or interrupting its action for superfluous comment. Blinded by victory and the thought of his triumph in which she is to figure, Octavius is clay in her hands, infatuated in a sense and to a degree that she and her lover never were. She twists him, as it were, around her little finger. If this still be acting, it is acting of another order. It is no longer "art" vaingloriously exhibited as personal triumph or the pride of personal power. It is art, rather, tragically impressed in the service of death. Those who think that Cleopatra is driven to suicide only when she is certain that if she does not kill herself she will be shown in Caesar's triumph are taken in by her as badly as is Caesar himself.

The text corroborates this interpretation to the point of supererogation. Antony in almost his last words begs Cleopatra to seek of Caesar her honor and her safety. "They do not go together," she replies with a ringing finality. Trust none about Caesar but Proculeius, Antony adds.

My resolution and my hands I'll trust;
None about Caesar.

Who cannot hear the tone in which that "none" is uttered, and who can fail to understand from that reference to her hands that her determination to do away with herself is already taken? Antony dies, and no one will ever debate, as in the case of Lady Macbeth, whether the swoon into which Cleopatra falls is genuine or not. It is as if in those few moments of unconsciousness she visits some other world and comes back divested forever of all mere earthly royalty. Now for the first time she is a woman—and not Woman.

No more but e'en a woman,

are her first words as consciousness returns,

> and commanded
> By such poor passion as the maid that milks
> And does the meanest chares.

It is as if she must compensate for having been queen by being not merely a woman, but the humblest of women, a menial, a servant. And as the fourth act ends, she confirms to Iras and Charmian the promise she made to Antony before he expired:

> We'll bury him; and then, what's brave, what's noble,
> Let's do it after the high Roman fashion,
> And make death proud to take us. . . .
> Ah women, women! come; we have no friend
> But resolution, and the briefest end.

Resolution: it is the same word she had used to Antony. This Egyptian has become a Roman, not an imperial Roman like Caesar, but a noble Roman like the angel of her own Emperor—

Noble, courageous, high, unmatchable.

The change in Cleopatra is again confirmed in the first words we hear from her in the last act:

> My desolation does begin to make
> A better life.

Better!—a word, in that sense, not in the lexicon of the original Cleopatra. The rapidity of the change going on within her is registered in another word in the message she sends by Proculeius to Caesar:

> I *hourly* learn
> A doctrine of obedience.

Caesar, poor fool, thinks, as she intends he shall, that it is obedience to his will that she is hourly learning. But it is obedience to her own new self and to her own Emperor, Antony, to which she of course refers. The very words with which she hoodwinks Octavius most completely are made to express, on another level, the highest fidelity to her own soul. When Caesar first enters her presence, she kneels to him:

> *Caes.*: Arise, you shall not kneel.
> I pray you, rise; rise, Egypt.

He wishes to dupe her into thinking she can still remain a queen. But to be a queen in that sense is the last thing that she wishes.

> *Cleo.*: Sir, the gods
> Will have it thus; my master and my lord
> I must obey.

"You, Caesar, are now my lord and master; I have no choice but to kneel and obey," Caesar thinks she means. It sounds like obeisance to the point of prostration. But what Cleopatra is really saying is that she now listens only to divine commands. She must obey her master and her lord, her Emperor Antony, not the mere emperor of this world to whom she is kneeling in mockery.

The interlude with her treasurer Seleucus is to the undiscerning overwhelming proof that Cleopatra is still angling for life, if she can only get it on her own terms. But surely this is the old histrionic Cleopatra placing all her art at the disposal of the new Cleopatra who is bent only on death and immortal life. Whether this little play within the play was planned in advance in consultation with Seleucus and he too is acting, or whether it is a piece of inspired improvisation on her part alone, struck off at the instant of her treasurer's betrayal of her, makes little difference. The reason Cleopatra kept back some of her treasures is the same in either case: to throw the gullible Caesar off the track of her intention. How completely he is deluded by her hint that she is planning to sue with gifts for the mediation of Livia and Octavia! It is the old wily Cleopatra of course who knows how to devise this trap, and her undertone of exultation at her success in springing it is heard almost to the end. But the wily Cleopatra is now the mere servant of another Cleopatra who is intent only on her own freedom, to whom traps for others are nothing except as they help her to escape from the trap that has been set for her.

Caesar is so beguiled that he makes a fulsomely magnanimous speech in which he thinks he is finally ensnaring his victim but in which he is really only entangling himself. His comparisons and metaphors, as usual, fairly blurt out the very truth he is trying to conceal. "Caesar's no merchant," he protests, revealing that a merchant is precisely what he is at heart. "Feed, and sleep," he advises—as if

Cleopatra were a beast being fattened for the slaughter and he were already licking his lips at the prospect. "My master, and my lord!" once more, is all she says. To him the words confirm her abject submission. To her—however aware she may be of the irony—they are no less than a prayer to Antony for strength. "Not so," says the overconfident Caesar, seeming to reject her obeisance, as he goes out. The two words, as he means them, are the mark that his self-stultification is complete. But, in a sense he could never divine, they are the very truth echoed from Cleopatra's heart.

> He words me, girls, he words me, that I should not
> Be noble to myself,

she cries the moment she is alone with her women. His pretended mercy has not fooled her.

> But hark thee, Charmian,

and she whispers in her maid's ear. What she tells her of course is that she has already ordered the instrument of death, the asp.

> I have spoke already, and it is provided,

and bids her "Go, put it to the haste." This tiny incident is calmly left out of account by those who think that Cleopatra has been seriously debating between life and death in the previous scene and that the interlude with her treasurer is just what it seems to be—a provision for avoiding death if a way of escape with safety to her person should present itself at the last moment. Caesar, as I said, is not the only one these scenes deceive.

Shakespeare sees to it that it is only *after* this sending for the asp, with its clear implication that the die is cast, that Dolabella—with one exception the last of many men to come under Cleopatra's spell—confides to her the fact that Caesar does indeed intend the worst. The effect of the information is merely to fortify further what needs no fortifying.

Left alone with Iras, Cleopatra draws a final picture of the fate she has escaped. Charmian returns from her errand.

> Now, Charmian,

she cries without a second's hesitation,

> Show me, my women, like a queen; go fetch
> My best attires; I am again for Cydnus
> To meet Mark Antony. . . . Bring our crown and all.

Here, it will be said, Cleopatra gives the lie to everything I have just been saying. Here, once for all, she proclaims herself actress, first, last, and forever. As if she were about to appear upon the stage, she calls for her costume, her robe and crown. Once more she will assume the role of queen—in her "best attires." She will play-act the very act of death. The woman is an incorrigible exhibitionist.

On the contrary, it is the extreme opposite of all this, I believe, that Shakespeare intends. We become new not so much by rejecting the old as by imparting to the old a new meaning. So here. What we have is not the old Cleopatra reverting to the theatrical and all its meretriciousness, but a new Cleopatra, rather, aspiring to make the symbol indistinguishable from the thing, to rise into that region where art is lifted into life and life into art, the goal, alike, of art and life.

As the clown brings the asp, she cries:

> I have nothing
> Of woman in me; now from head to foot
> I am marble-constant, now the fleeting moon
> No planet is of mine.

What follows confirms this inversion and reversal. (And we can be the more confident of this interpretation because, strangely, however much more swift, the change in Cleopatra parallels a change of like character in her creator, who, as in the cases of Falstaff and Hamlet, has endowed her with not a little of his own dramatic genius. Shakespeare, by his own confession, was at one time almost "subdued" by the theater, and his evolution traces his successful effort to elude its grasp. From *The Comedy of Errors* to *Antony and Cleopatra*, the story is one of the gradual subjection of the theatrical to the poetical. Cleopatra's development is a sort of parable of Shakespeare's. "Shakespeare led a life of allegory: his works are the comments on it.")

Four times, in her haste to be rid of him, Cleopatra says "farewell" to the loquacious clown who has brought the asp. When he is gone and Iras has returned, she begins her own farewell:

> Give me my robe, put on my crown; I have
> Immortal longings in me. Now no more
> The juice of Egypt's grape shall moist this lip. . . .

As she renounces the intoxicants of earth a celestial intoxication comes over her—she feels herself being transmuted from earth into fire and air. Whoever, as he listens to her, does not feel, in however diminished degree, a like effect within himself, misses, I believe, one of the supreme things in Shakespeare. The atmosphere of sunset—which Charmian's single phrase, "O eastern star!" turns into sunrise—the universal character of every image and symbol, and above all perhaps the sublimity of the verse, conspire with the action itself to produce this alchemic effect. Here, if ever, is the harmony that mitigates tragedy, the harmony, better say, that creates it.

VIII

Whoever questions or is insensible to all this should consider the contrast between the two meetings of Antony and Cleopatra at "Cydnus," the earthly meeting as described by Enobarbus, and the spiritual meeting to which the death scene is the vestibule. Around these two passages, as we can see fully only when we have finished the play and hold it off in perspective, the drama is described as an ellipse is about its two foci. The antithesis between them is complete: the "poetry" of the senses versus the poetry of the imagination. In the first we have Cleopatra as the earthly Venus, enveloped in incense, waited on by everything from the winds to the populace, conscious to the last degree, we cannot but feel, of the universal adulation. Antony is absent, and is brought in at the end almost as an afterthought. In the second he is in a sense more present than she is, and she unconscious of everything save him, her Emperor, whom she is about to meet—of him, and of the courage with which his love has endowed her. The only memories that cross her mind of a world that "is not worth leave-taking" are those of its emperor that by contrast serve to make her Emperor great. "Ass unpolicied"! It is her Last Judgment on all Caesars—hers and Shakespeare's—the revenge of poetry, which is the politics of heaven, on empire. For the rest, what unprecedented words on the lips of Cleopatra: "husband," "baby," "nurse"! Even that "kiss" which it is to be her heaven to have is of another order from the many thousand kisses that Antony once placed upon her lips, of which his dying one, he thought, was the "poor last." The first meeting at Cydnus, as Enobarbus gives it to us, is like an immense tapestry or historical picture, a word painting, just the overdecorated sort of thing that the world mistakes for supreme art. The second is more than the greatest art. It is an apocalypse.

IX

Yet, even after this, Shakespeare, incredibly, has something in reserve, the most miraculous single touch in the whole play, a touch that, like a flash of lightning at night, illuminates everything.

Caesar enters. He is first told the truth and then looks down upon it. The sight seems to lift him outside of himself. Quite as if he had overheard those earlier words of Cleopatra,

I dream'd there was an Emperor Antony.
O, such another sleep, that I might see
But such another man,

and had come to declare that prayer answered, he exclaims:

> she looks like sleep,
> As she would catch another Antony
> In her strong toil of grace.

Another Antony indeed, her Emperor! Whatever has happened elsewhere, here on earth, in those perfect words, the lovers are reunited. And Octavius, of all men, spoke them!

Many, including Bradley (who says that to him they sound more like Shakespeare than Octavius), have declared the lines out of character, entirely too imaginative for this boy politician whom Cleopatra herself derided so unmercifully. They are. And yet they are not. And when we see why they are not we have seen into the heart of the play.

Caesar, practically alone, has shown himself immune to the fascination of this woman, and only now is he in a position to realize how utterly, even at his own game, she has outplotted and outwitted him, led him, as it were, by the nose. Conqueror as he is, she has dragged him behind the chariot of her superior insight and power. But all that now is nothing to him, less than nothing, not even remembered, and, gazing down as if entranced, this man, who had been cold to her and to her beauty while she lived, utters the most beautiful words ever spoken of her. Dead, she proves more powerful than the most powerful of men alive. She makes him realize that there is something mightier than might, something stronger than death. She kindles the poet within him. She catches him in her strong toil of grace. She leads him in her triumph!

X

Nothing in his works perhaps illustrates better than the conclusion of *Antony and Cleopatra* what I have called the integrity of Shakespeare, by which I mean the psychic interdependence of those works and their consequent power to illuminate one another.

The imaginative germ of *Antony and Cleopatra* is found in Romeo's opening speech in the fifth act of *Romeo and Juliet*:

> I dreamt my lady came and found me dead—
> Strange dream, that gives a dead man leave to think!
> And breath'd such life with kisses in my lips
> That I reviv'd and was an emperor.

So specific is this, down even to the conception of a spiritual emperor, that it not merely presages the situation at the end of *Antony and Cleopatra* but is a perfect comment on and interpretation of its transcendental meaning.

Cleopatra and Othello seem incongruous figures to connect. Yet Cleopatra in the end is in the same position as Othello: she has killed the one she loves, not with her own hand, to be sure, as he did, but not less actually. And in one respect her situation is far worse. He did his deed under a complete delusion, but in good faith. She did hers by a lie that was wantonly selfish. But if Cleopatra and Othello make strange companions, Antony and Desdemona make even stranger ones—the greatest soldier in the world and the simplest and most modest girl. Yet here the link is even closer—and we remember Othello's greeting, "O my fair warrior!" Desdemona dies with no reproach for the wrong he has done her, and when he discovers the truth he is shaken to the foundation by a profound spiritual change. Similarly, not one word, not one thought, of the part Cleopatra has played in his death crosses Antony's lips, or his mind, in his last moments. Instead he merely says:

I am dying, Egypt, dying; only
I here importune death awhile, until
Of many thousand kisses the poor last
I lay upon thy lips.

Here is the counterpart of Desdemona's last words:

Commend me to my kind lord. O, farewell!

and here the only conceivable cause commensurable with the change effected in Cleopatra. If it seems a more incredible change than that which occurs in Othello, it is because Othello had from the first a nobility to which the earlier Cleopatra could make no claim. The motif of the transcendental reunion of the lovers, which is only faintly hinted at and kept wholly in the overtones in *Othello*, becomes the main theme, openly announced and developed like music, at the end of *Antony and Cleopatra*. It is as if what the violins vaguely suggested there were played here by the full orchestra. At last we know that we were not deceived in what we hardly dared believe we heard in the earlier play.

But it is *King Lear* that comes closest of all. King Lear, summing up a dozen figures that preceded him, shows that it is greater to be a man than to be a king, greater to be a king in the imaginative than in the worldly sense. Antony's story says the same. He refuses to sacrifice to the Roman Empire his heritage as a man. He shows that it is greater to be an Emperor in Romeo's and Cleopatra's sense than to be emperor of the earth. "A man needs but six feet of ground," an old proverb has it, and though he has owned the whole earth six feet is enough when he has become a corpse. Even having been a universal landlord will not help him. "The earth I have seen cannot bury me," said Thoreau in one of the most astonishing sentences that even his genius ever struck off. The conclusion of *Antony and Cleopatra* makes clear what he meant.

The analogy between King Lear and Cleopatra is even more striking than that between King Lear and Antony, if for no other reason than that a contrast between the sexes is here involved. Just as Lear had to lose his title and recognize that he was only

> a very foolish fond old man
> Fourscore and upward, not an hour more or less,

before he could regain his kingdom as spiritual King, so Cleopatra had to realize that she was

> No more but e'en a woman, and commanded
> By such poor passion as the maid that milks
> And does the meanest chares,

before she could become a spiritual Queen worthy to meet her Emperor. Through humility both Lear and Cleopatra discover their humanity. Anger and violence in him are tamed to patience. Pride and passion in her are lifted to love. So faithful even in detail is Shakespeare to his earlier pattern that Lear's crown and robe of weeds and common flowers is the very counterpart of Cleopatra's symbolic robe and crown which she puts on before her death. And yet—what could be more splendidly different from the piercingly swift and simple ending of *King Lear* than the prolonged sunset glory of *Antony and Cleopatra*? The difference corresponds precisely to the two characters. But the likeness goes deeper than the difference. The end of the earlier play gives us a single lightning-like glimpse into heaven; that of the other ushers us to its very threshold.

Further plays, *Troilus and Cressida* especially, afford more comparisons and contrasts. But we must restrict ourselves to a last one, a link with *Hamlet* which is of another sort. When the Prince of Denmark discovers the truth about the poisoned rapier and realizes that he is trapped, he turns it on the King with the cry,

> The point envenom'd too!
> Then, venom, to thy work.

Cleopatra, as she applies the asp to her breast, exclaims:

> Poor venomous fool,
> Be angry, and dispatch.

It is as if Shakespeare had chosen the dying Cleopatra to make his ultimate comment on the dedication to the most futile of human passions, revenge, of the most gifted character he ever created.

XI

Antony and Cleopatra may be taken not only by itself, but as the final part of Shakespeare's Roman trilogy—*Coriolanus, Julius Caesar, Antony and Cleopatra*—last not in order of composition but in historical sequence. Coriolanus, Brutus, Antony; Volumnia-Virgilia, Portia, Cleopatra: the men, and even more the women, give us a spiritual history of Rome from its austere earlier days, through the fall of the republic, to the triumph of the empire. What lights and shadows, what contrasts and illuminations this immense canvas affords, surpassing even those in each of the separate plays! Only in the light of the whole, for instance, is the full futility of the conspiracy of Cassius and Brutus evident. This is Shakespeare's historical masterpiece.

Considered as three related Tragedies or even as a tragic trilogy, there are notes of triumph and even of hope to redeem the suffering at the end of each play and at the end of the whole. But considered as a single history or as the story of the evolution of imperialism, there is little but disillusionment and a sense of the predestined tendency of freedom, when it has once been wrested from slavery, to return again to slavery as if in a perpetual circle.

Can anyone doubt for a moment whether Shakespeare considered the tragic-poetical or the historical-political the profounder way of regarding life? Certainly the last thing Shakespeare was offering us at the end of his trilogy was any doctrine of "all for love" in the cheap popular sense of that phrase as suggested by the title of Dryden's famous version of the story of Antony and Cleopatra. But he certainly is saying that there is something in life in comparison with which battles and empires are of no account. As statesman and soldier it was Antony's duty to fight to the bitter end at the Battle of Actium for his half of the empire. If he had, at the price of depriving the world of the story of Antony and Cleopatra—including Shakespeare's play—is it certain that the world would be better off? The destiny of the world is determined less by the battles that are lost and won than by the stories it loves and believes in. That is a hard saying for hardheaded men to accept, but it is true. Stories are told, grow old, and are remembered. Battles are fought, fade out, and are forgotten—unless they beget great stories. We put up massive monuments to military heroes because otherwise their very names will be erased. We do not need to put up monuments to great poets nor to those heroes they have made immortal.

Antony was at times a pitiably weak man. His conduct at Actium was ignominious and shameful. But instead of trying to deify that weakness, saying foolish things like Richard II and the later Hamlet about angels and divinities, and killing under their supposed sanction, in the end he forgot, like Desdemona and Cordelia, that he had been sinned against and went on loving the one who had injured him. Was that not better than winning the Battle of Actium or any other battle? He that ruleth himself is better than he that taketh a city. And the weaker the man is, Shakespeare seems to add, the greater the victory.

NOTES

1. Shakespeare slips in an illuminating contrast here. When Enobarbus deserts *from* Antony, Antony accepts the act as if he were himself to blame and sends his friend's treasure after him to Caesar's camp. But when Alexas deserts *to* Caesar, and induces the Jewish Herod to shift his allegiance with him, Caesar hangs him for his pains.

2. Compare the 33d sonnet for alchemy at sunrise.

1972—Anne Barton. " 'Nature's Piece 'Gainst Fancy': The Divided Catastrophe in *Antony and Cleopatra*," from *An Inaugural Lecture* (to the Hildred Carlile Chair of English Literature in the University of London tenable at Bedford College)

Anne Barton is a fellow of Trinity College, Cambridge, and a highly respected Shakespearean scholar. She is a frequent contributor to the *New York Review of Books* and the author of *Shakespeare and the Idea of the Play* and *Essays, Mainly Shakespeare*, among other books.

When Ajax, in Sophocles' play, announces that from now on he will humble himself before heaven, that he is going down to the sea to cleanse himself of blood and to bury Hector's unlucky sword, it seems for a moment that there will be no tragedy. The hero's words, however, were double-edged. When he reaches the sea, Ajax buries the sword of Hector in his own heart. Abruptly, the rejoicings of the Chorus turn to lamentation. Tecmessa discovers and shrouds her husband's body. Ajax's brother Teucer points bitterly to the ineluctable nature of divine will. The tragic movement of the play appears, at this point, to have completed itself. We have lived through a reversal and a discovery and, whatever Aristotle really meant by *catharsis*, it seems that we have had the experience or something like it: have participated in and been changed by pity and fear. It seems positively perverse that Sophocles should not only extend his tragedy beyond this climactic moment, but extend it for almost four hundred lines. Why, when he could have ended with Ajax's heroic death and the valedictions of Teucer and the Chorus did he insist upon a long, unpredictable final movement occupied entirely by the struggle between Teucer, Menelaus, Agamemnon and Odysseus over the issue of whether Ajax's body should be buried properly, or simply left above ground to rot?

Some very unkind things have been said over the years about the construction of Sophocles' *Ajax*. Indeed, "broken-backed" is a comment that can still be heard. The trouble is that Sophocles seems to have had a puzzling predilection for these severed spinal columns. Of the seven complete tragedies which survive, no fewer than three are "broken-backed" or, to use a term that I personally much prefer, possess a "divided catastrophe." The first three quarters of *The Women of Trachis* concerns Deianira, the neglected and ageing wife of Heracles. When her son tells her that the "love-charm" she sent to her husband has destroyed him, she says farewell to the household things which symbolised her marriage, and then kills herself with a sword. Her body is displayed to the horrified Chorus of Trachinian women, and an ending seems imminent. Instead, the tragedy lurches forward again as Heracles himself, a character hitherto present only in name, suddenly arrives in Trachis to die. Not only is the last movement of the tragedy wholly taken up with Heracles: it dismisses and diminishes Deianira in a way for which neither the title of the tragedy nor its previous development has left the audience prepared. Heracles is not even interested in the revelation that his wife was innocent, deceived by the centaur, and that she now is dead. She is important, to him and to everyone else, only as the agent of his fate.

On the whole, the Antigone has been more lavishly admired than either the *Ajax* or *The Women of Trachis*. It too, however, achieves a tragic climax and then, without warning, presses on beyond it. Antigone gives her name to the tragedy, and dominates most of it. Sophocles sends her to her death with full tragic honours. Then, almost slightingly, he forgets her to focus on Creon: a man who has appeared previously as an oppressor riding for a fall, but not really as a tragic protagonist whose annihilation could carry the whole, concluding section of the play. Sophocles even frustrates expectation by refusing to bring Antigone's body on stage at the end, to join the bodies of Creon's wife and son. It is as though he feared that, by allowing her to take her logical and natural place in this final tableau of death, he might blur the double, the essentially divided nature of the catastrophe.

No one, and most certainly not Sophocles, constructs plays in so eccentric a fashion out of carelessness or dramatic ineptitude. The risks are too obvious, the difficulty of making a divided catastrophe effective too great. It would seem more sensible to inquire into the rewards offered by a procedure so wayward, so consciously determined to defeat an audience's normal conviction that tragic action will wind itself up—as it does in Sophocles' *Oedipus Rex*—to a single, unmistakable catastrophe in which subsidiary disasters (like Jocasta's suicide) resemble the moons which circle round Jupiter: more or less simultaneous attendants, not planets in their own right. I think myself that a dramatist is likely to experiment with a divided catastrophe when he wants and needs, for some reason, to alter the way his audience has been responding to the experience of the play. Basically, it's a way of forcing reappraisal, a radical change of viewpoint just at that penultimate moment when our complacency is likely to be greatest: when we are tempted as an audience to feel superior or even dismissive because we think we understand everything.

It is important here to distinguish between the divided catastrophe and the use of the deus ex machina. When the deified Heracles descends to break the deadlock at the end of Sophocles' *Philoctetes*, when the sun-chariot comes for Medea, or Apollo forcibly prevents arson and murder at the end of Euripides' *Orestes*, we feel that the play has simply been picked up by the scruff of the neck and artificially reversed. These endings are enormously effective, but they are also ostentatiously fictional. Particularly in the hands of Euripides, the deus ex machina ending parades its own falsehood. It reminds us of the gap between the myth as it has traditionally been told and the more dispiriting and untidy but also more convincing truth of the play. A coda rather than an organic final movement, this sudden intrusion of the supernatural operates in most cases to reinforce the first, or realistic, conclusion: a conclusion expressed in terms of uresolvable human muddle and mess.

Both the deus ex machina and the divided catastrophe are ways in which dramatists can grapple with the immemorial problem of endings in fiction. Conclusions, as Frank Kermode has stated in his brilliant book *The Sense of an Ending*, are really satisfactory only when they "frankly transfigure the events in which they were immanent." Otherwise, they are likely to seem negative, an artificial absence of continuation reminding us uncomfortably that the shapeliness and pattern which art imposes upon life is unnatural anyway, and never more so than in the false finality, the arbitrarily unified focus, of most tragedy fifth acts. The deus ex machina ending deals with the problem by admitting that it is a spurious transfiguration: self-consciously fictional. The divided catastrophe operates differently. In its unpredictability, its very untidiness, it seems to reflect not the dubious symmetries of art but life as we normally experience it in a world where events invariably straggle on beyond the point that art would regard as climactic. When used with skill, the divided catastrophe achieves a genuine transfiguration of the events in which it was immanent. It imposes a new angle of vision, an alteration of emphasis which, while it need not conflict with the previous development of the tragedy, will certainly modify our understanding of that development from a point beyond it in time.

Because, for all their apparent disjunctiveness, endings of this kind rise out of, and qualify, an entire and particular dramatic complex, no two divided catastrophes are exactly alike. In the case of the *Ajax*, Sophocles obviously wanted his audience to respond fully and emotionally to Ajax himself as a great, almost superhuman figure. E. R. Dodds was at least partly right when he described this play as a unique example of a shame-culture as opposed to a guilt-culture tragedy. Ajax himself never regrets the fact that, purely out of wounded pride, he has attempted treacherously to murder all the other Greek leaders: he regrets only that, because of the intervention of Athena, he missed. So dominant is Ajax through most of the play, so engrossing and persuasive as a tragic hero, that we accept his selfishness and passionate individualism, even as we accept behaviour on the part of the heroes in *The Iliad* which, in another context, would seem outrageous. There is no rival standard, or at least there is none until the second catastrophe, when Odysseus suddenly emerges as a kind of counter-hero. The man whose behaviour in the opening moments was positively pusillanimous, who was physically terrified of approaching Ajax's tent even under the protection of Athena, stands firm now against both Agamemnon and Menelaus. Odysseus goes on insisting until he wins that the body of Ajax, his own bitterest enemy, must be honourably buried. The reasons he advances are not Teucer's, nor are they reasons that Ajax himself could have stomached, or even understood. What Odysseus sees, in effect, is that no man is an island. The predicament of being a human is common to us all, the potentiality for tragedy universal, the end the same. Ajax must be buried, whatever his sins, because (as Odysseus says) "I too shall come to that necessity." Agamemnon misinterprets this as blatant self-interest but the selfishness of Odysseus is, paradoxically, a form of generosity. Sophocles poises it against the heroic individualism of Ajax in the first catastrophe, not in order to denigrate or cancel out that catastrophe, but to modify our comprehension of it. There are other kinds of heroism, other ways of regarding the self and one's relationship to others. In the light of Odysseus's behaviour in the second catastrophe, Ajax becomes in retrospect something of a glorious anachronism: an epic hero whose attitudes we see as limited without for a moment ceasing to recognize that they were great.

Antony and Cleopatra appeared originally in the Shakespeare First Folio without act and scene divisions. This omission, as A. C. Bradley remarked, is of no particular consequence. In fact, the tragedy divides logically and inevitably into five acts. Within this overall structure, Shakespeare has created a divided catastrophe, split between acts 4 and 5. Antony's crushing defeat at Actium comes in act 3. In act 4, scenes 4 through 8, there is for him a moment of respite. Not only does he seem, momentarily, to regain his lost, heroic identity: he moves towards a reconciliation within himself of the warring values of Rome and Egypt. May it not be possible after all to be a soldier, a triumphant workman in "the royal occupation" during the day, and still return to feast and sleep with Cleopatra in the night? Scenes 7 and 8 in particular are scenes in which we delude ourselves into thinking that there will be no tragedy. Caesar is beaten back. Antony discovers that Antony can be "himself . . . but stirr'd by Cleopatra." That formula for the reconciliation of opposites which, when it appeared in the first scene of the play, so patently rang false, here becomes almost true. And, for reasons buried deep in our own psychology and in that of the play, we want terribly to believe it. After all, beneath the surface of this tragedy lies one of the great Renaissance wish-dreams: the dream not only of harmony but of exchange and union between the masculine and feminine principles.

Shakespeare's use of the Heracles/Omphale myth—Antony tricked out in Cleopatra's tires and mantles whilst she wore his sword Philippan—always seems to be regarded by the play's critics through the cold eyes of Octavius: as an indication of Antony's utter degradation. He "is not more manlike / Than Cleopatra; nor the queen of Ptolemy / More womanly than he." The indictment here seems clear-cut. The image of a transvestite Antony is not only comic in itself, it seems to epitomise the destruction of his masculinity at the hands of Cleopatra. Almost nothing in this play, however, up to the point of the final scene, is either simple or easy to judge. It is important to balance against the censure of Octavius other and more complicated Renaissance attitudes. In *Arcadia*, Sidney had treated Pyrocles' long disguise as a woman as educative, if perilous: a search for full emotional maturity. Even Artegall's shaming captivity in female dress in the castle of Spenser's Radigund was an oddly necessary part of his quest, preparation for his eventual and tempering union with Britomart, a woman who finds it natural to set out in search of her lover wearing full armour and disguised as a man. Shakespeare may or may not have been aware of the iconographical tradition of synthesis, the blurring of identity between Venus and Mars, about which Edgar Wind writes in *Pagan Mysteries in the Renaissance*. He was, however, the author of "The Phoenix and the Turtle."

The heroic Antony of past time, the one recollected by Octavius, Pompey, Philo and Demetrius, was intensely male. On one level, it is clearly bad that Cleopatra has made him womanish. On another, his Egyptian bondage asks to be read as an attempt to regain the kind of wholeness, that primal sexual unity, about which Aristophanes is half joking, half deadly serious, in Plato's *Symposium*. Certainly there is something not just unattractive but maimed about the exclusively masculine world of Rome in this play. It emerges in that distasteful all-male party on board Pompey's galley in act 2, a party which ripens towards an Alexandrian revel but never gets there, as it does in the desperately public, chilly ostentation of Caesar's affection for his sister. Octavia, it seems, is the only woman in Rome and, unlike Portia and Calpurnia, Virgilia and Volumnia, she exists only in order to be manoeuvred and pushed about by the men.

Cleopatra is as quintessentially feminine as the younger Antony was male. Left alone among women and eunuchs after Antony's departure, she finds that life is scarcely worth living. This, one would expect. And yet she does try, particularly in the second half of the play, to become a kind of epic, warrior maiden. She is not exactly cut out to be a Britomart. When she tries to act as Antony's male body-servant in act 4, she merely succeeds in putting his armour on the wrong way round. She must have looked preposterous wearing his sword. At Actium, she announces that she will appear "for a man" but, when the battle is joined, it is as a fearful woman that she runs away. Nevertheless, it is important that she should at least have tried to participate in Antony's masculine world, that he should feel that one of her rebukes to him for military delay "might have well becom'd the best of men." Like Desdemona in Cyprus, she seems for a while to reconcile opposites, to become Antony's "fair warrior."

This moment of harmony is brief. As is usual in the fourth acts of Shakespeare's tragedies, a door is left temptingly ajar to reveal the sunlit garden of a possible happy ending, and then slammed shut. What is unique about *Antony and Cleopatra* is that this door closes where it opened, in act 4, and not—as in the other tragedies—in act 5. In scene 12 of the penultimate act, Antony loses the third and climactic battle. This time, there can be no recovery. He also loses all conviction of his own identity and all faith in his grasp of Cleopatra's let alone any belief that the values of masculine Rome and feminine Egypt might, after all, be united. Only the false report of her death can restore Cleopatra for him as a person. His own identity, from the very first scene of the play a persistent source of question and debate for the characters who surround him, now becomes for Antony himself as cloudlike and indistinct "as water is in water." For him, as for Sophocles' Ajax, the way to self-definition, to the recovery of the man that was, seems to lie through heroic suicide. Unlike Ajax, however, Antony bungles his death. The greatest soldier of the world proves to be less efficient then Eros, a former slave. Antony fails to kill himself cleanly, and no one will respond to his requests for euthanasia. Decretas simply steals his sword and carries it to Caesar in the hope of promotion. Wallowing on the ground in agony, Antony receives the equivocal news that his serpent of old Nile has once again demonstrated what Enobarbus called her remarkable "celerity in dying"—and in reviving again at a propitious moment. Because Cleopatra is too frightened to leave her monument, Antony must be hauled up to her, slowly and unceremoniously, with ropes. He finds it almost impossible to make the queen listen to his dying words, so obsessed is she with her tirade against fortune and Octavius. The advice he gives her to trust Proculeius is, characteristically, misguided. With a last attempt which, under the circumstances, seems pathetic rather than convincing, to reestablish his heroic identity as "the greatest prince o' the world . . . a Roman, by a Roman valiantly vanquish'd," he expires in his destroyer's arms.

By comparison with that of Ajax, this is not really a glorious or even a very controlled end. But it does feel distinctly like an end, in a sense that goes beyond Antony's individual death. Even at this point, this is already a long play; it positively seems to hanker after conclusion. The whole tragedy, after all, has been focussed on Antony far more than on Cleopatra. He has been the character standing, like Heracles at the cross-roads, with an important choice to make. He has done the journeying, while she stayed put in Egypt, and these journeys have not been simply geographical, but the pilgrimages of a divided mind. Rome or Egypt, virtue or vice, the active life or the life of pleasure, the Antony of the past or the sybarite of the present: these are the great antinomies between which his will has vacillated and swung and the movement has been, to a large extent, the movement of the play. Now that he is dead, the world seems almost as vacant and still as Cleopatra imagines: a "dull world, which in thy absence is / No better than a sty." There is room for tragic obsequies—"The crown o' the earth doth melt." "O, wither'd is the garland of the war"—but not, as one feels, for tragic continuation. It is true that Cleopatra remains to be accounted for, but that conclusion seems to be foregone:

> We'll bury him: and then, what's brave, what's noble,
> Let's do it after the high Roman fashion,
> And make death proud to take us. Come, away,
> This case of that huge spirit now is cold.
> Ah, women, women! come, we have no friend
> But resolution, and the briefest end.

No matter how well one knows the play, it is difficult not to be tricked at this point into believing in that "briefest end." Surely Cleopatra will send out on the spot for a commodity of asps and follow Antony without delay. What we are emphatically not prepared for is a second catastrophe sharply divided from the first: a catastrophe, moreover, which is going to occupy an entire fifth act and more than four hundred lines of the tragedy.

Historically and in Shakespeare's main source, Plutarch's life of *Marcus Antonius*, Cleopatra's death was divided from Antony's by a gap of time. I do not myself think that this is a serious consideration. Drama is an art of temporal compression. The Shakespeare who could take the liberties he did with the historical time of Hall and Holinshed in his English histories, who had already collapsed ten years of Plutarch into the playing time of *Antony and Cleopatra*, was scarcely going to worry about this piddling kind of inaccuracy. There was nothing to prevent him from doing what he had already done in *Romeo and Juliet* and *Othello*: sending the lovers to death within minutes of each other, and in the same final scene. This was the structure which Dryden adopted later in *All for Love*, where Cleopatra sinks lifeless into the arms of an Antony who has ceased to be only a short time before. Nor did Cinthio, Jodelle, Garnier and Daniel, all of whom wrote plays on the subject before Shakespeare, come any closer than Dryden to creating a divided catastrophe.

Cinthio's *Cleopatra*, published in 1583 but acted in the 1540s, opens after Actium. It concentrates on Cleopatra, although the prologue promises that some attention will be paid to Antony as well. In fact, Antony's appearances are confined to three scenes and he encounters his mistress in only one of them, the first of act 2, at which point he is already dying. The rest of the play concerns Cleopatra's preparations for her own death, preparations which cannot take long because the queen finally expires of a broken heart while conducting the funeral rites over Antony's as yet unburied corpse.

Jodelle's tragedy *Cléopatre Captive*, first presented in 1552, published in 1574, occupies itself with the last day of its heroine's life. Antonie, very recently dead, appears only at the beginning, as a singularly vindictive Senecan ghost. It seems that he is yearning for his lady's company in the underworld, not so that they may couch together on flowers or exchange reminiscences with Dido and Aeneas, but simply because he wants her to suffer hellish torment too. After this ferociously moral opening, it comes as something of a surprise to discover that Antonie's temptress is presented quite sympathetically: queenly and proud, honourable, and still deeply in love with Antonie. When, after completing her lover's obsequies, she manages to outwit Caesar and kill herself, offstage, Proculeius waxes rhapsodic about this reunion in death. Remembering the savage remarks of the ghostly Antonie, one feels that the poor queen is in for a shock.

Garnier's tragedy *Antonie* appeared in 1578 and was translated into English by the Countess of Pembroke in 1590. Like Cinthio's play, it opens after Actium, with Antonio's downfall assured, and the lovers estranged. In fact, we never see them together until the last scene, when Antonie is dead. Cléopatre, an honest and tender-hearted woman, collapses over his corpse. Apparently she has, in the politest way imaginable, willed herself to die, and done so, after completing her final couplet.

The most important of these four tragedies, from the point of view of Shakespeare's own achievement, is Samuel Daniel's closet drama *Cleopatra*, conceived as a companion piece to the Countess of Pembroke's *Antonie*, and published in 1599. Almost certainly, Shakespeare knew and was influenced by this play. A number of specific parallels between Shakespeare and Daniel, alterations or additions to the story as Plutarch told it, have been identified by Willard Farnham, Geoffrey Bullough and Kenneth Muir. It seems to have been Daniel, for instance, who suggested to Shakespeare that Cleopatra was ageing and worried about it, and also that her death scene re-created the glory of Cydnus. Of more interest to me, however, is a connection which seems to have gone unnoticed, perhaps because it is something relatively simple and verbally quite explicit in Daniel which, in Shakespeare, has not only become infinitely more complex, but also more generalised and diffuse: an underlying assumption conveyed not through direct statement but, to a large extent, through structural, visual and metaphoric means.

Daniel's Cleopatra makes a confession in her opening soliloquy which, as far as I know, is unique to this play. She states that she has been loved by so many men in her life that "I to stay on Love had never leisure." Antony was different from these other men, because he loved the autumn of her beauty: loved her indeed when she was no longer what she had been. During his lifetime, she took this love for granted, failed to distinguish it from that of a Caesar or a Pompey. Now that Antony is dead, she sees it truly and, for the first time in her life, she herself genuinely loves.

> Now I protest I do, now am I taught
> In death to love, in life that knew not how …
> For which in more than death, I stand thy debter,
> Which I will pay thee with so true a minde,
> (Casting up all these deepe accompts of mine)
> That both our soules, and all the world shall find
> All reckonings cleer'd, betwixt my love and thine.

This motive for suicide runs parallel through Daniel's play with Cleopatra's horror of being led in Caesar's triumph: indeed, you cannot separate them. When the Messenger enters to describe her last moments, how Honour scorning Life led forth "Bright Immortalitie in shining armour," he puns significantly on the words *part* and *touch*:

>   she performes that part
> That hath so great a part of glorie wonde.
> And so receives the deadly poys'ning touch;
> That touch that tride the gold of her love, pure,
> And hath confirm'd her honour to be such,
> As must a wonder to all worlds endure.

The acting imagery here—and there is a good deal more of it in the Messenger's account—obviously caught Shakespeare's imagination. But so, I think, did Daniel's association of the poisonous touch of the asp with the touchstone that distinguishes true gold. Daniel's Cleopatra alters her attitude towards Antony after she has lost him. In her own death, she sets out to transform their story: in effect, to do the impossible, and remake past time. It is true that Daniel could not do a great deal with this idea. He was hampered, for one thing, by his obligatory French Senecanism. Shakespeare, on the other hand, did not have the Countess of Pembroke breathing down his neck, and he could exploit it fully. I think myself that his reading of Daniel's play impelled him towards the one use, in all his tragedies, of the divided catastrophe.

As a structural form, the divided catastrophe is decidedly rare in Elizabethan and Jacobean tragedy. (Its use in comedy is far more frequent, but entirely different in effect.) Ford employed it in *The Broken Heart*, when he altered what had seemed to be the settled perspective of the play, and even the meaning of its title, by pressing on beyond the deaths of Penthea and Ithocles and the sentencing of Orgilus to the unexpected and cunningly delayed love-suicide of Calantha: a princess we have been led to regard as a kind of Fortinbras or Malcolm, restoring order to the shattered state, and not as the last and, in a sense, the most important of its tragic victims. Webster, even more daringly, conducted his Duchess of Malfy to death in act 4 and then devoted a long fifth act to a demonstration of how the world—like the garden in Shelley's "The Sensitive Plant" after the death of the Lady who was its Genius—festers and becomes poisonous, good and evil tumbled together and rendered equally impotent, once she has ceased to exist. It is not only Bosola but the theatre audience which is forced into a new understanding of what the Duchess was and what she signified after the tragic climax (as it seems at the time) has already taken place.

Apart from *The Broken Heart* and *The Duchess of Malfi*, I can think of no non-Shakespearean examples of the divided catastrophe in tragedies of the period. Certainly, Cinthio, Jodelle, Garnier and Daniel avoided it in dramatising the story of Antony and Cleopatra, even as Dryden did later. All five of these plays pick up the story late in its development. They tend (Dryden excepted) to concentrate on Cleopatra at the expense of Antony, and they are very chary of showing us the lovers together. All of them dignify Cleopatra herself, for reasons that obviously have something to do with the requirements of neoclassical decorum. The trivial or discreditable features of her character as outlined by her enemy Plutarch are smoothed away. She becomes, even in Daniel, a simple and straightforward woman: a great queen, who ought to have restrained her passions, certainly, but whose loyalty to Antony is beyond question. Lies do not come easily to this Cleopatra. Garnier is the only dramatist of the five who allows her to send the false report of her death to Antony, and even he goes out of his way to excuse and explain it. When it comes to the point of her suicide, there is nothing but respect and compassion. Indeed, this response almost seems inherent in the story. Cleopatra would not, after all, seem a particularly likely candidate for inclusion in Chaucer's *Legend of Good Women*, but hers is the first story that the poet tells. He makes it clear, moreover, that she stands beside Alcetis and Philomela, Ariadne and Hypermnestra and Lucrece, solely because of the way she kept faith with Antony in her death. Even Spenser, of all people, could be grudgingly respectful of this death. Although he puts Egypt's queen in the dungeon of Lucifera's House of Pride in book 1 of *The Faerie Queene*, his description of "High-minded Cleopatra that with stroke / Of Aspes sting herselfe did stoutly kill" is at least half admiring.

As a result of their sympathetic treatment of Cleopatra, all five tragedies are to some extent morally ambiguous. Certainly, it is difficult to reconcile the attitude adopted towards her, and in particular towards her suicide, with the official commentary on the story provided by the prologues to these plays, or by those innumerable choruses of depressed Egyptians concerned to point out that the wages of lust are death, not to mention a great deal of public misery. Even

Dryden, although he did without choric commentary of this kind, and rashly subtitled his play "The World Well Lost," was careful to declare in the preface that, for him, the principal appeal of the subject lay in "the excellency of the moral." It is not easy, in face of the play itself, to see just what he means.

Shakespeare, of course, greatly complicated the situation by transferring this moral ambiguity to Antony and Cleopatra themselves. As characters, they become singularly hard to assess or know. Part of their opacity springs from the fact that she has nothing even resembling a soliloquy until the last scene of the play and that Antony is not much more forthcoming about his private intentions. This reticence contrasts sharply not only with the inveterate mental unburdenings of the protagonists in Daniel or Garnier, but with Shakespeare's own, earlier tragic practice. Emrys Jones has argued, in *Scenic Form in Shakespeare*, that the construction of *Antony and Cleopatra*—the wasteful, drifting movement of all those short scenes—reflects the haphazard nature of phenomenal experience, that it seems more like the life process itself than like formal tragedy. I think that this is true, and that the effect is one that Shakespeare reinforces through his handling of the protagonists. With Romeo and Juliet before, with Othello and Desdemona, even with Macbeth and his wife, evaluation of the two individuals concerned and of their relationship had not only been encouraged: it was possible. With Cleopatra and Antony, on the other hand, it simply cannot be managed. They are as mysterious and contradictory as people known in real life. Our place of vantage is basically that of Charmian and Enobarbus: people sufficiently close to their social superiors to witness informal and often undignified behaviour, without participating in motive and reflection like the confidantes in Garnier or Jodelle. It is true that we see more of the picture in range, if not in depth, than these attendant characters. They cannot move, as we can, from Rome to Egypt and back again within an instant, nor are they present in all the scenes. Our perspective upon the affairs of Antony and his mistress is wider than theirs, but this very breadth makes judgment more instead of less difficult.

In this tragedy, other characters are continually trying to describe Cleopatra and Antony, to fix their essential qualities in words. This impulse generates several of the great, set speeches of the play: Enobarbus's description of Cleopatra at Cydnus, or Caesar's account of Antony crossing the Alps, like a lean stag inured to privation. It also makes itself felt in less obvious ways. Because of the constant shifting of scene, the protagonists are forever being discussed by bewildered rivals or subordinates while they themselves are away in Egypt or in Rome. The results of this unremitting attempt at evaluation are bewildering. In the course of the tragedy, Antony is called "the noble Antony," the "courteous Antony," the "firm Roman," "Mars," a "mine of bounty," the "triple pillar of the world," "the demi-atlas of this earth," the "lord of lords, of infinite virtue," the "crown o' the earth," and "the garland of the war." These are only a few of the celebratory epithets. He is also "poor Antony," a "libertine," "the abstract of all faults that all men follow," a "gorgon," a "sworder," an "old ruffian," a "doting mallard," the "ne'er lust wearied Antony" and a "strumpet's fool." There is no progression among these epithets, no sense of alteration in Antony's character during the play as there is, for instance, with Macbeth. Macbeth begins his tragedy as "worthy Macbeth" and ends it as "this dead butcher." The space between the two descriptions is that of his tragic development. Antony, on the other hand, is all the contradictory things that people say he is more or less simultaneously. Nor is there any neat division of the celebratory and the pejorative between Antony's friends and Antony's enemies. Enobarbus and Octavius are alike in acknowledging both sides of the moon: the bright as well as the dark.

Cleopatra's situation is similar. She is "great Egypt," "dearest queen," a "rare Egyptian," a "triumphant lady," "Thetis," "this great fairy," "day o' the world," "nightingale," "eastern star," a "most sovereign creature," a "lass unparallel'd"—but also a "foul Egyptian," the "false soul of Egypt," a "witch," a "gipsy," a "strumpet," a "whore," a "trull," "salt Cleopatra," a "boggler," a "morsel cold upon dead Caesar's trencher," Antony's "Egyptian dish," the "ribaudred nag of Egypt," and "a cow in June." One may begin to feel that language used so indiscriminately to describe a single personality becomes meaningless and self-defeating, that one would do better to adopt Antony's method when he described a different serpent of old Nile to the drunken Lepidus. "What manner o' thing is your crocodile?" And Antony replies:

It is shap'd, sir, like itself, and it is as
broad as it hath breadth: it is just so high
as it is, and moves with its own organs. It
lives by that which nourishes it, and the
elements once out of it, it transmigrates.

It's of its own colour too, and the tears of it—like Cleopatra's—are wet.

The situation is made more acute by the fact that all the other characters in the play are, for Shakespeare, remarkably monolithic. Enobarbus surprises us somewhat in his death, but up to that point we are never tempted to depart from the general consensus that he is "good Enobarb," "strong Enobarb," a soldier and a blunt, honest man. Even Cleopatra can see that Octavia is "patient." For everyone else, Caesar's sister is also holy, modest, still, and a little cold. When Cleopatra, in her jealous rage, tries to add a few spurious qualities, to make out that her rival must also be dull of tongue and dwarvish, we recognise the falsehood at once—even as we do when Caesar announces smugly that he has got rid of Lepidus because Lepidus was grown too "cruel." For Caesar himself, the epithets are again consistent: "scarce-bearded Caesar," "the young man," "blossoming Caesar," "full fortuned Caesar," "the novice," the "young Roman boy." References to his youth and rising star may be made in envy or in scorn but, regardless of whether one admires it or not, there is no real ambivalence about his character.

When it comes to the vital task of assessing one another, Cleopatra and Antony seem as uncertain as everyone else. When Cleopatra learns of Antony's Roman marriage, she tries to arrive at judgment, but fails.

Let him for ever go, let him not—Charmian,
Though he be painted one way like a Gorgon,
The other way's a Mars.

This Janus-faced image of Antony derives from Elizabethan perspectives: trick paintings in which the identity of the picture, the very nature of the object represented, transformed itself according to the angle from which it was viewed. Cleopatra finds that she must put up with two contradictory, but equally real images of Antony: on the one hand a Mars, "a god in love to whom I am confin'd," on the other an uncouth Gorgon with a heart of stone. Antony too wavers continually up to the point of his suicide in his estimation of Cleopatra. Is she his "most sweet queen," or a "triple-turn'd whore?" He can never be sure of her, only of his own irrational fascination, and even that has its ebbs and flows. He loses faith again and again, mildly at the end of act 1, violently after Actium and when he catches her with Caesar's messenger in act 3, catastrophically in act 4. Cleopatra rules his life, but he remains uncertain as to just who she is. A man does not react with the hysteria of Antony at the mere sight of a messenger kissing his lady's hand unless he has hidden doubts.

We too have doubts. At the beginning of the play Antony tells Cleopatra that his love is beyond reckoning, vaster than heaven and earth. A few minutes later, he is seeking ways to break off from "this enchanting queen." What really was in his mind when he agreed so readily to marry Octavia? Is he telling the truth when he assures Caesar's sister that "I have not kept my square, but that to come / Shall all be done by the rule?" Or a moment later when he admits that "i' th' East my pleasure lies?" Cleopatra's behaviour is even more ambiguous. What was she intending to do in that scene with Thidias in act 3, when she agrees smoothly that she has never loved Antony, but merely been forced into being his paramour? Was Caesar right to think that she could be bribed to murder her lover? Again, is she betraying Caesar, or Antony, in the quarrel with Seleucus in act 5 when, after so many protestations of her intent to follow Antony in death, we find her, a boggler to the last, trying to conceal the true amount of her treasure from Octavius?

These are questions which elude resolution. Continually, the play directs one back to Cleopatra's perspective, to the monster who is also a Mars. With these two people, the same quality tends to exact contradictory descriptions, to become a vice or a virtue depending upon the position of the viewer or the particular moment of time. So, Cleopatra's infinite variety, the thing which holds Antony captive in Egypt for so long, both is and is not the same as her regrettable propensity to tell lies. Enobarbus himself, that shrewd and cynical commentator, cannot distinguish between her charm and her deceit at a number of crucial moments in the play. Nor, alas, can he separate Antony's extravagance, that culpable waste about which Caesar is so censorious, from Antony's bounty: the godlike generosity of spirit which makes Antony send Enobarbus's treasure after him when he defects to Caesar, and breaks the soldier's heart. Antony's behaviour, as Philo complains in the opening scene, "o'erflows the measure," but the very phrase reminds us that when the Nile does exactly this it showers largesse and prosperity on everyone around. Caesar's "bounty," on the one occasion when the word is associated with him, in the second scene of act 5, is a meaningless abstraction: a political lie invented by Proculeius in the hope of deceiving Cleopatra. Antony's "bounty" is not like this. A protean and mercurial thing, it is as stunning and unnecessary as the spontaneous leaps of the dolphin, and as difficult to order or assess. The worst things about Cleopatra and her lover are also, maddeningly, the best.

Like the vagabond flag of Caesar's image, *Antony and Cleopatra* up to the point of its final scene, "goes to and back, lackeying the varying tide, / To rot itself with motion." This restlessness is expressed not only in terms of a continual shifting of place, from Alexandria to Rome, to Misenum, to Athens, to Parthia, to Rome again, to Egypt, but also of the vacillation of the perspective picture, Mars dissolving into the Gorgon and then again becoming Mars. By the end of act 4, we long for stasis, for the movement to stop. But it does not. Most of act 5 is taken up with Cleopatra's hesitation and delay. Indeed, all of its dramatic tension derives from our uncertainty as to whether, despite all her protestations, she will keep her word and follow Antony in death. And, oddly enough, in a way for which there is no parallel in any other Shakespearean tragedy, we want Cleopatra to die. The reaction is one that flies in the face of normal tragic convention. After all, most of the suspense generated in the fifth act of *Hamlet* springs from our hope that somehow Hamlet himself will manage both to kill Claudius and to escape alive. In *Othello*, there remains the tantalizing possibility that the Moor will see through Iago and recognize Desdemona's innocence before it is too late, or, in *Romeo and Juliet*, that Juliet will wake before Romeo takes the poison. Only in *Antony and Cleopatra* do we long for a protagonist who has not, like Macbeth, been a villain to decide to die and do so.

Shakespeare's reason for employing the double catastrophe was, I think, precisely to elicit this unconventional reaction from the audience, and then, to gratify our desires in a way that modifies our feelings about the entire previous development of the tragedy. As Cleopatra wavers and procrastinates, we see that there can be only one way of putting doubt and ambiguity to rest. This love story has hovered continually between the sublime and the ridiculous, the tragic and the comic. We have never been able to decide which of the two sets of perspective images was the right one, or to reach any compromise between them. Only if Cleopatra keeps faith with Antony now and dies can the flux of the play be stilled and their love claim value. The act itself is indeed one that "shackles accident and bolts up change," and not merely in the sense that it will free Cleopatra herself from mutability and time. It will also transform the past, remake it in terms more far-reaching than anything envisaged by Daniel's Cleopatra. The vagabond flag will come to rest, leaving the triple-turned whore a lass unparallel'd, the Gorgon an immutable if injudicious Mars. It may even be possible to adumbrate a reconciliation between masculine Rome and feminine Egypt more lasting than the one achieved so briefly in act 4: one which will diminish Caesar forever as half-human by comparison.

Caesar, of course, is the enemy. He wants passionately to get a living Cleopatra back to Italy because, as he says, "her life in Rome / Would be eternal in our triumph." If only he can do this, he will fix the qualities of the story forever in his own terms, which are those of the strumpet and the gorgon, not the lass unparallel'd and the Mars. Cleopatra will fade into a mere parody queen in the epic pageant of his own imperial greatness, and Antony become the brother-in-arms who deserted his superior for a light woman and got what he deserved. This threat makes it imperative not only that Cleopatra should die, but that she should die in the way she does: ostentatiously as a tragedy queen. Shakespeare makes us understand that the achievement was difficult. Cleopatra at last makes up her mind. Despite her apparent duplicity with Seleucus, her anxious enquiries as to Caesar's intentions, and her own fear of physical pain, she does finally recognise and repudiate Octavius's plan: "He words me, girls, he words me, that I should not be noble to myself." She understands what will happen in Rome:

> the quick comedians
> Extemporally will stage us, and present
> Our Alexandrian revels; Antony
> Shall be brought drunken forth, and I shall see
> Some squeaking Cleopatra boy my greatness
> I' th' posture of a whore.

If she does not die well, this is the way her story, and Antony's, will be told for all of time that matters. The puppeteers, the ballad-makers and the quick comedians will cheapen and impoverish a love which was flawed at best, but never just absurd.

Appropriately, the last obstacle Cleopatra faces on her way to death is Comedy: personified by that ribald and garrulous countryman who brings her asps concealed in his basket of figs. Patiently, she listens and even responds to the clown's slanders about women, to a kind of sexual innuendo that threatens to diminish the whole basis of love tragedy. When he cautions her that the worm is not worth feeding, she asks humorously: "Will it eat me?" and one realises that she has brought together and reconciled in death two warring images of herself from earlier in the play: the positive one in which she was "a morsel for a monarch," but also Antony's savage description of her as mere broken meats: "a morsel cold upon dead Caesar's trencher." When she finally persuades the clown to depart—and the woman committed to tragedy has to ask comedy to leave no fewer than four times—we feel that precisely because she has walked through the fire of ridicule, the thing she most dreads and potentially the thing most deadly for her, she has earned the right to say, "Give me my robe, put on my crown, I have / Immortal longings in me." And she does so at once, without a break or a mediating pause. Comedy simply flowers into tragedy.

"Immortal," of course, was one of the words that the clown stumbled over most comically: "I would not be the party that should desire you to touch [the worm]," he cautioned, "for his biting is immortal: those that do die of it, do seldom or never recover." It must have taken courage for Cleopatra to use that word "immortal" again, so differently, within so short a space of time. She succeeds, however, in winning it back as part of the vocabulary of tragedy. Indeed, she even imposes, in retrospect, a truth upon the clown's blunder that he never intended: the biting of this particular asp will indeed be "immortal," the agent of Cleopatra's, and through her of Antony's, undying fame.

Cleopatra dies perfectly, as a tragedy queen. In doing so, she not only redeems the bungled and clumsy nature of Antony's death in act 4 by catching it up and transforming it within her own, flawless farewell; she crystallises and stills all the earlier and more ambiguous tableaux of the play—Cydnus, her appearance throned in gold as the goddess Isis, even the dubious spectacle presented to the Roman messenger in the opening scene. This is a divided catastrophe of a very special kind. Not only does it alter the way we feel about the previous development of the tragedy, hushing our doubts about Cleopatra's faith, it makes us understand something about historical process. After all, there does seem to have been something about Cleopatra's death as the story was perpetuated in time that made it impossible for Cinthio and Jodelle, Garnier and Daniel, not to mention Chaucer and Spenser, to condemn her, whatever the overall moral pattern of the poem or play in which she appeared. There are no satirical comedies about Antony's infatuation with an Egyptian whore.

Shakespeare's second catastrophe stands as a kind of explanation of this phenomenon. Cleopatra's death, as he presents it, demonstrates how the ending of this story transfigured its earlier, more suspect stages. The modification of feeling which it imposes upon us as an audience is a repetition and reenactment of what has happened within historical time. In the play itself, we watch as Octavius acquiesces to Cleopatra's tragedy, consents (indeed) to become its Fortinbras. Here will be no parody queen led in triumph before a hooting mob, no bawdy Roman ballads, no comic puppet-shows presenting and coarsening the revels of Alexandria. Instead,

> She shall be buried by her Antony.
> No grave upon the earth shall clip in it
> A pair so famous . . . . Our army shall
> In solemn show attend this funeral,
> And then to Rome. Come, Dolabella, see
> High order in this great solemnity.

Because Cleopatra has left him no real choice, Caesar consents to become an actor in her tragedy. Indeed, his order that the Roman army should, "in solemn show," attend her funeral merely extends and develops Cleopatra's final pose.

Does it diminish Cleopatra in our eyes that the last scene of her life was just that: a tragic pose? That she assumes costume and a role, gathers Iras and Charmian as minor players around her, ransacks the treasuries of rhetoric, and confronts Caesar and his soldiers when they break in upon her with a contrived and formal tableau of death which they understand as such? I think not. When he remembered Cleopatra at Cydnus, Enobarbus said that the sight "beggar'd all description." As she lay in her pavilion, she o'er-pictured "that Venus where we see / The fancy outwork nature." That is, the living Cleopatra surpassed a picture of Venus in which art itself had outdone reality. Cleopatra herself develops this favorite Renaissance paradox when she tells Dolabella, shortly before her death, about the mythical Antony of her dreams: "His legs bestrid the ocean, his rear'd arm / Crested the world: his voice was propertied / As all the tuned spheres." Asked if there "was or might be such a man / As this I dreamt of," Dolabella answers literally: "Gentle madam, no." And Cleopatra flashes out:

> You lie up to the hearing of the gods.
> But if there be, or ever were one such,
> It's past the size of dreaming: nature wants stuff
> To vie strange forms with fancy, yet to imagine
> An Antony were nature's piece 'gainst fancy,
> Condemning shadows quite.

An Elizabethan cliché, the conceit of an art more realistic than reality itself, acquires in the second catastrophe of *Antony and Cleopatra* a very special meaning. Cleopatra here bestows upon Antony an heroic identity so colossal, but also in a sense so true—after all, those kingdoms dropping like plates, unregarded, from his pockets summon up the careless Antony we have always known—that it will defeat Time. She is also working towards her own death scene, a fictional masterpiece of another kind which is going to outclass the normal fictions of tragedy by also being real. In this death, reality will borrow the techniques of art as a means of fighting back against oblivion. Moreover, it will be victorious. Hitherto, all the images of stasis offered by a tragedy yearning towards rest have been either distasteful, like Caesar himself and his "universal peace" spread through a silent world from which everything remarkable has departed, or else obviously fragile: "the swan's down feather, / That stands upon the swell at the full of tide, / And neither way inclines." We know that, in the next moment, the tide will ebb. It is Cleopatra who finally arrests the eddying of the vagabond flag, who gives to the swan's down feather an immutable poise. She does so by creating a tableau, "still and contemplative in living art," which transfigures and quiets the events in which it was immanent in a way that Sophocles, surely, would have understood.

1974—Rosalie L. Colie. "The Significance of Style," from *Shakespeare's Living Art*

Rosalie L. Colie (1924–1972) was a professor of English at Barnard College, Wesleyan University, and Brown University. Her books include *Paradoxia Epidemica: The Renaissance Tradition of Paradox*, *"My Echoing Song": Andrew Marvell's Poetry of Criticism*, and *Shakespeare's Living Art*, which was published posthumously.

In *Antony and Cleopatra*, the problem of style, although equally telling, is set entirely differently [than in *Julius Caesar* and *Coriolanus*]. Oratory and public speaking are not at issue in this play, are not the plot-elements they are in both *Julius Caesar* and *Coriolanus*. Nor is style displayed at the outer surface of the play, as in *Love's Labour's Lost* styles are animated into personality. Nonetheless, its peculiar language is a major force in the play, as critics from Dr. Johnson to Maurice Charney have pointed out; in comparison to the plainer speech of the other Roman plays, the verbal richness of *Antony and Cleopatra* demands attention not only for its spectacular imagery but also as a function of the play's subject. As in *Julius Caesar*, where the economical style seems properly mated to its severe subject, so in *Antony and Cleopatra* the abundance of the language seems to match the richness of its subject, the fertility of the Egyptian setting, the emotional largesse of hero and heroine. The play's language bursts with energy and vigor; figures abound; of figures, as Charney so cleverly shows, hyperbole is particularly common, that overreacher of the figures of speech. Indeed, the figures are so numerous and so rich that at times they seem almost to crowd out other meanings, to stop the action and the plot, to force attention to their resonances alone. Enobarbus's speech on Cleopatra is one example, the most famous of the play's set-pieces; Cleopatra's memories of the absent Antony, her paean to Dolabella, Antony's evaluations of his own emotional and worldly situations raise speech above the movement of plot.

Magniloquence fascinates both hearers and speakers. Antony's "normal" decisions to undertake his Roman responsibilities as triumvir and husband vanish in the hue and cry raised by his emotions and expressed immediately in the language he uses. More markedly, Enobarbus's famous detachment gives way before his recognition of Cleopatra's sources of power. In his great comment on her qualities his magniloquence rolls out to contrast with the plainness and irony of his previous speeches about her. In that speech, Enobarbus abandons himself to Cleopatra, and thereby gives himself away: from his response to her, apparently so out of character, we feel the force of her enchantment. Indeed, Enobarbus's giving way to grandiloquence seems an almost sexual abandon before her; the cynical and experienced Roman soldier, suspicious of Egypt and its ways, cannot and will not contain his climactic praise of the Queen.

Though the language seems at times to crowd out action and judgment, it does not crowd out meaning, for much of the meaning of this play, as one critic has argued, resides in the characters' attitudes to the language they use. The stated, plotted action of the play is in itself grand enough to require no rival in language: the range of the play is epic, over the whole Mediterranean world which was, in the Roman context, the whole world altogether. Action and scene oscillate between the poles of Rome and Egypt. From the beginning, in Philo's first speech, Rome and Egypt are set off against one another, in the shapes of Caesar and Octavia on the one side, Cleopatra on the other. The two locales, with their properly representative dramatis personae, seem to struggle for domination over Mark Antony's spirit and will. Like his great ancestor, the god Hercules, Antony stood at the crossroads of duty and sensuality, of self-denial and self-indulgence. Rome is duty, obligation, austerity, politics, warfare, and honor: Rome is public life. Egypt is comfort, pleasure, softness, seduction, sensuousness (if not sensuality also), variety, and sport: Egypt promises her children rich, languorous pleasures and satisfactions. Rome is business, Egypt is foison; Rome is warfare, Egypt is love. Egypt is "the East," where the beds are soft—and what "beds" can mean is never scanted in this play. To keep us aware of Cleopatra's power, the Romans, in their own eyes contemptuous of her life, show themselves as fascinated by Cleopatra's reputation as a bedfellow as Antony is by the actuality. Egypt is florid, decorated, deceitful, artful, opulent, sensual, idle; is "inflatus," "solutus," "tumens," "superfluens," "redundans," "enervis," "inanus." I took this list of Latin adjectives from various critiques, not of the fleshpots of Egypt, but of the Asiatic style; these epithets can, within the frame of this play, be transferred to the loose, ungirt life in Alexandria, the life to which, according to the source, Antony was inclined by temperament and which, in the end, he chooses as his own.

The question at issue is another dimension of style from those already discussed: not style as garment, or as chosen rhetoric or self-presentation, not style as manipulative instrument, but style as fundamental morality, style as life. Style of speech necessarily reveals personality, values, and ethics: one recognizes both the rectitude and the chilliness of Octavia, the silliness of Lepidus, the policy of Dolabella, from the way they speak as well as from what they say. In the speeches of Antony, Cleopatra, Octavius, Enobarbus, we recognize not just the varying moods of the speakers but their complex inner natures as well. How otherwise, indeed, could we ever assume anything about dramatic characters? Language must act to indicate quality and character, but here it does more: by reaching to the heart of the moral problems faced by Antony and Cleopatra, the language of their play makes us realize anew the ingrained connection between speech and style of life. The "square" of Roman speech and Roman life has its values, which we recognize the more easily as we see those values betrayed by Romans; the "foison" of Egypt, both its fertility and its corruption, find expression in the agon. If one felt that the play were only an essay in style as life-style, then one might draw back from it as superficial and trivial; but *Antony and Cleopatra* seems to be more than a presentation-play of theatrical and unpersoned types, more also than the psychomachia to which it is occasionally reduced. One thing that makes the play so compelling is that it is all these things—show, morality, exercise of power; it is a study in cheapness as well as in extravagance and costliness. Its chief characters are undisguisedly selfish and often trivial; in what lies its force? The language is one indicator, again, for the very style, with its grandioseness and hyperbolical explosions, finally points to the real problem: the efforts of two powerful, wilful, commanding personalities to bring their styles of living, their ingrained alien habits, into line with one another, for no reason other than love.

In a sense quite different from that of the morality-play, *Antony and Cleopatra* is about morality, about mores and ways of life—not by any means just about sexual morality, although problems of sexuality are not ignored—but about lives lived in moral terms. "Style" is—especially in the Attic–Asiatic polarity—a moral indicator, but here displayed as deeply thrust into the psychological and cultural roots of those ways of life. In this play, a given style is never merely an alternative way of expressing something: rather, styles arise from cultural sources beyond a character's choice or control.

At the beginning of the play, this does not seem to be the case: Antony doffs and dons Egyptian and Roman styles, of speech and of life, apparently at will and at need. By the play's end, he has settled for a manner of speech and behavior proved by his decisive final actions to be the signature of his inmost nature. That is to say, his style can be seen not only to express his deepest sense of self, but also to relate to the consequences of his life-choices. It is possible—indeed, it was the classical view, which Plutarch tried hard to present—to see Mark Antony's life as ruined by Cleopatra, to see the play, then, as a struggle between *virtus* and *voluptas* in which Antony fails to live up to his ancestor Hercules' example *in bivio*. But as Plutarch takes pains to tell us, and as Shakespeare in *Julius Caesar* lets us know clearly enough, there was much in Antony's temperament, bred though it was in Rome, to explain why the pull of Egypt was so strong upon him, and from Enobarbus we know how strong that pull was on anyone. Though there is a structural and thematic contrast in the play between Rome and Egypt, the scenes alternating to give us that strong sense of oscillation between these poles, the play is not so simple as a straight contest between their different values.

Seen from one perspective, Rome dominates the play: Rome's wide arch covers the epic scene, Roman policy decides the order of events and the order therefore of these important private lives. The play begins and ends with expressions of the Roman point of view; by Roman standards, Antony perishes for his failure as a Roman. But seen from another angle, Egypt commands the play, where the action begins and ends and where all the major episodes take place. In this respect, the oscillation between the two localities makes it difficult to identify a single and certain source of power. Further, the two areas are not really kept polar: Rome and Egypt interpenetrate each other, just as past history continually penetrates the play's present. Rome's impact on Egypt has helped make Cleopatra what she is; and Antony's Romanness flaws his pleasure in Egypt, even as his Egyptian experience dulls his Roman arrangements. Together and apart, Antony and Cleopatra recall their own and each other's past; Octavius speaks of Antony's and his shared past; Pompey takes the action he does because of events long over before the play begins. We see Antony unwillingly come to accept the fact that his present has been shaped by his past behavior, or that his "Rome" can never be an unqualified value again. Cleopatra dies as a Roman, or so she thinks—but does so in a decor undeniably Egyptian, and by a means particularly local. Her attributes, the iconographical details she chooses for her last tableau, are entirely Egyptian, but her suicide is itself the final Roman gesture consciously chosen.

Nor is the mixture of Rome and Egypt in her accidental: deep in her experience lay the same Julius Caesar who had such a marked effect on both Mark Antony and Octavius Caesar. Before the play's beginning, Cleopatra and her Egypt had been Romanized; by its end, she is once more Romanized, and her Egypt has finally fallen to Roman rule. Indeed, throughout the play, Egypt is constantly open to Rome: Cleopatra's relation to Julius Caesar, to Pompey, to Antony, even her efforts to charm Octavius, are symbolic of her country's dependency upon Rome's dominion. The presence at her court (a court "hers" only by the conqueror's grace) of so many Romans, full of what she calls with distaste "Roman thoughts," assures that the force of Rome upon Egypt is never unfelt, even at the height of Egyptian wassail.

However he may think of himself, Antony is a Roman soldier; Roman soldiers are always with him, even at the moment of his death. When he is away from Egypt, Roman messengers bring Cleopatra news of him and of affairs in Rome. He himself was sent to Egypt as a political administrator; he is succeeded at the play's end by Caesar himself, the last of a series of Romans proclaiming the dominion of the empire, Thidias, Dolabella, Proculeius. People die *à la romaine*: Enobarbus, Eros, Antony, Cleopatra, Charmian, Iras. Antony is borne to die his long-drawn-out death after the high Roman fashion; Cleopatra promises a like death, in which she shall be "marble constant" at the end of a life lived, publicly and privately, in significantly "infinite variety." There is no altering Roman historical destiny, however captivating Egypt and the Egyptian way of life may be.

As the play begins, we are instructed to take Roman virtues for granted as the measure from which Antony has fallen off, but as it develops, we are shown more and more to criticize in Rome. No one could be sillier than Lepidus, one of the triple pillars of the world, grosser and more clownish than any Egyptian; nor more opportunistic than Menas, whose master regrets only that Menas forced him to veto his schemes. Octavius calculates ever; Pompey seeks his own ambitious ends; Octavius's relation to Roman polity is hardly self-subordinating. Further and most important, when he is "Roman," Antony is at his least attractive—in his relations to his Roman wives, Fulvia and Octavia, both dismissed in his mind's economy as terms of political function. As the play advances, the notion of Rome becomes more and more tarnished, particularly in the great orgy-scene in which even Octavius's tongue "splits what it speaks," and Lepidus is carried drunk to bed (a scene unmatched in the play by the "sensual" Egyptians so constantly criticized by these same Roman tongues). In that scene, the grossness of Rome is unequivocally displayed in the unbending ambitions of Caesar, the jealousy of the triumvirs, the thinness of Pompey's honor, Menas's crude hankering after power, the heroes' dancing to their roundsong. Into such hands the world has been delivered. Of course "Egypt" offers no moral improvement over this—Cleopatra lies from first to last, to others and to herself. We are never in doubt of her duplicity, but its naturalness comes to seem worthy in comparison to the slyness of Octavius and of the "trustworthy" Proculeius. Cleopatra's is a consistent and therefore honest duplicity: her policy is innocence itself compared to the masterful and automatic deceptions of the politic Octavius. More: life in its natural spontaneity is set against machination, as Cleopatra faces Octavius symbolically and in fact. Against such an opposition, all the more obviously can Cleopatra be seen to satisfy a universal human need: though she makes hungry where most she satisfies, both hunger and satisfaction are natural enough. The Roman hunger for power can never be filled; in it there is always something barren, inhuman, and perverse—but Cleopatra can allay, even as she rekindles, one Roman's hunger for the satisfactions of love.

The question at issue is not so much the value of Rome set against the value of Egypt, clear as these are, as it is the private relation between Antony and Cleopatra, a relation always colored by their different backgrounds and local loyalties. Normally speaking, it is not considered admirable, nor even sensible, for a man of public position to jeopardize his career for a woman. When the man is Antony, well-married in Rome and well-supplied elsewhere, and the woman Cleopatra, full of experience and of years, it is easy enough to see the matter with Roman eyes as a dissolute business between middle-aged sensualists having a last fling while they can, sinking into sloth and indolence and letting the affairs of empire go hang. Further, there is opportunism even in this love affair—that Cleopatra's political position was immensely strengthened by Antony's presence in Egypt, Caesar's sharp observations make plain. The suspicion certainly exists that she loves Antony for what he can do for her as well as for what he is to her.

The play begins with a Roman inductor, who takes the worst for granted. Philo (what a name for him!) evaluates the major characters according to accepted Roman standards; his critical speech breaks off as Antony and Cleopatra enter to act out what he has just, so degradingly, described as their typical behavior:

> Nay, but this dotage of our general's
> O'erflows the measure: those his goodly eyes,
> That o'er the files and musters of the war
> Have glow'd like plated Mars, now bend, now turn
> The office and devotion of their view
> Upon a tawny front: his captain's heart,
> Which in the scuffles of great fights hath burst
> The buckles on his breast, reneges all temper
> And is become the bellows and the fan
> To cool a gipsy's lust.
>   Look, where they come:
> Take but good note, and you shall see in him
> The triple pillar of the world transform'd
> Into a strumpet's fool: behold and see. (1.1.1–13)

The hero and heroine then enter, to act out their tableau of mutual absorption. They behave with freedom towards each other—perhaps with abandon, indeed—but *not* as strumpet and fool. Their language, that of lovers bent on ideal expression, is thus quite counter to Philo's assessment of them:

> *Cleopatra.* If it be love indeed, tell me how much.
> *Antony.* There's beggary in love that can be reckon'd.

Cleopatra. I'll set a bourn how far to be belov'd.
Antony. Then must thou needs find out new heaven, new earth. (1.1.14–17)

The inflation of their language may strike us, but hardly as exceptional in any pair of lovers mutually absorbed. Rather, theirs is the common rhetoric of love, unspecified and generalized, seeking to express inexpressible heights and depths of feeling. Cosmic analogies are habitually called up by lovers less involved than these in the "real" world; the fact that Antony and Cleopatra are so deeply involved in the factual political world lends poignancy, irony, and a kind of accuracy to their occupational hyperbole. The "new heaven, new earth" of their love, created by them for themselves alone, must substitute for the real geography around them, the Mediterranean world over which their influence and the play's action range. Symbolic geography is invoked, with its real referents: Rome, Alexandria, Athens, Sicily, Sardinia, Parthia, Judea, Media, Mesopotamia, Syria, Armenia, Cyprus, Lydia, Cilicia, Phoenicia, Libya, Cappadocia, Paphlagonia, Thrace, Arabia, Pontus all testify to the reach of Rome, whose "universal peace," proclaimed by Caesar, was endangered by Antony's withdrawal from the world scene in wilful, careless, selfish pursuit of private satisfactions.

All this real world, then, was insufficient for these two—but more important than that, it was also too much for them. To keep their love safe, they must shut out the actual world in hopes of finding a new space for themselves small enough to exclude occupations other than love, large enough to contain their exalted imaginations. In this play, the common literary metaphor of lovers' giving up the world for love is taken as the literal donnée: meaning pours back to give substance to the cliché, as the play teaches something of the human cost involved in neglecting the serious public world, the glories and woes of war and administration, for love of one woman.

Antony and Cleopatra speak "excessively" from the beginning, in an idiom familiar enough in love-poetry. But it is worth noting that they are not alone in this habit of overstatement: Philo's initial speech is wholly cast in terms of excess. He degrades the amorous exploits of his commander with Egypt's queen, certainly: his account of that commander's military accomplishments is as excessive as his contumelious commentary on Antony's amatory achievements. Antony's eyes in war "glow'd like plated Mars"; "his captain's heart . . . burst the buckles on his breast." Caesar's speech too follows the pattern of overstatement: he makes the same kind of contrast of Antony's "lascivious wassails" and "tumblings on the bed of Ptolemy" to his astonishing endurance at Modena and on the Alps (1.4.55–71). Whatever Antony does, it seems, "o'erflows the measure"—but the Romans can *recognize* excess only in Antony's un-Roman acts: the heroic rest is, to them, natural in a Roman. Excess, then, is culturally conditioned: men recognize as excessive only what they regard as "too much," so that Romans who valued military extravagance as much as Cleopatra valued extravagant pleasures could find in her Antony much to praise. When Octavius denounces Antony's self-indulgence, he calls him "A man who is the abstract of all faults / That all men follow." Who could be more than this, an epitome of ill? Taking exception to Octavius's statement, Lepidus casts his comments in terms equally hyperbolical:

> I must not think there are
> Evils enow to darken all his goodness:
> His faults in him, seem as the spots of heaven,
> More fiery by night's blackness. (1.4.10–13)

What are we to make of Antony, then? What are we to make of his present love-experience, judged by Philo as tawdry and low, judged by the lovers as quite past the reach of expression? In fact, what do Antony and Cleopatra *do*? We are told (by Romans) how they pass their time, in behavior characterized as "Asiatic" in the extreme. Egypt is, certainly, "the East," regularly so designated in the play. As queen, Cleopatra is often addressed by her country's name; when she dies, she is called "the eastern star," that is, the planet Venus. What Antony and Cleopatra do, evidently, is live by the attributes of the Asiatic style; they act out, they and the Romans tell us, a life-style gaudy, loose, ungirt, decorated, artful, contrived, and deceitful. The Egyptian court is an idle, opulent, sensual, Asiatic place, where men are effeminate and women bold. Mardian the eunuch exists to remind us of what can happen to a man in such an environment, and we see Antony unmanned in various symbolic ways. Normal decorum is constantly breached by this general, this queen. Drunk, Antony will not hear his messages from Rome; playing with Cleopatra, he relinquishes his armor to her and dresses in her "tires and mantles." She takes his sword away, and though she returns it before their battle, she disarms him entirely in the midst of a real battle, by more critical means. Publicly she ignores him, however preoccupied with him privately. Nor is she manly, for all the dressing in armor and proclaiming herself a man's equal before the last battle. At Actium she flees out of fear, and retires in the last pitch as well: when Antony is dying before her eyes, she will not emerge from her monument, nor even open its doors that he may easily be brought in to her—because, she says, she is afraid.

In Egypt men feast and sleep. "The beds in the East are soft" in many ways. Both defeat and victory are celebrated in Egypt by one other gaudy night, and Caesar seems to acknowledge this Egyptian need for self-indulgence when, to reassure the captive Cleopatra, he urges her to "Feed and sleep." Though the meanings of "sleep" deepen radically by the end of the play, at the beginning and for the most part, "sleep" is a sign of Egyptian indolence and womanishness. Festivities are unmanly too; Caesar says of his great competitor:

> From Alexandria
> This is the news: he fishes, drinks, and wastes

The lamps of night in revel; is not more manlike
Than Cleopatra; nor the queen of Ptolemy
More womanly than he. (1.4.3–7)

His last comment may indicate Caesar's limitations as a judge of human character, but it also sums up the Roman attitude to Egypt, a place merely of "lascivious wassails." The way most Romans think of Cleopatra, it is no wonder that she shrinks, at the end, from being carried through Rome to see "some squeaking Cleopatra boy my greatness / I' the posture of a whore." She knows how she is named in Rome, because in his rage Antony tells her:

I found you as a morsel, cold upon
Dead Caesar's trencher; nay, you were a fragment
Of Gnaeus Pompey's, besides what hotter hours,
Unregister'd in vulgar fame, you have
Luxuriously pick'd out. (3.13.116–20)

Again and again, "appetite" is a word used to cover all satisfactions. Feasting and love (or, better, sex) are equated, as in the passage just quoted. Cleopatra is often reduced to food—by Enobarbus, speaking of Antony, "He will to his Egyptian dish again"; by herself, in her youth "a morsel for a monarch," although those were, as she says, her "salad days," when she was both greener and colder than she later became. Pompey speaks man-to-man to Antony of "your fine Egyptian cookery" (2.7.63–65) and, later, of the "cloyless sauce" that Egypt proves for Antony.

Unquestionably the preoccupation with sex and with the shared sexuality of Antony and Cleopatra runs as an undercurrent through the play. The difference between Egyptian and Roman talk of sex is instructive: Charmian and the Soothsayer, Cleopatra and the Eunuch, speak playfully and naturally; Enobarbus speaks cynically to and about Antony, on "death," on horses and mares; and the other Romans show their prurience and crudity when they speak, as they compulsively do, about the subject. The imagery too carries its sexual meanings: Cleopatra's "sweating labour" joins with the imagery of bearing and of weight to remind us of the woman's part in the act of love. This language in turn conjoins with the marvelous and varied horse-imagery which reaches its peak as she imagines the absent Antony on horseback: "O happy horse, to bear the weight of Antony!" Such language assumes sexuality to be a normal part of life; the Nile-imagery, with its "quickenings" and "foison" references, suggests procreation and creation as part of a natural cycle. Nature provides reproductive images for sexuality, and war another sort. The constant reference to swords, in fact as in image, keeps manliness ever at the forefront of our awareness, as it is at the forefront of the dramatic characters' awareness, too.

There is more than the suggestion, then, that love is no more than appetite or a drive; if that were all there was to love, the Roman view of this affair would be correct, Cleopatra simply a whore and Antony besotted, "ne'er lust-wearied." But can a man remain "ne'er lust-wearied" by the same woman, however infinite her variety, if she is merely a whore, however aristocratic her birth? Enobarbus, in so many ways faithful to Antony and Cleopatra in spite of his disapproval of their behavior, sees something more in her and tries to say what that "more" is. Once again, significantly, he speaks in terms of food—"Other women cloy / The appetites they feed, but she makes hungry, / Where most she satisfies." Mere sexuality, strong sexual love, idealized love: however it is described, the emotions shared by Antony and Cleopatra challenge the heroic world of Roman military organization.

This miracle of love (or whatever it is) we do not see acted out onstage. Indeed, we never see Antony and Cleopatra alone, as we do Romeo and Juliet, Desdemona and Othello. What we see is something quite different: a man and a woman playing, quarreling, making up; a woman sulking, pretending to anger, flying into real rages, running away from danger, flirting even in deep disgrace and danger. Except on Roman tongues, there is little that can be called shameless or lascivious in Cleopatra's or Antony's utterances about love: her language on this preoccupying subject is remarkably clean—which is not the case with Roman commentators on these spectacular lovers.

To make so commonplace, so vulgar a mixture into a woman worth losing the world for is a considerable task for any playwright. Our playwright accomplishes it by fairly simple, even domestic, means. His Cleopatra has, among other things, a girlish, hoydenish companionability. She is obviously amusing company; she will try anything once. She has a lovely imagination and considerable command of language. She tries to rise to occasions, and sometimes she does. We hear much of Cleopatra's whoredom, and we see Antony blundering after her, twice fatally; we hear him speak of the less pleasant side of his love, of the "Egyptian fetters" which tie him in Alexandria, of his "dotage," and later, when he misses her in Rome, of his "pleasure" with Cleopatra. There is every reason to think very little of Cleopatra—although, to balance her crudities (as when she had a salt-fish attached to Antony's line), we are made to see that even in her breaches of decorum, her riggishness, her foolish middle age, she is delightful. She is earthy, and down-to-earth; her sudden accessions of realism puncture both the romanticizing of the lovers and Antony's simplistic view of love and Cleopatra as satisfaction to his appetite. This woman is something more:

> Sir, you and I must part . . .
> Sir, you and I have lov'd. (1.3.87–88)

In praising Antony, I have disprais'd Caesar . . .
I am paid for't now. (2.5.107–9)

Think you there was, or might be such a man
As this I dreamt of? (5.2.93–94)

>   Antony
> Shall be brought drunken forth, and I shall see
> Some squeaking Cleopatra boy my greatness
> I' the posture of a whore. (5.2.218–20)

When her ironical common sense pierces her own theatricals, her charm is irresistible: though she rarely acts on that knowledge, we see that at moments she knows herself and the precarious, politicking world she lives in. It is this side of her, the practical, real woman, that is picked up in Charmian's farewell epithet: to "a *lass* unparallel'd." Age, apparently, could not wither her, nor a rakish life, nor childbearing.

But in her first parting from Antony, as in her exchange with Dolabella after Antony's death and just before her own, Cleopatra's common sense rises to something greater:

Sir, you and I must part, but that's not it:
Sir, you and I have lov'd, but there's not it.

The facts are clear enough—but they do not provide Cleopatra with an explanation for the pressure of her feelings, that this love for Antony is unduly significant, that parting from him must radically diminish her. Her sentence loses its direction as she seeks to express the "more" of her feeling for him:

That you know well, something it is I would,—
O, my oblivion is a very Antony,
And I am all forgotten! (1.3.89–91)

As she later says, she wants to sleep out "the great gap of time" that Antony is away from her; in his absence, even by herself, she is, imaginatively, "forgotten" and therefore does not exist. Both Antony and Cleopatra speak feelingly and movingly about their sense of identity lost. Part of their tragedy lies in Antony's feeling himself dissolve when he is with her, and Cleopatra's feeling her "nothingness" when he is not with her.

Cleopatra makes clear that her love for Antony is fully sexual; but, as has been noted, this emphasis comes in reverie, not in lascivious action or exchange. What is significant, surely, is that in a life given to sexual conquest and enjoyment, her relation to Antony means more to her than anything else. It is not that Cleopatra does not want to be reminded of her old connection with Caesar; it is that she knows its qualitative difference from the connection with Antony. Certainly Cleopatra does not shirk the facts of her sexual past; however giddy and irresponsible her behavior with Antony, though, she knows that for him, she has quit being a rake. For her, sexuality is never just the "pleasure" that Antony implies early in the play it is for him. It has (at last, one has the impression) risen above itself to become love of a sort that defies definition in psychological ways, not just in "literary" ways. Indeed, in literary ways, the lovers' extreme preoccupation with one another is almost *too* resonant to the conventional language of love: as in *Othello*, but in an entirely different context, the Petrarchan mixture of love and war has here been actualized in the necessary conditions, unmetaphored into actuality, of everyday life for this general and this queen. But the love-poet's transcendent aim is the same as theirs: how to express the indefinable love they share, a love that to unsympathetic onlookers seems ordinary enough, vulgar enough, but to the lover experiencing it inexpressibly glorious and valuable. Their language is pitched at the familiar literary goal, to make the "new heaven, new earth" of lovers' cliché into a universe for their exclusive dwelling. Their *folie à deux* is in part a matter of language, manipulated to record heightened experience and to displace both conventional and particular renditions of their experience by others.

Cleopatra's imagination particularly works at this task: if sex is the reality and imagination the fantasy of love, then the two fuse in Cleopatra's speech in Antony's absence from her, when she imagines him as he at that very moment actually *is*:

> Stands he, or sits he?
> Or does he walk? or is he on his horse? (1.5.19–20)

Her sexual memories crowd into the single line, "O happy horse, to bear the weight of Antony!" Her images of weight, realistic enough in any woman's experience of love, come to their culmination in the terrible scene of Antony's death, as she draws him into her monument:

> How heavy weighs my lord!
> Our strength is all gone into heaviness,
> That makes the weight. (4.15.32–34)

The reality is there, although not displayed to us, of the children she has borne him; "the lap of Egypt's widow," as Pompey so rudely said, has actually held Antony and known what it was to do so. Finally, to her "demi-Atlas" she attributes more weight than any man can carry; she turns her love into an even more colossal personage than the world will recognize or can, in the person of Dolabella, accept.

In this habit of stretching expression, of trying to say more than words or figures habitually allow, lies some clue to the effect on each other of these lovers. They make each other feel that age is no bar to living fully; they make each other feel, not still alive, but more than usually alive, a feeling, however illusory, which can exercise curious power over a man and a woman more than commonly experienced. The connection between them, obviously, is quite different from other experiences they have had; Cleopatra knows this from the beginning of the play, and we witness Antony coming to know it too. It is precisely his marriage to Octavia, with all its chilly merits, that teaches him what Cleopatra is to him. In their view of each other, Antony and Cleopatra are more than life-size. So Cleopatra speaks truth in her great speech of hyperbole about Antony:

> I dreamt there was an Emperor Antony.
> O such another sleep, that I might see
> But such another man! . . .
> His face was as the heavens, and therein stuck
> A sun and moon, which kept their course, and lighted
> The little O, the earth. . . .
> His legs bestrid the ocean, his rear'd arm
> Crested the world: his voice was propertied
> As all the tuned spheres, and that to friends:
> But when he meant to quail, and shake the orb,
> He was as rattling thunder. For his bounty,
> There was no winter in 't: an autumn 'twas
> That grew the more by reaping: his delights
> Were dolphin-like, they show'd his back above
> The element they liv'd in: in his livery
> Walk'd crowns and crownets: realms and islands were
> As plates dropp'd from his pocket. (5.2.76–92)

Antony has then finally turned into that "new heaven, new earth" he had told Cleopatra in the first scene she must find as the appropriate bound of their love. Microcosm and macrocosm change places: the earth is smaller than this man, as the common cosmic metaphor expands into all space and more-than-time in the images of ever-ripe autumn and a creature, the dolphin, transcending his natural element. Correspondence imagery involving worlds in different scales—the cosmos, however thought of, macrocosm and microcosm; stars and eyes—is so common in sixteenth- and seventeenth-century poetry as to be mere cliché, and certainly at one level, all Cleopatra is doing in this magnificent speech is making more extravagant a notion already hyperbolical at its base. But in this particular case of lovers, the standard hyperbole has its peculiar reality to "match" this particular psychological and political situation. In the imagery, the larger world has been contracted into the limits of Antony's body (normally a microcosm), and Antony's body in turn enlarged encompasses and surpasses the macrocosm to which originally it had been likened. In fact, this is what happened to these lovers: "the world," in this case half or a third of the civilized world which was under their control, was rejected in favor of the "little world," quite literally, of man. "Bodies" are very important in the play, and although Antony and Cleopatra speak with remarkable delicacy about each other's bodies and their own bodily sensations in love, this speech gives the literary justification for that physical love. Hyperbolic metaphor that it is, this speech at the same time unmetaphors its literary content by making plain the crucial importance to these lovers of their finite, particular, well-worn bodies.

Cleopatra does not linger on the fantasy, but asks Dolabella, with the realism characteristic of her:

> Think you there was, or might be such a man
> As this I dreamt of? (5.2.93–94)

To that, Roman Dolabella can only respond, "Gentle madam, no"—which serves to arouse Cleopatra to still more immense reaches of imagery, to language rejecting anything nature can offer as fit comparison to the wonder that Antony was. This time momentary realism touched off, as it habitually does not, the reassertion of hyperbole's value. Hyperbole becomes "true"—and yet even that hyperbolical language is not "enough" for the intense feelings between these two overreachers of life. In the references within the play, they are always more than merely human, more than triumvir and queen: Cleopatra was, we hear, more beautiful than the most beautiful picture of Venus. Art cannot render her, nor can nature's works render Antony. In her eulogy of him, Cleopatra never denies his manhood—"My man of men," she says, and she should know—but the manhood she attributes to him no ordinary mortal can aspire to. His bounty was endless—and his treatment of Enobarbus suggests that this is so—his delights transcendent. His empire was to be prodigal of imperial power—"as plates dropp'd from his pocket." Compare that magnificence with Caesar's careful accounting of Mark Antony's distribution of empire in act 3, scene 6: for Caesar, these political entities which Mark Antony gave away were no mere "plates" but the extended possessions of Rome, to be protected, at cost, for Rome's sake.

Cleopatra's imagination is as bountiful as Antony's generosity. Her language is rich as her habitat, and she is, as both detractors and admirers point out, histrionic to a degree. She stages herself at Cydnus; she stages herself as dead for Antony; she stages herself for her death. She speaks and is spoken of in theatrical terms of scene, act, and stage; she is a creature of impulse and whim, which she tries out on her audiences, acting to Dolabella, to Caesar, to Antony, acting even with her familiar maids. That habit of acting stands her in good stead in her determination to outwit Caesar at the end. Reversing Marx's famous quip, this play first acts out in farce what becomes tragedy a second time through. Cleopatra pretends to be dead—trivially, but with horrible results for Antony—before she dies in earnest. The theme of death echoes throughout the play—the lovers know, long before the crisis, the cost of their choice. Enobarbus plays on the slang term, "death," for sexual intercourse, when Antony first tells him he must be gone; his cynicism can seem justified to an audience which sees Cleopatra feign illness and death. Her coquetry, charming within the domestic protections of her court, is fatal on the battlefield. It is worth noting that for the deceit which cost him his life, Mark Antony never reproaches her; instead, he promises to be "A bridegroom in my death, and run into 't / As to a lover's bed." She too equates love and death: "The stroke of death is as a lover's pinch, / Which hurts, and is desir'd." She dies to join Mark Antony—"Husband, I come"—as his wife, taking for granted the meaning of a simple act which could never take place in the Roman world during their lives. Put in the simplest terms, the word "death" is gradually ennobled by what happens in the play—but not before its seamier implications have all been laid before us.

So the play begins to live up to itself. As Philo's crudity is submerged under the lovers' flood of words, again and again the nasty turns out to have its noble aspect too, the Gorgon indeed becomes Mars. Because the playwright never shirks the unpleasantness, the triviality, even the occasional brutality of the lovers, because he always allows them to recognize and to reveal the compulsiveness of their love, its literal extremity, that love's peculiar force begins to take its confirmation from the radical action and the extreme language. As we watch the hyperbole coming true, we recognize a maturing of emotions more than life-size to begin with, commanding a space of their own making, relying on their mutual respect for their own worth. The simplicity, singleheartedness, and intensity of this faulty human love, magnificent in spite of the lovers' politics and duplicity, in spite of the inevitable deceits of their world, come to seem a far greater achievement, against greater odds, than the successful Roman quest for power.

And for this, as we shall see, there is theoretical precedent in Longinus's defense of the style Antony and his acquaintances used, a style designed to express generosity, magnitude, magnanimity; a style, as he put it, "with the true ring of a noble mind." Though Shakespeare does not slight the cultural structure and construction of any style—Roman, Egyptian here, Navarrese elsewhere—he is concerned in this play with the significance of a personal style within the cultural matrix, with what Longinus called "magalofrosune." Though we know, from Philo's initial speech, of Antony's capacity for greatness and perceive, in his dealings with Enobarbus and Cleopatra, his magnanimity in the face of terrible losses, he still has to live up to the nobility of his soul and to the elevation of his speech. Still more Cleopatra, unused to Roman gestures of magnanimity: from riggish, rakish queen who plays tricks with a man's honor and his life, she must grow into the moral capacities her hyperbole seems to make light of.

The risks are great—how does a man, how can a woman, leave off grandiose and bombastic play-acting, even to the roles of god and goddess, to die as heroes? The lovers set their sights high from the start: chose as their models superhuman figures from Roman mythology—Antony in the play's first speech is likened to Mars, Cleopatra unmistakably to Venus. They act out that archetypal coupling throughout their lives, even to receiving mockery like the gods of Venus and Mars. Cleopatra is a goddess of love in her disguises, both the Roman Venus and the Egyptian Isis: she celebrated her greatest political triumph, over Antony and by his means over Rome, dressed "in the habiliments of the goddess Isis," as Caesar in outrage reports. Isis was also a moon-goddess, whose variability, reflected in the feminine psychology, is made much of in the play; her "habiliments," as Plutarch tells us in another place, are varicolored, to show her involvement with all nature—with light as well as dark, fire as well as water, life as well as death, beginning as well as ending. These robes are singularly appropriate to Cleopatra: they symbolize all matter and "afford many disclosures of themselves, and opportunities to view them as they are changed about in various ways." Cleopatra is too much a woman, variable and faulty, to "be" either Venus or Isis, but she takes the part of both of them; posing as these goddesses, she occasionally takes on some of their meanings, as Antony on occasion takes on some of the meanings attributed to Mars and Hercules. In addition, this pair is too intermingled in one another for such an interpretation: whatever their natural attributes making them godlike, Antony and Cleopatra are a man and a woman to each other and to the world.

Although it is as a man that she most values him, Cleopatra symbolically and actually unmans Antony. We hear of her dressing him in her clothes, as Omphale did Hercules. His decline from perfect manhood to something less than that is part of Antony's tragedy. In this play, however, the facts of the Roman idea of manhood are examined again and again and found wanting, particularly in respect to the very quality Antony so lavishly displays, magnanimity. He was a generous, a prodigal man, but always a man large of spirit. Largesse is his attribute, in all senses. He gave away his goods to his soldiers in defeat; his graciousness drove the defected Enobarbus to his shamefast death. To Antony's naturally great character Octavius stands in cheerless contrast; and no one in Rome, ever, is shown as rising to Antony's heights of grace. Again and again we are brought up against the hard realization that if to be a Roman is to be so narrow and calculating as Octavius, so vulgar as Pompey, so divided as Enobarbus, then Antony has surely chosen the better part. Octavius speaks beautifully of Antony's death:

> The breaking of so great a thing should make
> A greater crack. The round world
> Should have shook lions into civil streets,
> And citizens to their dens. The death of Antony
> Is not a single doom; in the name lay
> A moiety of the world. (5.1.14–19)

Beautiful words indeed to eulogize a dead colleague and opponent—but Caesar cannot help calculating the man's worth: "A moiety of the world." That coveted demi-monde is at last his; the reckoning is over, the world brought under Caesar's universal landlordism. The "boy" has become, as Cleopatra names him, "Sole sir of the world." After the briefest respite in honor of his dead "mate in empire," Caesar turns back to the business of the world and lays his plans for the future. To such a man, it is difficult not to prefer the prodigal old ruffian, who can assert, and mean it, "There's beggary in love that can be reckon'd," who can risk and lose his moiety (or his third) of the world for something which, however flawed, he valued above himself.

For Antony is no standard Roman, as the Romans testify. Men *speak* of his greatness of character and action, his stature in virtue and in vice. Men *act* to honor those qualities: his soldiers love him; his servant kills himself rather than stab his master; Enobarbus dies of having betrayed him. Philo can speak of him only in hyperbolical terms; so, in spite of themselves, can Caesar and Lepidus. In everyone's mind, this man was aggrandized and enlarged above the commonalty of men. Like his ancestor Hercules, Antony does things no other man can do, on a scale on which no other man can do them. It is not Cleopatra alone who feels this, but everyone who knows him. When we compare this Antony with the man duped twice by Cleopatra, or with the man causing Caesar's messenger to be beaten, or the man feasting, joking, and making love with Cleopatra, we see the range of the problem Shakespeare set himself and we must suspect that some of this hyperbole is merely bombast. But when his imagination is fired by Cleopatra, Antony *can* do great deeds at arms. He conquered the entire East and redistributed its countries (without consulting Rome) among Cleopatra and her children. When she arms him, he defeats the Romans at odds, and returns to tell her his "gests" that day. At his death, when an ordinary man might well have nagged, he looks to an Elysium in which he and she shall outdo Aeneas and Dido; he warns her to look after her safety and, like the great lover he is, dies on a kiss. No trace remains of his rage at her, no trace of reproach for her false message: with his own life he was prodigal; with hers, he was generous.

These are the gestures to match an hyperbolical style, the behavior so admired by Longinus: the gestures of the overreaching man whose imagination is larger than the stage it must act upon. For Antony, the two "stand up peerless"; Cleopatra remembers that

> Eternity was in our lips, and eyes,
> Bliss in our brow's bent; none our parts so poor,
> But was a race of heaven. (1.3.35–37)

For her he was, finally, truly Herculean, a "demi-Atlas," a colossus whose "legs bestrid the ocean"; he was greater than the arch of empire itself: he was her world. For him, she could make herself into Venus and Isis, could "be" ageless and infinitely desirable, immortal, more than human. They read their stature from their mutual view of one another. Their ideas of themselves and of each other may have been unrealistic, vain, self-flattering, and self-deceitful, but they reflected what can never be readily explained, the peculiar sense of well-being and power a man and woman in love can give each other. So their clumsy games, their open lovemaking and open quarreling, their flirtations, their drinking, their mockery, turn somehow from nonsense and bombast into legitimate hyperbole, into a language forever on the stretch to express what had not been expressed before. Far from ideal lovers, Antony and Cleopatra demand a language for their love which rejects conventional hyperbole and invents and creates new overstatements, new forms of overstatement. In the language itself, we can read the insatiability of their love, as the language seems to make hungry, too, where most it satisfies. Nothing is enough for these two, not even the most extravagant figures of speech.

The language Antony and Cleopatra use, the language others use about them, is stretched at its upper and lower limits, to express their high and low gestures as bigger than life-size. It is interesting that Antony and Cleopatra do not bewitch others' imaginations only by their charismatic presence; their great qualities are praised, described, referred to, and criticized mostly in their absence. These two are watched by a world fascinated even when disapproving; they are staged in a play of their own making, with the world as their willing audience. But they do not really play for that audience: their imaginative acting is all for each other, and in their mutual absorption they do not care who happens to look on at the spectacle. Of course the Romans cannot keep their eyes off them; beneath the language of official disapproval, one can see Roman fascination with this un-Roman style of life, with this abundant, prodigal, excessive manner of doing things. Their bounty knows no winter but is, in Antony's word, always "foison."

Ripeness, overripeness: certainly the images of fertility, in particular the Nile-imagery, stresses life-giving, fecundity, creation; and, with these good qualities, also corruption and rotting. Action can corrupt; so can inaction. In Caesar's image for the variable Roman people, the famous "vagabond flag" passage, we read of one kind of rotting; in Antony's inaction we see another. The flag is dissolved in the stream's current; "solutus," dissolved, was one word of disapprobation applied to the Asiatic style, and (as Charney points out) images of dissolution and deliquescence abound in the play. We see things dissolve and resolve—the liaison with Cleopatra, the marriage with Octavia. Antony vacillates between his Roman alliances and his Egyptian delights, choosing now the one, now the other. The tide is against him, literally at Actium, figuratively on land as well. And yet one is not surprised at this particular literalization of water-images of dissolution, for the metaphor has gained power through the play until, in Antony's great speech about himself, we see that he thinks of himself as formless, his shape lost. The metaphor of dissolution is overtly made use of through the play—"Let Rome in Tiber melt," Antony cries at the beginning; "Authority melts from me," he says near the end of his life. Cleopatra too speaks in this image: "Melt Egypt into Nile." If she should ever play him false, then "dissolve my life." Both use the neologism "discandy," Cleopatra in a hyperbolical assertion of love, Antony in connection with his melting authority:

> The hearts
> That spaniel'd me at heels, to whom I gave
> Their wishes, do discandy, melt their sweets
> On blossoming Caesar. (4.12.20–23)

The most important of the dissolution passages is Antony's speech about himself as a cloud in which shapes continually shift, dissolve, and reform until "The rack dislimns, and makes it indistinct, / As water is in water." When he finds his Roman form again and dies "a Roman, by a Roman / Valiantly vanquish'd," Cleopatra says of him, "The crown o' the earth doth melt," into a nothingness she feels as palpable. To mark Cleopatra's death, Charmian calls for cosmic dissolution, "Dissolve, thick cloud, and rain, that I may say / The gods themselves do weep" (5.2.298–99).

Peculiarly enough, other words characteristically applied in denigration to the Asiatic style are picked up and openly developed in the powerful imagery of this play. "Enervis" is such a word—Antony and Cleopatra taunt each other with idleness (1.2.113–14, 127; 3.8.90–92), and Antony accuses himself of "slackness" (3.7.27). The notion of effeminacy is related to the notion of idleness and, in Enobarbus's last speech to Antony, is explicitly connected with melting. Enobarbus weeps ("I, an ass, am onion-eyed"), and asks Antony to stop talking—"for shame / Transform us not to women" (4.2.35–36). "Inanis," empty, is another word played in the imagery: "vacancy" occurs, in connection with voluptuousness (1.4.26), and in Enobarbus's attempt to praise Cleopatra

(2.6.216). By all odds the most significant use in the play of such a term is the imagery and the practice of enlargement, of blowing up. The Asiatic style was "inflatus": we have seen how Cleopatra continually enlarged her idea of Antony, until in her paean to Dolabella of Antony's greatness she outdid her hyperbolical habits of rhetoric. There is, too, much about inflation in the play's language. In the first speech of Philo, in which so much of the play's implications, sexual and other, lie coiled, Antony is said to have "become the bellows and the fan / To cool a gipsy's lust." Primarily, the bellows blows up, the fan cools: but *both* can actually blow up and both can cool. On her barge, Cleopatra has magical fans, apparently, also both blowing and cooling: the "winds did seem / To glow the delicate cheeks which they did cool, / And what they undid did." (2.2.203–5). Breathless, Cleopatra breathes forth her power; in her, Enobarbus assures his hearers, defect becomes perfection. Antony and Cleopatra, then, "inflate" each other—or, to put the same thing more gracefully, they inspirit each other. For those Atticists who polemicized against the Asiatic style, such "inflation" was bad because it was untrue to nature and gave false impressions of fact. Now, Antony and Cleopatra may have had, and have fostered, false impressions about themselves and each other; but they were trying to do something else, something highly respectable and highly poetic: to give utterance to their own convictions and sensations of being larger than life, which in turn demanded a style of expression more spacious than that used by the ruck of mankind. By means of the style, ever on the reach for an undefined "more," the infinite longings of these figures can be understood: but, furthermore, by means of this twice-heightened speech, the play examines not only the values of an enriched style, but the values of the life it seeks to match. The play is a study in richness and ripeness, necessarily also a study in overripeness as well, a study even of corruption. But never may we conclude, in morality vein, that these last qualities are valueless, that the people who speak so are simply megalomaniac and self-deluded. Indeed, what emerges from the play is something quite different, the affirmation of the values, qualified by an awareness of its dangers, of such a way of life.

As one works through the play, several things become clearer: at the beginning, Antony speaks hyperbolically, bombastically: his honest heartfelt emotions, mingled with an ironic self-criticism, are reserved for his realization of Fulvia's death. It is Cleopatra who checks his overstatement, questions the sincerity of his hyperbole ("Excellent falsehood"; "Hear the ambassadors"). Mocking him, she is still besotted with him; no less than Antony is she manipulable by her love. Both Antony and Cleopatra suffer from self-surpassing rages, she at the messenger, he at her apparent and real betrayals of him; hyperbole operates there in both language and gesture. By the third act, something has begun to happen which demonstrates the identity of the lovers: the hyperbolical style with which Antony began the play now issues from Cleopatra's mouth:

> Ah, dear, if I be so,
> From my cold heart let heaven engender hail,
> And poison it in the source, and the first stone
> Drop in my neck: as it determines, so
> Dissolve my life; the next Caesarion smite
> Till by degrees the memory of my womb,
> Together with my brave Egyptians all,
> By the discandying of this pelleted storm,
> Lie graveless, till the flies and gnats of Nile
> Have buried them for prey! (3.13.158–67)

It is Antony now who says, "I am satisfied," evidently needing that assurance to go on with the "chronicle" of which he feels himself to be a part. Early in the play, Antony and Cleopatra are separately hyperbolical; as their unity grows, they adapt to each other's modes of speech. These lovers are in many ways temperamentally alike, and they become more so as their meaning for each other becomes more conscious and more motivating in their lives. In the third act, as they pitch their lives together once more, their most hyperbolical speeches of love are signs of their deepening unity with one another, the more poignant for their violent and frequent misunderstandings.

To speak as they do, so grandly, so magnificently, so frankly in hyperbole, is in Antony's and Cleopatra's nature. They are true to one aspect of the Attic (or "Senecan") prescription, after all, in that they express "themselves" truly in their language—this is to say, then, that their style *must* in honesty be bombastic, which according to Attic prescription should mean that their style matches the variability and shoddiness of their characters, discovers beneath their bluster and shouting mere fustian cheapness, secondhand emotions, and sleazy intentions. Longinus was fully aware of how close the elevated style was to bombast: it is almost as if Shakespeare set himself to examine Longinus's problem fully in this play, to test out against human actions and human speech the human aspiration for sublimity.

Antony's habits of speech reach toward and respond to the fundamental grandeur of his nature, as his actions increasingly confirm the propriety and integrity of his grand style. That Enobarbus adopts the hyperbolical mode—that Plutarch adopts it, indeed—to render Cleopatra's magnificence, tells us much about the "real" application of an inflated and hyperbolical style. In Enobarbus's mouth we are invited to recognize things as they are: Enobarbus knows *ping* from *pong*, Rome from Egypt. For better and for worse, Enobarbus is a Roman, speaks as a Roman, acts as a Roman. Yet to this man is given the great speech about Cleopatra, its figures stretching farther and farther as the speech goes on and as he realizes the difficulties involved in making anyone who has not experienced her charm understand what this woman is. Like his master, vacillating between Rome and Egypt in his own life, Enobarbus seems to opt for Rome against Egypt. At his end he chooses neither place, but rather chooses a man, a human being involved with both symbolic places and, for him, transcending both. From his relation to Mark Antony, Enobarbus took his final definition, to die with his betrayed master's name on his lips. By the pull of hyperbole, of overstatement, of inflation, and of magnanimity on such a man, we can measure the power of Antony for Cleopatra—and, just because of his greatness, can measure her power for him. The two lovers confirm each other and themselves—so much we might expect. Enobarbus, with his excursions beyond his habitual style and behavior, not wanting to do so, nonetheless confirms them from outside themselves.

In his set-speech on Cleopatra, Enobarbus had called upon a natural miracle to attest to her power:

> Antony
> Enthron'd i' the market-place, did sit alone,
> Whistling to the air; which, but for vacancy,
> Had gone to gaze on Cleopatra too,
> And made a gap in nature. (2.2.214–18)

Even in figure, though, this miracle cannot take place; there is no gap in nature, nor in this play, however crowded things are by the space Antony and Cleopatra take up, by the bruit of their presence, the bustle of their companionship. To stretch the metaphor, the play's dominant style is not one of vanity, although there are vanities enough blatantly set forth in the protagonists' characters. They are self-centered and self-indulgent—but they are not self-satisfied. They look to each other forever for more; they criticize each other and themselves. In their lives, however lived out in the Asiatic style, in dissoluteness, inflation, swelling, enervation, slackness, effeminacy, and idleness, these two do *not* decay. Their satisfactions breed hunger; their desire neither stales nor cloys, not even at the moments in which they die. Finally, their desire can be seen to be a particular kind of love, a kind of love rarely made romantic, firmly based in shared sexual experience. Out of such love, each can think only of the other at the time of death.

Even when they are idle, Antony and Cleopatra make a stir in the world. This is perhaps part of the tragedy (though not in Renaissance terms): that public figures cannot afford private joys. In the modern jargon, there is no solution to their problems either of aspiring temperament or of historical situation. They could not do without each other and, their world being what it was, they could not live comfortably with each other. But imagine alternative solutions: suppose Antony *had* gone back to live in Rome with Octavia and their daughters (present in Plutarch but excised from the play); the political struggle with Caesar could hardly have failed to come to a head, for Caesar, if not Antony, had to find opportunity for quarrel. Suppose Cleopatra had gone back to her philanderings with Eastern potentates and Roman ambassadors: could she have restrained herself from political troublemaking, out of boredom if nothing else? Or, turning the matter about still more, how could Antony have lived among Romans whose view of Cleopatra was as extreme as his own, though at quite the other end of the scale? Could he have endured the silliness of Lepidus, the calculations of Octavius, the prurience of Menas and the rest, their eagerness to vulgarize personal experiences beyond their capacities to imagine? Character has something to do with "fate"—the struggle with Caesar would have come in the end, without the satisfaction for Antony of having chosen for Cleopatra, without the heroics at his death which, self-deceiving or not, eased him into Elysium with the conviction that his life had been worth its trouble and pain, and that his final disgrace was canceled by his grandiose final gestures of love.

This is a curious play, resting on an ambivalent concept of love impossible to sum up, to categorize, or to define. We learn throughout that desire can remain insatiable, that vacillation breeds corruption, that rewards in one sphere exact penalties in another. Cleopatra's fans heated where they cooled, what they undid, did. So Cleopatra: she undid Antony, but also she made of him not so much what she wanted him to be—indeed, in that she failed—as what *he* wanted to be. Certainly one cannot draw as a general conclusion from this play that an intense connection between a man and a woman justifies all else, justifies all the neglect, the idleness, the betrayals, the prodigality of lives and honor. Shakespeare shows us, unmistakably, that it does not, by the play's eternal balancing of one thing against another, its long vacillation between the bombastic and the sublime, its constant qualification of virtue by fault, of vice by virtue. But on balance, it is obvious that those experiences, from whatever source, which can elevate human beings are judged more favorably than those which do not; that those human beings who can be elevated are nobler than those whose nature is too small to permit such enlargement. With all its qualifications and all its defects admitted, proclaimed, displayed, the love of Antony and Cleopatra is nonetheless affirmed, the strumpet and the strumpet's fool grow into the imaginative warrior and the theatrical queen. There is no denying their excesses, which are examined, studied, and reassessed both by the speakers within the play and by the audience watching the excesses demonstrated onstage. We learn that in such excess, life itself can reside. Though it threatens to rot, and seems at times to have corrupted the lovers, their style of living affirms their life—and that despite the deaths of the proceedings.

Indeed, in the deaths we see the value of the lives. Antony says that he dies as a Roman, but he bungled his death all the same, both by letting Eros die before him, and by not killing himself outright. However significant the "elevation" of Antony into Cleopatra's tomb, it is an awkward business; the queen's failure to open the tomb lays stress, just at the worst moment, on the weakest side of her nature. Antony's dying skirts bombast the while, and we may assume that his failure to die efficiently in the Roman style is one mark Egypt laid upon him.

His beauty of character, though, emerges clearly through this uncomfortable death-scene: in spite of the clumsiness, what we remember is Antony's magnanimity and Cleopatra's high poetry. Antony affirms in his manner of dying both the Roman and the Eastern sides of his nature; Cleopatra too comes to accept Roman ways, even to embrace them in her own death. Her contemptuous fear of "Roman thoughts" in the first act gives way before her desire to emulate Antony and to die, like him, "in the high Roman fashion." Her suicide, though, cannot be said to be pure Roman: she had done research into painless ways to die; she chose the Nile worm as a suitable weapon; she arranged the spectacle of her death with a care and love inappropriate to Roman suicide. In both suicides, a Roman pattern has been expanded and enriched by Egyptian opulence and Egyptian decoration, not least in the ornate style in which both Antony and Cleopatra take leave of their world. The actual world has shrunk away from them; in expectation of Elysium in each other's company, they affirm the larger world of their fantastic and extravagant imagination, which their love had brought into being. The play's language affirms that determination to enlarge life: even at the end, Cleopatra speaks as woman, lover, and mother. After all, it is only by Roman tongues that the hero and heroine are spoken of as mere voluptuaries, softened and weakened by self-indulgence and excess. Antony's and Cleopatra's speech is consistently vigorous, various, copious, vivid, liveliest in those remarkable passages where excessive behavior, excessive sensation, excessive emotions are given their due.

Even though it threatens to do so, this hyperbolical play does not get out of hand: its images are as closely controlled as those of the other late tragedies. Further, the richness and decoration of the language, in passages of passionate disgust as in passages of grandiloquent elevation, match the richness of temperament which confers upon their characters the privilege of an equal elevation. What at first sounds like bombast in Antony's speech is naturalized in the course of the play, until his way of speaking becomes a standard against which other men are judged. Of effeminacy, slackness, or idleness, Antony's behavior may sometimes be accused—but never his language, nor Cleopatra's. From first to last what emerges is its affirmation of activity, of creativity, of unending and unendingly interesting emotional process. Till their very last breaths, these persons change and develop, to involve the audience in that development toward greatness. During the course of the play, then, Antony and Cleopatra grow into their rhetorical measure. At the play's start, Philo had called a spade a spade, or even a shovel; in contrast, Antony and Cleopatra spoke in love's arrogant, idealized overstatements. By the end of the play, Philo's linguistic practice is blocked out by Antony's hyperbole coming true, until we too believe that "the nobleness of life" is for such lovers to embrace. Until the very end, we are never quite sure of Cleopatra, such is the oscillation of the play and the woman between extremes, from rejection to reunion, from reviling to reaffirmation, from lie to truth, from denigration to encomium.

By their manner of dying, these figures are known: the Roman world, with all its real space, could not house the love of Antony for Cleopatra. That Antony lost his place in the real world, lost that world altogether, is made to seem unimportant beside the imaginative satisfactions of his emotional life. What Antony and Cleopatra do and say represents them: for all their own vacillation and oscillation, they turn out to be true in their ultimate commitment to each other. Antony dies with energy and (oddly enough) enthusiasm; Cleopatra looks to her last moment and beyond it, both on earth and in Elysium—she remains alive, feeling, imagining, to her last breath. Both catch and express their visions of the new heaven, new earth, seen always in terms of each other and of being with each other. They die as they had lived, beyond definition, in expectation of more. It is the strength, the vividness, the vigor of excess which this play presents, examines, criticizes, and ultimately, with full understanding, confirms, in a language of hyperbole built to match the size and scope of the subject. In the *ping* and *pong* of plain and grandiloquent styles, now one seeming to lead and now the other, Shakespeare manages to show us the problem and the problematics, in moral as in literary terms, at the heart of style. By sinking the notions associated with the Asiatic style back into life itself, in the play's dramatic action he can examine and assess both the style and the style of life in terms of each other, and to see them as one. He can demonstrate, then, by the peculiarly literary device of a stylistic agon, the moral problematics of dimension, can manage to make acceptable—more, to make admirable and comprehensible—the values of an honestly ostentatious style.

⸺◦/▵/◦⸺ ⸺◦/▵/◦⸺ ⸺◦/▵/◦⸺

1986—Northrop Frye. "Antony and Cleopatra," from *Northrop Frye on Shakespeare*

The Canadian scholar Northrop Frye (1912–1991) was one of the most influential literary critics of the twentieth century. Harold Bloom has called him "the largest and most crucial literary critic in the English

language" since Walter Pater and Oscar Wilde. One of Frye's most
famous books is *The Anatomy of Criticism*.

I've talked about *Hamlet* as the central Shakespeare play for the nineteenth and
early twentieth centuries, when so many cultural factors revolved around the
difficulties of uniting action and the consciousness of action. In the existentialist
period of this century this theme was still in the foreground, but, with a growing
sense of the absurdity of trying to rationalize a world set up for the benefit of
predatory rulers, *King Lear* began to move into the centre in its place. I don't
know what play will look most central in the twenty-first century, assuming we
get there, but *Antony and Cleopatra* is, I think, the play that looks most like the
kind of world we seem to be moving into now.

History goes in cycles to a large extent, and in our day we're back to the
Roman phase of the cycle again. It's amazing how vividly Shakespeare has
imagined a world so much more like ours than like his. There's no Tudor anxiety
about who the Lord's anointed is or who his successor should be. We can see
what the power relations are like in the conference on Pompey's galley. The
Roman Empire has reached the stage of the second "triumvirate," or control
by three leaders, Antony, Caesar and Lepidus. Lepidus, who holds a third of
the world but not his liquor, is only a cipher, and as soon as the time is right
he is swept into prison on a trumped-up charge by Caesar. Caesar and Antony
are making an alliance, to be cemented by Antony's marriage to Caesar's sister,
Octavia, but we realize that they are only postponing a showdown. Enobarbus
says so, speaking on Antony's side; Antony tells him to be quiet, but Caesar
expresses his agreement, and remarks again after Antony's death that two such
leaders "could not stall together" in the same world. After the conference ends,
the triumvirate goes off the ship, because Pompey lacks the nerve to murder the
lot of them and become master of the world himself. Having missed his chance,
the officer who suggested it to him deserts him in disgust.

The defeat of Antony by Caesar does not centralize authority in the way
that, for example, the defeat of Richard III centralizes authority in the House of
Tudor. We're not in a closely knit kingdom anymore: there's only one world, so
there's no patriotism, only more or less loyalty to the competing leaders. Late in
the play the demoralized Antony challenges Caesar to a duel; and we see how
clearly the creator of Tybalt understands that in *this* world personal duelling is
an impossibly corny notion. There are any number of messengers in the play, and
the air is thick with information and news, but nothing much seems to be getting
communicated, although when something does happen it affects the whole
world at once. But while there is one world, there are two aspects of it: the aspect
of "law and order" represented by Rome, and the aspect of sensual extravagance
and licence represented by Egypt. The lives and fortunes of millions depend,
quite simply, on the whims and motivations of three people. The fact that two of

them are lovers means that what is normally a private matter, the sexual relation, becomes an illuminated focus of contemporary history.

The historical Cleopatra was a highly cultivated woman who spoke seven languages and had had the best education her time afforded. It's true that she used her sex as a political weapon, but Queen Elizabeth used her virginity as a political weapon. All the efforts of Roman propaganda failed to disguise the fact that she was the one person the Romans were really afraid of. When the news of her death reached Rome, even the normally stodgy Horace was prompted into something like enthusiasm:

> Nunc est bibendum, nunc pede libero
> pulsanda tellus . . .

Now's the time to drink and dance, because Cleopatra's dead and everything's going to be wonderful. Virgil was more restrained, but even he puts the word *nefas*, shameful, into his allusion to her in the *Aeneid*. The spectre of an enemy equipped, not merely with an open female sexuality, which was frightening enough, but with terrible secret weapons like intelligence and imagination, was gone forever. (I'm not idealizing her—she was a tough and dirty fighter—but her qualities had survival value in her world.) Shakespeare's treatment of her is not historical: for one thing, the historical Cleopatra was Greek, not Egyptian, and we have to forget that in this play, where she's the very essence of Egypt. But we can see from the play why she still haunts history as well as literature.

Of the two aspects of the Roman-Egyptian world, Caesar belongs consistently to the Roman side, Cleopatra consistently to the Egyptian one, and Antony vacillates between the two. Near the beginning of the play, with Antony in Egypt, Cleopatra remarks sardonically: "A Roman thought hath struck him." But Antony, at least then, knows what a Roman thought is, and Cleopatra, quite genuinely, does not. The Roman way of life makes no sense of any kind to her, despite her previous experience of it, when she was attached to Julius Caesar. The most elementary way of misreading this play is to turn it into either a moral or a romantic melodrama, against or for Cleopatra. The moral view identifies Rome with the virtues of Rome, and Egypt with the vices of Egypt, and says what a pity it was that so great a man, instead of living up to his historical destiny, allowed himself to be debased by a sexy woman. The romantic view is expressed in the title of the second most famous play on the subject in English literature: John Dryden's *All for Love, or The World Well Lost*. (The play itself is better balanced.) Both views are cop-outs: what we have to make sense of is a tragedy, not a morality play or a sentimental love story.

We've seen Shakespeare working, in *Hamlet* and *King Lear*, on well-known stories that had been treated in earlier plays. In *Antony and Cleopatra* he was dealing with one of the best-known stories in the world, one that everybody had heard of and that was endlessly alluded to in every kind of literary genre. There was an earlier play (one of many) on this subject too: Samuel Daniel's *Cleopatra* (1594), which deals with events occurring after the death of Antony. According to Ben Jonson, "Samuel Daniel was a good honest man, had no children; but no poet." You may gather from this, correctly, that Jonson's judgments were not always notable for fairness. Shakespeare found a good deal of poetry in Daniel's play, and probably found in him too the emphasis on the horror of being part of Caesar's triumph in Rome as the main motive for Cleopatra's suicide. For the rest, Shakespeare's main source was Plutarch's *Lives*, which was available to him, in those easygoing days, in an English translation made from a French translation of the Greek. The incidents of the play almost all come straight from Plutarch, except that the impression of Antony we get from Plutarch is one of a rather brutal gangster: I hope the reasons why Shakespeare gives so different an impression of him will become clearer as we go on. For this, and for all the rest of the plays in this course, we have the Folio text only. Modern printed texts, where you get involved with Act IV, Scene xv, may give the impression of a cumbersome play, but any good production will show that the speed and economy of Shakespeare's storytelling are still at top level. Caesar and Antony also appear in Shakespeare's earlier play *Julius Caesar*, but I think it's a mistake to read our present play as a sequel, though we could look at a few details here that refer back to the earlier time.

Julius Caesar had set up the triumvirate pattern earlier in his career, when he got control of the western part of the Roman world, leaving Pompey in control of the east. Crassus, a slum-landlord profiteer, supplied the money and was the third member. Looking for a more heroic role, he led an expedition against the Parthians, on the eastern frontier of the empire: the Parthians captured and murdered him, and poured molten gold down his throat—the only evidence we have of what the Parthian sense of humour was like. I mention it only because Cleopatra uses the image as one of the things she would like to do to the messenger who brings the news of Antony's marriage. Pompey was murdered in Egypt, but his son, who had become a pirate, is still an influential figure in the world of *Antony and Cleopatra*. The rebels against Julius Caesar, Brutus and Cassius, were defeated and killed at the battle of Philippi by an army led by Mark Antony and Octavius Caesar, as he was then called. In this play Antony has a good deal to say about how much the Philippi victory depended on him and how little on his colleague, but in *Julius Caesar* he and Octavius both seem rather mean-minded and cynical, co-opting Lepidus but determined to treat him as a "property," always ready (especially Antony) to manipulate a crowd with tear-jerking speeches, but using the impetus of revenge for Julius Caesar's death to get power for themselves.

Both of them are relatives of Julius Caesar: Octavius was born his nephew, but was adopted as his son. The fact that Cleopatra had been Julius Caesar's mistress, and had borne him a son, Caesarion, makes an additional complication to the later play. Caesar tells his lieutenants how Cleopatra and Antony were publicly enthroned in Alexandria, along with "Caesarion, whom they call my father's son." We notice how often tragedy includes as a central theme a rupture within a family, as in *Hamlet* and *King Lear*, and in this play Caesar, and Antony by virtue of his marriage to Octavia, are both involved in inter-family feuds. There is, of course, a considerable difference between Roman and Egyptian views on what constitutes a permanent sexual relationship. In Rome there is no obstacle to Antony's marriage to Octavia because Cleopatra has no legal status as a wife; but in the closing moments of the play, when Cleopatra plans her entrance into the next world, it never occurs to her that anybody in that world would be stupid enough to regard Antony as still married to Octavia. Her only problem, as she sees it, is to get into the next world before her attendant Charmian, so that she won't have to get Antony pried loose from somebody else. The point here is not how primitive her views of the next world are, but the fact that she can't conceive of any world at all where she wouldn't continue to be Cleopatra.

I've often spoken of the theatre as the central character in all of Shakespeare's plays, and this play revolves around Cleopatra because she's the essence of theatre. Besides having the fattest female role in the entire range of drama, she's a woman whose identity is an actress's identity. One wonders how the lad who first attempted the part got along, and how much he liked expressing Cleopatra's contempt of having "Some squeaking Cleopatra boy my greatness"—a line that in any case took the most colossal nerve on Shakespeare's part to write, even if the context is logical enough. One occasionally hears some such question about the play as: "Did Cleopatra really love Antony or was she just play-acting?" The word "really" shows how wrong the assumption underlying the question is. Cleopatra is not an actress who can be Vivien Leigh or Elizabeth Taylor offstage: the offstage does not exist in her life. Her love, like everything else about her, is theatrical, and in the theatre illusion and reality are the same thing. Incidentally, she never soliloquizes; she talks to herself occasionally, but someone else is always listening and she always knows it.

The most famous description of her is in the speech of Enobarbus describing her appearance in the royal barge on the Cydnus. Enobarbus is a character who in this age of Brecht might be called an alienation character: it's part of his function in the play to comment on how the principals are doing as theatrical figures. He has several other aspects, one of them being a plain blunt Roman soldier, and one wonders if a plain blunt soldier would really talk about Cleopatra in the terms he does if he were not half in love with her himself. At the same time, he calls her Antony's "Egyptian dish," and has earlier commented to Antony himself about her carefully manufactured tantrums. He comes close to the centre of his own feelings, however, when he says that "vilest things / Become themselves in her," echoing Antony's earlier remark that she is someone "whom everything becomes." To translate this simply as "she can get away with anything" would be inadequate: it means far more than that. Pascal remarked in one of his aphorisms that if Cleopatra's nose had been an inch shorter the history of the world would have been different. But Shakespeare's Cleopatra could have coped very easily with a snub nose (actually the historical Cleopatra may have had one, as some of her coins suggest). She doesn't depend on any conventional attributes of beauty. The whole of Cleopatra is in everything she expresses, whether splendid, silly, mean, grandiloquent, malicious or naive, and so her essential fascination comes through in every mood. She has the female equivalent of the kind of magnetism that makes Antony a born leader, whose soldiers will follow him in the face of obvious disaster.

Of course there is a price to be paid for being in contact with such a creature, the price of being upstaged by someone who is always centre stage. At the beginning of the play we have this little whispered exchange among her attendants:

Hush! here comes Antony.
    Not he: the queen. (I.ii. 75)

The words could not be more commonplace, yet they tell us very clearly who is number one in that court. Her suicide is motivated by her total refusal to be a part of someone else's scene, and she needs the whole fifth act to herself for her suicide show. Apart from Julius Caesar, who is a special case, Mark Antony is the only major hero of Shakespeare who dies in the fourth act. An obsolete proverb says that behind every great man there is a devoted woman, but Cleopatra is not a devoted woman and she's not standing behind anybody. Octavia, now, is the kind of woman who does exactly what she should do in a man's world, and she bores the hell out of Antony.

There is no character in Shakespeare whom Cleopatra resembles less than Falstaff, and yet there is an odd link between them in dramatic function. Both are counter-historical characters: they put on their own show oblivious to the history that volleys and thunders around them. But the history of Falstaff's time would have been the same without him, and Cleopatra, though very conscious of her "greatness" in her own orbit, hardly seems to realize that she is a key figure in *Roman* history as well. Her great betrayal of Antony comes in the middle of the battle of Actium, when she simply pulls her part of the fleet out of the battle. What is going on in her mind is probably something like: "What silly games these men do play: nobody's paying any attention to me at all." She may not even be aware that her action would lose Antony the battle, or that it would make any difference if it did. She says to Enobarbus, "Is Antony or we in fault for this?", and it seems clear that it is a real question for her, even though she's obviously dissatisfied with Enobarbus's patriarchal Roman answer that the fault was entirely Antony's for paying attention to a woman in a battle. We may still wonder why she insisted on entering the battle in the first place: the reason seems to be that Caesar was shrewd enough to declare the war personally on her, putting her in the spotlight of attention. So, although Antony could have won handily on land, she insists on a seafight, because there would be nowhere to see her in a land operation.

Let's look at Antony's death scene, in which, after a bungled attempt at suicide and mortally wounded, he makes his way to Cleopatra's monument and asks her to come down and give him her last kiss. But Cleopatra has already started on her private war to outwit Caesar's plan to make her part of his triumph in Rome. It sounds like a restricted operation, but it's as important to Cleopatra as the mastery of the world is to Caesar. So she apologizes to Antony, but she's afraid she can't come down "Lest I be taken." She must stay in the protection of a monument that would hold up a cohort of Roman legionaries for about a minute and a half. There's no help for it: "we must draw thee up." What follows is a difficult scene to stage, but nobody can miss the humiliation for Antony of this grotesque manoeuvre, to say nothing of the physical agony of the ordeal for a dying man. "Here's sport indeed! How heavy weighs my lord!" says Cleopatra. Our minds go back to an earlier scene, when, with Antony absent and Cleopatra stupefied with boredom, she proposes to go fishing, as she used to do with Antony:

> my bended hook shall pierce
> Their slimy jaws; and as I draw them up,
> I'll think them every one an Antony,
> And say "Ah ha! y'are caught" (II.v. 12–15)

To Antony's exhausted murmur, "Give me some wine, and let me speak a little," her answer is, "No, let me speak, and let me rail." When Antony is finally going, she says first, "Hast thou no care of me?", and then breaks into the tremendous rhetoric of her lament for her dead lover. I'm taking phrases out of their contexts a bit, and of course Shakespeare's really intense scenes are so delicately balanced that emphasizing and overemphasizing any single aspect are almost the same thing.

The reason why Antony is in this situation, and mortally wounded, is that when his fleet surrendered to Caesar he assumed that Cleopatra had betrayed him, and Cleopatra had to counter this threat with the most dramatic action possible: of sending to Antony, by her eunuch Mardian, a report of her death, which Mardian was urged to "word piteously." All of which still does not show that Cleopatra is a monster of selfishness. Selfishness is a product of calculation, and Cleopatra, at least at the moment of Antony's death, is not calculating. Her reactions are too instinctive to be called selfish: she's just being Cleopatra. And she's still being Cleopatra when, a few scenes later, she thinks of the humiliation of being in Caesar's triumph, and says with the utmost horror (echoing a phrase Antony had used earlier): "Shall they hoist *me* up?" (emphasis mine, but doubtless hers as well).

From now on, her whole strategy is directed to baffling Caesar's intention to include her in his triumph in Rome. She first has to make sure that this is his intention. The dying Antony has said to her: "None about Caesar trust but Proculeius." It would not occur to Cleopatra to trust anybody: what she does with all the people she meets is to ascertain, within a few seconds, whether she can get what she wants from them or not. Proculeius, precisely because he is trustworthy, walks into her monument and takes her prisoner; then Dolabella comes in. It is to him that she utters a prodigiously exaggerated eulogy of Antony: he doesn't fall for that, of course, being a Roman, but he's dazzled by her all the same, and in no time she's extracted the information she wants.

Caesar certainly does want Cleopatra to be part of his victory procession in Rome: her presence there "would be eternal in our triumph," he says. He has her under close guard, and keeps two of her children as hostages, dropping a veiled threat about their fate if she should fool him. That falls flat: Cleopatra is one of the least motherly heroines in literature, and hardly even knows that she has children. There is a scene (which I'm reading the way it usually is read and produced) in which, with Caesar present, she pretends to be outraged with her treasurer, Seleucus, for exposing some minor cheating of hers, reserving for herself some "trifles" that were part of the Roman loot. Caesar is amused by this, but assumes that if Cleopatra still wants such things she can hardly be meditating suicide, which is precisely what she hoped he would think. Then she arranges for a clown to bring a basket of figs to her past the Roman guard, poisonous serpents being under the figs.

This clown, brief as his scene is, is extraordinarily haunting: as with the more elaborate gravediggers' scene in *Hamlet*, he represents almost our only contact with the population of survivors on whose backs all these masters of the world are sitting. As a clown, he mixes up his words, as clowns conventionally do, but the way he mixes them makes him an eerie and ghoulish messenger from another world, and not at all the kind of world Cleopatra thinks of herself as entering. He hands on a recommendation to Cleopatra from a woman who has sought the same remedy for life: "how she died of the biting of it, what pain she felt; truly, she makes a very good report o' the worm." At the same time he strains Cleopatra's nerves nearly to the breaking point: he's garrulous; he doesn't want to shuffle off the stage; he knows very well what he's carrying and what it's for, and at any moment he could wreck her whole scheme. However, the stage is finally clear: her scheme has succeeded; the "worm" is ready to do its job. She wishes that the serpent, like its ancestor in Eden, could speak, and call "great Caesar ass." It's hardly necessary to add that she's greatly underrating Caesar: there isn't a syllable of disappointment or baffled rage from him when he discovers he's been circumvented. That's how things go sometimes, is his only reaction. Let's give them both a big funeral and attend it "in solemn show." They've earned that, at least.

All of which seems merely to be accumulating evidence that Cleopatra was Antony's evil genius. It's true that she herself doesn't seem to be really evil, in the way that Goneril and Regan are evil. No doubt she'd be capable of it, in some contexts. But what we see is a woman possessed by vanity, and vanity, whatever the moralists say, is a rather disarming vice, in a way almost innocent, exposing the spoiled child under the most infuriating behaviour of the adult. And sometimes we even wonder if she's such a simple thing as an evil genius at all. In the second scene of the play a "soothsayer" is introduced, making a not very glamorous living telling the fortunes of a group of giggly attendants on Cleopatra. We know that Shakespeare would never introduce such a character unless he were going to use him later, and later he duly appears, to tell Antony that his real evil genius is Caesar. (He's Egyptian, of course, but that seems to have nothing to do with it.) The mysterious quality called "luck," so important and so frequently mentioned in tales of legendary heroes, only works for Antony, the soothsayer says, when he's out of Caesar's range. Within Caesar's orbit, Caesar will have all the luck. So the really fatal misstep that Antony makes is not returning to Cleopatra but marrying Octavia. In his last days there's a temporary rally in his favour, and Cleopatra says to him:

O infinite virtue, com'st thou smiling from
The world's great snare uncaught? (IV.viii. 17–18).

The world's great snare is war generally, and war with Caesar in particular. The point is that most moralists would say that the world's great snare for Antony was Cleopatra herself, and Cleopatra's use of such a phrase means that she has a different point of view on the subject, perhaps one to be respected.

There's also a curious scene at the beginning of the third act, when one of Antony's generals, named Ventidius, has done what Antony should have been doing all along: fought with and defeated the Parthian army. One of his subordinates suggests that he follow up the victory in a way that will knock the Parthians out for much longer, but Ventidius says he's done enough. If he makes a more impressive victory than he has made, he'll be threatening Antony's "image," as we call it now, and Antony will find some way of getting rid of him. We're back to the smaller, calculating Antony of *Julius Caesar*, and the episode seems to be telling us that if Antony really did his Roman duty we'd find him a rather commonplace character, not the unforgettable tragic hero of this play.

There are different levels on which characters can be presented to us in literature. In pure myths characters may be gods or divine beings, though since

Classical times this has been rather uncommon. Or they may be heroes of romance like the knights of Arthur's court, or like what Don Quixote dreamed of being, capable of incredible feats of strength, endurance and love. Or they may be leaders like Othello or King Lear or Bolingbroke, with nothing strictly supernatural about them, but with authority and a power of speech denied to ordinary mortals. Or they may be people roughly on our own level, or they may be unfortunate or foolish or obsessed people whom we feel to be less free than ourselves, and whom we look down on (I mean in perspective, not morally). At the beginning of the play Caesar and Antony are on the third level, social and military leaders. Caesar's greatest strength is his limitation to that role: he is single-mindedly devoted to leadership, and lets nothing else get in his way. He has gods, of course, but he seems to be indifferent to them, and one would never guess from this play that he himself was deified after his death. Thus:

     1. Divine being, hero descended from gods, hero who is a protégé of the gods, etc.

     2. Romantic hero and lover, human but not subject to ordinary human limitations.

     3. Kings and other commanding figures in social or military authority.

     4. Ordinary people.

     5. Foolish, obsessed, unfortunate people; people assumed to be in a state of less freedom than we are.

Antony is a leader, we said, but he has a heroic dimension that makes him a romantic legend, on the second rather than the third level, even in Caesar's eye, as when Caesar recalls his tremendous powers of endurance in his earlier campaigns, drinking "the stale of horses" and the like. A bystander remarks that his soldiership is "twice the other twain," meaning Caesar and Lepidus, whatever Lepidus may count for. His immense physical vitality (Plutarch calls him the "new Bacchus" or Dionysus) and his great personal magnetism mean that any army following him feels drawn together into a fighting community. In front of the most certain defeat, his men, or some of them, are still fighting with high morale and joking about their wounds. In his last wretched days, when he is only, as his soldiers call him, the ruin of Cleopatra's magic, he still seems like a kind of force of nature. Even his blunders are colossal, and, as Enobarbus says, there is a glamour in being part of so majestic a lost cause.

The story of Enobarbus is the clearest illustration of Antony's power as a leader. Enobarbus, we said, is a commentator on the action; his detachment makes him use rational categories, and causes him to be especially sensitive to the decline of rationality in Antony. He contrasts the courage of Caesar, guided by a cool head, with the courage of Antony, which is increasingly guided by panic, "frighted out of fear," as he says, so that in a sense Antony's reason has been taken prisoner by Caesar. He then draws the inference that the rational thing for him to do would be to desert to Caesar. But his reason has betrayed him. He finds himself at once in the deep cold hell of the deserter, no longer trusted by those he has left, never to be trusted by those he is trying to join. Then comes the news that Antony, aware of his desertion, has sent on all his possessions and his "treasure." What he discovers in that moment is that his identity consisted of being a part of Antony's cause, and that he is now nothing, just as a hand severed from the body is no longer a hand. It's significant, I think, that he does not commit suicide: he simply lies down in a ditch and stays there, because he's already dead.

The great romantic heroes are normally great lovers too, and Antony's love for Cleopatra gives him again a dimension that puts him beyond the usual human categories. We may look at the extraordinarily concise opening scene. Two fairly anonymous Romans speak of Antony's "dotage" and his spending his energies in cooling a "gipsy's lust" (the Gypsies were believed at that time to have come from Egypt, and the term is Roman racism). Then they eavesdrop on the first encounter we have between Antony and Cleopatra. The important part of it for us is Cleopatra's "I'll set a bourne how far to be beloved," and Antony's response, "Then thou must needs find out new heaven, new earth." However the scene is staged, it's framed by the two visiting Romans, so that it's in a deliberately confined area, yet out of this confined area comes the declaration of a love that bursts the boundaries of human experience altogether. The two Romans, like most tourists, have seen and heard what they expect to see and hear, and have no notion of what they really have seen and heard, which is a statement of what another very great love poet, John Donne, calls "Lovers' Infiniteness."

As for Cleopatra, the queen of Egypt *was* a goddess, an incarnation of Isis, the goddess of the sea, in whose "habiliments," according to Caesar, she publicly appeared. She is also described by Enobarbus as enthroned on her "barge" on the water, as though she were a kind of Venus surrounded by love spirits. The effect she produces is so close to being that of an incarnate love goddess that Enobarbus speaks of how even the holy priests "Bless her when she is riggish [sexually excited]." It is after Antony dies that in her laments for him she speaks of him as a divinity whose legs bestrid the ocean and whose eyes were the sun and moon. We may, with Dolabella, consider this just the rhetorical grief of a very rhetorical person, but then there is that curious episode of soldiers hearing a mysterious music which means that Hercules, Antony's patron, has deserted him.

This scene, Act IV, Scene iii, is the only moment in the play that looks in the least supernatural, and we may think it at first a bit out of key: something that Shakespeare found in Plutarch and thought maybe he ought to include, but that doesn't really belong. I don't think that critical judgment will quite do. If one is explicitly writing romance or myth, characters can go into extrahuman categories without trouble, according to the conventions of what's being written; but *Antony and Cleopatra* is on the historical level of credibility. On that level, anything above the human may be suggested, but it must almost always be associated with failure. The desertion of Antony by Hercules means that Antony has failed to become a pagan incarnation, a Hercules or Dionysus walking the earth. Such heroic incarnations always fail: that's one of the things Greek tragedy is about. Agrippa, on Caesar's side, remarks that the gods always give great spirits flaws to keep them on the human level. There's a truth in this I want to come back to, but not all tragedy is about heroes who had flaws preventing them from living up to their heroism. Some tragedies are about heroes whose "flaws" *were* their virtues, whose heroism was simply too destructive a force to the world around them to survive in it. Antony was perhaps not one of those, but he comes so near to being one that what emerges from the deepest centre of this immensely profound play is Cleopatra's bitter complaint:

> It were for me
> To throw my sceptre at the injurious gods,
> To tell them that this world did equal theirs,
> Till they had stolen our jewel. (IV.xv. 75–78)

What is true of heroism is true of love as well. There are no superhuman lovers, and all attempts at such love have been tragic. Antony's page, who kills himself to avoid having to kill Antony, is named Eros, and it seems clear that Shakespeare uses the name for the sake of its resonances, and for the aspect of the play in which it is a tragedy of Eros:

> Unarm, Eros, the long day's task is done,
> And we must sleep. (IV.xiv. 35–36)

In one of his more manic phases in the same scene, Antony speaks of himself and Cleopatra as becoming the model for lovers in the next world, gazed at by all as the two who, so to speak, made it:

> Dido, and Aeneas, shall want troops,
> And all the haunt be ours. (IV.xiv. 53–54)

The reference to Dido and Aeneas is deeply ironic, as it's both right and wrong. Aeneas rejected Dido's love; she burned herself on a funeral pyre; Aeneas went on to Italy but had first to visit the lower world to gain a prophecy of the future greatness of Rome; he met Dido in the lower world; she cut him dead and went off to find her first husband. Nevertheless, Dido is one of the most famous lovers in literature, and Aeneas is famous by virtue of his association with her. The Aeneas who went on to Italy and made a dynastic marriage with someone called Lavinia is, despite Virgil's best efforts, almost an antihero. Antony's tragedy is in many respects like the tragedy of Adam as seen later by Milton. Adam falls out of Eden because he would rather die with Eve than live without her: theologically he may have been wrong, but dramatically everyone applauds his decision. Success in heroic love being impossible, better to fail heroically than to succeed in mediocrity.

Here we have to return to Agrippa's observation. There is a character in one of Blake's Prophecies who says, at the end of a long poem, "Attempting to become more than man we become less." It is because Antony is so much bigger a man than Caesar that he is also, at other times, so much smaller. Along with Cleopatra, he is often not simply ordinary but silly and childish. Caesar never descends to that level, because he never rises above his own: he has no dreams of divinity, and so no awakenings into the "all too human," as Nietzsche calls it. Cleopatra is often spoken of as though she had charms or love potions or magic spells or other apparatus of a witch. She hasn't any of these things: what gives the illusion of them is the intensity of her humanity, and the same thing is true of Antony. But intense humanity is a two-way street.

One yardstick to contrast Rome and Egypt, and which this time does illustrate the superiority of Rome, is the treatment of messengers. Caesar is invariably courteous to his messengers, and so is Antony at the beginning of the play, when the messenger who brings the bad news from the eastern front is even encouraged to include a comment on Antony's lackadaisical response. But Cleopatra's treatment of the messenger of the marriage to Octavia shows her at her impossible worst, and Antony soon shows that he has caught the infection, when he orders Caesar's messenger Thidias to be flogged. There is, it is true, another element here: it almost looks as though Cleopatra, feeling that Antony's number is up, would be ready to do a deal with Caesar, and of course her repertoire of deals is very limited. Enobarbus, one feels, also suspects that Cleopatra is ready to come to some kind of terms with Caesar, and this is the moment when he decides to leave Antony. The childish petulance in Antony's action comes, first, from the fact that it's obviously Cleopatra that he wants to take the whip to, and, second, that he's reacting in a small-minded way to disaster, by retreating from the present into fantasy and reminiscence of the past. Antony never recovers his original control, and later tells the eunuch Mardian how close he has come to death for bringing the (false) news of Cleopatra's death. But still his lowest moment in the play is the pitiful complaint in his speech to Thidias:

> He [Caesar] makes me angry with him. For he seems
> Proud and disdainful, harping on what I am
> Not what he knew I was. (III.xiii. 141–43)

One pattern of imagery that runs all through the play is the contrast of land and sea, of a solid and a liquid world, an imagery that reinforces the contrast between Rome and Egypt. I spoke of the first scene, where a Roman begins the play with:

> Nay, but this dotage of our general's
> O'erflows the measure. . . (I.i. 1–2)

This is a Roman view of someone taken over by Egypt, the land that owes its fertility, in fact its very existence, to the annual overflowing of the Nile. The metaphors associated with Rome are often geometrical, as in Antony's apology to Octavia, "I have not kept my square," implying something solid. On Pompey's galley there is a discussion between Enobarbus and Pompey's lieutenant, Menas, in which the words "land" and "sea" echo like a cuckoo clock; and Cleopatra, the "serpent of old Nile," as Antony calls her, is constantly associated with seas and with two rivers, the Nile and the Cydnus. It is she, as is said earlier, who insists that the battle of Actium should be a sea fight, and it is the fleet that finally betrays Antony.

I said a moment ago that in tragedy we sometimes get forms of heroism that are too big for the world as we know it, and so become destructive. If the wills of Antony and Cleopatra had been equal to the passions they express in their language, there wouldn't have been much left of the cosmos. "Let Rome in Tiber melt," says Antony at the beginning of the play; "Melt Egypt into Nile," says Cleopatra later. From the scene of Antony's attempted suicide on, the play is full of images of the world dissolving into chaos, of the sun burning its sphere, of cloud shapes becoming as indistinct "As water is in water." The chaos is social as well as cosmic, because with the loss of such a leader the hierarchy on which all existence depends collapses, as Lear's world after his abdication collapses into the world symbolized by the storm. Cleopatra says of Antony:

> The soldier's pole is fall'n: young boys and girls
> Are level now with men: (IV.xv. 65–66)

The entire history of the word "standard," which is not even used, lies behind these images. The images of dissolution point to the fact that Caesar becomes master of the world because he knows the substance, location and limits of the world that can be mastered: for a short time, one may master anything that will stay in place. Antony has fallen into the world of process and metamorphosis, a far bigger world than Caesar's, but a world that no one can control unless he can also control death itself. Cleopatra comes to feel that to choose death with Antony is a greater destiny than Caesar, who is "but Fortune's knave," can ever reach; and she speaks of transcending the world of the moon and of the corruptible elements below it:

> I am fire and air; my other elements
> I give to baser life. (V.ii. 288–89)

difficult as it is to envisage a discarnate Cleopatra.

One cannot read or listen far into this play without being reminded that the action is taking place about thirty years before what Shakespeare's audience would have considered the turning point of history, the birth of Christ. There are references to Herod of Jewry, which are in Plutarch but have overtones for the audience that they would not have for Plutarch, and Caesar, with his victory practically in sight, remarks, "The time of universal peace is near," where again the audience knows more of his meaning than he does. It would have been strange if Christ had been born into a world whose temporal master was a protégé of Hercules, ruling the world probably from Egypt. It is partly in this context that the upper limits of Antony and Cleopatra become so significant: of Antony as a failed pagan or heroic incarnation, of Cleopatra as a goddess of love, of the sea, and of the overflowing Nile. The Egypt of this play is partly the Biblical Egypt, whose Pharaoh was called in the Bible "the great dragon that lieth in the midst of his rivers," and whose ruler here is the serpent of old Nile whom we last see nursing a baby serpent at her breast.

There are some books on mythology that tell you things about the actual grammar of mythology that you won't find in more conventional handbooks. I referred earlier to Robert Graves's *The White Goddess*, a book that appeared about forty years ago, which tells us of a goddess personifying the fertility of the earth, who takes a lover early in the year, then turns him into a sacrificial victim, then erases the memory of him and starts the next year with a new lover. We remember that Cleopatra hates to be reminded that she once was the mistress of Julius Caesar, and she apparently does not react to the name Herod, though she had been involved with him too. And when she is finally dead—at least so far as our knowledge of such things goes—Caesar looks down on her and comments that:

> she looks like sleep,
> As she would catch another Antony
> In her strong toil of grace. (V.ii. 344–46)

The old dispensation, as the theologians call it, has rolled by, carrying its symbols of the skin-shedding serpent, the sea, the dying and renewing life of the earth. And, whatever happens to human fortunes in the next thirty years, it is still there, ready to roll again.

1988—Laura Quinney. "Enter a Messenger,"
from *William Shakespeare's "Antony and Cleopatra"*

Laura Quinney is associate professor of English at Brandeis University.
She is the author of *The Poetics of Disappointment* and *Literary Power and the
Criteria of Truth*.

***

> All their words are like coals of fire.
> —Pirke Avoth

For a long stretch of *Antony and Cleopatra*—until the battle at Actium, late in
act 3—Antony's presence in the play is curiously pervasive but abbreviated. He
appears in only half the scenes, and, while Cleopatra appears in even fewer, he
seems particularly elusive, since so many of the scenes from which he is absent
concern his absence itself. As long as he shuttles ambivalently between Rome
and Egypt, the question of his whereabouts remains crucial, and a puzzle. Caesar,
Pompey, and Cleopatra all spend their time waiting for him and thinking on
him. They speculate on his doings with more or less frustration and anxiety.
They invoke his name with more or less respect, affection, and resentment. The
host of these apostrophes to Antony both make his presence pervasive, and, with
their epitaphic drive, imperil it. When he does appear on stage (the first scene
excepted), he seems composed and capable, at once too solid and too vulnerable
a figure for the demanding investment in him that others have manifested in
their apostrophes. The surprising modesty of his grandeur carries over into the
ease and the equanimity of his discourse. He is almost equally comfortable
in proclaiming his love, parleying at a diplomatic summit, and quibbling at a
drinking bout. While Antony is still a pillar of the world, his language shares in
the contented dexterity of his power. But after his fall at Actium—from which
point, until his death, he dominates the stage—his language suddenly comes into
a range and an urgency that it had not had, at the same time that he comes into
a fragility prophesied by the other characters' insistent apostrophes to him. His
language escapes from subordination and utility when he becomes tenuous to
himself, and it becomes tenuous to him.

With Antony's defeat at Actium, his word loses performative power, as he
is the first to remark: "Leave me, I pray, a little: pray you now, / Nay, do so; for
indeed I have lost command, / Therefore I pray you" (3.11.22–24). Now that his
political sovereignty has disintegrated, he cannot issue commands, but can only,
like the powerless and outcast, beg that his small, privative requests should be
heard and respected. Yet at the end of this scene, his language claims for itself
a performative power more comprehensive than an emperor's: "Fall not a tear, I
say; one of them rates / All that is won and lost" (11.69–70). The performative

power that Antony's language assumes here is of a different order from that which he has forfeited. This power is as ungrounded as it is expansive—language affirming itself in the absence of the subject's empirical authority. And Antony is himself moved by this transformation in his relationship to his own language. With "Fall not a tear, I say," his mood changes utterly; the spirit of shame, anguish, and recrimination dissolves, and in its place rises quiet acceptance: "Give me a kiss; / Even this repays me" (11.70–71).

He seems to step into the stride and assurance of his language; and yet his anxiety emerges as his language flares. These lines express, after all, the pathos of life and desire constricted to the smallest scope—to a tear, a kiss. The pathos of such a minimalism lingers as Antony struggles toward the soothing surface of activity; he wavers between pursuing the continuity of mundane life, and attending to the absorbing heaviness of his spirit: "We sent our schoolmaster: / Is a come back? Love, I am full of lead. / Some wine, within there, and our viands!" (11.71–73). His anxiety is here strangely coterminous with the exuberance of his language, as if this exuberance sprung from, but also sustained, his sense of dislocation. Antony's political displacement results in his displacement from his own language; and his language then reveals, not a perfect autonomy from him as the speaking subject, but an alterity that makes it at once distant and free. With "Fall not a tear, I say," Antony can be both affirmative and sad, because he has here discovered the impotent generosity of language.

This is the discovery, and the life, given to those whom "Fortune" has abandoned. The play is littered with the casualties of imperial conflict and consolidation; and when they lose their political viability, these preterite figures turn to seek in language the elusive space of their survival. In this space there emerges what Maurice Blanchot, in his book *L'Entretien infini*, calls "the other rapport," a rapport with that impersonality and impossibility whose existence is obscured by power and place. That Antony's relationship to his language should change in this way is prefigured by Pompey's brief appearance. An early and easy casualty of the battle over the empire, Pompey suffers for his fatal incompetence with the ways and the rhetoric of imperial powerplay. He may claim nobility for his purposes in a bold and censurious speech (2.6.8–22), and he may scoff at the compromise the triumvirate has offered him (11.34–39), but all this brave rhetoric is vitiated when he sheepishly concedes, "Know then / I came before you here a man prepared / To take this offer" (11.40–41). His rhetoric is characteristically more sovereign than it can justify; he pitches it high, but he wears it ill. Caesar observes coldly, "Since I saw you last / There's a change upon you," to which Pompey retorts, "Well, I know not / What counts harsh fortune casts upon my face, / But in my bosom shall she never come / To make my heart her vassal" (11.51–56). Though valiant, his words are sadly untrue, since his despair has already caused him to "laugh away his fortune" (2.6.105), as Menas bitterly remarks. Pompey's high rhetoric collapses, because his situation and his spirit cannot sustain it. His naive and uneasy handling of rhetoric, like his residual attachment to "honor," make him a doomed anachronism.

At his entrance, then, the play encourages us to take Pompey for an awkward and empty boaster. Yet when Pompey falls to his weakest, after he dismisses his last chance for power, and so guarantees his disappearance from the political arena, as from the play, he suddenly steps into the stride of language. At the climax of the boisterous celebration on his galley, this figure, shadowed by defeat and coming extinction, suddenly speaks out with urgency and longing: "O, Antony, / You have my father's house. But what, we are friends!" (2.7.130). With its (not unambivalent) burst of generosity, and its undercurrent of forlorn appeal, this line seeks a new rapport, outside the domain of diplomacy and imperialism. Aspiring to an intimacy for which there is no room, it becomes the refuge of Pompey's life, at the same time that it confines his life to this (last) moment of language.

In the final soliloquies of Enobarbus—who follows Pompey in homoerotic mourning for Antony—this changed relationship to language becomes even more vividly opulent and hopeless. Enobarbus speaks these soliloquies as a shunned pariah, not to be mentioned again, nor mourned himself. His position of utter loss transforms the character of his language; it loses the balance of shrewd, rational appraisal, and becomes, instead, expansive and supplicating. Enobarbus is moved and grieved by Antony's unexpected generosity to him; it is not only unwarranted, but an instance of that noble excess in Antony, which allows him to go on "o'erflowing the measure" even after he has been stripped. "Your emperor / Continues still a Jove" (4.6.28–29), as the soldier says, who brings Enobarbus's treasure, with Antony's "bounty overplus." Now that he has been stripped to his word, Enobarbus finds a similarly impossible excess, and repays Antony in the only means at his disposal—the wealth of hyperbole: "O Antony, / Thou mine of bounty, how wouldst thou have paid / My better service, when my turpitude / Thou dost so crown with gold" (4.6.31–34). Antony's bounty overflows into the generosity of Enobarbus's language. At the very end, his comparisons break from symmetry: "O Antony, / Nobler than my revolt is infamous / Forgive me in thine own particular" (4.9.18–20). When the space and time of Enobarbus's life shrink to that of his language, he invests it with the urgency and power of action, or, as Blanchot puts it in "La Mésure, le suppliant," "lorsqu'il y a défaut de tout, l'homme abîme dans le malheur est en mesure de parler, car c'est-là sa vraie mésure." But the expansiveness of his language strays from Enobarbus himself, and his apostrophes go unheard by the one to whom they appeal; despite the vocabulary of "wealth" and "payment" used here, the phenomenon described is not an economic or compensatory one. The space of the subject reduced to the word becomes a space of isolation and futility.

Much of the sadness in *Antony and Cleopatra* arises from Antony's gradual reduction to this space. In the climactic departure of Hercules, for example, the spirit of Antony's isolation materializes. On the night before battle, his soldiers on watch hear a supernatural, fading music whose mystery troubles them. They huddle together, anxiously wondering, "What should this mean?" until one among them declares grimly, "'Tis the god Hercules, whom Antony loved / Now leaves him" (4.3.14–16). The soldiers' anxiety and fatalism spill over from Antony's own, which he had manifested in the crisis pitch of the previous scene. There, in a flushed and restive mood, he makes an elaborate farewell to his servants. His sense of his own deterioration, both in fortune and in psychological integrity, stirs him to this gratuitous and extravagant gesture. In the grip of his apprehension, Antony feels an aura of fatality envelop him, out of which he can appeal to his servants, to cherish and secure this ghost of him still living: "Tend me tonight: May be it is the period of your duty. / Haply you shall not see me more: or if, / A mangled shadow, . . . I look on you / As one that takes his leave" (4.2.23–29). He feels himself to be so abstracted, so insubstantial that he is already fading from the world, his presence more tenuous not only than his servants', but than that of the "mangled shadow" to be memorialized in the alien imperviousness of death. And yet only in these other presences can Antony find an intimation of his own attenuated self, as if he were a figure in a mirror seeking a body to reflect. He enters into such a specular relationship with his own language when it seems to harbor in itself the "I" fast fading from him: "I look on you as one that takes his leave." His anxiety, which is coterminous with this sense of himself as residualized and isolated, overflows from the one scene to the next, where it conjures up the sadness of departing music, and where that departure certifies the emergence of the other rapport.

The spirit of abandonment in this scene colors the rest of the play. Hercules' departure underscores a transition recognized by everyone, including Antony and Cleopatra: history belongs to Caesar, and to them belongs only a space of time and of language. Antony and Cleopatra are acutely aware of surviving into this limbo, where they sustain themselves at preternatural length. Hercules' abandonment is, oddly enough, followed by a temporary upswing in Antony's fortunes—his one thriving day of battle—and by Antony and Cleopatra's tenderest moments. But the spirit of abandonment has so touched the play that this ephemeral success seems "wild"—a grace as exuberant as it is fragile and surprising.

This is the sense in which Antony and Cleopatra take their victory. Antony understands his single triumph to be so much against the trend of history that his celebration of it leaps to apocalyptic terms: "Trumpeters, / With brazen din blast you the city's ear, / Make mingle with our rattling tambourines, / That heaven and earth may strike their sounds together, / Applauding our approach" (4.8.35–39). In their victory Antony and Cleopatra take a joy as buoyant and fleeting as the victory was wild. Their intimate moments become unassuming and gentle in the light of this fragility. They wake up in bed, and Cleopatra helps Antony dress for battle, while he tries to share his proud excitement: "O, love. /

That thou could'st see my wars today. and knew'st / The royal occupation: thou should'st see / A workman in't" (4.4.15–18). The sweetness of these moments arises from the fragility in which Antony and Cleopatra now live, the fragility of the world formed in the moment of language. Thus their sadness lingers at the height of celebration. Cleopatra greets Antony, returning triumphant from battle, with these dark, joyous words: "O Lord of lords, / O infinite virtue, com'st thou smiling from / The world's great snare uncaught?" and Antony replies in the same cadences of haunted affirmation, "Mine nightingale, / We have beat them to their beds. What, girl! Though gray / Do something mingle with our younger brown" (4.8.17–20). In their isolation, signified by the withdrawal of a listening god, the space of their lives turns to words, at the same time that words, now the locus of the other rapport, open out only to absence.

For Antony, language comes to harbor a confidence like the lost substantiality of the self, but at a distance infinitely remote. This is its generosity, the source of affirmation in the play, and its limitation, the source of tragic affect. This generosity emerges as if it were a movement in language answering to the survival of Antony's "heart." "Heart" should carry here its full Shakespearean resonance, so that it means not only courage and affection, but the spirit from which these spring, the residue of the self that perseveres in a buoyant autonomy from its worldly fate. It is a center that, after Actium, is continually displaced in Antony, which he is always seeking, and which is always eluding his grasp. In his language he hears the recovery of his "heart," though, harbored there, it remains elusive and estranged. He invokes this distant echo when, recovering from his bout with Thidias, he asks, "Where hast thou been, my heart?" (3.13.171), and when he tells Cleopatra, helping him arm for battle, "Ah, let be, let be. Thou art / The armorer of my heart" (4.4.6–7). Because it seems as displaced from him as his own heart, his language can offer him its failed generosity. When he has reached the ebb of loss, where he feels himself to be as attenuated and amorphous as a cloud, even then his words take on an assurance far removed from his own experience of disintegration: "My good knave Eros, now thy captain is / Even such a body: here I am Antony, / Yet cannot hold this visible shape, my knave" (4.14.12–14). In offering Antony all the impersonal resources of its wealth and assurance, his language responds to, but does not answer, his own experience of attenuation; the remote alterity of language only makes it more acutely felt. This alterity is dramatized not only in Antony's changed relationship to his words, but in his changed relationship to the play's messengers and messenger-figures.

II

Antony and Cleopatra includes a startling number of messages and messengers. In *The Common Liar*, Janet Adelman points out that among the dramatis personae there are eight nameless "messengers" and another seven characters who act primarily as messengers (Alexas, Varrius, Thidias, Mardian, Proculeius,

Dolabella, and Antony's schoolmaster). To their number I would add what I call the "messenger-figures": the Soothsayer, Diomedes, and the Clown. The play's central conflicts—which lie in the characters' imperialist struggles and psychological ambivalence—are represented in terms of the manipulation and treatment of messengers. They are spurned, beaten, sent to lie, and sent to ensnare. They bear news that, whether galling or welcome, rapidly turns obsolete in the flux of ambivalence and powerplay. Yet in the course of *Antony and Cleopatra*, the role of the messenger is so transformed that this figure comes to have its own thematic. The messengers begin as messengers, but end as angelloi; they are at first merely representatives, but, for Antony at least, they finally develop an autonomous presence, ushering in a rapport that is anonymous and otherworldly. Standing on the threshold between subject and language, they are not quite characters, not psyches, yet they have autonomous will and feeling. Because they maintain this liminal position, they can exemplify the quasi-human, but impersonal and anonymous traits of the alterity of language—its generosity, intimacy, and distance.

To Caesar and his messenger-agents belongs the sterile impersonality of the bureaucrat. Caesar adopts the role of a faceless and efficient administrator, who consolidates his power by skillfully deploying a legion of methodical operatives. This political style originates in, and fulfills, Caesar's brilliant imperialist imagination, by which Antony is scourged and defeated, as it is, in turn, a symptom of Antony's failure that he should find the other anonymity in his rapport with the messenger. Unlike Antony, Caesar pursues a canny utilitarianism in his relationship to the messengers. His opening scene dramatizes this relationship, when an envoy enters to assure him, "Thy biddings have been done, and every hour, / Most noble Caesar, shalt thou have report / How 'tis abroad" (1.4.34–36). Through a network of messengers which operates as an information police, Caesar supervises the terrain of expanding empire and accelerating political conflict. In this panoptical extension of himself, he is made preternaturally ubiquitous, disseminated across myriad points of reconnaissance, along which, "every hour," the news flies.

Caesar knows this self-dissemination to be the principle of his radical, ineluctable ascendency. In his climactic encounter with Octavia, returning from her brief marriage, Caesar rises to a curious and telling moment of energy in his customarily dry speech. He is unusually excited throughout this scene, rather cruelly insisting to his sister, despite her own attempts to maintain dignity, that she is Antony's "castaway," "an abstract 'tween his lust and him," an abandoned wife who has had to enter Rome like "a market maid" (3.6.40, 61, 51). Though happy to reappropriate his beloved Octavia, Caesar thrills even more to find that, with Antony's misbehavior, he is free to unleash his own imperial designs, as well as his primal hatred for "our great competitor." But he is most energized to recall the means and assurance of his triumph, when he presses Octavia by saying, "Where is [Antony] now?" and declares with a sinister confidence:

> I have eyes upon him,
> And his affairs come to me upon the wind. (3.6.62–63)

This moment proves so keen for the temperate Caesar because in it he experiences the nature of his own power—as a man all eyes, an impersonal intelligence that ranges as if supernaturally diffused and incorporeal. He is the spirit of bureaucratic anonymity—invisible, ubiquitous, omniscient—that has dissolved into a racing, multifarious power. The play corroborates this view of Caesar, and reproduces his excitement, when it has him advance on Antony and Cleopatra with the speed of a superhuman and selfless force. News of his swift course reaches Antony and his generals, stirring in them a worried confusion over this antagonist who is strangely nebulous yet saturating: "This speed of Caesar's / Carries beyond belief." "Can he be there in person? 'Tis impossible; / Strange that his power should be." "While he was yet in Rome / His power went out in such distractions as / Beguiled all spies" (3.7.74–75, 56–57, 75–77). The play represents Caesar as uninhibited by temporal and spatial constraints, unlike Antony and Cleopatra, because his power is not located in him, but diffused among proxies.

Caesar's political style speeds the rise of imperialism, where Antony and Cleopatra's faith in charisma and personal loyalty suffers the fate of a static anachronism. The cult of charismatic personality falters more and more miserably, until it finally lapses into such ineffectual challenges as Antony's demand for single fight ("His coin, ships, legions / May be a coward's, whose ministers would prevail / Under the service of a child as soon as Caesar. I dare him therefore" [3.13.20–22]). In his archaic attachment to personal nobility, Antony does not see that Caesar has triumphed precisely because he has abandoned individualism, and established the rule of the "ministers"; his empire waxes strong on the structural solidity of a power network efficient unto itself, and so appropriate for the maintenance of a vast, disparate territory. Antony and Cleopatra are defeated in the same way by Caesar's imperialist mode of articulating politics and representation. Caesar designs and exploits the propagandistic value of documentation and "shows" in which he effaces himself, while drawing others into his chosen representation of history. Meanwhile, Antony and Cleopatra produce themselves as theatrical spectacle, a display that goes to demonstrate their personal distinction and to reaffirm the status quo. "Show me, my women, like a queen" (5.2.227), Cleopatra proclaims, where Caesar harps on "What I can show in this" ("this" being his innocence in Antony's death; [5.1.77]). The conflict between these two modes of political theatre finally culminates in the specter of Caesar's triumphal pageant—a propagandistic drama of imperialist enslavement which Antony and Cleopatra regard in the light of the most acute personal humiliation.

Yet because Caesar makes such productive use of his "ministers" and "representatives," he would not recognize, and his proxies do not in fact develop, the autonomous presence and the other anonymity that attends on Antony, when he encounters the more gravely marginalized and powerless of the messenger-figures. For this reason, the play's most elaborate messenger scene—Antony's tantrum at Thidias—does not participate in the disjunctive rhythms of the other messenger scenes. As a purposeful representative of Caesar, Thidias is easily drawn into the pattern of identification and ambivalence which causes Antony to lash out at him. Uncanniness only arises in the angelloi, those orphaned and otherworldly figures invisible in the blaze of power.

In the play's first scene, the messengers appear as the intrusive agents of Caesar, as ciphers for his summons to legal duty and obligation. Antony treats them as vexatious reminders, and impatiently spurns them, as if that were to escape what they represent. The agitation that their appearance excites in him he projects outward, into the apocalyptic collapse of this intrusive world, against which he can then contrast, and renew, his imaginary refuge: "Let Rome in Tiber melt, and the wide arch / Of the ranged empire fall! Here is my space" (1.1.33–34). The space of this delicate idyll would be one in which messengers could mediate intimacy, not empire, and imperial rulers could become anonymous flaneurs:

> Fie, wrangling queen!
> Whom everything becomes—to chide, to laugh,
> To weep; whose every passion fully strives
> To make itself, in thee, fair and admired.
> No messenger but thine; and all alone
> Tonight we'll wander through the streets and note
> The qualities of people. Come, my queen;
> Last night you did desire it. [*To Attendants*] Speak not to us.
> *Exeunt Antony and Cleopatra with the Train.* (1.1.49–55)

In Plutarch, Antony and Cleopatra actually do disguise themselves as ordinary people, and go to mingle with the crowds in the streets of Alexandria. But Shakespeare recasts this activity in the mode of "desire," of a daydream in which their intimacy could have the oblivion it is not allowed in the play: the two never appear "all alone," but are always accompanied and observed by an audience of waiting-women, eunuchs, generals, and so on. Even after this speech, with its appeal to privacy, and its rebuff, "Speak not to us," Antony and Cleopatra are in their sweeping exit encircled by "the Train." The wish for a private intimacy remains a fantasy because it is not, in fact, true to the style of Antony and

Cleopatra. They are regal figures who thrive on public admiration, and who do not distinguish between political and intimate life, which they subject to the same project of self-dramatization. Antony can exact the wonder of a universal audience even in this scene ("I bind / On pain of punishment, the world to weet / We stand up peerless" [37–39]), and can imagine such an attentive public even in the shadowiness and impersonality of the underworld ("Where souls do couch on flowers, we'll hand in hand, / And with our sprightly port make the ghosts gaze" [4.14.51–52]).

Like the first, the second scene also involves the repudiation of messages. Here, Charmian and Iras make bawdy of the Soothsayer's enigmatic prophecies. Removed from the action, blank of character and history, the Soothsayer is the pure spirit of the messenger, a remote and grave presence imbued with the anonymous wisdom of the otherworldly. He is the most emblematic of the messenger-figures who, early on, reveal their capacity for chilling detachment and the strangely impersonal intimacy it makes possible. But because these figures are as yet anomalous, their audience now either overlooks or, shaken, retreats from their preternatural austerity.

The Soothsayer's appearance works to cast an aura of uncanniness over the messenger-figure, as we feel a few moments later, when Antony determines to hear the envoys he had shunned in the previous scene. The first messenger is talkative and sympathetic, but the second is terse and dark. He materializes suddenly, in answer to the call for news "From Sicyon." Looking up from a distracted meditation, Antony gasps, "What are you?" (1.2.117), as if this nameless functionary had a piercing air. The messenger replies starkly:

Fulvia thy wife is dead. (1.2.118)

He ignores Antony's question, and omits the softening speeches of his predecessor. Handing Antony a letter, the messenger adds, as if it were the power of his impersonal office to fathom all priorities and needs, "Her length of sickness, with what else more serious / Importeth thee to know, this bears" (1.2. 120–21). His distant and austere familiarity fulfills the promise of uncanniness in Antony's spellbound "What are you?"

This intimacy can be paradoxically remote and impersonal because it arises between a subject and a spirit void of a subject. In the first half of the play, this anonymous spirit makes its most dramatic approach with the second and final appearance of the Soothsayer, this time before Antony. The Soothsayer opens with the same disjunctive and terse severity as the messenger from Sicyon:

Antony. Now, sirrah, you do wish yourself in Egypt?
Soothsayer. Would I had never come from thence, nor you thither.
(2.3.11)

He is empowered to speak with a disinterested authority and candor. His prophecy can claim that it is closer to Antony's fate than Antony himself, and can describe this fate with an accuracy as grim as it is rigorous: "Thy daemon, that thy spirit which keeps thee, is / Noble, courageous, high, unmatchable, / Where Caesar's is not. But near him thy angel becomes afeard, as being o'erpowered: therefore / Make space enough between you" (2.3.19–24). But there is no masterful subject behind this knowledge and assurance. The Soothsayer's grandly precise and dispassionate rhetoric produces its own spirit of austerity; and the anonymous figures who speak this rhetoric, the figures whose dramatic lives work only to speak it, diffuse the chilling aura of this language. The Soothsayer and the messenger from Sicyon appear as uncanny presences not only because they speak a cold message in cold words, but because they uncannily assume the character of these words; they enter not as subjects, who can command or fail to command their own language, but as the impersonal spirit of that language itself. At this point, Antony himself recoils from such a strange phenomenon; he hurries the second messenger out with "Forebear me," while he anxiously tells the Soothsayer "Speak this no more," and "Get thee gone."

In the play's first scene, the messengers appear as an encroaching public, whose intervention stirs Antony to an illusive wish for anonymity; but when Antony's fortunes have irrevocably deteriorated, he will find the spirit of anonymous intimacy in the messenger figures. The change in Antony's relationship to the messengers comes just after the battle at Actium, in the scene immediately following Antony's speech, "Fall not a tear, I say," with its appeal to the generosity of language. A representative appears at Caesar's camp to bargain for the lives of Antony and Cleopatra. Having never encountered this lowly subject of his new empire, Caesar must ask, "Know you him?" and Dolabella tartly identifies him as Antony's schoolmaster, "An argument that he is plucked, when hither / He sends so poor a pinion of his wing, / Which had superfluous kings for messengers / Not many moons gone by" (3.12.1–6). Dolabella takes the relative anonymity and unimportance of the messenger to indicate a poverty in Antony. When the schoolmaster enters, he seems to corroborate this view, but what he says in fact completely reverses its tenor and affect. This "poor," unknown figure speaks in a first person which is peacefully emptied out; his is the fidelity of the insignificant and anonymous, free to affirm Antony's "bounty" as if it still continued into the present:

> Such as I am, I come from Antony.
> I was of late as petty to his ends
> As is the morn-dew on the myrtle leaf
> To his grand sea. (3.12.7–10)

With the quiet expansiveness of these lines, the messenger becomes more than a messenger, though still less than a subject; he becomes the spirit of an impersonal intimacy waiting on the "heart" in Antony that survives his worldly decay. His generosity springs from the groundless exuberance of his language, just as this exuberance itself resembles the generosity of an insignificant and anonymous person. Out of Antony's entry into the alterity of language, there materializes this messenger who, unlike his predecessors, is not austere, but gifted with the impersonal kindness and generosity of the other rapport.

When Antony falls to his lowest ebb, he can welcome the alterity of this intimate distance, and can requite the grave generosity of the messenger. After Eros foils Antony's suicide, Antony's own guard flees from him in panic and dismay. Only Decretas pauses long enough to steal the bloody sword which he hopes will "enter" him with Caesar, and he is so furtive in this opportunism that he ignores Diomedes' question, "Lives he? / Wilt thou not answer, man?" (4.14.115). Antony's dying seems destined to take place amid hysteria, betrayal, and then lonely silence. He has been left wretchedly begging to be dispatched when Diomedes enters, fulfilling the wish made long ago for "No messenger but thine." With Diomedes' first words, the atmosphere of the scene changes from anguish to quiet concentration. For with Diomedes enters the spirit of calm and disinterested attentiveness. Antony's exchange with him is pared down to the fewest words, whose weight each knows, so that he speaks with a familiar brevity, as without now superfluous affect:

> *Diomedes.* Most absolute lord,
> My mistress Cleopatra sent me to thee.
> *Antony.* When did she send thee?
> *Diomedes.* Now, my lord.
> *Antony.* Where is she?
> *Diomedes.* Locked in her monument. (4.14.116–17)

Diomedes responds to Antony's change of tone without surprise, as Antony responds to his news without anger or bitterness. Stages of feeling are simply ellipsed, as if irrelevant, and the two figures share instead a muted understanding and regret. When Diomedes comes to tell of his mission, he acknowledges its failure, but touches on it as lightly as Antony's mood is quiet. He describes the tragedy he has found with gentle understatement:

> She had a prophesying fear
> Of what hath come to pass; for when she saw
> (Which never shall be found) you did suspect
> She had disposed with Caesar, and that your rage

Would not be purged, she sent you word she was dead;
But, fearing since how it might work, hath sent
Me to proclaim the truth, and I am come,
I dread, too late. (4.14.120–26)

This sentence slows to its subdued and careful end. The "and" which introduces the last, grim reflection ("and I am come") mutes the potential for melodrama; no climactic transition is marked, but only a soft fall into the heaviness of "too late." Antony matches the messenger's calm austerity when he confirms and echoes his words, as if in intimate, lyrical refrain:

> and I am come,
> I dread, too late.
> Too late, good Diomed.

This scene, with its unexpected turns of feeling, and its close, elliptical dialogue, takes on the form of an intimate encounter. Antony finds a delicate and evanescent rapport with a figure who, though named, is nonetheless fleeting and anonymous, a creature of the moment of language. (Diomedes has not appeared before, and will appear only once more, to answer Cleopatra's question, "How now? Is he dead?" with a bleak precision: "His death's upon him, but not dead" [4.15.5–6]). The messenger emerges from his utilitarian function, and the anonymity of the functionary, to manifest an autonomous presence and a different kind of anonymity—that of a spirit not human, available only in the mode of an impersonal and distant intimacy displaced from the world, when Antony himself is displaced from it.

But it is with Cleopatra that the play irradiates the alterity of language and its intimacy, for she welcomes this alterity without the mediation of the angelloi, and even more luminously than Antony can ever do. Amid the flux of events, she remains oddly unchanging and removed. Neither her character nor her language undergo the dramatic transformation of Antony's. From her two scenes with the envoy bearing news of Antony's marriage, it is clear that the affect associated with the angelloi already belongs to Cleopatra, in whom it has advanced beyond the influence of messenger figures. She is from the beginning what she will be—the play's most intent and moving speaker, a figure given over to the space of language and the other rapport. Her word has an exuberant solitariness all its own until late in the play—when Antony's joins hers in this, after his collapse at the battle of Actium.

Cleopatra is vigorously self-dramatizing, and correspondingly keen in her awareness of the theatricality of other people's rhetoric. She can puncture Antony's expansive, "Let Rome in Tiber melt," with the tart riposte, "Excellent falsehood!"; and when he attempts to take a stately leave of her, she can mock his high rhetoric: "Good now, play one scene / Of excellent dissembling, and let it look / Like perfect honor" (1.3.75–77). As Anthony Brennan has argued in his essay, "Excellent Dissembling: Antony and Cleopatra Playing at Love," their intimacy involves understanding and responding to one another's self-dramatizations. But the relationship between intimacy and self-dramatization is not unmediated. Cleopatra's language often seems to be pitched above her audience (including us), opening outward as if in appeal to an attention more comprehensive and an intelligence more perfectly sympatico with her production of herself. Such attention and intelligence do not exist; and this appeal to absence gives her language its solitary grandeur. Her frenzied encounter with the messenger bearing news of Antony's marriage ends in such a moment of majestic exile:

> *Cleopatra.* In praising Antony I have dispraised Caesar.
> *Charmian.* Many times, madam.
> *Cleopatra.* I am paid for't now. (2.5.107–8)

The grave justice of "I am paid for't now" is not quite addressed to Charmian, but to a disengaged silence and distance. Her language appeals to this other rapport when she says wonderingly, "Though age from folly could not give me freedom, / It does from childishness. Can Fulvia die?" a capacious but enigmatic question elided by Antony's response, "She's dead, my queen" (1.3.58–59). But it is not only in moments of shock or abandonment that her language appeals to the other rapport, for she manifests, from beginning to end, the knowledge of her own stature and isolation. She can address even Antony in words that, though supplicating, seem distracted from him, as if their distance and futility were what he ought to love in her:

> Courteous lord, one word.
> Sir, you and I must part, but that's not it:
> Sir, you and I have loved, but there's not it:
> That you know well. Something it is I would—
> O, my oblivion is a very Antony,
> And I am all forgotten. (1.3.86–91)

This speech is strangely aware of a remoteness from its listener, and a solitary communication with the elusive spirit of a nonhuman intelligence. This sense of her world's isolation allows Cleopatra to speak, when she wishes to, with the precision and austerity of the messengers, as when she asks Antony, "Not know me yet?" or replies to Caesar's "I'll take my leave" with the bracing truth, "And may, through all the world: 'tis yours" (5.2.133–34).

It may seem odd that, with its distance and difficulty, her question, "Not know me yet?" should appear in the play's most commanding representation of intimacy, in the moment of intense conference after Antony's violent attack on Thidias.

> *Antony.* To flatter Caesar, would you mingle eyes
> With one that ties his points?
> *Cleopatra.* Not know me yet?
> *Antony.* Cold-hearted toward me? (3.12.156–58)

This dialogue has the antiphonal rhythm and elliptical expression of an intimate exchange, but it is also oddly disjunctive. With their brave solitude, the words of Antony and Cleopatra join the elliptical expression of intimacy and the isolation of language opening out to the other rapport. Here, to be humanly intimate means to be moved by the anonymous intimacy of the other's language.

Cleopatra's "last conquest" takes this form of intimacy, when she brings Dolabella to speak a language that corresponds to her own in heroic sincerity, and corresponds to it especially because he denies her words, when she herself knows this denial to be just:

> *Cleopatra.* Think you there was or might be such a man
> As this I dreamt of?
> *Dolabella.* Gentle madam, no. (5.2.92–93)

It testifies to the summoning power of Cleopatra's poetry that she can make this agent of the clammy Caesar emerge into the austerity and distant familiarity of the angelloi. In this context, Stephen Booth has engagingly argued that the actor playing Antony doubled for Dolabella. Whether or not Booth's claim is accurate, his view illuminates this moment: the intimacy between Antony and Cleopatra here resurfaces uncannily as a rapport touched by the spirit of the angelloi, and mediated by the remote alterity of language.

The absent rapport summoned up by the rhetorical power of Cleopatra's language constantly makes us feel the impoverishment of the play's world, with its incorrigible binary oppositions and its stingy imperialist ethos, just as the generosity of her language produces the sense of buoyant affirmation in the play. Critics generally try to say what is being affirmed, whether it is a mystical union of love and death (Knight), the imaginative vision of love (Adelman), or the creation of private value (Eagleton). But the sense of affirmation comes first from Antony and Cleopatra's language, before an object of affirmation can be found. The solitariness of Cleopatra's language is, curiously enough, not bleak, but the source of an exuberance which gives sweep and buoyancy even to speeches whose content is not altogether happy, like "My salad days . . ." (1.4.73–end), and even to those spoken at the bleakest moments: "O sun, / Burn the great sphere thou mov'st in: darkling stand / The varying shore of the world. O Antony / Antony, Antony!" (4.15.9–12). From the beginning, Cleopatra knows and loves this impotent generosity of language—which explains the strange tonality of the last act, with its leisurely pace and its strange, erotic happiness. In this act, which Cleopatra has all to herself, she can receive with perfect equanimity the most fantastic of the messenger-figures, a peasant bearing the asps and the eerie salutation, "I wish you joy o'th'worm" (5.2.279); and can free her words, with their call elsewhere, to the most startling affirmations: "go fetch / My best attires. I am again for Cydnus, / To meet Mark Antony" (5.2.226–28).

※ — ※ — ※

1988—Harold Bloom. "Introduction," from *William Shakespeare's "Antony and Cleopatra"*

Harold Bloom is Sterling Professor of the Humanities at Yale University. He has edited many anthologies of literature and literary criticism and is the author of more than 30 books, including *The Western Canon* and *Shakespeare: The Invention of the Human*.

Freud taught us that the therapy-of-therapies is not to invest too much libido in any single object whosoever. Antony at last refuses this wisdom and in consequence suffers what must be called an erotic tragedy, but then Cleopatra, who has spent her life exemplifying the same wisdom, suffers an erotic tragedy also, on Antony's account, one act of the drama more belatedly than he does. *The Tragedy of Antony and Cleopatra* is unique among Shakespeare's plays in that the tragedy's doubleness, equal in both man and woman as it was with *Romeo and Juliet*, takes place between equally titanic personages. Each truly is all but everything in himself and herself, and *knows* it, and neither fears that he or she is really nothing in himself or herself, or nothing without the other. Both consciously play many parts, and yet also *are* those other parts. Both are adept at playing themselves, yet also at being themselves. Like Falstaff and Hamlet, they are supreme personalities, major wits, grand counter-Machiavels (though overmatched by Octavian, greatest of Machiavels), and supreme consciousnesses. They fall in love with one another, resist and betray the love repeatedly, but finally yield to it and are destroyed by it, in order fully to fulfill their allied natures. More even than the death of Hamlet, we react to their suicides as a human triumph and as a release for ourselves. But why? And how?

The crucial originality here is to have represented two great personalities, the Herculean hero proper and a woman of infinite guile and resource, in their overwhelming decline and mingled ruin. A destruction through authentic and mutual love becomes an aesthetic redemption precisely because love's shadow is ruin. We have no representations of this kind before Shakespeare, since a Euripidean vision of erotic ruin, as in the *Medea*, permits no aesthetic redemption, while Virgil's Dido, like Medea, is a solitary sufferer. Antony and Cleopatra repeatedly betray one another, and betray themselves, yet these betrayals are forgiven by them and by us, since they become phases of apotheosis that release the sparks of grandeur even as the lamps are shattered.

From act 4, scene 14, through to the end of the play, we hear something wonderfully original even for Shakespeare, a great dying fall, the release of a new music. It begins with the dialogue between Antony and his marvelously named, devoted follower, Eros:

> ANTONY. Eros, thou yet behold'st me?
> EROS. Ay, noble lord.
> ANTONY. Sometime we see a cloud that's dragonish,
> A vapor sometime like a bear or lion,
> A [tower'd] citadel, a pendant rock,
> A forked mountain, or blue promontory
> With trees upon't that nod unto the world,
> And mock our eyes with air. Thou hast seen these signs,
> They are black vesper's pageants.
> EROS. Ay, my lord.
> ANTONY. That which is now a horse, even with a thought
> The rack dislimns, and makes it indistinct
> As water is in water.
> EROS. It does, my lord.
> ANTONY. My good knave Eros, now thy captain is
> Even such a body. Here I am Antony,
> Yet cannot hold this visible shape, my knave.
> I made these wars for Egypt, and the Queen,
> Whose heart I thought I had, for she had mine—
> Which whilst it was mine had annex'd unto't
> A million more (now lost)—she, Eros, has
> Pack'd cards with Caesar's, and false-play'd my glory
> Unto an enemy's triumph.

Nay, weep not, gentle Eros, there is left us
Ourselves to end ourselves.

There is a deliberate touch of the cloud-watching Hamlet in Antony here, but with Hamlet's parodistic savagery modulated into a gentleness that befits the transmutation of the charismatic hero into a self transcendent consciousness, almost beyond the consolations of farewell. The grandeur of this transformation is enhanced when Antony receives the false tidings Cleopatra sends of her supposed death, with his name her last utterance:

Unarm, Eros, the long day's task is done,
And we must sleep.

The answering chorus to that splendor is Cleopatra's, when he dies in her arms:

The crown o'th'earth doth melt. My lord!
O, wither'd is the garland of the war,
The soldier's pole is fall'n! Young boys and girls
Are level now with men; the odds is gone,
And there is nothing left remarkable
Beneath the visiting moon.

Antony touches the Sublime as he prepares to die, but Cleopatra's lament for a lost Sublime is the prelude to a greater sublimity, which is to be wholly her own. She is herself a great actress, so that the difficulty in playing her, for any actress, is quite extraordinary. And though she certainly loved Antony, it is inevitable that, like any great actress, she must love herself all but apocalyptically. Antony has a largeness about him surpassing any other Shakespearean hero except for Hamlet; he is an ultimate version of the charismatic leader, loved and followed because his palpable glory can be shared, in some degree, since he is also magnificently generous. But Shakespeare shrewdly ends him with one whole act of the play to go, and retrospectively we see that the drama is as much Cleopatra's as the two parts of *Henry IV* are Falstaff's.

Remarkable as Antony is in himself, he interests us primarily because he has the splendor that makes him as much a catastrophe for Cleopatra as she is for him. Cleopatra is in love with his exuberance, with the preternatural vitality that impresses even Octavian. But she knows, as we do, that Antony lacks her infinite variety. Their love, in Freudian terms, is not narcissistic but anaclitic; they are propped upon one another, cosmological beings who are likely to be bored by anyone else, by any personality neither their own nor one another's. Antony is Cleopatra's only true match and yet he is not her equal, which may be the most crucial or deepest meaning of the play. An imaginative being in that he moves the imagination of others, he is simply not an imaginer of her stature. He need not play himself; he is Herculean. Cleopatra ceases to play herself only when she is transmuted by his death and its aftermath, and we cannot be sure, even then, that she is not both performing and simultaneously becoming that more transcendent self. Strangely like the dying Hamlet in this single respect, she suggests, at the end, that she stands upon a new threshold of being:

> I am fire and air; my other elements
> I give to baser life.

Is she no longer the earth of Egypt, or the water of the Nile? We have not exactly thought of her as a devoted mother, despite her children by Julius Caesar and by Antony, but in her dying dialogue with Charmian she transmutes the asps, first into her baby, and then apparently into an Antony she might have brought to birth, as in some sense indeed she did:

> CHARMIAN. O eastern star!
> CLEOPATRA. Peace, peace!
> Dost thou not see my baby at my breast,
> That sucks the nurse asleep?
> CHARMIAN. O, break! O, break!
> CLEOPATRA. As sweet as balm, as soft as air, as gentle—O
> Antony!—Nay, I will take thee too:
> [*Applying another asp to her arm.*]
> What should I stay—*Dies.*

As Lear dies, Kent cries out "Break, heart, I prithee break!" even as Charmian does here, not wishing upon the rack of this tough world to stretch Cleopatra out longer. When Antony's men find him wounded to death, they lament that "the star is fall'n," and that "time is at his period." Charmian's "O eastern star!" associates one dying lover with the other, even as her echo of Kent suggests that the dying Empress of the East is in something like the innocence of Lear's madness. Cleopatra is sucked to sleep as a mother is by a child, or a woman by a lover, and dies in such peace that Octavian, of all men, is moved to the ultimate tribute:

> she looks like sleep,
> As she would catch another Antony
> In her strong toil of grace.

Bewildering us by her final manifestation of her infinite variety, Cleopatra dies into a beyond, a Sublime where actress never trod.

ANTONY AND CLEOPATRA
IN THE TWENTY-FIRST CENTURY
⌇

As the first decade of the twenty-first century draws to a close, it is not obvious what direction thinking about *Antony and Cleopatra* will take. But in an era of global economies, global warfare, global clashes of competing cultures and values, and global figures who are projected as both heroic and frightening, *Antony and Cleopatra* seems to be a play perfectly suited for the times. The essay below, by Jacqueline Vanhoutte, examines the theme of suicide in the play in the context of traditions in Shakespeare's day, of those in Roman times, and of today's thinking on the subject.

2000—Jacqueline Vanhoutte. "Antony's 'Secret House of Death': Suicide and Sovereignty in *Antony and Cleopatra*," from *Philological Quarterly*

Jacqueline Vanhoutte is an assistant professor of English at the University of North Texas. Her principal area of scholarly expertise is early English drama, including Shakespeare. She is the author of *Strange Communion: Motherland and Masculinity in Tudor Plays, Pamphlets, and Politics* (2003) as well as numerous critical essays.

Just after Antony dies from a self-inflicted wound, Shakespeare's Cleopatra asks, "is it sin, / To rush into the secret house of death, / Ere death dare come to us?" The question appears to be rhetorical; Cleopatra soon announces her intention to prove her "resolution" by pursuing "the briefest end" (4.15.91). This decision earns her the homage of her most assiduous critic: Caesar, fond of describing the living Cleopatra as a "whore" (3.6.67), refers to the dead one as "bravest at the last" and "royal" (5.2.333–34). Readers of the play have followed suit. The queen of Egypt herself is the subject of conflicting commentary, but her "end" typically earns critical applause. Even those who denounce Cleopatra's conduct as sinful tend to find her suicide splendid. She is, to paraphrase Antony's comment about Fulvia, good choosing death.

As Cleopatra's question suggests, we judge suicide by precise ethical standards; as her answer about "the high Roman fashion" reveals, these standards are also culturally contingent. In Tudor England, those who had access to education, and therefore to classical literature, might indeed judge a suicide "brave" and "noble" if done "after the high Roman fashion" (4.15.86–87). The classical tradition concerning suicide provided the only widespread and coherent interpretative challenge to absolute condemnation of the act in early modern society. But for most people living in sixteenth- and early seventeenth-century England, suicide was unquestionably a sin. Under the designation of "self-murder," it was regarded as a transgression against the laws of God, of nature, and of the state.

Far from being rhetorical, then, Cleopatra's question calls attention to the difficulty of judging a suicide that does not conform to "Roman fashion." Prompted by the "poor passion" (4.15.74) that she suffers as a result of Antony's death, her question refers as much to his death as to her own. And Antony's final moments have earned less acclaim than hers, in part because Antony improvises a death that comprises elements of the "high Roman" and early modern models of suicide, but that cannot satisfactorily be explained by reference to either. In his treatment of Antony's suicide, Shakespeare inhibits both praise and condemnation, the two responses associated respectively with classical and early modern ideas about suicide. The ensuing ambiguity suits the story well: the pagan setting precludes strictly Christian readings of suicide, while Antony's status as history's most famous deserting soldier undermines Roman readings. Capitalizing on the potential of his source, Shakespeare overturns the categories by which suicide was understood in the early modern period; he evokes these categories only to demonstrate their inadequacy when it comes to describing Antony's tragic death.

Antony's refusal to follow a recognizable pattern in his suicide might account for the discomfort occasioned by his death among the play's critics. While from Cleopatra's perspective Antony has rushed into "the secret house," his critics have more frequently chastised his slowness in dying. Even Phyllis Rackin, whose reading of the play is sympathetic to its protagonists, considers Antony's suicide "a messy affair"; other scholars more categorically describe it as "bungled" or "botched." Antony's motivations appear conflicted and his means suspect: he "cannot properly manage" his own death, he is "diminishe [d] . . . in the eyes of the audience," he behaves "like a gulled, ineffectual comic figure." Again and again, Antony's dying body elicits such condescension and confusion. Like Antony's guards, who upon discovering their bleeding master flee the room, critics eager to salvage Antony's reputation rush over the embarrassing particulars of his suicide and focus instead on its aftermath. Cleopatra's eulogies enable readings that emphasize Antony's achievement of some kind of transcendent "new heaven" (1.1.17). Such readings, however, privilege another character's view of Antony's death over his own experience of it. Yet Shakespeare demonstrably calls our attention to the actual details of Antony's dying; for the better part of two scenes, Antony "importune[s] death" (4.15.19).

Significantly, none of the surviving characters comments negatively on Antony's failure to achieve a brief "end." When modern critics denounce the "botched" nature of Antony's suicide, then, they seem to be applying to it an aesthetic standard more attuned to late Romantic sensibilities than to those of the early modern period. Like Ibsen's Hedda Gabler, they want their hero's suicide to "shimmer with spontaneous beauty." Antony fails to meet that standard and indeed fails to meet any other recognizable standard. His suicide is "shap'd" only "like itself" (2.7.41). This morphology manifests itself in the extraordinary stage business that attends Antony's dying. It is also apparent in the fact that he finds a "secret house" in a world where there is "no time for private stomaching" (2.2.9) and in the way that he bears his dying body into the public sphere where he presents it as an emblem of his sovereignty: "not Caesar's valor hath o'erthrown Antony, / But Antony's hath triumph'd on itself" (4.15.14–15). To borrow a phrase from Elaine Scarry's work on torture, Antony's death is a "piece of compensatory drama," a ritual purgation of the public world generally and, more specifically, of the excess signification that his body has been made to bear in it. It is comic only in that it celebrates the brief reunion of what Antony calls his "spirit" (4.15.58) and the body from which, over the course of the play, he becomes increasingly alienated. It is transcendent only in that Antony momentarily overcomes the dynamics by which his body has become a form of cultural property.

Cleopatra's domestic metaphor (the "house of death") implies that suicide, like Antony's body, is private, even though it calls to itself public meaning. Instead of signaling a failure, then, the "great gap of time" (1.5.5) required for Antony's death provides Shakespeare with the opportunity to investigate this discrepancy more closely. As John Donne notes, any conclusions reached about a suicide's state of mind are "doubtfull" at best, since they reflect the "scandaliz'd" sensibilities of those who presume to judge rather than the actual experience of the suicide, who can no longer be interrogated. Donne calls attention to the distance between the suicide's private experience and the public judgment passed on that experience. Shakespeare exploits this gap in his representation of Antony's death. Antony's prolonged death emphasizes the disjunctions between his experience and the culturally validated models for understanding that experience. His case, in other words, points to the limitations in the deterministic paradigms governing early modern responses to suicide.

By the time Shakespeare wrote *Antony and Cleopatra,* suicide had become a source of intense cultural concern. For various reasons, the Tudor institutions of church and state produced increasingly stringent definitions of and sanctions against self-murder. In their study of suicide in early modern England, Michael

MacDonald and Terence Murphy record a steady increase in convictions for *felo de se*: whereas from 1485 to 1499 only six persons were convicted, from 1540 to 1549, 499 were convicted, and from 1600 to 1609, 873. According to MacDonald and Murphy, this increase does not reflect an actual rise in the number of suicides; instead, it signals an increasing socio-cultural censoriousness about suicide. Because of "the early coincidence of governmental and religious reform," early modern English society developed "a common stereotype of self-murder, shared by men and women of every rank, [which] determined the response to the deed."

The stereotype represented the suicide as alienated, deprived of divine grace, and dangerous to human communities; consequently, the response to suicide tended to be condemnatory. Both stereotype and response evolved from a combination of popular superstition, church doctrine, and legal persecution. Legal and popular attitudes towards suicides focused on the deed as it affected the larger community—self-murder was a political sin as well as a religious one. A commonplace analogy, here in Montaigne's version, expresses the period's dominant paradigm for understanding suicide:

> without the expresse commandment of him, that hath placed us in this world, we may by no meanes forsake the garrison of it, and that it is the hands of God only, who therein hath placed us, not for our selves alone, but for his glory, and others service, when ever it shall please him to discharge us hence, and not for us to take leave: That we are not borne for our selves, but for our Countrie . . . it is against nature, we should despise, and carelessly set our selves at naught.

The analogy of the suicide to a deserting soldier emphasizes the religious and political dimension of the crime, because the soldier's post is assigned by God but involves responsibility to "others service" and to the state. Like witchcraft, suicide violated the order of "nature" and was frequently attributed to diabolic intervention.

Classical culture—in particular Roman culture—did make more positive valuations of suicide available. Ever contradictory, Montaigne praises Cato's death, cites the Roman stoics in defense of suicide, and opines that "the voluntariest death is the fairest." The classical paradigm tended to select for praise those, like Cato, who killed themselves to preserve honor or communally held values. Thus, whereas the common suicide retreated dangerously from public responsibility, the heroic suicide in effect affirmed his or her commitment to communal life. But such heroic figures had little enough to do with most suicidal individuals. The idealizing tendencies of the classical view of suicide could therefore coexist peacefully with the demonizing tendencies of the early modern view despite the apparent contradictions between the models.

Shakespeare's plays attest to his familiarity with the two dominant interpretations of suicide. In fact, his representations of suicidal characters typically rely on cultural commonplace. Macbeth's suicidal despair, for example, is the consequence of his disregard for the laws of nature, God, and state. To accentuate the extent to which his hero's transgressions are supernatural, Shakespeare has Macbeth call on the aptly named Seyton while he despairs of Divine grace. The same suspicion that suicide is not only sinful but diabolical informs Edgar's treatment of his father in *King Lear*; Edgar "cures" his father of suicidal despair by staging a mock-suicide complete with imaginary devil. Shakespeare treats Brutus, on the other hand, to the "high Roman fashion": he dies nobly and efficiently, affirming to the last the values of honor and country, and earning the public praise of his enemies Antony and Octavius.

In *Antony and Cleopatra*, Shakespeare uses these familiar strategies to present the deaths of Enobarbus and Cleopatra. He applies the early modern model of suicide to Enobarbus's miserable and lonely death: having lost faith in Antony, the deserting soldier succumbs first to Caesar's empty promises and then to suicidal despair. In Shakespeare's adaptation of Christian ideas about suicide, the triad of good general, soldier, and enemy general replaces the more traditional triad of God, soul, and devil. Although the religious implications of suicide disappear, the political ones are stressed. Enobarbus deserts Antony's "garrison," enters instead in Caesar's service, and finds himself "the villain of the earth" (4.6.30). Evidence of Antony's continuing magnanimity serves only to deepen the old soldier's despair, for it underlines the extent to which he is unworthy of the one system—service to Antony—guaranteed to bring him "Joy" (4.6.20). Ranking himself "a master-leaver, and a fugitive" (4.9.22), he finds a "ditch, wherein to die" (4.6.38). In his final moments, Enobarbus experiences the self-hatred, melancholia, alienation, and despair commonly attributed to suicides in the early modern period. His choice of a grave further condemns him, for suicides were buried in England face-down in a pit by the highway. Shakespeare leaves little doubt that, in Enobarbus's case, rushing into the "secret house" is "sin."

Shakespeare's treatment of Enobarbus's death makes use of one aspect of his culture's dualistic thinking about suicide, and his treatment of Cleopatra's death reflects the other. Her death is untinged by desertion, despair, or self-hatred; like Brutus, she maintains her dignity. Although she manages to keep her intention a secret from Caesar, the suicide itself is not a private act. Instead, like Brutus's suicide, it derives its nobility from its public nature. Death, for Cleopatra, is an opportunity for one more controlled display of theatrical power, one more extravagant political self-assertion. It works: Caesar finally acknowledges "her strong toil of grace" (5.2.346). More importantly, Cleopatra forces Caesar to abandon his own habitual misogyny and come to terms with her as a political agent. The man who believes that "women are not / In their best fortunes strong; but want will perjure / The ne'er touched vestal" (3.12.29–31) recognizes in

Cleopatra's death the defeat of his own stratagems. "She levell'd at our purposes," he observes, "and being royal / Took her own way" (5.2.334–35). This is high praise, for the Romans generally refuse Cleopatra her position as "president of [her] kingdom" (3.7.17); and Caesar himself calls into question her royalty earlier in the scene when, ignoring the visible signs that distinguish Cleopatra from her serving maids, he asks, "which is the Queen of Egypt?" (5.2.111). Cleopatra's suicide answers him. Her resolution in death expresses her continued engagement in the politics of the play and her absolute commitment to the values she has espoused throughout. When the First Guard echoes Cleopatra's question about the ethical validity of suicide—"Is this well done?" (5.2.324)—Charmian responds without hesitation: "It is well done, and fitting for a princess / Descended of so many royal kings" (5.2.325–26). Here, Charmian implies, lies the noblest Egyptian of them all.

Antony's death is flanked by the deaths of Enobarbus and Cleopatra. It occurs, literally, "midway / "Twixt these extremes" (3.4.19–20). Such placement invites comparison, and indeed, Antony's suicide comprises aspects of the other deaths. It originates, for example, in private despair but it ends in public display: Antony kills himself in a room and dies at a monument. In his desire to "unarm" and to be "no more a soldier" (4.14.35–42), Antony, like Enobarbus, calls to mind the analogy of the soldier. But, like Cleopatra, Antony takes his own death to be a triumph; as Robert Miola points out, some aspects of Antony's suicide are "recognizably Roman." This interweaving of apparently incompatible positions on suicide is further complicated by the fact that although Shakespeare goes out of his way to invoke both familiar patterns, he also inhibits the standard response to either. Neither praise nor condemnation seems an appropriate reaction to Antony's experience.

By attributing Antony's initial suicidal impulse to despair, Shakespeare strays from his source and strips the suicide of some of its classical connotations. Plutarch's Antonius behaves as a Roman should. He hears that Cleopatra has died; and, refusing to be outdone by a woman, he dies by manfully "thrust[ing] his sword into his bellie." In *Antony and Cleopatra*, Antony displays no such laudable resolution, no single-minded commitment to a motivation—and certainly not to the one cited by Plutarch, since Antony's first suicidal thoughts precede by two scenes the false report of Cleopatra's death. Instead, Antony contemplates suicide when he suspects that Cleopatra has betrayed him with Caesar. His loss of faith in Cleopatra is tainted by the Roman view of her; he calls her, famously, a "triple-turn'd whore" (4.12.13). But the self-destructive thoughts that this despair inspires owe nothing to the "Roman fashion" concerning suicide. Enraged, Antony invokes the memory of Hercules' death:

> The shirt of Nessus is upon me, teach me,
> Alcides, thou mine ancestor, thy rage.

Let me lodge Lichas on the horns o' the moon,
And with these hands that grasp'd the heaviest club,
Subdue my worthiest self. . . .   (4.12.43–47)

The analogy that Antony makes between his putative ancestor's demise and his own desire for self-destruction is instructive in a number of ways. By using Hercules' Greek name (for the first time in the play), Antony underlines the extent to which his suicidal rage is not a manifestation of his Roman identity. Suicide, at this time, appears shameful to him. Far from safeguarding integrity and honor, it entails the destruction of his "worthiest self." Moreover, implicit in Antony's analogy is the recognition that his rage is misdirected: whereas Alcides vents his anger against the innocent Lichas, Antony prepares to vent his against Cleopatra.

In its earliest appearance, Antony's suicidal impulse resembles the despair experienced by characters like Macbeth and Enobarbus. Antony's analogy implies, in any case, that his inherited suicidal rage is inescapable, like the fate that Macbeth routinely blames. Like Macbeth, Antony believes that he has been driven so far because a "witch" has "beguil'd" (4.12.28) him. Enobarbus succumbs to despair because he lacks faith in Antony; Antony follows suit when he loses faith in Cleopatra. Both servant and master have what they take to be sufficient evidence to justify their skepticism, and neither can tolerate living with that skepticism. But whereas new evidence of Antony's generosity plunges Enobarbus farther into despondency and self-hatred, Antony's despair is short-lived. He raises the idea that Cleopatra is a "witch" with supernatural power only to dismiss it, conclusively. When he does finally throw himself on his sword, he has overcome his despair. Further evidence of Cleopatra's trickery does not disturb the equanimity with which he faces his death, nor does he mention again the ways in which she has failed him. Antony's despair over Cleopatra brings the idea of suicide to his mind, but it is not what makes him kill himself.

Antony's bewildering improvisation of motives undermines Shakespeare's initial presentation of him as a soul in despair, and it equally undermines Decretas's later presentation of his master as a noble Roman. In considering suicide, Antony cites, in chaotic succession, his rage at Cleopatra, his fear that Cleopatra and Caesar are colluding, his love for Cleopatra, his desire to emulate her, his desire to emulate Eros, and his refusal to become a trophy in Caesar's triumph. Only the latter qualifies as a "Roman" justification for suicide, but its presence among so many others gives it the ring of rationalization rather than motive. Indeed, as circumstances force Antony to recognize that a motivation is not valid, he simply exchanges it for a new one. His commitment to suicide is constant; the reasons that he adduces for it are not.

Near death, Antony asserts that he was once "the greatest prince o' the world, / The noblest" (4.15.53–54). He cannot, however, affirm anything categorically about his own suicide. At first he does find that he has done his "work ill" (4.14.105) because he survives the actual deed. But the private work ill begun ends in a sense of public triumph at Cleopatra's monument. There, he expresses his achievement in a series of negatives, assuring Cleopatra that "not Caesar's valour hath o'erthrown Antony, / But Antony's hath triumph'd on itself," and that

> . . . [I] do now not basely die,
> Not cowardly put off my helmet to
> My countryman: a Roman, by a Roman
> Valiantly vanquish'd . . . (4.15.55–58)

The Latinate words that he chooses—valor, vanquish, valiant—underscore his claim. They suggest not the private despair of the alienated individual, but the glorious victory of the classical hero. The way in which Antony puts these words together, however, cancels out Roman meaning even as it is invoked: "valor" destroys "valor" and "Roman" annihilates "Roman." The suicide may or may not have subdued Antony's "worthiest self," but it has certainly destroyed his Roman identity. The two, as we shall see, are not the same.

The instability of Antony's motivations restrains both "scandaliz'd" and laudatory responses, because both rely on a stable sense of motive. The amalgam of Christian and classical motifs that characterizes Antony's suicide further impedes pat ethical judgment. No easy label can adequately convey the complexities of Antony's experience as Shakespeare represents it. As a result, it becomes difficult to answer Cleopatra's question—"Is it sin?"—with any certainty.

By inhibiting both praise and condemnation, Shakespeare may be encouraging what Donne, in *Biathanatos*, calls a "charitable interpretacion" of Antony's suicide. The subtitle of Donne's treatise gives a good indication of its content: *A Declaration of that Paradoxe or Thesis, that Selfe-homicide is not so naturally Sinne, that it may neuer be otherwise. Wherein The Nature, and the extent of all those Lawes, which seeme to be violated by this Act, are diligently Surueyd.* "Is it sin?" Not always, says Donne; and his treatise, by contesting the arguments that describe suicide as sin, cautions against totalizing judgments on the subject. Shakespeare's treatment of Antony's death stresses ambiguity and uncertainty and thus delivers a similar caution. Certainly, we are asked to withhold judgment for the considerable time that it takes Antony to make his decision, to implement it, and, finally, to die. Shakespeare does not idealize or ridicule Antony's suicide; instead, he depicts it in agonizing detail. The stunned reactions of the on-stage witnesses give some indication of the potentially intense effect of the dying scenes. Eros kills himself to "escape the sorrow / Of Antony's death" (4.14.94–95), and Antony's guards initially run from the room. But the rest of us must look on while Antony "cure[s]" himself "with a wound" (4.14.78).

Shakespeare leaves us no choice but to come to terms with the sorrow of Antony's death, and the business with Eros and the guards provides us with a means for doing so. Antony requests assistance from Eros and from the guards: he tells the guards "let him that loves me strike me dead" (4.14.108). Both refuse and thus prolong his agony—Eros because, as his name indicates, he loves Antony too much, and the guards because, as their response indicates, they do not love Antony enough. Antony's plea calls attention to the guards' cowardly failure in charity; despite their recognition of the momentousness of the occasion, they withdraw. In making the plea for cooperation, Antony assumes that his suffering will elicit a loving response. The success of the suicide, in other words, momentarily hinges on Antony's ability to provoke a "charitable interpretacion."

Although the guards disappoint Antony, his assumption concerning the possibility of such an interpretation is not necessarily faulty. It involves steering a course "midway / 'Twixt these extremes" of idealization and denigration, loving too much and loving not enough. Antony himself paves the way for a "charitable" response when he refers to the suicide as a cure (4.14.78). The suggestion that suicide heals suffering tends to provoke sympathetic responses in early modern commentators. For example, Montaigne notes that "the common course of any infirmitie, is ever directed at the charge of life: we have incisions made into us, we are cauterized, we have limbes cut and mangled, we are let bloud, we are dieted. Goe we but one step further, we need no more physicke, we are perfectly whole." Momentarily, Montaigne withholds judgment as he considers the possibility that suicide might be a radical act of self-healing, a making "whole" of that which has been rent. Suicide returns agency to the traumatized subject: after being prodded, mangled, cut, bled, and cauterized by some unknown agent, the "we" of the sentence triumphantly takes charge at the moment of suicide. By grounding suicide in the common somatic experience of pain, Montaigne briefly asks us to identify with, rather than disassociate ourselves from, the suicide.

The idea that suicide returns agency to the subject also sustains Donne's "charitable interpretacion," which is based in part on an acknowledgement of his own suicidal tendencies. In Donne's self-analysis, the categories by which early modern society understood suicide are evident, despite his desire to resist them; he blames his suicidal tendencies on his exposure to the discredited Catholic religion and on "the common Enemy." But as he progresses in his search for cause, other possibilities present themselves. The mention of "braue scorn" evokes a classical approach to suicide, and while Donne describes suicide first as an "affliction," it quickly becomes a "remedy." As in Antony's case, the idea of suicide sustains a number of contradictory and culturally specific meanings. But these meanings cancel each other out in order to leave only Donne's desire for sovereignty—"methinks I haue the keyes of my prison in myne owne hand."

The triumphant sense of recovered agency in Donne and Montaigne calls to mind Antony's sense of triumph in death, his insistence that his suicide be understood as a self-referential act ("Not Caesar's valor . . . but Antony's"). In fact, the desire for agency over his own body informs not only Antony's determination to cure himself with a wound but also his behavior throughout the play. Shakespeare, in other words, does not limit his representation of Antony as a suicidal figure to the scenes immediately preceding his death. From the beginning, Shakespeare presents Antony as a soldier eager to desert the competing cultures—Rome and Egypt—that claim agency over his body. Antony's assertions of sovereignty at Cleopatra's monument make sense within the context of his broader struggle to regain possession of his own body.

Antony and Cleopatra opens with an inventory of Antony's body parts: while condemning Antony's "dotage," Philo describes his "goodly eyes," "his captain's heart," and "his breast" (1.1.2–8). Philo's attention to Antony's physical traits recalls the conventional blazons of Renaissance sonnets. As such, Philo's speech forms an appropriate introduction to a male hero whom the playwright consistently represents in terms of his superabundant carnality. Carnality is more habitually associated with women in the period; indeed, many readers of *Antony and Cleopatra* have associated it with Cleopatra. But Shakespeare never insists on Cleopatra's body in the way that he insists on Antony's. Antony's physicality overwhelms all the other characters' conversations about him. Cleopatra spends his absence wondering "Stands he, or sits he? / Or does he walk? Or is he on his horse?" Her attempts to imagine Antony's body culminate, notoriously, with her envy of his horse: "O happy horse to bear the weight of Antony" (1.5.19–21). Cleopatra's erotic yearning underlines Antony's status as an object of desire in this play. The form that desire takes is culturally contingent; Antony's "weight" signifies differently in Egypt than in Rome. But the validity of his body as cultural capital is never in question.

Both Rome and Egypt have a political stake in Antony; both Romans and Egyptians consequently show themselves determined to take advantage of Antony's expansive carnality. He is, as Cleopatra notes, "the greatest soldier in the world" (1.3.38), and he can be made to bear a number of ideologically inflected meanings. To Cleopatra, he is not just a lover, but a "soldier, servant" (1.3.70), the means by which she converts sexual into political power. Accordingly, Antony's departure from Egypt strikes Cleopatra as a political offense; she finds that he has committed "treasons" against her as a queen (1.3.26). Even so, he continues to be significant enough to her politics that she finds criticism of him to be equally treasonous (1.5.7). Cleopatra needs Antony's "inches" in order to show "there were a heart in Egypt" (1.3.40–41). Long after he leaves his post, she continues to use those "inches" as evidence of her own power.

The Romans have their own ideas about what Antony's "inches" mean; and in his predilection for Egyptian queens and Egyptian dishes, Antony challenges those ideas. He deviates from Roman standards of masculinity that emphasize masculine control over somatic impulses—standards that, paradoxically, he also embodies. By a perverse logic, Antony best represents ideal Roman masculinity because he has the most body to control. In fact, his name has become the Roman culture's byword for honor and valor, and the Romans find only his own past example to indict his current behavior. Even in the act of condemnation, for example, Philo attests to the way in which Antony's body sustained Roman readings: his "goodly eyes" once "glow'd like plated Mars," his "captain's heart . . . in the scuffles of great fights hath burst / The buckles on his breast" (1.1.2–8). Caesar similarly relies on Antony's past to castigate Antony for his "lascivious wassails" in Egypt (1.4.56). He demonstrates the transgressive nature of Antony's current "voluptuousness" (1.4.26) by contrasting it to his previous willingness to drink the "stale of horses" and to "eat strange flesh, / Which some did die to look on" (1.4.62–68) in the line of duty. Even under such a regimen, Caesar notes approvingly, Antony's "cheek / so much as lank'd not" (1.4.70–71). Antony's unnatural feedings stand in Rome for masculine honor, for the extent, that is, to which the body can be subjected to spirit and material need can cede to the needs of the state. Despite its reductiveness—masculinity here becomes little more than a form of gastronomic self-flagellation—Caesar's description supplies the surest definition of Roman honor in *Antony and Cleopatra*.

The Romans resent Antony's desertion precisely because Antony occupies such a privileged position. While Philo means to pay homage to the way in which Antony's body signified Roman honor, the image that he invokes—of this body exploding the constraints of Roman armor—is ambiguous. Antony's body "overflows" (1.1.2); Roman armor or Roman interpretation cannot ultimately contain it. And Antony's resistance to Roman interpretation confuses Philo because it threatens his basic cognitive categories. To Philo, honor and Antony are so closely identified that a separation between them would dissolve both quantities: "when he is not Antony, / He comes too short of that great property / Which still should go with Antony" (1.1.57–59). The "great property" is by definition Antony's; if "he is not Antony," then the property has nowhere to go. In abandoning his post as Roman soldier par excellence, Antony leaves a troubling vacuum in Roman discourse. Although all the feats of Roman honor discussed in the play occur in the past—occur in fact in Antony's past—the value remains central to Roman cultural identity. By staying alive without retaining the "great property" which he embodies, Antony threatens that identity. From the Roman perspective, he has deserted a long time before he orders Eros to "pluck off" (4.15.37) the armor that binds what Philo calls his "captain's heart."

As his first great speech demonstrates, Antony himself views his stay in Egypt as an escape from the determining forces of Rome. In response to Cleopatra's teasing accusations that his blush "is Caesar's homager" and that his "cheek pays shame" to Fulvia (1.1.30–31), Antony asserts his sovereignty:

> Let Rome into the Tiber melt, and the wide arch
> Of the rang'd empire fall! Here is my space,
> Kingdoms are clay: our dungy earth alike
> Feeds beast as man; the nobleness of life
> Is to do thus. . . . (1.1.33–36)

As Cleopatra observes, the speech is "an excellent falsehood" (1.1.40), for Egypt is not in fact a depoliticized "space" Antony may define as his own but a "kingdom" in which he must act the part of a subject. Antony has exchanged Roman overdetermination for its Egyptian counterpart; and, afraid to "lose [him]self," he eventually reverses the process to break his "Egyptian fetters" (1.2.113–14). Nevertheless, he briefly finds in Egypt a position from which to criticize the Roman association between nobility and somatic repression; as he kisses Cleopatra, he privileges his own pleasure momentarily over the competing claims that the Roman and Egyptian states have on his "inches." "To do thus" for Antony is to create a gap in language and to reclaim his body as independent from the public representations of it that proliferate in the play. He deserts so as to assert his own power (however imperfectly, however fantastically) over his body and its significations. Antony's "excellent falsehood" allows him briefly to "be himself" (1.1.43).

It is within this context, provided by Antony's first speech, that I suggest we understand his decision "to do thus" (4.14.102) later in the play, when he kills himself. Antony's belief that doing "thus" once again guarantees "nobleness" (4.14.99) confirms the connectedness of these two moments in the play; the kiss and the sword stroke are parallels of a sort. Moments before he stabs himself, Antony fears that his body is disintegrating, like a cloud given brief shape by the imagination:

> *Ant.* That which is now a horse, even with a thought
> The rack dislimns, and makes it indistinct
> As water is in water.
> *Eros.* It does, my lord.
> *Ant.* My good knave Eros, now thy captain is
> Even such a body: here I am Antony,
> Yet cannot hold this visible shape, my knave. (4.14.9–14)

As his analogy indicates, Antony perceives his body as shaped by others' thoughts: he is still Antony, but it no longer belongs to him. He proposes the suicide as a remedy to his sense that he "cannot hold" his own body together. His suicide is thus an attempt to reassert control over his "visible shape" by removing himself from the determining cultural pressures that he thinks are destroying him. With a "wound," Antony creates a gap in culture where he can make his body his own again.

Like Donne and Montaigne, Antony discovers sovereignty in a suicidal thought. The representational practices of Rome and Egypt have alienated him from his body by making it bear an excess of signification. Antony experiences this alienation as a somatic disintegration. But he can make himself "whole," to use Montaigne's term, by effecting his own death; in doing "thus," he proves that his "inches" are indeed his and that his "cheek" pays homage to none. For Antony, suicide replicates, with a difference, the dynamic that Elaine Scarry has identified in torture. Scarry argues that torture

> is a condensation of the act of "overcoming" the body present in benign forms of power. Although the torturer dominates the prisoner in both physical and verbal acts, ultimate domination requires that the prisoner's ground become increasingly physical and the torturer's increasingly verbal, that the prisoner become a colossal body and the torturer a colossal voice . . . with no body, that eventually the prisoner experience himself exclusively in terms of sentience and the torturer exclusively in terms of self-extension.

Suicide collapses torturer and prisoner into one; by subjecting his body to "sentience," the suicide may paradoxically experience a "self-extension." Given the right conditions, the suicide may in fact experience himself or herself as both "colossal body" and "colossal voice," so that he or she may overcome the other voices that seek domination over the body and thus establish "ultimate domination."

Antony's suicide culminates in such a scene of domination. His final moments are marked both by sentience and by self-extension. "How heavy weighs my lord!" (4.15.31), exclaims Cleopatra as she hoists up the dying Antony to her monument. W. B. Worthen argues that the comment "draws our attention to [Antony's] body," and so do the other carnal puns in which the scene abounds. The focus on Antony's body in his death-scene momentarily inactivates ideological readings—those within the play of that body and those within the audience of his suicide. Poised between heaven and earth, Antony's body offers itself as an object of contemplation throughout the scene, insistently drawing attention to its own heaviness, its carnality, and its pain. His range of physical activity, meanwhile, establishes that body's continued capacity for the more pleasurable forms of sentience. He kisses, he drinks, and, punningly, he comes. While his body hangs, his expansive carnality becomes his own. Antony's extraordinary death makes his body present as a "colossal body," the huge "case of that huge spirit" (4.15.89) bestriding, if not the ocean, at least the extremes of carnal experience.

The audience's extended confrontation with this dying body serves several functions. First, the recognition of Antony's pain should encourage a sympathetic response: Shakespeare suspends his hero in order to encourage us to suspend our judgment. Plutarch's description of "poore Antonius" at the monument emphasizes the fact that those who "were present to behold it, said they never saw so pitiefull a sight." Shakespeare follows his source by evoking pity; however, he carefully avoids the negative connotations of "pitiefull" by distancing his triumphant Antony from Plutarch's "crying" Antonius. As Leslie Thomson notes, Antony's death scene prompts us "to agree that he 'do[es] . . . not basely die.'" Moreover, the extent to which Shakespeare represents Antony's pain in terms of his capacity for pleasure forces an acknowledgment of Antony's singular individuality, stripped now of political meanings. Whereas the rest of the play has trained us to think of Antony's body in terms of its ideological use, in the death scene, it becomes, as it were, pure body. The heavy eroticism of this scene at the same time transforms us into voyeurs. Our gaze in the death scene is invasive and therefore transgressive. Our voyeuristic shame (the embarrassment so common to critical discussions of the scene) paradoxically confirms Antony's ownership of his body because it transforms his politicized body into a private body. And if Antony owns his body—if that body does not, in fact, belong to Egypt or to Rome, to the "countrie" or to God—then his suicide cannot be a sin.

Wearied by the aftermath of Actium, Antony earlier expressed his desire to "breathe between the heavens and the earth, / A private man" (3.12.14–15). By entering the "secret house of death," Antony briefly enacts that desire: he finds the "midway / 'Twixt extremes." In transition between heaven and earth, life and death, Roman guards and Egyptian queen, Antony's body emblematizes his search for a private "space" where "kingdoms are clay." The suicide rejects politically constructed meanings and substitutes a jubilant sense of sovereignty. Twice, Antony claims that his voluntary death constitutes an act of overcoming. The inarticulateness of his claims reveals the extent to which he has removed himself from the play's public discourses. His assurances to Cleopatra—that his "valor," not Caesar's, has overcome his "valor" and that though undefeated by a "countryman," he is a "Roman, by a Roman" vanquished—also emphasize his erasure of his own submission to culture. Antony forces the cancellation of Rome within himself. His pain is "world-ridding"; (39) it obliterates all evidence of Romanness and of Caesar.

Paradoxically, Antony's death also frees the Romans to rehabilitate his reputation and reappropriate his past. The suicide allows the Romans to restore the link between Antony's "great property" and Antony, and thus to restore Antony to his previous position as the paragonal Roman soldier. When Decretas notifies the Roman generals of Antony's death, he connects the suicide directly to Antony's glorious past, thereby imputing to Antony a consistency that he has lacked and erasing altogether the Antony whom we have seen in the play:

> ... that self hand
> Which writ his honour in the acts it did,
> Hath, with the courage which the heart did lend it,
> Splitted the heart. This is his sword,
> I robb'd his wound of it: behold it stain'd
> With his most noble blood. (5.1.21–26)

Decretas imagines Antony's suicide as Antony's final inscription of Roman honor on his body—he writes his honor on his splitted heart—and this pleases the assembled Roman potentates enormously. Where shortly before they had regarded Antony as an "old ruffian" (4.1.4), they now characterize him as the rarest "spirit" that "did steer humanity" (5.1.31–32); Caesar himself finds in the dead Antony a "friend," a "mate," a "companion" (5.1.43–44).

But Decretas's interpretation of Antony's suicide is perforce limited and limiting. Unlike us, he does not witness Antony's ultimate moments or attend to his final speeches; he barges into the room and remains only long enough to take the sword embedded in the still-living Antony. When he mentions having "robb'd his wound of it," Decretas does not speak metaphorically, and his interpretation of the suicide is tainted by the cold-blooded opportunism of the gesture that enables it. Decretas has no idea why Antony committed suicide. His only concern is that "this sword but shown to Caesar with this tidings / Shall enter me with him" (4.14.112–13). As the unfortunate pun reveals, the sword, in facilitating Decretas's entry with Caesar, has taken on a quite different signification than it had had in Antony's body. It becomes the occasion for Caesar's cunning reappropriation of Antony and of his body: the rebellious voluptuary thus becomes "the arm of [Caesar's] own body" (5.1.45) and his story may usefully be rehabilitated to inflate "his glory which / Brought [Antony] to be lamented" (5.2.359–60). To drive an "old ruffian" to suicide is hardly creditable labor; however, to encourage a wayward hero to kill himself in an ultimate tribute to the value of "honor" is work fit for an emperor. To use Donne's term, the Romans' judgment concerning Antony's suicide is "doubtfull" at best. The "tidings" Decretas so carefully prepares for Roman consumption are nothing but the serviceable fictions of a grave-robber and the culture he wishes to re-"enter."

The habit of imposing ideologically useful readings on still-warm corpses is not peculiar to Romans; indeed, Cleopatra manages successfully to use her dead lover to further her own ends. Once she overcomes the "poor passion" that turns her into "no more but e'en a woman" (4.15.73–75), she transforms the suicide into proof of her own transfigurative powers. Initially, she views Antony's suicide not just as an act that guarantees his status as the "noblest of men" (4.15.59) but also as an act of selfishness and desertion: she asks her dying lover, "Hast thou no care of me?" (4.15.60). Cleopatra experiences his death first as an abandonment, a fissure in their carefully sustained public identity as a "mutual pair" (1.1.36). In dying too soon, Antony has moved beyond her decidedly unsecret public representations of their relationship. Only by keeping him alive artificially in her visionary speeches does she manage to give credence to the assertion that she will join him. Her eulogies of Antony, delivered to Dolabella, are prologue to her own "immortal longings" (5.2.280). She "imagine[s] / An Antony" (5.2.98–99) so as to seduce a Dolabella, and through him, posterity. Cleopatra's handling of Antony's death is far more attractive than Decretas's but no less opportunistic.

Shakespeare suggests that judgments such as Decretas's and Cleopatra's are more likely to reflect on the ethical nature of the judge than on that of the dead person. The misreadings of Antony's suicide that proliferate after his death underscore the difficulty of judging an act of such complexity. These misreadings point also to the ultimate failure of Antony's enterprise. Although his suicide allows him a moment of unfettered sovereignty, it finally feeds the ideological forces that he had attempted to defeat. And in that irony lies the "sorrow of Antony's death."

———

BIBLIOGRAPHY

Adelman, Janet. *The Common Liar; An Essay on Antony and Cleopatra*. Yale Studies in English, 181. New Haven: Yale University Press, 1973.

Alvis, John. "The Religion of Eros: A Reinterpretation of *Antony and Cleopatra*." *Renascence* 30 (1978): 185–198.

Barroll, J. Leeds. *Shakespearean Tragedy: Genre, Tradition, and Change in "Antony and Cleopatra."* Washington, D.C.: Folger Books, 1984.

Battenhouse, Roy. "*Antony and Cleopatra*: Comment and Bibliography." In *Shakespeare's Christian Dimension*, edited by Roy Battenhouse, 494–496. Bloomington: Indiana University Press, 1994.

Bradley, A.C. "Shakespeare's *Antony and Cleopatra*." In *Oxford Lectures on Poetry*, 279–305. London: Macmillan, 1909.

Brown, John Russell. *Shakespeare: Antony and Cleopatra*. Casebook series. London: Macmillan, 1968.

Charney, Maurice. *Shakespeare's Roman Plays; The Function of Imagery in the Drama*, 125–141. Cambridge, Mass.: Harvard University Press, 1961.

Davidson, Clifford. "*Antony and Cleopatra* and the Whore of Babylon." *Bucknell Review* 25 (1980): 36–39.

Drakakis, John. *"Antony and Cleopatra": William Shakespeare*. New Casebooks series. New York: St. Martin's Press, 1994.

Dusinberre, Juliet. "Squeaking Cleopatras: Gender and Performance in *Antony and Cleopatra*." In *Shakespeare, Theory, and Performance*, edited by James C. Bulman, 46–67. London and New York: Routledge, 1996.

Fawkner, H. W. *Shakespeare's Hyperontology: "Antony and Cleopatra."* Rutherford, N.J.: Fairleigh Dickinson University Press, 1990.

Fichter, Andrew. "*Antony and Cleopatra*: The Time of Universal Peace." In *Shakespeare Survey* 33, edited by Kenneth Muir, 99–111. London: Cambridge University Press, 1980.

Fitz, Linda T. "Egyptian Queens and Male Reviewers: Sexist Attitudes in *Antony and Cleopatra* Criticism." In *Shakespeare Quarterly* 28 (1977): 297–316.

Goddard, Harold C. "Antony and Cleopatra." In *The Meaning of Shakespeare*, vol. 2, 184–208. Chicago: University of Chicago Press: 1951.

Granville-Barker, Harley. "Antony and Cleopatra." In *Prefaces to Shakespeare*, vol. 1, 87–119. Princeton: Princeton University Press, 1946.

Kastan, David Scott. "More Than History Can Pattern." *Cithara* 17 (1977): 31–33.

Parker, Kenneth. *Writers and Their Work: "Antony and Cleopatra."* London: Northcote House, 2000.

Rackin, Phyllis. "Shakespeare's Boy Cleopatra, the Decorum of Nature and the Golden World of Poetry." *PMLA* 87 (1972): 201–212.

Rosenberg, Marvin. *The Masks of Antony and Cleopatra.* Newark: University of Delaware Press, 2006.

Seaton, Ethel. *"Antony and Cleopatra* and the Book of Revelation." *Review of English Studies* 22 (1946): 219–224.

Singh, Jyotsyna. "Renaissance Anti-theatricality, Anti-feminism, and Shakespeare's *Antony and Cleopatra." Renaissance Drama* 20 (1989): 99–121.

Tennenhouse, Leonard. *Power on Display: The Politics of Shakespeare's Genres.* New York: Methuen, 1986.

Wood, Nigel, ed. *Antony and Cleopatra.* Theory in Practice series. Buckingham, U.K., and Bristol, Pa.: Open University Press, 1996.

ACKNOWLEDGMENTS
❦

Twentieth Century

Knight, G. Wilson. "The Diadem of Love: An Essay on *Antony and Cleopatra*." In *The Imperial Theme: Further Interpretations of Shakespeare's Tragedies Including the Roman Plays*, 263–326. 1931. Reprint, London: Methuen, 1972. © 1931 by G. Wilson Knight. Reprinted by permission.

Goddard, Harold C. "Antony and Cleopatra." In *The Meaning of Shakespeare*, vol. 2, 184–208. Chicago: University of Chicago Press: 1951. © 1951 by The University of Chicago Press.

Barton, Anne. " 'Nature's Piece 'Gainst Fancy': The Divided Catastrophe in *Antony and Cleopatra*" from *An Inaugural Lecture* (to the Hildred Carlile Chair of English Literature in the University of London tenable at Bedford College, October 1972). © 1973 by Anne Barton. Reprinted by permission.

Colie, Rosalie L. "The Significance of Style" (originally titled *"Antony and Cleopatra*: The Significance of Style"). In *Shakespeare's Living Art*. Princeton, N.J.: Princeton University Press, 1974. © 1974 Princeton University Press, 2002 renewed PUP. Reprinted by permission of Princeton University Press.

Frye, Northrop. "Antony and Cleopatra." In *Northrop Frye on Shakespeare*, 122–139, edited by Robert Sandler. New Haven: Yale University Press, 1986. © 1986 by Northrop Frye. Reprinted by permission of Yale University Press.

Quinney, Laura. "Enter a Messenger." In William Shakespeare's *Antony and Cleopatra*, edited by Harold Bloom. Modern Critical Interpretations series. New York and Philadelphia: Chelsea House, 1988. © 1988 by Laura Quinney. Reprinted by permission.

Bloom, Harold. "Introduction." In William Shakespeare's *Antony and Cleopatra*, edited by Harold Bloom. Modern Critical Interpretations series. New York and Philadelphia: Chelsea House, 1988. © 1988 by Harold Bloom.

281

Twenty-first Century

Vanhoutte, Jacqueline. "Antony's 'Secret House of Death': Suicide and Sovereignty in *Antony and Cleopatra*." *Philological Quarterly* 79, no. 2 (2000): 153–176. © 2000 by Jacqueline Vanhoutte. Reprinted by permission.

INDEX

aging of Antony and Cleopatra, xi, 77–78, 106, 110, 195–196

Agrippa, 42

Ajax (Sophocles), 188–191

Alexander, Peter, 1, 43

All for Love, Or The World Well Lost (Dryden), 49–50, 54, 67, 187, 194, 198, 231

Antonie (Garnier), 195

Antony, Mark. *See also* Antony, Mark, suicide of; Eros
  as power seeker, 172–273
  Bloom on, 260
  Bradley on, 102–104
  character of, 41, 61, 228, 228–229
  Cleopatra's betrayal and, 79–80, 146–147, 234–235, 259
  Cleopatra's dream of, 152–153, 177, 216–218
  Colie on, 220–221
  compared to Hamlet, 173, 260
  compared to Octavius, 172–173
  compared to Sophocles' Ajax, 193
  destruction of by Cleopatra, 102–104
  epithets describing, 198–199
  Frye on, 241, 246–247
  Goddard on, 172–173
  hyperbolical speeches of, 225
  in image of transvestite, 192
  likened to the sun, 175–176

linked to Desdemona, 185
linked to King Lear, 185–186
physicality of, 192, 272–273
Quinney on, 244–245
Schlegel on, 61
style of, 207–208
Tate on, 51
weakness of, 187–188

Antony, Mark, suicide of
  beauty of character and, 228–229
  bungling of, xi, 193, 235, 264–265
  Cleopatra and, 146–147, 260
  final moments of, 275–278
  motivations for, 269–270, 274–275
  Roman aspects of, 268–269

"Antony and Cleopatra," (Frye), 229–243
  overview, 230–231
  Act IV, Scene iii, 239–240
  Antony as romantic legend, 238–240
  Antony's death, 235–236
  misreading the play, 231
  play revolves around Cleopatra, 233–235
  scope of play, 240–243
  war with Caesar, 237–238

"Antony and Cleopatra," (Goddard), 163–188

Antony and Cleopatra (Shakespeare).
  See also *Julius Caesar* (Shakespeare)
  as finest of historical plays, 62, 67
  as most comprehensive work, xii
  Coleridge on, 59, 92–93, 94
  construction of, 94, 160
  contrast with "famous four," 95,
    96–97, 108, 163–164
  Davies on, 57–58
  Dryden on, 49–50
  dualism in, 161–162
  Gentleman on, 56–57
  harmonious complexity of, 133
  Henry IV, Part I and, xii
  Hill on, 54–55
  historical masterpiece, 187
  myth rather than history, 176–177
  opening scene, 96, 100–101, 239
  pathos in, 72
  productions of, xii, 85
  realism in, 84, 110–111, 162
  relevance to world of today, xii
  Shaw on, 85–92
  stillness in, 160–161
  style of, 92–93
"Antony's 'Secret House of Death':
  Suicide and Sovereignty in *Antony
  and Cleopatra*" (Vanhoutte), 263–278
  suicide of Cleopatra applauded,
    160, 263
Arden, Mary, 1
Asp as instrument of Cleopatra's
  death, 181. *See also* Cleopatra,
  suicide of

Barton, Anne, 163–188. *See also*
  "Nature's Piece 'Gainst Fancy': The
  Divided Catastrophe in *Antony and
  Cleopatra*" (Barton)
Bathurst, Charles, 60, 69–70
Bell's Edition of Shakespeare's Plays
  (Gentleman), 56–57

Blackfriars (theater), 49
Blanchot, Maurice, 245
Bloom, Harold, xi–xii, 258–263
Bradley, A. C., 92–110
Brandes, Georg, 60, 75–81
Broken Heart, The (Ford), 196–197
Burbage, James, 2

Caesar, Octavius
  on Antony's death, 113–114, 221
  Bradley on, 166
  character overview, 41
  Cleopatra and, 145, 164–167, 180,
    184
  Cleopatra's contempt for power of,
    171
  at Cleopatra's death, 159–160,
    183–184, 203–204, 243, 261
  description of, 199–200
  failure of Cleopatra's attempt to
    ensnare, 153–154
  Frye on, 237–238
  leadership greatest strength, 238
  messenger agents of, 249, 251
  role of, 164–167
  selling of sister to Antony, 174,
    192
Caesar and Cleopatra (Shaw), 83, 85
Caesarion, 232–233
Canidius, 42
Catastrophes, divided. *See* "Nature's
  Piece 'Gainst Fancy' The Divided
  Catastrophe in Antony and
  Cleopatra"
Characterization
  Barton on, 198–199
  Bathurst on, 69–70
  Bloom on, 258–259
  Brandes on, 75–81
  conflicting assessments of,
    200–201
  Dowden on, 71

first meeting of lovers, 48–49
friendliness of characters, 111
Jameson on, 67–69
Characters, list of, 41–43. See
also *names of specific characters*
(e.g., Eros)
Characters of Shakespear's Plays
(Hazlitt), 62–66
Charmian, 43, 154, 158–159
Chaucer, Geoffrey, 197
Cinthio, Giraldi, 194–195
Cleopatra. *See also* Cleopatra,
suicide of
afterlife view of, 233–234
Amazon courage of, 142–143
at Antony's death, 147–148, 178–
179, 278
as divinity of play, 149–150
as evil, 155, 237
as warrior maiden, 192–193
as "wonderful piece of work," 115
birth-day of, 146
Bloom on, 260–261
Bradley on, 93, 95, 105–107
character of, 41, 62–63, 66, 67–68,
80–81, 133
clown on, 155–156
Colie on, 208–209, 214–216, 218
contemplation of death by, 151–
152, 154–155
death faked by, 128, 193, 218–219,
241
dream of Antony by, 152–153, 177,
216–218
epithets describing, 199
Frye on, 232–237
Goddard on, 174–175, 177–179,
182
historical, 231
insincerity of, 73–74
Knight on, 144–145, 149, 151
linked to Desdemona, 193

linked to Falstaff, xi, 234
linked to King Lear, 186
linked to Othello, 185
Octavius Caesar and, 153–154,
165–166, 171
Quinney on, 255–257
Schlegel on, 61
seductive arts of, 61
sympathetic treatment of in
sources, 197–198
theatricality of, 233–234, 260
Cleopatra (Cinthio), 194–195
Cleopatra (Daniel), 195–196
Cleopatra, suicide of
as erotic tragedy, 258
clown and, 202–205
death and love identical,
130–131
motivations for, 80–81
preparation for, 181
resolution in death, 267–268
Roman aspects of, 228–229
sublimity of, xi, 69, 74–75, 157–
158, 261
Cléopatre Captive (Jodelle), 195
Clown, 43, 155–156, 182, 202–203
236, 235
Coleridge, Samuel Taylor, 59, 66–67,
92–93, 94
Colie, Rosalie L., 205–229. *See also*
"Significance of Style" (Colie)
Coriolanus (Shakespeare), compared to
Antony and Cleopatra, xi, 205
Cydnus meeting of lovers, 48–49, 183,
233

Daniel, Samuel, 49, 195–196, 232
"Dark Lady as a Model—The Fall of
the Republic a World-Catastrophe"
(Brandes), 75–81
Decretas, 42, 254, 276–277
Demetrius, 42

"Diadem of Love: An Essay on
  Antony and Cleopatra" (Knight),
  110–163
  Amazon courage of Cleopatra,
    141–142
  Antony's farewell to Cleopatra,
    135–138
  as divinity of play, 149–150
  on Cleopatra, 144–145
  Cleopatra alone with thoughts of
    Antony, 138–140
  Cleopatra as all Shakespeare's
    heroines in one, 133–135
  Cleopatra as all womankind, 144–
    145, 149
  Cleopatra's death scene, 157–158
  Cleopatra's dream of Antony,
    152–153
  Cleopatra's flirtation with
    messenger, 141–142
  death as positive, not negative, 132
  death faked by Cleopatra, 128, 193,
    218–219, 241
  death not tragic in play, 160
  ebb and flow as theme, 119–125,
    132, 143–144
  Enobarbus on Cleopatra, 150
  Enobarbus reports Cleopatra's
    treachery, 145
  Enobarbus's common-sense
    commentary, 115–117
  on evil of Cleopatra, 155
  loyalty as theme, 111–114
  messenger brings news of Antony's
    marriage, 141
  Octavius Caesar and Cleopatra,
    153–154
  realism in play, 84, 110–111, 132,
    162
Diomedes, 43, 254–255
Divided catastrophes. *See* "Nature's
  Piece 'Gainst Fancy' The Divided

Catastrophe in Antony and
  Cleopatra"
  in *Ajax*, 190–191
  in *Antony and Cleopatra*, 191–192
  examples of, 196–197
  Shakespeare's reason for using,
    201–202
Dolabella, 43, 204, 218, 253, 257,
  278
Donne, John, 270, 271
Dowden, Edward, 60, 71–75
Drunk scene (Pompey's gallery),
  167–169, 192
Dryden, John, 49–50, 54, 67, 187, 194,
  198, 231
Duchess of Malfy, The (Webster), 197

Effeminacy, 223–224
Eighteenth-century criticism,
  53–58
  overview, 53
  Davies, 57–58
  Gentleman, 56–57
  Hill, 54–55
  Johnson, 55–56
Enobarbus
  Bradley on, 106
  character of, 42, 49, 58, 199
  on Cleopatra, 150, 174, 225–226,
    239
  Cleopatra's death scene and,
    108nA, 130–131
  Colie on, 206, 218
  in defense of Cleopatra, 115–117
  deserts from Antony, 173, 188n1
  on effeminacy, 223–224
  function of in play, 233–234,
    238–239
  meeting at Cydnus described by,
    48–49, 183, 233
  on proposed duel between Antony
    and Octavius, 167

repentance after treachery, 66
reports Cleopatra's treachery, 145
soliloquies of, 223, 246
suicide of, 66, 267
"Enter a Messenger" (Quinney),
  244–258
  on Antony, 244–245
  on Cleopatra, 255–257
  Cleopatra's "last conquest,"
    257–258
  first scene of play, 251–252, 253
  messengers and messenger figures,
    248–249
  transition with Hercules' departure,
    247–248
Eros, 42, 65, 173, 240, 259, 270–271

Failure of love as theme, 127
Figures of speech, use of, 205
Ford, John, 196–197
Frye, Northrop, 84, 229–243. See also
  "Antony and Cleopatra" (Frye)

Gallus, 43
Garnier, Robert, 49, 195
Gentleman, Francis, 56–57
Globe, The, 2
Glyn, Eleanor, 59
Goddard, Harold C., 163–188
Graves, Robert, 243
Greene, Robert, 1
Groatsworth of Wit, A (Greene), 1

Hamlet linked to Antony and Cleopatra,
  173, 186–187, 260
Hazlitt, William, 60, 62–66
Heracles/Omphale myth, 192, 220
Herbert, Mary, 49
Hill, John, 54–55
Historical background, 5, 47–49, 96,
  230–231, 232
Humanism, 132, 160, 162

Humor, 164
Hyperbole, use of, 205, 210–212, 217,
  218, 219–222, 224–226

Imagery. See Hyperbole, use of
"Introduction" (1988) (Bloom),
  258–259
"Introduction" (this volume) (Bloom),
  xi–xii
Iras, 43, 154, 158–159

James I (king), 1
Jameson, Anna Murphy Brownell, 60,
  67–69
Jodelle, Athena, 195
Johnson, Samuel, 55–56, 57
Jonson, Ben, 3
Julius Caesar (Shakespeare), 61, 66–67,
  71, 97, 187, 205, 232

Kermode, Frank, 190
Key passages, 19–40
  Act I, i, 14–17, 19–20
  Act I, i, 1–2, 19
  Act I, i, 19–24, 20
  Act I, ii, 147–157, 20–21
  Act I, iii, 6–10, 21
  Act III, i, 12–17, 24–25
  Act II, ii, 241–246, 22–23
  Act II, iii, 19–24, 23
  Act III, v, 22–23, 25
  Act III, vi, 3–19, 25–26
  Act III, vi, 65–79, 82–91, and
    98–99, 26–27
  Act III, vii, 1–6 and 17–20, 27
  Act III, xi, 7–24, 28–29
  Act III, xii, 27–33, 29–30
  Act III, xiii, 43–46, 30
  Act III, xiii, 74–78, 30–31
  Act III, xiii, 154–167, 31
  Act II, v, 20–23, 23–24
  Act I, iv, 25–33, 21–22

Act II, vii, 75–82, 24
Act I, v, 42–50, 22
Act IV, i, 1–6, 32
Act IV, ii, 23–45, 32–33
Act IV, v, 2–17, 33–34
Act IV, xii, 31–39, 34
Act IV, xiii, 3–4, 35
Act IV, xiv, 2–22, 35–36
Act V, i, 14–20, 36
Act V, ii, 21–34, 36–37
Act V, ii, 42–46, 37
Act V, ii, 107–111, 38
Act V, ii, 139–178, 38–39
Act V, ii, 210–224, 39–40
Act V, ii, 280–291, 40
King Lear linked to *Antony and
    Cleopatra*, 185–186
Knight, G. Wilson, 115. *See also*
    "Diadem of Love: An Essay on
    Antony and Cleopatra" (Knight)

Lectures on Dramatic Art and Literature
    (Schlegel), 61
Legend of Good Women (Chaucer), 49,
    197
Leigh, Vivien, 85, 233
L'Entretien infini (Blanchot), 245
Lepidus, 41, 168, 170, 230
*Lives of the Noble Grecians and
    Romans* (Plutarch), 47, 194, 232, 251,
    252–253
Love, use of term, 171–172
Loyalty, 111–113

Maecenas, 42
Marc Antoine (Garnier), 49
Mardian, 43
Menas, 42, 168
Menecrates, 42
Montaigne, Michel Eyquem De,
    271

"Nature's Piece 'Gainst Fancy': The
    Divided Catastrophe in *Antony and
    Cleopatra*" (Barton), 188–205
    overview, 188–191
    Antony compared to Sophocles'
        Ajax, 193
    characterization ambiguity in,
        198–201
    Cleopatra's artful tableau at death,
        204–205
    Cleopatra's death scene after clown,
        202–204
    Heracles/Omphale myth, 192–193
    Shakespeare's reason for using
        divided catastrophe, 201–202
Nineteenth-century criticism, 59–81
    Bathurst, 69–70
    Brandes, Georg, 75–81
    Coleridge, 66–92
    Dowden, 71–75
    Hazlitt, 62–66
    Jameson, 67–69
    Schlegel, 61
North, Sir Thomas, 47
"Notes on the Plays" (Johnson), 55–56

Octavia
    as Antony's "castaway," 249
    as Antony's wife, 232–233, 237
    given to Antony by brother, 41,
        141–142, 170, 174
Othello (Shakespeare), 185
outward conflict effects, 99–100

Pagan Mysteries in the Renaissance
    (Wind), 192
Passages, key. *See* Key passages
Philo, 42, 210–211, 219, 224,
    272–273
Plutarch, 47, 194, 232, 251, 252–253.
    See also Sources

Pompey, 41, 167–169, 192, 232,
    245–246
Power, satire on, 167–169
Power, thirst for, 164
Proculeius, 43
Puritanism, 2

Quinney, Laura, 244–258. *See also*
    "Enter a Messenger" (Quinney)

Realism, 84, 110–111, 132, 162
*Remarks on the Differences in
    Shakespeare's Versification in Different
    Periods of His Life* (Bathurst), 69–70
Roman trilogy of Shakespeare, 187
Romeo and Juliet (Shakespeare), 184

Scarus, 42
Schlegel, August Wilhelm von, 59–60,
    61
Schoolmaster, 42, 253
Seleucus, 43
Sense of an Ending (Kermode), 190
Seventeenth-century criticism, 47–51
    overview, 47–48
    Dryden, 49–50
    Tate, 50–51
Shakespeare, William
    biographical information, 1–3
    Brandes on, 75–81
    genius of, xii, 62, 66
    Shaw on, 85–92
    Tate on, 51
*Shakespeare, with Introductory Remarks
    on Poetry, the Drama, and the Stage*
    (Coleridge), 66–67
"Shakespeare's *Antony and Cleopatra*"
    (Bradley), 92–110
*Shakespeare's Heroines: Characteristics of
    Women, Moral, Poetical, & Historical*
    (Jameson), 67–69

Shakespeare's Life and Art (Alexander),
    1
*Shakespere: A Critical Study of His
    Mind and Art* (Dowden), 71–75
Shaw, George Bernard, 83, 85–92
"Significance of Style" (Colie),
    205–229
    Asiatic lifestyle of lovers, 212,
        222–224
    Cleopatra stages her death,
        218–220
    Cleopatra's dream of Antony, 177,
        216–218
    death theme throughout play,
        218–219
    deaths beyond definition, 228–229
    Enobarbus adopts hyperbolical
        mode, 225–226
    epic range of play, 206–207
    hyperbolical use of language,
        210–212
    language magniloquence fascinates,
        205–206
    language on denigration of Asiatic
        style, 222–224
    love of Antony and Cleopatra
        confirmed, 227
    lovers match hyperbolical style,
        219–222
    Octavius speaks at Antony's death,
        220–221
    Rome and Egypt mixture, 208–209
    sexuality runs throughout play,
        213–215
    style as moral indicator, 207
Silius, 42
"Some Remarks upon the New-revived
    Play of *Antony and Cleopatra*" (Hill),
    54–55
Soothsayer, 43, 172, 174, 237,
    252–253

Sophocles, 188–191

Sources, 5, 47–49, 194–198, 251–253

Style in play. *See* "Significance of
  Style" (Colie)

Suicide. *See also* Antony, Mark, suicide
  of; Cleopatra, suicide of
    attitudes in sixteenth century on,
      266
    Donne on, 270, 271
    Montaigne on, 271
    in Shakespeare, 267
    in Tudor England, 264, 265–266

Summaries. *See also* Historical
  background
    Act I, 5–8
    Act II, 8–11
    Act III, 11–15
    Act IV, 15–17
    Act V, 17–18

Tate, Nahum, 50–51

Taurus, 43

Themes
    as world catastrophe, 75–81
    death, love, and life associated,
      131–132
    double moral, 57
    dying for love, 162n
    ebb and flow, 119–125, 132,
      143–144
    failure of love, 127
    humanism, 132, 160, 162
    interplay of sexes, 143

loyalty, 111–114
    realism, unfaithfulness, death,
      hatred, evil, 110–111
    thirst for power, 164
    transcendental reunion of lovers,
      185

Thidias, 42

Tragedie of Antonie (Herbert, tr.), 49

Tragedie of Cleopatra (Daniel), 49, 232

Treachery between Cleopatra and
  Antony, xi, 66, 145

Twentieth-century criticism
    overview, 83–85
    Barton, 84, 163–188
    Bloom, 85, 258–263
    Bradley, 92–110
    Colie, 84–85, 205–229
    Frye, 84, 229–244
    Goddard, 84
    Knight, 84, 110–163
    Quinney, 85, 244–258
    Shaw, 83, 85–92

Twenty-first-century criticism,
  263–278

Vanhoutte, Jacqueline, 263–278

Varrius, 42

Ventidius, 42, 237

Webster, John, 197

White Goddess, The (Graves), 243

Wind, Edgar, 192

Women in Shakespeare, 155–156